Medical Ethics in China

Drawing on a wide range of primary historical and sociological sources and employing sharp philosophical analysis, this book investigates medical ethics in China from a Chinese-Western comparative perspective. In doing so it offers a fascinating exploration of both cultural differences and commonalities exhibited by China and the West in medicine and medical ethics.

The book carefully examines a number of key bioethical issues in the Chinese socio-cultural context including: attitudes towards fetuses; disclosure of information by medical professionals; informed consent; professional medical ethics; health promotion; feminist bioethics and human rights. It not only provides insights into Chinese perspectives, but also sheds light on the appropriate methods for comparative culture and ethical studies. Through this pioneering study, Jing-Bao Nie has put forward a theory of "trans-cultural bioethics," an ethical paradigm which upholds the primacy of morality whilst resisting cultural stereotypes, and appreciating the internal plurality, richness, dynamism and openness of medical ethics in any culture.

Jing-Bao Nie is an Associate Professor at the Bioethics Centre of the University of Otago in New Zealand and Furong Visiting Professor at the Centre for Moral Culture of Hunan Normal University in China. His publications include *Behind the Silence: Chinese Voices on Abortion* (2005), *Japan's Wartime Medical Atrocities: Comparative Inquiries in History, Science and Ethics* (chief editor) (Routledge, 2010), three chapters in *The Cambridge World History of Medical Ethics* (2009), and numerous journal articles and other book chapters.

Biomedical Law and Ethics Library
Series Editor: Sheila A.M. McLean

Scientific and clinical advances, social and political developments and the impact of healthcare on our lives raise profound ethical and legal questions. Medical law and ethics have become central to our understanding of these problems, and are important tools for the analysis and resolution of problems—real or imagined.

In this series, scholars at the forefront of biomedical law and ethics contribute to the debates in this area, with accessible, thought-provoking, and sometimes controversial ideas. Each book in the series develops an independent hypothesis and argues cogently for a particular position. One of the major contributions of this series is the extent to which both law and ethics are utilized in the content of the books, and the shape of the series itself.

The books in this series are analytical, with a key target audience of lawyers, doctors, nurses, and the intelligent lay public.

Available titles:

Human Fertilisation and Embryology (2006)
Reproducing Regulation
Kirsty Horsey & Hazel Biggs

Intention and Causation in Medical Non-Killing (2006)
The Impact of Criminal Law Concepts on Euthanasia and Assisted Suicide
Glenys Williams

Impairment and Disability (2007)
Law and Ethics at the Beginning and End of Life
Sheila McLean & Laura Williamson

Bioethics and the Humanities (2007)
Attitudes and Perceptions
Robin Downie & Jane Macnaughton

Defending the Genetic Supermarket (2007)
The Law and Ethics of Selecting the Next Generation
Colin Gavaghan

The Harm Paradox (2007)
Tort Law and the Unwanted Child in an Era of Choice
Nicolette Priaulx

Assisted Dying (2007)
Reflections on the need for law reform
Sheila McLean

Medicine, Malpractice and Misapprehensions (2007)
Vivienne Harpwood

Euthanasia, Ethics and the Law (2007)
From Conflict to Compromise
Richard Huxtable

Best Interests of the Child in Healthcare (2007)
Sarah Elliston

Values in Medicine (2008)
The Realities of Clinical Practice
Donald Evans

Autonomy, Consent and the Law (2009)
Sheila McLean

Healthcare Research Ethics and Law (2009)
Regulation, Review and Responsibility
Hazel Biggs

The Body in Bioethics (2009)
Alastair V. Campbell

Genomic Negligence (2011)
An Interest in Autonomy as the Basis for Novel Negligence Claims Generated by Genetic Technology
Victoria Chico

Health Professionals and Trust
The Cure for Healthcare Law and Policy
Mark Henaghan

Medical Ethics in China
A Transcultural Interpretation
Jing-Bao Nie

Forthcoming titles include:

Abortion Law and Policy
An Equal Opportunity Perspective
Kerry Petersen

Bioethics
Methods, Theories, Scopes
Marcus Düwell

Birth, Harm and the Role of Distributive Justice
Burdens, Blessings, Need and Desert
Alasdair Maclean

Medicine and Law at the Limits of Life
Clinical Ethics in Action
Richard Huxtable

The Jurisprudence of Pregnancy
Concepts of Conflict, Persons and Property
Mary Ford

About the Series Editor

Professor Sheila McLean is International Bar Association Professor of Law and Ethics in Medicine and Director of the Institute of Law and Ethics in Medicine at the University of Glasgow.

Medical Ethics in China

A Transcultural Interpretation

Jing-Bao Nie

Routledge
Taylor & Francis Group
LONDON AND NEW YORK

First published 2011
by Routledge
2 Park Square, Milton Park, Abingdon, Oxon OX14 4RN

Simultaneously published in the USA and Canada
by Routledge
711 Third Avenue, New York, NY 10017

Routledge is an imprint of the Taylor & Francis Group, an informa business

First issued in paperback 2013

© 2011 Jing-Bao Nie

The right of Jing-Bao Nie to be identified as author of this work has been asserted by him in accordance with sections 77 and 78 of the Copyright, Designs and Patents Act 1988.

All rights reserved. No part of this book may be reprinted or reproduced or utilised in any form or by any electronic, mechanical, or other means, now known or hereafter invented, including photocopying and recording, or in any information storage or retrieval system, without permission in writing from the publishers.

Trademark notice: Product or corporate names may be trademarks or registered trademarks, and are used only for identification and explanation without intent to infringe.

British Library Cataloguing in Publication Data
Nie, Jing-Bao, 1962-
Medical ethics in China : a transcultural interpretation / Jing-Bao Nie.
p. cm. -- (Biomedical law & ethics library)
ISBN 978-0-415-68949-6 (hardback) -- ISBN 978-0-203-13817-5 (e-book) 1. Medical ethic--China--Cross-cultural studies. I. Title.
R725.5.N54 2012
174.2--dc23
2011028413

Library of Congress Cataloging in Publication Data
A catalog record for this book has been requested

ISBN 978-0-415-68949-6 (hbk)
ISBN 978-0-415-72456-2 (pbk)
ISBN 978-0-203-13817-5 (ebk)

Typeset in Garamond
by Saxon Graphics Ltd, Derby

To my three Ls, with love

Contents

Foreword by Robert M. Veatch xi
Prologue: "Supping with foreign devils" xiv

Introduction: the search for a transcultural bioethics 1

PART I
Beyond stereotypes and stereotyping 19

1 Communitarian China versus the individualistic West: a popular myth and its roots 21
2 The fallacy of dichotomizing cultures 37
3 China as the radical other of the West, or a misconstruction of Foucault: sexual excess as a cause of disease in China and the United States 51
4 Excursion: "false friends" in cross-cultural understanding, or a misjudgement of Needham: refuting the claim that the ancient Chinese discovered the circulation of the blood 69

PART II
Truths of cultures 87

5 Taking China's internal plurality seriously 89
6 The complexity of cultural differences: the forgotten Chinese tradition of medical truth-telling 98
7 The "cultural differences" argument and its misconceptions: the return of medical truth-telling in China 116
8 Is informed consent not applicable in China?: further intellectual flaws of the "cultural differences" argument 134

PART III
Cultural norms embodying universal values   147

9 Human rights as a Chinese value: a Chinese defense and critique of UNESCO's Universal Declaration on Bioethics   149

10 Women's rights in the Chinese context: toward a Chinese feminist bioethics   163

PART IV
Chinese wisdom for today   179

11 After *cheng* (sincerity or truthfulness): the professional ethics of traditional Chinese medicine   181

12 "Medicine as the art of humanity" and the physician as a general   196

13 Exploring the core of humanity: a Chinese-Western dialogue on personhood   206

14 Beyond individualism and communitarianism: a yin-yang model on the ethics of health promotion (*with Kirk L. Smith*)   214

Conclusions: toward the uncertain future   225
Epilogue: thus spoke *Hai Ruo* (The God of the North Sea)   230

Bibliography   235
Acknowledgements   253
About the author   259
Index   261

Foreword

Biomedical ethics as an interdisciplinary field of study emerged in Western, primarily American, culture about 1970. At that time of turmoil an outmoded, professionally-generated system of ethics tracing back to the Hippocratic Oath and, more importantly, many independent attempts of physicians to control the ethical conduct of members of the profession were supplanted by efforts grounded in a broader cultural set of norms coming from political philosophy (the Western liberal tradition), law, religion, and diverse belief systems. It was all scholars of the Western bioethical revolution could do to pay attention to their own national and regional trends.

American scholars of bioethics were rightly accused of having too narrow a gaze, but the critics were often urging only modest expansion of the horizon to other English-speaking countries, to Europe, and perhaps to Latin America. All this time we had an uneasy awareness that there was more to the world, including the world of biomedical ethics, than Western culture. We understood the importance of Japan and were vaguely aware of rich, long traditions in other parts of Asia including, most critically, China.

We tapped scholarship influenced by anthropology from the German scholar Paul Unschuld, whose horizon-expanding *Medical Ethics in Imperial China* gave us our first serious glimpse of the rich and complex alternatives to Western medical ethics complete with some excerpts from the ancient texts. More recently that exploration has been advanced by the next generation including the important contributions by Ole Doering. From within China we learned of scholars trying to survive the difficult times of the Cultural Revolution studying Western philosophy and the Chinese traditions of medical ethics. Ren-Zong Qiu exposed many Westerners to the basics of Chinese medical ethics.

Both Western and Chinese scholars of biomedical ethics, however, necessarily confronted serious limitations. They were clearly rooted in one culture and communicating to another as outsiders. They looked in on another culture and helped begin the bridging. With Jing-Bao Nie's *Medical Ethics in China: A Transcultural Interpretation*, everything changes. We have a breakthrough to a new level of communication that will enrich not only the study of the relation between Chinese and Western medical ethics, but the entire field of cross-cultural and transcultural study of ethics.

Nie is the first person in medical ethics who can seriously claim to be at home as an insider in both Chinese and Western thought. He was born and raised in China, trained in traditional Chinese medicine, and is in every way a product of the events of China's rapid change during the twentieth century. But he is also comfortable as a resident of Western culture studying sociology at Queen's University in Canada, obtaining his doctorate in the University of Texas Medical Branch (then the only PhD program in medical humanities in the world), and working as a postdoctoral fellow at the important bioethics program at the University of Minnesota, and now for the past decade playing a unique and active role as a faculty member at the Bioethics Centre at the University of Otago in New Zealand (a leading bioethics program in the Australasia and Pacific region). At the same time, he retains professorial affiliations at both Hunan Normal University and Peking University in China.

He is the first, really the only, scholar of medical ethics of China who I find comfortable thinking, feeling, and analyzing as a Westerner while simultaneously retaining his deep and abiding commitment to his original culture. He writes in English comfortably, gracefully, beautifully. He, for example, understands that usually scholars in English speak of "medical ethics" in the singular ("Medical ethics is a rapidly changing discipline") much as Aristotle might speak of politics in the singular as a field of thought. At the same time he knows when to refer to medical ethics in the plural ("The medical ethics in China and the United States are often quite different"). Nie reflects a grasp of the subtleties of English well beyond many native speakers. His facility with the language enriches the text immeasurably.

We have had a foretaste of Nie's potential contribution to a new level of understanding of Chinese-Western relations in his earlier journal essays, book chapters, and edited volumes dealing with topics that might frighten a lesser scholar: the atrocities of World War II perpetrated not only by the Germans, but also by the Japanese and Americans. His co-edited volume, *Japan's Wartime Medical Atrocities: Comparative Inquiries in Science, History and Ethics*, raises to a new level the transcultural analysis of a major issue in international medical ethics. He has previously taken on the ultra-sensitive issues of abortion and population in China, informed consent, and human experimentation, but this is the volume we have been waiting for. It is the comprehensive, comparative exploration of medical ethics in China from an unrelenting transcultural perspective as only Jing-Bao Nie could provide.

He covers all the major topics of medical ethics: fetal life, sexuality, truth-telling, informed consent, women's rights, theories of personhood, and health promotion. He looks at a wide range of perspectives from that of the traditional Chinese doctor to that of the modern feminist.

There is something more important here, though, and this makes the book important even to those who claim no special interest in Chinese medical ethics. The volume advances the understanding of doing cross-cultural and transcultural comparative ethics. It is not only the most ambitious study of Chinese-Western medical ethics ever undertaken, but also one of the truly significant events in the history of transcultural medical ethics taken more globally. He taps into a recent movement in Western medical ethics to find a grounding of medical ethics into what some Westerners are calling a "common morality" from scholars from Tom Beauchamp, Ruth Macklin, and Bernard Gert to critics like Tristram Engelhardt and Leigh Turner. Proponents of a common morality have maintained that underlying all our cultural diversity and obvious linguistic differences, there is a pretheoretical convergence around a small set of moral norms that are accepted by all reasonable people, at least if their view is not distorted by parochial bias. At the same time, this is no naïve claim that everyone agrees on all moral judgments. Not only do different facts and circumstances lead to differing judgments even if the same basic norms are applied, more critically different cultural understandings may lead to apparent variations in judgment and different weightings of conflicting norms even though the same, underlying, basic norms are the ground of the judgment.

This is a claim not easily refuted by simple empirical observation of obvious cultural differences. It is an analysis that Nie advances with a sophisticated exploration of the interplay of underlying commonly held norms and empirical factual variations. Calling his approach "interpretative," he affirms simultaneously rich cultural complexity, internal plurality within any culture, similarities among cultures, the possibility of dialogue, and, most critically, the necessity and primacy of moral judgment. He contributes to the recognition of a fundamental convergence of ethics even while affirming cultural diversity not only between, but, at least as importantly, within, cultures. His methodology is an important advance in the development of this complex and crucial topic. It is a joy to have Nie's volume available.

Robert M. Veatch
Professor of Medical Ethics and Former Director
The Kennedy Institute of Ethics
Georgetown University
Washington, DC

July 2011

Prologue:
"Supping with foreign devils"

While I was trying to devise a catchy title for this book, philosopher and neurosurgeon Grant Gillett, a colleague at the Bioethics Centre of the University of Otago in New Zealand, suggested "Supping with foreign devils"—a reference to the English proverb, "He who sups with the devil should have a long spoon." I smiled at the time, and have been greatly tempted to use this provocative phrase. Although my final decision for a title was made on straight-out academic grounds, it is admittedly less imaginative.

I don't know what led Grant to come up with such a phrase. However, it immediately brought back memories of my childhood and youth during the 1970s when Westerners, in particular Americans and Britons, were often called "foreign devils" (*yangguizi* or *waiguo guizi*) in official propaganda, and even in children's games. Among these foreign devils, the Japanese were in a class of their own; Chinese people still retain strong historical memories of the war, the national humiliation it brought about, and the massive social suffering that Japan imposed on China in the 1930s and 1940s. Putting aside the international political environment of the Cold War, references to Westerners—the English, for example—as foreign devils had been circulating in China since at least the first half of the 19th century. A large group of associated terms includes such choice epithets as "foreign devils" (*yangguizi*), "devil slaves" (guinu), "barbarian devils" (*fangui*), "island barbarians" (*daoyi*), "blue-eyed barbarians" (*biyan yinu*), "red-haired barbarians" (*hongmaofan*), "raw barbarians" (*shengfan*), and the latter's apparent opposite, "cooked barbarians" (*shufan*). A Chinese textbook about the English language was simply entitled *Devils' Talk* (for a study of racial prejudice by Chinese, see Dikötter 1992). A series of military defeats and unfair treaties imposed on China by the imperialist West, including two opium wars with Great Britain and the looting of Beijing by the armies of eight Western allies led by Great Britain and France, greatly increased the circulation of these apparently uncomplimentary phrases. In Cantonese, the term "devil or ghost foreigners" (*guilao*) is still used in everyday conversation, not necessarily with negative connotations. Culturally speaking, there has been a tendency toward ethnocentrism and chauvinism in China from ancient times. The cultural superiority of Chinese (*hua*) in relation to foreigners or barbarians (*yi*) has often been assumed. In classic Chinese, special (often derogatory) terms have been widely used to refer to the barbarian peoples of respectively the East, South, West and North surrounding the Divine or Middle Kingdom.

However, this personal and general experience of China at a particular historical period, as well as the long-held chauvinist attitudes to foreigners and foreign cultures, should not be misinterpreted so as to reinforce the widespread stereotype which portrays China as an isolationist culture that resists all foreign influences. From the beginning, Chinese civilization has been very curious about, and open to, foreign ideas and material goods. Indeed, the greatness of Chinese civilization lies partly in its openness to the outside world. The acceptance and transformation of Buddhism by the Chinese since the first century AD constitutes a salient example of China's willingness not just to passively accept, but also to actively learn from peoples in foreign lands and their cultural achievements. For centuries—as vividly depicted in one of the handful of classic Chinese novels (and the most popular Chinese novel for children from any period), *Xiyou Ji* (The Journey to the West)—Chinese monks and scholars were willing to overcome *qiannan wanxian* (innumerable hazards and hardships) to travel to India, the "near West" of China, in order to learn Buddhism and bring back Buddhist scriptures and other texts for translation and study. Over the past few centuries, learning from the "far West"—Europe and North America—has been one of the most fundamental themes of Chinese cultural and political life. Far from isolationist, the attitude of the Chinese has been so open at times that the idea of "wholesale Westernization" has received varying degrees of support from both the intelligentsia and the general populace. As a major phenomenon of our times, the Chinese state policy (and social practice) of openness (*kaifan*) since the late 1970s has transformed not only China, but the rest of the world (for a recent account of China's attempts to integrate elements of other Asian cultures, in addition to the West, over the past two millennia, see Waley-Cohen 2005).

Ever since the extravagant reports of the great Italian traveller Marco Polo in the 13th century, many different images of China have been developed and circulated in the West. These images range from the positive and romantic ("plentifulness" or "an example and model for the West") to the negative and discriminatory ("a people of eternal standstill" and a branch of the "Yellow Peril"). (For studies of the variety of Western perceptions of China, see Dawson 1967; Mackerras 1989; Spence 1998: for Asian influences on the making of modern European cultures, see the monumental work of Lash and van Kley 1965–98.) The stances adopted by two German thinkers illustrate the variety of responses. For Leibniz, the West needed "missionaries from the Chinese" to teach it moral excellence. He emphasized "how often strangers have better insight into the histories and monuments of a nation than their own citizens" (cited in Spence 1998, 85–6). To J. G. Herder, the Enlightenment philosopher who advocated moral and political pluralism and appreciation of the unique features of different cultures, the Chinese nation was like "an embalmed mummy, wrapped in silk, and painted with hieroglyphics" and governed by "unalterably childish institutions." And there was nothing the Chinese could do to alter their destiny: "Planted" on their particular spot on the globe, they could never become Greeks or Roman. Chinese they were and will remain: a people endowed by nature with small eyes, a short nose, a flat forehead, little beard, large ears and protuberant belly." (Ibid, 99)

This book is not about the cultural stereotypes and racial prejudice shown by one group against another, in either China or the West. Rather, it deals with medical ethics in China from a Chinese-Western comparative perspective. It is, nevertheless, concerned to show that, in the context of medical ethics, many old cultural stereotypes—and the mentality of "having a long spoon" when encountering other cultures—are never very far away. In this book, I critique a number of empirical viewpoints and normative positions—both Western and Chinese—regarding medical ethics in China and Chinese-Western cultural differences in bioethics. I would like to point out at the very start that I have adopted this stance not just in order to be "different" (*biaoxin liyi*, proposing or doing something unconventional merely for the sake of being different)—a common vice that, for centuries, both Confucianism and the professional ethics of traditional Chinese medicine have spoken out against. In fact, my criticism here is not so much a critique of others as self-criticism, as I myself have subscribed to most, if not all, of these viewpoints and positions at one time or another. But, for the reasons presented in the following chapters, I can no longer believe in them. I sincerely hope that, to borrow a phrase commonly used by Chinese authors to preface or conclude their works, my book will serve as "a brick to attract jade."

My purpose in exposing some common pitfalls encountered in cross-cultural bioethics is to clear the ground for the emergence of constructive ways of moving beyond these widespread stereotypes and intellectual barriers, enabling us—Westerners and Chinese as well—to arrive at a better understanding of medical ethics in China and deal more adequately with the challenges of the East-West encounter. Above all, I aim to demonstrate the necessity and possibility of a transcultural bioethics—an ethics that is rooted in particular cultural experiences but seeks to transcend their limitations by following the dictates of ethical ideals and moral imperatives.

This book is a work of interpretation, written from a particular perspective. It is commonplace wisdom that things can look very different when seen from different perspectives, a truth expressed in a Chinese household poem about one of the best-known mountains in China by the great 11th-century writer Su Shi:

> From the side, a mountain range; from the end, a single peak;
> Far, near, high, low, no two parts alike.
> Why can't I tell the true shape of Mount Lu?
> Because I myself am in the mountain.

A similar point was made at another time, on another continent and in a very different context by the great French thinker, mathematician and scientist Blaise Pascal:

> A town, a country-place, is from afar a town and a country-place. But, as we draw near, there are houses, trees, tiles, leaves, grass, ants, limbs of ants, in infinity. All this is contained under the name of *country-place*.
> (*Pensées* #115; italics original)

Indeed, any mountain and any rural locality or country-place, like any other landscape, can appear very different when seen by different individuals, at different times, from different angles, or even when viewed by the same observer in different moods.

The same perception is as true, if not more so, of medical ethics in China, in the West, and indeed universally. Medical ethics in every society, just like any other dimension of human culture and civilization, can be approached, examined and presented from innumerable points of view. While Su Shi's poem perhaps encourages us to see things from the outside, the external view should not be privileged, any more than its opposite. Both have their own advantages and disadvantages. Like awesome landscapes, the strength of medical ethics in China—historical and contemporary, traditional and modern—is partly revealed by its capacity to stimulate very different, even opposing, interpretations from outsiders as well as insiders.

The benefits and difficulties of understanding one culture from the standpoint of another are obvious. While Czech writer Franz Kafka never set foot in China, his short story "The Great Wall of China," and the mini-parables within the story, powerfully demonstrate the challenges and complexities involved in gaining an intimate understanding of China, not only by foreigners but also by Chinese themselves. On the one hand, Kafka's work should be read primarily *not* as a story about the Great Wall or China per se, but as an insightful metaphor of the universal conditions of human existence—a story about cultural and political authority and the place of the individual, and about the struggle to make sense of the absurdity of life and the ambiguities of the particular social and historical contexts in which we all find ourselves. At the same time, in the surreal style typical of Kafka, the story can been read as a realistic portrait of China as symbolized by the building of the Great Wall. By adopting the persona of a knowledgeable and contemplative Chinese, Kafka has produced one of the most perceptive works ever written on Chinese society and culture. Through a narrative told by a southerner near the Tibetan Highlands who helped build the wall thousands of miles to the north—a Chinese man given life and voice through the genius of a Western artist—"The Great Wall of China" has become a testament to the fascinating, mystifying, challenging, alienating and inspiring power that China has exercised on people living outside as well as inside its borders. Among Kafka's many insights in the story is the following:

> So vast is our land that no fable could do justice to its vastness, the heavens can scarcely span it—and Peking is only a dot in it and the imperial palace less than a dot.
>
> (Kafka 1993, 382)

Kafka was acutely aware of the elaborate internal diversity, the innumerable ironic contradictions and elusive cultural characteristics of this vast and varied land with its immensely long history. While China is not so vast that the heavens can scarcely span it; while in contemporary China Beijing and Zhongnanhai (the headquarters of the Communist Party and Government) adjacent to the Forbidden City have been far from a mere dot with regard to the power that they have exercised over the Chinese people and the natural environment, Kafka's point that official discourse is just one voice among many, and that no one fable can do justice to the immensity of China, should be borne in mind for anyone writing about China or interested in knowing more about it.

Furthermore, one should always bear in mind a more general difficulty in any efforts to study morality in any part of the world, comparative ethics in particular, a difficulty acutely observed by nineteenth-century Swiss historian Jacob Burckhardt (1990, 271):

> The relation of the various people of the earth to the supreme interests of life, to God, virtue and immortality, may be investigated up to a certain point, but can never be compared to one another with absolute strictness and certainty. The more plainly in these matters our evidence seems to speak, the more carefully must we refrain from unqualified assumptions and rash generalizations.

Burckhardt continued, "This remark is especially true with regard to our judgement on questions of morality." "The ultimate truth with respect to the character, the conscience and the guilt of a people remains for ever a secret." (Ibid) This warning, nevertheless, does not mean that we should not strive hard to understand better human morality, medical ethics included, from a comparative perspective.

This book is written by a Chinese "native," a southerner from a remote village far distant from the Tibetan Highlands, who has been in self-imposed exile in the West, first in North America and now in New Zealand, for nearly two decades. It offers a report from a curious traveller who is simultaneously an insider and an outsider, both intellectually and geographically, with respect to bioethics and culture in China and the West. He will be satisfied if his hard labour—scarcely as glorious an endeavor as participating in building the

Great Wall—will help to overcome some of our long-held cultural stereotypes, such as defining "others" as radically different from "ourselves" and thus having to resort to a "long spoon" when meeting them. Actually, he will be satisfied if his efforts to promote an enhanced cross-cultural dialogue about medical ethics in China and the West go some way to tear down the various invisible "walls" that stand among and between people from different cultures. We may all be seen as "foreign devils" by some of our fellow human beings or other living creatures. Morally and humanly speaking, when supping together it's better to use chopsticks, forks or simply one's hands, and leave the long spoon in the kitchen drawer.

Introduction: the search for a transcultural bioethics

Bioethics, as both an academic field and a public discourse on an international scale, has developed extremely rapidly over the past few decades. This is not surprising, as bioethical issues touch everyone in one way or another and raise many challenging moral, socio-political, religious and cultural questions. As a result of this growing interest, in the English-speaking world increasing attention is being given to medical ethics in China and cross-cultural bioethics in general.

The increasingly large-scale and intimate interactions between and among different cultures and civilizations is a phenomenon that distinguishes our times from previous eras. The question of how cultural differences should be addressed poses a persistent challenge for both ethics and politics, especially in this age of globalization and multiculturalism. While cultural differences are obvious, real, ever-present and deeply rooted, what these differences really mean morally and intellectually and how they ought to be handled practically are far from always being clear. It is from this broad socio-historical context that the need for a comparative Chinese-Western medical ethics, as well as the possibility of a transcultural bioethics, has emerged.

Cultures and bioethics in the new Axial Age

According to German philosopher Karl Jaspers, if there has ever been a phase of human history that can be defined as an "Axial Age," then it should be the period around 500 BCE—from 800 to 200. For in those few hundred years, a remarkable—and to some extent, miraculous—phenomenon occurred around the globe: the intellectual and spiritual foundations of humanity were "simultaneously and independently" laid in the major civilizations that arose in China, India, Persia, Palestine, and Greece (Jaspers 2011 [1953]). During this period, humankind produced the basic socio-cultural categories by which we still live today, created the moral and political principles and ideals we still live by and aspire to, and formulated—through a combination of higher revelation and advanced human wisdom—the world religions which still command enormous allegiance around the globe.

Disease—an unavoidable element of life—is far older than the human race; health care, seen in terms of the biological and social practices involved in the struggle against illness, is at least as old as human history; and morality was present at the birth of human civilization. Thus, the moral problems connected with health, disease, and healing have always puzzled people. Rooted in particular social, political, economic, cultural, and religious conditions, the medical ethics that have arisen in different societies, or in different historical periods of the same society, can exhibit very different content and take very different forms—but may also exhibit common features and even shared foundations.

In China, medical ethics, or deliberation on moral issues in medicine, dates back to the Axial Age. This period produced the earliest Chinese works on disease and healing, from which the paradigmatic classics of traditional Chinese medicine such as *Huangdi Neijing* (The Yellow Emperor's Classic of Medicine)—still essential reading for today's traditional-style practitioners—were compiled in later centuries. It was in this era, too, that the fundamental orientations and basic vocabulary of Chinese socio-cultural life were established through the teachings of the major schools of thoughts including Confucianism (Kong Zi or Confucius, Meng Zi or Mencius, and Xun Zi), Daoism (Lao Zi, Zhuang Zi), Moism (the doctrine of universal love) (Mo Zi), Egoism (Yang-Zhu), Legalism (statism and totalitarianism), and the Yin-Yang theory. Fragmentary discussions of subjects that are defined today as medical ethics are found in both the medical and non-medical literature of this period: the moral character of physicians; the nature of life and illness; the management of dying and death; the practice of telling the truth about terminal illness directly to the patients; the nature of medicine as both an art and a science. From the intellectual and spiritual innovations of the Axial Age (and earlier), China has developed its philosophical thoughts, moral-political traditions, healing systems, and medical moralities (see, e.g., Fung 1952–53; Hsiao 1979; Roetz 1993; Unschuld 1979; Zhou 1983; He 1988; Nie 2009).

Cultural and medical interactions between different cultures and civilizations have been occurring from a very early stage of human history, more actively than we are led to think. The major human civilizations in the Axial Age might not have arisen as independently as Jaspers believed (for the Eastern influence on the classical civilizations of Greece and Rome, see Burkert 1998; McEvilley 2001). As for medical ethics in China, five major traditions can be discerned, with three having their origins in other lands: Confucianism, Daoism, Buddhism, socialism and Christianity. And this is not to mention the contributions of Islam and other ethnic and religious minorities. Without taking account of the enormous influence of these foreign or imported traditions, medical ethics in China would be scarcely imaginable.

Humankind has been experiencing a New Axial Age since the fifthteenth and sixteenth centuries, especially the late nineteenth and early twentieth centuries. If relative independence was the defining characteristic of the major civilizations of the first Axial Age and of the human history that flowed from it, the most significant feature of the New Axial Age is the direct, large-scale and in-depth meeting of different civilizations and cultures at all levels of human life. All the major international events and developments of the past few centuries—such as the great voyages of discovery, the rise and expansion of capitalism, the ascent of modern science and technology, and the globalization of the world's religions—need to be seen from this perspective if we are to gain a better understanding of their origins and implications.

Over the past few centuries, the West has dominated the world politically, militarily, economically and culturally. The aggressive expansion of the West in China has posed the most serious challenges ever encountered by an ancient civilization, resulting in a collective crisis of Chinese identity and a profound loss of cultural confidence and superiority which had been taken for granted for centuries. Partly as a result of these powerful foreign stimuli, and partly because Chinese civilization has never eschewed change, since the early twentieth century China has seen itself as immersed in the age of *geming* (revolutions). Revolutions, one after another, have swept a path across almost every area of political, economic, social and cultural life, including government, the economy, education, language, science and technology, medicine and health care, and medical ethics. The famous phrases used by Marx and Engels in *The Communist Manifesto* to describe the features that distinguish the modern ("bourgeois") epoch from its predecessors in the West can equally be applied to twentieth-century and contemporary China: "uninterrupted disturbance of all social conditions, everlasting uncertainty and agitation." "All fixed, fast-frozen relations, with their train of ancient and venerable prejudices and opinions, are swept away, all new-formed ones become antiquated before they can ossify. All that is solid melts into air, all that is holy is profaned" (Marx and Engels 2002 [1888]). One of the central themes in modern and contemporary China, medical ethics included, is how China can learn from the West without losing its own cultural identities and distinctive traditions.

Despite the persistent hegemony of the West, America in particular, the meeting of medical ethics traditions from diverse cultures constitutes the most visible and salient feature of what has been broadly described as "bioethics"—the contemporary designation of medical ethics—whether in the academic field or the public domain. There is a large and growing body of literature on the cross-cultural and international challenges faced by the discipline, discussing among other things how these challenges should be met, and the ways in which different cultural groups are responding to the ethical issues posed by contemporary health care practices, life sciences and advanced biotechnologies. This vast literature includes influential textbooks (e.g., Veatch 2000 [1989]; May, Wong and Delston 2010 [1994]) and overviews of bioethics as practised in different parts of the world (Peppin and Cherry 2003). Other studies cover particular countries or regions such as Latin America (e.g. Salles and Bertomeu 2002). Many works have focused on particular bioethical issues such as human cloning (Roetz 2006), human embryonic stem cell research (Gottweis, Salter and Waldby 2009), genetics and eugenics (Wertz and Fletcher 2004), end-of-life decision-making (Blank and Merrick 2007), human finitude (Rehmann-Sutter, Düwell and Mieth

2006), and the globalization of medical care and biomedical research (Green, Donovan and Jauss 2009). Research involving human subjects is a major sub-area of contemporary bioethics, as is cross-cultural and international bioethics (Emanuel et al. 2008), especially regarding medical research in developing countries (Macklin 2004; Lavery et al. 2007). One of the central debates concerns the desirability or possibility of a universal or global bioethics, with some arguing in favor of the notion (Macklin 1999) and in support of the discipline's transcultural dimensions (Pellegrino, Mazzarella and Corsi 1992), while others oppose it (Tao 2002; Engelhardt 2006). Almost all the studies in this highly selective list are collections of essays by scholars from both Western and non-Western countries. China is frequently, though not always, discussed in these works.

Feminist bioethics is one of the most rapidly developing areas in the expanding field of bioethics. International and cross-cultural issues have figured strongly in a number of anthologies in this major sub-field of bioethics, with contributions from feminists—both female and male—from countries throughout the world (e.g. Tong, Anderson and Santos 2001; Tong, Donchin and Dodds 2004; and Scully, Baldwin-Ragaven and Fitzpatrick 2010). China has been represented in these pioneering collections of essays in international feminist bioethics which are often associated with the International Network on Feminist Approaches to Bioethics (the most prominent sub-group of the International Association of Bioethics).

Bioethics in Asia has also become a thriving sub-field, as reflected in a growing body of literature in the English language, with many studies having significant content on China. There are now two English-language journals that focus specifically on Asia: *Asian Bioethics Review* (peer-reviewed and launched in 2008) and *Eubios Journal of Asian and International Bioethics* (non-peer-reviewed and launched in 1990; this is the official journal of the Asian Association of Bioethics). The established book series, "Medicine and Philosophy," has produced a sub-series entitled "Asian Studies in Bioethics and the Philosophy of Medicine," in which six collections of essays have been published to date (Fan 1999; Tao 2002; Englehardt and Rosmussen 2002; Qiu 2004; Lee 2007; Tao 2008). A number of publications cover a variety of contemporary bioethical challenges in Asia (Fujiki and Macer 1998; Qiu 2004; Macer 2004; Tai 2008). A casebook for multicultural learners on biomedical ethics in Asia has recently appeared (Akabayashi, Kodama and Slingsby 2010). Many studies have focused on particular bioethical issues; examples include an Eastern-Western comparative study of personhood (Becker 2000), the role of the family in medical decision-making and biotechnology (Lee 2007), the political and cultural dimensions of Asian bioscience and biotechnology (Ong and Chen 2010), an historical study of eugenics in China and Japan (Chung 2002), human genomics (Sleeboom-Faulkner 2008a), the human genetic biobank (Sleeboom-Faulkner 2008b), genetic and predictive testing (Sleeboom-Faulkner 2010), and an Eastern-

Western comparative study of the ethics of population engineering (Nie forthcoming[a]). Some works have explored the bioethical perspectives of different Asian cultural traditions such as Buddhism (Keown 2001 [1990]) and Hinduism (Crawford 2003; Bhattacharyya 2006). Other publications have focused on particular Asian countries, such as Singapore (Elliott, Ho and Lim 2010). Using the Philippines as a case study, authors have proposed moving "beyond a Western bioethics" (Alora and Lumitao 2001). Many studies have a clear Japanese focus, addressing subjects such as abortion (LaFleur 1992; Hardacre 1997), Japanese bioethics compared to Western bioethics (Hoshino 1997), advance directive and surrogate decision making in Japan in comparison with Germany and the United States (Sass, Veatch and Kimura 1998), and life-and-death issues (Takahashi 2005).

Just as humane behavior and human moral pursuits cross cultural boundaries, so also, unfortunately, do inhumanity and the violation of the most basic ethical norms. Attention in this area has been directed to the counterpart of Nazi medicine in the East: the atrocities carried out in the areas occupied by the Japanese army before and during the Second World War, especially the extensive programmes of biological warfare implemented throughout China and the barbaric human experiments carried out upon Koreans, Russians, Americans and (mostly) Chinese (Nie, Tsuchiya and Li 2009). In order to monopolize the data acquired by the Japanese scientists and other war criminals involved, the American government committed complicity after fact by making a deal with Japanese perpetrators after the war (Nie 2006). This subject—one that bioethics in Asia can never afford to ignore—has been covered in both journalist investigations (Williams and Wallace 1989; Barenblatt 2004) and systematic historical studies (Harris 2002 [1994]). One cross-cultural study of one of medicine's darkest sides—the rationalizing of unethical medical research—included the activities of the now infamous Unit 731 (LaFleur, Böhme and Shimazono 2007). Comparative historical, sociological and ethical inquiries into Japan's wartime medical atrocities and their international aftermath have been the focus of a recent collection of essays (Nie, Guo, Selden and Kleinman 2010), and will be further examined in a forthcoming monograph (Nie forthcoming [c]).

This select list of book-length studies of bioethics in Asia, undertaken by scholars from various academic disciplines—philosophy, anthropology and the social sciences in particular—raises some very big questions. They include, but are not limited to, the following: How are people, countries and cultural groups in Asia responding to the thorny bioethical dilemmas arising from the conditions of contemporary health care and advances in life sciences and biotechnology? Is there an "Asian bioethics" and, if so, what are its distinctive features? How should bioethics in the Asian context respond to the principles and achievements of bioethics in the West? What contribution can the Asian indigenous traditions make to contemporary bioethics? All these questions are highly relevant to bioethics in China.

Over the past few decades, China has increasingly come under the international spotlight. An interest in medical ethics in China has also been growing in the West. There is a proliferation of journal articles and special journal issues on the subject, and there seems to be no end in sight. Yet, there are only a handful of books in print in English on medical ethics in China, including an historical study of professional ethics in imperial China (Unschuld 1979) and a work on bioethical challenges in contemporary China (Döring and Chen 2002). There are studies of the bioethical perspectives offered by particular Chinese traditions such as Confucianism (Fan 1999, 2009) and of particular topics for example human genetics (Döring 1999), medical ethics education (Döring 2002), nursing ethics (Pang 2003), abortion in mainland China (Nie 2005) and Taiwan (Moskowitz 2001), and health-care policy and social confidence in a market economy (Tao 2008). The BIONET project (a Sino-European co-operation on the ethical governance of biological and biomedical research) has produced a report (BIONET 2010) as well a stimulating anthology (Döring 2009) regarding the Chinese and European perspectives on the ethics of life sciences and the possibility of productive dialogue (both are freely available online). In addition, Ole Döring has published a pioneering study of bioethics in China from cross-cultural and philosophical perspectives in German; it is not available in English (Döring 2004).

China's ambitious and invasive birth control programme—which aims at "controlling the quantity and improving the quality" of the population—has acquired significant academic attention in the West, in addition to enormous media coverage. Although a systematic and in-depth ethical analysis of this massive project of social engineering is yet to be undertaken (Nie 2010b, 2010c, forthcoming b), some of the existing sociological, anthropological, historical and demographic studies of the subject have a significant ethical component or implications (Aird 1990; Milwertz 1997; Dikötter 1998; Greenhalgh and Winckler 2005; White 2006; Greenhalgh 2008).

All this activity reflects the most salient feature of our New Axial Age: the large-scale cross-cultural dialogue now taking place across the globe. At the same time, and as one aspect of this phenomenon, a Chinese-Western dialogue on medical ethics has been going on, likewise on a grand scale. Despite this, however, no book-length work in the English language has yet appeared which approaches medical ethics in China from an explicitly Chinese-Western comparative perspective (for an initial Chinese work see Xu, Cheng, Li and Zheng 1998). And no study has yet taken on the task of establishing the contours of a distinctive "transcultural bioethics" and suggesting ways of developing a more adequate Chinese-Western cultural dialogue on medical ethics.

Toward a transcultural bioethics

My overall aim in this book is to begin the process of formulating a transcultural bioethics through the investigation of medical ethics in China from a Chinese-

Western comparative perspective. Theoretically and methodologically, my approach can be characterized as "interpretative" or "interpretivist." Along with the American bioethicist and medical humanist Ronald Carson (1990, 1995) I believe that bioethics is "fundamentally an interpretive enterprise." For Carson (1999), when assessing the practices of other cultures, especially those that seem unfamiliar and even "strange," an interpretative approach is not just more effective but a moral imperative. German sinologist and philosopher Ole Döring (2000, 2004) has similarly argued for the central role that hermeneutics should play in global and Chinese/East-Asian medical ethics. In an earlier study, I employed this approach as a way of making better sense of a very strange practice in traditional Chinese medicine—using a range of human body parts such as pubic hair, nails and even flesh as medicine (Nie 1999b; for the Chinese practice, see Li 1988 [1592], Vol. 52). I took the same approach, for the same reasons, to the complicated Chinese moral world of abortion—soliciting various voices, different viewpoints and personal experiences to break down the apparent public silence on this deeply contested issue (Nie 2005).

Whatever name we give to this approach—"interpretative" cross-cultural bioethics and "transcultural" bioethics are two possibilities—it is fundamental to the theoretical and methodological orientation of this book, and has produced a focus on five broad themes: 1) the complexities of cultural differences; 2) the internal moral plurality that exists within every culture; 3) the similarities or commonalities manifested in a wide range of cultural differences; 4) the possibility of effective dialogue between different cultures; and 5) the necessity of normative judgments, or the primacy of morality. In today's world, a transcultural or interpretative approach moves against a series of powerful currents: a deeply rooted proclivity for stereotyping both non-Western and Western cultures; a belief in the inevitable clash or war of cultures; the endorsement of the tyranny of cultural practices and norms over ethics or morality; and various versions of cultural and ethical relativism.

Let me present these five major themes of a transcultural bioethics one by one.

Overcoming stereotypes to appreciate the complexities of cultural differences

Growing out of and reinforcing some widespread stereotypes of Chinese society and cultures (the plural form is significant), a number of empirically problematic, normatively misleading and politically contentious characterizations of Chinese medical ethics have gained currency, both outside and within China. These persistent (mis)perceptions of China and Chinese medical ethics include: thinking about Chinese and Western cultural differences in a series of dichotomous terms; treating China as "the radical Other" of the West; characterizing Chinese cultures and medical ethics as homogenous and communitarian in contrast to the diverse and individualistic West; privileging the mainstream or official position as the only authentic cultural representative of the diversity of China; setting up Western cultural achievements as the sole standard of evaluation; and appealing to perceived "cultural differences" to oppose such values as informed consent and human rights as being incompatible with Chinese culture. Before such misconceptions can be replaced, the first task of an adequate cross-cultural bioethics is to expose these stereotypes and stereotypical ways of characterizing cultural differences, whether in overt or disguised forms.

A transcultural approach first of all maintains that Chinese-Western cultural differences in medical ethics are far more complex, subtle, intriguing—and thus more difficult to grasp and articulate—than the facile generalizations, sweeping assertions, ready-made assumptions and simplistic contrasts that are all too commonly found in this area. They are also, as a result, far more fascinating.

Taking seriously the internal plurality within every culture

A transcultural bioethics appreciates and indeed cherishes the great internal plurality and even radically differing approaches to medical ethics *within* every culture. The moral plurality that flourishes within the diversity of Chinese cultures can hardly be overemphasized. "Taking cultural differences seriously" has become a resounding slogan in this age of globalization and multiculturalism, along with the more ominous "clash of civilizations." While the differences between cultures are often highlighted, differences or diversity within other cultures, particularly non-Western ones, are often downplayed. So much is made of Western—particularly American and British—pluralism and diversity that it is easy to overlook the fact that, throughout its history, China has been socially and culturally as diverse as the United States, if not more so. While the West, and the United States in particular, is said to epitomize the modern multiracial, multicultural, pluralist society, the many Chinas have long been treated as essentially homogenous. The obvious and profound plurality of Chinese cultures—including medical ethics—has never been taken as seriously as it deserves, outside as well as inside China.

There are many ways of appreciating the internal plurality and cross-cultural complexity of medical moralities in different cultures and societies. One process advocated in interpretative anthropology is "thick description" or thick narrative. According to the distinguished American anthropologist Clifford Geertz, an interpretive theory of culture depends on this ethnographic or thick description. For Geertz (1973), thick description possesses four significant characteristics: it is interpretive; the social discourse that is interpreted is always in flux; the purpose of interpretation to try to "rescue the 'said' of such discourse from its perishing occasions and fix it in pursuable terms;" and thick description is "microscopic"—i.e., it approaches both broad interpretations of whole societies and abstract analysis "from the direction of exceedingly extended acquaintances with extremely small matters." The purpose of thick description in cross-cultural bioethics is to understand how medical moralities actually work in health-care practice. Interpretive cross-cultural bioethics pays special attention to the experiences, perspectives and voices of non-mainstream or non-legitimate, unofficial and dissident groups and individuals. It investigates commonplace experiences, life stories, and local moral worlds and generates a thick description or thick narrative as a basis for critical understanding. The norms and practices of different medical moralities in different cultures may appear incommensurable. But, through the use of thick description and interpretation, similarities or comparabilities will emerge.

Focusing on both differences and commonalities

Thus, a transcultural approach focuses not only on differences, but also on similarities; more exactly, on the similarities in differences and the differences in similarities. Since both Chinese and Western medical moralities, like all other medical moralities in other cultures, are always plural, it is not sufficient to compare the two systems only by means of highly abstract and contrasting generalizations. A transcultural approach calls for comparisons and conversations between, for example, Chinese and Western perspectives on individualism, Chinese and Western communitarian views, and virtue-based medical ethics in both traditions. This approach is at odds with the popular postmodernist discourse in which the differences within and between cultures and civilizations are defined as so radical that they are incommensurable with each other and thus destined to clash.

Much has been written and said about the radical differences between cultures and their inevitable conflicts when they encounter each other. It is all too tempting to set up categories of total opposition. A French scholar of Chinese history has concluded that "the intellectual traditions, mode of thoughts and vision of the world of the Chinese differed markedly from those of Europe." Their differences are so radical and fundamental that Chinese cultures and people, rather than manifesting humanity under a different guise, belong to "a different kind of humanity" (Gernet 1985, 247).

However, the thesis that human cultures are so radically different from each other that there are no shared or common values among human societies overlooks some basic findings which have emerged from the enormous body of work that has been done on cultural differences. According to one British philosopher, a "striking unanimity" exists among superficially different cultures and societies:

> All human societies show a concern for the value of human life; ... All human societies regards the procreation of a new human life as in itself a good thing unless there are special circumstances. No human society fails to restrict sexual activities; ... All human societies display a concern for truth,

> ... all societies display a favour for the value of co-operation, of common over individual good, of obligation between individuals, and of justice within groups. All know friendship. All have some conception of *meum* and *tuum*, title or property, and of reciprocity. All value play, serious and formalized, or relaxed and recreational. All treat the bodies of dead members of the group in some traditional and ritual fashion different from their procedure for rubbish disposal. All display a concern for powers or principles which are to be respected as suprahuman; in one form or another religion is universal.
>
> (Finnis 1982, 83–4)

This description is certainly applicable to Chinese societies and cultures. Indeed, the universalist stance of the British philosopher, based on the Western natural law tradition, echoes an essential concept in Confucianism, best articulated by Mencius, the Confucian saint second only to Confucius himself. For Mencius, every human being shares certain basic moral sentiments. To illustrate this truth, he used the well-known scenario of a young child on the verge of falling into a well. Everyone, so long as he or she is a human being,

> would be moved to compassion, not because he wanted to get in the good graces of the parents, nor because he wished to win the praise of his fellow villagers or friends, not yet because he disliked the cry of the child.
>
> (Mencius 1970, 82)

The real reason is self-evident: the universal spirit of human compassion for someone in distress. It was this concept of a shared human morality and humanity that led some physicians in traditional China like Sun Simiao in the 7th century (known as the "king of medicine" in popular Chinese culture) to advocate that physicians should treat all patients—nobles or commoners, rich or poor, old or young, handsome or homely, abled and disabled, intelligent or simple-minded, Chinese or foreigners, relatives and good friends or enemies—on an equal moral footing.

Great intellectual efforts have been given to identify the common political and moral grounds in the Western, especially American context, including such prominent and potent notions as the "overlapping consensus" in political philosophy (Rawls 2005 [1993]) and the "common morality" in biomedical ethics (Beauchamp and Childress 2009). One effort has been made to articulate ethical universals in medicine and medical ethics in the midst of ubiquitous cultural diversity from the perspective of human rights (Macklin 1999). This approach has been criticized often by anthropology-trained bioethicists as having not taken seriously the diversity of human moral life (Turner 1998, 2003a, 2003b, 2005).

A transcultural bioethics recognizes that a common moral ground, or merely our shared common humanity (whether between China and the West, or any other group of cultures) is always present, and exists precisely in the midst of ubiquitous cultural differences—whether or not we recognize it, however insufficiently we have grasped it, however mistakenly we have represented it. Without acknowledging the existence of a common humanity, cultural differences can never be seen in their true perspective. Without acknowledging the existence of a common humanity, there would be no shared ground on which medical ethics in China and the West could learn from each other in order for each to expand its own horizons.

Promoting a deeper cross-cultural dialogue

A transcultural approach treats the "other"—the medical morality foreign to one's own—as a partner in dialogue, and fosters a deeper and richer dialogue than generally occurs between the different medical morality traditions. The other is neither a paradise nor a hell, neither a source of salvation nor an inferior being. The goal is neither to discover which medical morality is better, nor to resolve all the conflicts between various moral views. Rather, the primary goal is to know oneself better and to understand the other better through on-going conversation. By promoting long-term coexistence, continuous dialogue, reciprocal learning and criticism, on-going negotiation and mutual flourishing, as well as reasonable ways of dealing with dissimilarities and tensions between medical ethical systems, the interpretive approach cultivates—rather than overrides—the diversity of perspectives within and among different medical moralities. Of course, sustaining the dialogue between different traditions is anything but an easy task.

Although the dialogue between Eastern and Western medical moralities has long begun, it is far from being complete, even adequate. There are many reasons to expect more from this on-going conversation. One can only hope that some aspects of traditional Chinese medical ethics remain alive after the various useful arguments and tools of Western bioethics have been integrated into Chinese health care and medical morality. One day we may live in a world in which Western medical moralities are no longer as thoroughly "Western" as they are today, just as Western biomedicine is no longer only Western in character, but has been both influenced by and incorporated into the medical practices of other cultures including China. At the same time, Chinese medical moralities will no longer be as "Chinese" as they are today, just as already Chinese medicine is no longer only Chinese in nature, but has been appropriated by many people outside China. In other words, Chinese medical ethics will acquire more Western-ness and Western bioethics will have a greater degree of Chinese-ness in the process of their mutual globalization.

Upholding the primacy of morality

Lastly and most importantly, against the tendency to endorse the "tyranny of cultural practices over ethics," transcultural bioethics stresses the primacy of morality over cultural practices. In order to encourage productive dialogue, tolerance of, respect for, and curiosity about our differences are always necessary. Nevertheless, this is not to say that an interpretive approach to cross-cultural bioethics automatically rules out normative judgments. It is simply to say that understanding and interpretation must precede those judgments. Interpretive cross-cultural bioethics works from the bottom up. The first and most important question for this approach is how certain perspectives or practices in other cultures—especially those that are superficially alien and ethically problematic—are possible, and what is their cultural context. Only then can an informed ethical judgment be made. Engaged interpretations are essential to any normative judgment. *Either* simply applying normative ethical principles developed within a particular moral tradition to cross-cultural settings *or* merely respecting cultural differences and the particularity of the local is both practically dangerous and theoretically problematic.

In order to understand the reality on the ground and challenge its unethical aspects, bioethics must find a way to address *both* what really matters locally, especially for those who are culturally oppressed and socially deprived, *and*, at the same time, uphold the normative and (assumed) universal moral values we hold dear. To a degree, the interpretive approach complements the normative approach. For instance, interpretive cross-cultural medical ethics can help normative criticism to be culturally relevant by discovering similar moral norms in the culture being critiqued and by encouraging and empowering critical voices indigenous to that culture.

Studies of cultural factors and context can often provide important information on why and how a practice exists, without ethically justifying the practice. In fact, cross-cultural moral criticism and normative judgments are often insightful in identifying the moral blind spots that every society or culture has. In ancient Greece and Rome, and in early periods of U.S. history, the morality of slavery was rarely questioned. In patriarchal societies, including China, belief in the social, moral, and intellectual inferiority of women is rarely contested. In ancient China, as in many other imperial systems, the political and moral authority of the emperor over his subjects was rarely challenged. The moral blind spots in each of these societies were rarely questioned, as reigning social practices and customs were taken for granted, even seen as the "natural" order. Such moral blind spots may be so well embedded in everyday social practice and long-rooted customs that it is difficult to identify them. Human beings depend upon customs and practices to simplify life by reducing the need for individual decision-making about conduct in day-to-day living. Cross-cultural moral criticism and normative judgments can effectively reveal problems that hide, deeply rooted, in everyday practices.

In this age of Western political, economic, cultural and military hegemony, it is extremely important to respect different cultural practices, especially non-Western ones. Nevertheless, an ethical dilemma arises when cultural practices conflict with moral imperatives. In the lofty efforts to preserve and advocate for cultural differences, a moral danger exists—the temptation to privilege cultural practices over ethical mandates. It can be implied, if not explicitly held, that whatever is culturally authentic is automatically ethically defensible. This tyranny of culture over ethics can easily lead to moral relativism and even ethical nihilism. According to the logic of this moral reasoning, slavery in human history; gender discrimination and many other forms of discrimination, which are found in almost all human societies; the West's colonization of the non-Western world including China; the slavery of African Americans in the United States; the Third Reich in Germany; and foot-binding in Chinese history—to list just a few examples—are all ethically justifiable because all these practices are culturally genuine and even unique.

More crucially, an uncritical reverence for cultural norms and practices can actually work against the most fundamental values of a given culture and society. For both Confucianism and Daoism, the two major indigenous Chinese moral and political traditions, it is not existing cultural practices that should be privileged, but whatever is morally right. For Confucianism and Daoism, the most fundamental value is precisely the primacy of ethics and morality over existing social and cultural practices, rather than the other way around. The moral imperative of the Dao (Tao, literally "the Way") or the *Tianming* (the mandate of Heaven) is superior to the claims of any cultural and social practices, whether Western or Eastern. The basic task and highest calling of ethics, transcultural bioethics included, is, first of all, to identify which socio-cultural practices are morally justifiable and which are not; and then to begin the process of constantly reforming existing social and cultural practices, however accepted or privileged they are and however difficult it may be to change them, according to ethical ideals and moral imperatives.

It is in this sense that every culture, every medical ethics tradition, Chinese culture and bioethics included, is always an open system—open to new and creative interpretations of the past, open to incorporating positive elements from other systems, open to innovations whether originating from outside or within; above all, open to the aspirations of human morality and the calling of the great Dao.

The contents of this book

This is primarily a book about medical ethics in China. To provide insights into Chinese viewpoints and experiences, I draw on a wide range of primary and secondary historical and sociological sources, many of them unexpected in character. Also I will employ critical philosophical and normative analysis. With their help, I carefully examine a number of key topics in medical ethics including China's internal moral plurality; views on fetal life; the disclosure of information by medical professionals; informed consent; professional medical ethics; the nature of medicine; health promotion; attitudes towards sexuality; personhood; feminist bioethics; the UNESCO Universal Declaration on Bioethics; and human rights.

Medical ethics in China—as with each of the topics to be examined—are here approached from an explicitly Chinese-Western cross-cultural comparative perspective. In particular, I offer detailed comparisons—involving cross-cultural differences and similarities, including differences in similarities and similarities in differences—of a number of subjects including Chinese and Western approaches to medical truth-telling; ancient Chinese and nineteenth-century American medical attitudes to sexual overindulgence as a cause of morbidity and even premature death; and a Chinese-Western dialogue on women's rights, human rights, personhood, and health promotion in the context of bioethics. In this process, I will develop some more adequate methods for comparative culture and ethical research.

The book consists of fourteen chapters arranged in four parts. The four chapters in Part I critically examine some popular myth and stereotypes on Chinese cultures, Chinese medical ethics, Chinese medicine and Chinese-Western cultural differences. The first chapter presents the most widespread and persistent myths which characterize a homogenous Chinese culture and medical ethics as being radically different from the West, in particular, a collectivist or communitarian China versus the individualistic West. This myth is rooted in the "East is East and West is West" mentality and the age-old and still dominant dichotomizing way of thinking about the East and the West, about "us" and "them," about cultural differences in general.

In the second chapter, using medical truth-telling in China, Chinese views on fetal life, and a brief discussion of individualism in China and the West as examples, I have identified a series of grave intellectual and political problems involved with dichotomizing Chinese-Western cultures, or what I have called the "fallacy of dichotomization." A main task of this book is to further demonstrate the fallacy of dichotomizing cultures and seek ways to overcome this age-old and dominant habit of thought.

Using the method of cross-cultural historical comparison, in Chapter 3 I discuss some of the striking similarities and subtle differences between medical attitudes to sexual excess in nineteenth-century America and ancient China. In doing so, I offer a critique of the fashionable view of China as a "radical other" of the West, a mistake representatively committed by great poststructuralist French thinker Michel Foucault in his comparison of Chinese and Western attitudes to sexuality.

While most of this book is focused on Chinese-Western cross-cultural commonalities, it is important to acknowledge cross-cultural differences can be deeper than what we often assumed. On the opposing end of the "false opposites" (the assumed cross-cultural differences are not as dramatic as they appear to be) is another common vice in cross-cultural understanding, the problem of "false friends" (the perceived similarities are not as real as they appear to be). It treats cultural differences as only superficial, never fundamental and significant, and often uses Western standards to measure the value of particular cultural achievements and practices in other societies. Taking the form of an excursion, Chapter 4 illustrates the problem of "false friends" through a thoroughgoing refutation of the widely accepted claim that the ancient Chinese—in particular, the authors of *The Yellow Emperor's Classic of Medicine*—first described the circulation of the blood, a claim made most prominently by Joseph Needham, arguably the greatest China scholar in the West.

A major approach proposed in the entire book to overcome the popular myths and stereotypes about China, the fallacy of dichotomizing cultures in particular, is to take seriously China's great internal heterogeneity and pluralism—social, political, economic, cultural, religious, and moral. Chapter 5, the first one in Part II "Truths of Cultures," shows that just as there is no single and homogenous Chinese culture or morality, there is no single and homogenous Chinese medical morality. Great internal diversity and pluralism has always been an essential feature of Chinese civilizations and medical ethics in history and today.

In Chapter 6, I re-discover a long but forgotten Chinese tradition of medical truth-telling. In total contradiction to standard Chinese medical practice today and what has been universally assumed both inside and outside China, a great deal of primary historical evidence—including the biographies of ancient medical sages and celebrated physicians from many different dynasties—reveals a Chinese tradition of medical truth-telling that dates back at least twenty-six centuries. The longevity of this tradition is especially remarkable in comparison with the West, where full medical disclosure did not become the accepted standard until the 1970s or even later. Ironically, when seen in its historical context, the contemporary mainstream Chinese practice of nondisclosure has been strongly influenced by the earlier dominant Western norm of concealing hard medical truths. A more appropriate cross-cultural bioethics must pay close attention to the complexity of cultural differences whose character and meaning are rarely as straightforward as they appear.

In Chapter 7, I argue that, even if medical truth-telling were culturally alien to China, as is usually assumed, ethical imperatives exist to reform the contemporary mainstream Chinese practice of nondisclosure (or indirect disclosure through family members) as this practice can cause serious harm to patients as well as their families. Numerous surveys conducted throughout mainland China, like others in Hong Kong and Taiwan, indicate that the great majority of Chinese want truthful information in terminal cases. I also offer a traditional Confucian defense of truthfulness as a fundamental ethical principle and an essential personal and social virtue for physicians to practice. An historic shift toward honest and direct disclosure by physicians is now occurring in China. Culturally, this change is not so much an aping of Western (and thus foreign) ways, but a return to a long-neglected indigenous Chinese tradition.

When considering matters of cultural difference, empirically problematic perceptions, ethically dubious judgments, and practically contentious resolutions can easily become entangled. This shows most commonly in the appeal to perceived (often misperceived) cultural differences as an ethical justification for the rejection of norms with historical origins and strong support in the West—such as truth-telling by medical professionals, informed consent, patients' rights, women's rights and human rights in general—by non-Western societies and cultures including China. Despite its popularity and apparent plausibility, the "cultural differences" argument, just as that against medical truth-telling in China, is seriously flawed, both descriptively and normatively. It often obscures the real ethical issues at stake and promotes the tyranny of existing socio-cultural practices.

In Chapter 8, I discuss some further intellectual flaws involved in the "cultural differences" argument as it relates to informed consent. Rather than primarily as an issue of culture, informed consent is mainly concerned with the issue of power—balancing power relations between medical institutions and professionals on the one side and vulnerable patients on the other—a situation which exists in the West as well as in China. The "cultural differences" argument confuses the philosophical justification for informed consent, based on individualism and individual autonomy, with informed consent as a practical moral guide or principle for health-care practice and medical research. A communitarian justification of informed consent has been offered. In addition, I examine the sociological and economic reasons behind the phenomenon of "family consent" as widely practiced in China today, as well as some serious ethical problems associated with it.

Two chapters in Part III address the theme "Cultural Norms Embodying Universal Values." It is widely believed that the concept of human rights is, by and large, a Western cultural norm, often at odds with non-Western cultures and, therefore, not applicable in non-Western societies such as China. "The Universal Declaration on Bioethics and Human Rights" adopted by the United Nations Educational, Scientific and Cultural Organization in 2005 reflects this deep-rooted and popular assumption. Using Chinese cultures as an illustration, Chapter 9 points out the problems of this stereotypical view of culture and human rights and demonstrates that a commitment to human rights has long been a Chinese ethical value. It highlights the international nature of human rights and the often-ignored positive elements of Chinese cultures that promote and embody universal human values such as human rights. It is long overdue to give due recognition about these positive elements, especially the significant contributions made by people in China and other non-Western countries to international human rights.

Like most other societies, Chinese society is patriarchal in its fundamental social structures and embodies long-held prejudices against females. Although feminist approaches to bioethics largely remain a product of Western thought and social movements, they have attracted international attention, including in China. In Chapter 10, I argue that Western feminism, feminist bioethics and the feminist human rights discourse are highly relevant and significant for China. Collectively, they provide Chinese theorists and activists with useful conceptual lenses and powerful political strategies to better address the various forms of gender discrimination, whether overt or hidden, expressed in medical ethics as practiced in China. The ways to develop a Chinese feminist bioethics are also proposed.

If the purpose of Part III is to elaborate that, despite their Western origins, such values as informed consent, women's rights and human rights are relevant and applicable to China, in the final part of this book—"Chinese Wisdom for Today"—I present a number of case studies illustrating how traditional Chinese medicine, viewed in light of Chinese ethical and philosophical traditions, can offer us insights into the problems of contemporary medical ethics, whether in China or the West—provided that we are willing to attend carefully to this material and interpret it creatively.

Chapter 11 offers an introduction to professional medical ethics through a study of the most influential text in Chinese medical ethics, *Lun Dayi Jingcheng* (On the Proficiency and Sincerity of the Master Physician) by the great seventh-century physician Sun Simiao. The complex and multi-layered Confucian notion of *cheng* (sincerity, authenticity, or truthfulness) has important metaphysical and spiritual dimensions. From the perspective of a professional ethics based on *cheng*, the contemporary theory and practice of medical professionalism in the West has significantly neglected the central role not only of the inner disposition of the moral agent, but also of the metaphysical and spiritual dimensions of the moral life.

In Chapter 12, I present two more concepts—one on the nature of medicine and the other on the patient-physician relationship—from traditional Chinese medical ethics: the norm of "medicine as the art of humanity" and the metaphor of the physician as a general (with the patient as the king). The rich sources in the traditional Chinese professional ethics of medicine have the potential to contribute more to the positive development of medical professionalism in both China and the West. For instance, the ideal of medicine as the art of humanity can help to guard medicine—the oldest and newest profession of humankind—so as not to be metamorphosed into a slave, serving merely the interest of profit-making and the claims of nation-states.

The issue of personhood is a major theoretical issue in contemporary bioethics and moral philosophy. As a review of two pioneering works on Chinese and Western perspectives on personhood, Chapter 13 offers further illustration of one of the central points of this book—that effective cross-cultural dialogue can enrich not only "our" cultures, the cultures we are most familiar with, but also "their" cultures, the cultures we know little about. The result will be that we will all come to know ourselves, and our common humanity, in much greater depth.

An inherent and essential tension exists in human moral and political life, most concisely expressed in the opposition of the individual vs. community and society. As a consequence, many moral, political and bioethical issues have bifurcated into two conflicting versions, one stressing the element of individualism, the other communitarianism. This tension has been particularly manifested in the ethics of health promotion. Employing one of the basic concepts of Chinese thought and traditional Chinese medicine—the notion of *yin-yang*—Chapter 14, the final one of this book, offers a yin-yang dialectical model for health promotion in which the seemingly opposed claims of the individual and the community are weighed and reconciled and the essential identity of their interests revealed.

In "Conclusions: Ways Toward the Uncertain Future," I will recapture the main themes and conclusions of this book. First, a genuine cross-cultural dialogue is necessary and possible and the clash of cultures is not our destiny. Second, for China, taking its internal diversity seriously is an urgent task, more in practical terms than in intellectual ones. Indeed, the future of China depends on how well it will meet the most persistent challenge that she has always faced in history as well as today: to unify the vast nation politically and culturally while maintaining due respect for its great internal heterogeneity and pluralism.

In the prologue, I suggested that, despite the open character of Chinese civilization there is nevertheless a strong pull towards ethnocentrism and cultural chauvinism in China. In the epilogue, I recount a couple of telling parables and insights from the work of Zhuang Zi, a profound but humorous Daoist philosopher and story-teller, to offer readers a glimpse of an alternative discourse within Chinese culture which resists ethnocentrism and absolutism, advocates for difference and plurality, and argues for the necessity of mutual understanding among diverse peoples, however difficult this task may prove to be.

To sum up, in this book I set out to expose a series of common obstacles in the pursuit of cross-cultural bioethics and to develop an "interpretative" or "transcultural" approach to the subject. Drawing on a wide range of primacy sources and supplied with careful philosophical arguments, this book will take readers on a journey of exploration of the captivating cultural differences as well as the fascinating commonalities exhibited by China and the West in their respective (and various) traditions of medicine and medical ethics. I will show that, rather than being homogenous and static, as so often assumed, in China medical ethics has always been internally heterogeneous, full of diverse and contradictory elements, changing over time, influenced by and borrowing from foreign cultures, open to new possibilities, and subject to ethical scrutiny and developing moral ideals. Above all, I seek to put forward a theory—and some appropriate methods—for the development of a more adequate cross-cultural or transcultural bioethics: an ethics that resists cultural stereotypes, cherishes our common humanity, upholds the primacy of morality, and acknowledges the richness, internal diversity, dynamism and openness of medical ethics in every culture, whether in China, the West or elsewhere.

Part I

Beyond stereotypes and stereotyping

Chapter 1

Communitarian China versus the individualistic West

A popular myth and its roots

Since British poet Rudyard Kipling penned his famous lines, "Oh, East is East and West is West, and never the twain shall meet," in "The Ballad of East and West" (1895), the world has moved on. Whether people like it or not, the twain came together a long time ago. However, the mentality behind Kipling's words stubbornly refuses to go away. Deeply rooted stereotypes and myths die hard in bioethics, as in the public mind.

The most persistent and widespread myth sets up a static, homogeneous, and monolithic Chinese culture in radical contrast to a fluid and pluralistic Western culture—in its simplest and most popular version, a collectivist, communitarian or familist China versus an individualistic West. This dichotomy has achieved almost universal currency and permeated all levels of discourse. Underlying this myth is an age-old and still dominant way of thinking about cultural differences as "radical others": the dichotomizing of East and West, of "them" and "us." Accordingly, both outside and inside China, a unified, single and communitarian Chinese medical ethics is widely believed to exist in radical opposition to a Western bioethics, perceived as individualistic in character and in practice.

In this and the following chapter, I offer a critical study of this myth and expose the intellectual fallacy and political perils of dichotomization. I will discuss its enormous popularity, modes of expressions and the main intellectual or epistemological root of the myth not only in the West but also in China. As next and other chapters in this book will show, this myth and the dichotomous way of thinking about Chinese-Western cultural differences have brought about a series of grave consequences. Among the gravest ones are that cross-cultural similarities and commonalities are overlooked and that the great internal diversity and pluralism of cultures and medical ethics *within* China has been minimized and denied.

Western attitudes: two opposing ideologies, one shared myth

In the West, two apparently opposing attitudes can be distinguished on the subject of cultural differences. The first is what can be called the "modernist" or ethnocentric way of thinking about cultures. The modernist approach to Occidental and Oriental cultures was vividly depicted by the German author Thomas Mann through the character of Herr Settembrini in *The Magic Mountain*. Settembrini, an inmate of a tuberculosis sanatorium in Switzerland, is the intellectual guide of Hans Castorp, the young, questing hero of the novel. According to the "Settembrinian cosmogony," wrote Mann, two incompatible principles, one Asiatic and the other European,

> were in perpetual conflict for possession of the world: force and justice, tyranny and freedom, superstition and knowledge; the law of permanence and the law of change, of ceaseless fermentation ensuing in progress. One might call the first the Asiatic, the second the European principle; for Europe was the theatre of rebellion, the sphere of intellectual discrimination and transforming activity, whereas the East embodied the conception of quiescence and immobility. There was no doubt as to which of the two would finally triumph: it would be the power of enlightenment, the power that made for rational advance and development.
>
> (Mann 1969: 157)

For Settembrini, an Italian humanist zealot, the Asiatic principle has to be "crushed" for the sake of progress, science, and human reason. With "his suave smile," he foresaw that, in fulfilling this task and other "sublime exertions," the blessings of enlightenment would soon come to all of Europe and the whole of humankind, "if not on the wings of doves, then on the pinions of eagles" (Ibid).

This Eurocentric or chauvinist attitude was also manifested by the seventeenth-century Jesuit missionaries who were deeply disappointed to discover that the Chinese neither believed in God nor had any form of systematic logic; by the philosopher Hegel, who assumed that there was no real philosophy underpinning Chinese civilization; and by the scientist–philosopher Alfred Whitehead, who asserted that China had never made any progress in science and that the Chinese contribution to science was practically negligible.

A typically Western ethnocentric response to Chinese medical ethics was provoked by the earliest visit of Western bioethicists to China in 1979, just as the nation was launching its "revolutionary"—or "anti-revolutionary" according to Mao's ideology—state policy of "reform and openness." Organized by the Kennedy Institute of Ethics (one of the leading programs in contemporary bioethics), a group of American bioethicists, along with lawyers, theologians, and physicians, travelled for two weeks throughout China. This visit provided American specialists with their first opportunity for a serious and explicit evaluation of contemporary Chinese medical ethics.

However, disappointment awaited them. Far from what they expected, they discovered that no "bioethics" existed in China in comparison with the U.S. The group's spokesperson, H. Tristram Engelhardt, Jr., later reported that "in the real sense there is no bioethics in the PRC as a scholarly subdiscipline," and that the Chinese "failed to distinguish principles" from the "grounds" or "conceptual foundations" that justified those principles. The reasons Engelhardt gave for this absence of bioethical inquiry on the part of his Chinese hosts included "their lack of extended experience with a variety of moral viewpoints" and their "unfamiliarity with discussions focused primarily on discovering the comparative intellectual merits of varying moral viewpoints apart from any immediate concern to establish or maintain a single one." Other reasons suggested for the absence of bioethics in China were that the prevailing ideology of dialectical materialism denied the importance of moral reflection and emphasized the determining role of the economy, and that China lacked a well-developed philosophical tradition of "criticism and debate about the intellectual bases of social and moral policies." For the American team, their Chinese hosts "had their own positions, replete with implicit subtle distinctions. It is simply that they had not attended with a conceptual, analytical interest to the nature of those distinctions." (Engelhardt 1980: 8, 10)

Over the past few decades, a new approach to cross-cultural differences— one that can be called "postmodernist" or relativist—has been unfolding. Countering the negative view of the East, the postmodernist standpoint takes a positive attitude toward non-Western cultures. One of the many historical forces that have contributed to this postmodern turn is the radical criticism of modernity and such modern values as rationalism, universalism, liberalism, and scientism. The postmodern approach to thinking about cultures rejects the habit of judging the values and norms of one cultural system—non-Western cultures in particular—from the standpoint of Western culture.

Curiously, this postmodernist—or even romanticist—attitude has modern roots, at least with reference to China. It reminds us of the sixteenth-century Italian traveler Marco Polo, who described the material prosperity and moral superiority of China in high-flown prose; the Enlightenment philosopher Voltaire, who portrayed China as the ideal model of rationality in his attack on Christianity and theology; and the great twentieth-century historian of science Joseph Needham who, with his collaborators, argued eloquently in his voluminous works that Chinese science and civilization, especially the unique philosophy of the organism, constitute a beacon to the rest of the world.

The first real evidence of a positive attitude to medical ethics in China in the contemporary West was seen in a very influential article published by two American sociologists–bioethicists, Renée Fox and Judith Swazey. In 1981,

Fox and Swazey conducted six weeks of fieldwork in China, primarily at a Western-style urban hospital in Tianjin, a northern industrial city near Beijing. Unlike their counterparts at the Kennedy Institute of Ethics, they had set out for China with no plans to explore ethical issues in medicine.

Yet, on their return, the two sociologists brought back plentiful evidence of "medical morality"—the peculiar "form ... taken by medical ethical interest and activity" in China. They charged Engelhardt and his colleagues with an "inadvertent ethnocentricity"—seeing China in the same way as the Jesuit missionaries had done. They attributed this disturbing "cultural myopia" to the general cultural perspective of the American bioethicists, leading them to "ignore or misperceive the social and cultural matrices of their ideas." They told their readers:

> It was both surprising and satisfying to learn in a first-hand way that, despite the thousands of geographical miles and historical years that separate Chinese society and our own, and their very different cosmic outlooks, these aspects of Chinese thought are compatible with the conceptual and methodological framework in which we observe, analyze, interpret, and evaluate as sociologists."
>
> (Fox and Swazey 1984: 339)

They were in no doubt as to the existence of a Chinese medical ethics—one that, among other virtues, emphasizes a spirit of self-sacrifice and self-cultivation, a lofty sense of responsibility, modesty, self-control and devotion to family and nation, and other virtues.

Moreover, Fox and Swazey argued that, although strange to American eyes, many aspects of Chinese "medical morality"—such as the emphasis on personal virtues, holism, "two-legged dualism" (which always involves a chain of dualities: yin-yang, self and others, the individual and society, being "Red" and being "expert," preventive and curative medicine, modern Western and traditional Chinese medicine, and so forth), the principle of dynamic complementarity, pragmatism, and collectivism—could provide an effective antidote to many problems and deficiencies in American bioethics. At the same time, they criticized American bioethics and its intellectual assumptions with a series of observations on its narrowly gauged individualism, the dominance of rights language, its contractarian outlook, scientism, positivism, universalism, objectivism, materialism, rationalism, absolutism, secularism, and so on.

Indeed, the primary goal of Fox and Swazey was not so much to introduce their American audience to Chinese medical ethics as to use China as a comparative reference to analyze and illuminate the sociological characteristics of American bioethics—summed up in the phrase "rugged individualism." Their real purpose behind commending Chinese medical morality was to offer a cultural critique of the "American-ness" of bioethics—their aim was to push

American bioethicists to realize that "bioethics is not just bioethics, and is more than medical." In this sense, their basic approach was American-centred, not China-centred. In fact, this emphasis—American-centred-ness—has been a leading feature of American scholarship on China, especially the American historiography of China (Cohen 2010 [1984]).

These two contrasting American responses to medical ethics in China occurred thirty years ago. One might expect that, as a result of the dramatic socio-historical changes during the period since, some significant advances would have been made in the West's understanding of culture(s) and medical ethics in China. It is true that, over the past three decades, China and the West have experienced unprecedented interactions, both large-scale and intimate; bioethics has evolved into a well-established and institutionalized though still rapidly expanding academic field; and medical ethics in China has also undergone great transformations. Unfortunately, however, there is no evidence to show that the general understanding in the West of medical ethics in China has been much advanced by comparison with the views expressed by these two groups of American academics.

Today, there is no doubt that people in the West know more "facts" about medical ethics in China. And there is an emerging body of English-language literature on the subject, as briefly reviewed in the introduction. But, the development of an adequate general understanding is another matter. Some academic investigators have changed their position. For example, Engelhardt, now one of the best-known Western bioethicists in China, has long shifted his allegiance to the postmodernist camp and argued against any possibility of a global bioethics (2006). He promotes the idea of an Asian or Chinese versus a Western bioethics both in his own writing as well as by encouraging his Asian and Chinese students and colleagues to pursue the route of a thoroughly dichotomized East and West (Nie 2007). The assumed radical differences between Western and Asian (or other non-Western) cultures provide strong empirical "evidence" for a key concept of Engelhardt's bioethical theory (1996), the notion that "moral strangers" can never share what he calls a "contentful" moral life. In fact, his vision of a bioethics for the postmodern world presupposes these radical differences between belief systems—whether religious or secular—and cultures.

However, despite the apparent fact that modernist and postmodernist attitudes toward China and Chinese medical ethics take up opposing evaluative positions, they share a common outlook—what British China scholar Raymond Dawson long ago called the "East is East and West is West" mentality (Dawson 1967). Although the rise of the postmodern discourse has challenged modernist or ethnocentric evaluations of the Eastern "principle," it still views East and the West as two different worlds which are mutually inscrutable. In other words, although postmodernist discourse has totally reversed the negative stance of modern Orientalists towards the East, belief in the essential, dualistic and radical differences between East and West remains.

The most widely circulated generalization is that Chinese and Western cultures are dominated by collectivism (or authoritarianism) and individualism respectively—the former thought of as totalitarianism by its detractors and collectivism or communitarianism by its adherents.

Dichotomizing East and West

The oppositional way of thinking about East and West has a deep intellectual and historical root. Dichotomizing East and West has been a cornerstone of modern Occidental approaches to the Orient. As Edward Said has pointed out in his influential study of Orientalism:

> Orientalism is a style of thought based on an ontological and epistemological distinction between 'the Orient' and (most of the time) 'the Occident.' Thus a very large mass of writers, among whom are poets, novelists, philosophers, political theorists, economists, and imperial administrators, have accepted the basic distinction between East and West as the starting point for elaborating theories, epics, novels, social descriptions, and political accounts concerning the Orient, its people, customs, 'mind,' destiny, and so on.
> (Said 1994 [1979]: 2–3)

In 1958, the distinguished author of *The Logic of Scientific Discovery* and *The Open Society and its Enemies* delivered a public address in Zürich entitled "What does the West believe in?" For Karl Popper, as for Mill and Settembrini, the West properly believes in its own values: rationalism, progress, democracy as the least flawed and thus the best form of government and, most importantly, pluralism of ideas. In his words, "we can say proudly that we in the West believe in many and different things, in much that is true and in much that is false; in good things and in bad things" (Popper 1994: 212). Popper hints that, contrary to the West, where this diversity of thought is not only a prominent feature but also an ideal to be pursued, the East (as represented by Communism) is characterized by a monolithic unity of ideas and thus lacks diversity.

Although the "Cold War" political context of Popper's speech was historically unique and his hostile attitude to the "East" is no longer widely shared, this way of dichotomizing East and West is still commonplace. Ironically, many of the efforts aimed at overcoming the deficiencies of Orientalism—such as a Western postmodernist and a conservative Chinese (to be discussed in the next section) approach to medical ethics—still subscribe to the Orientalist epistemological distinction between East and West.

Historically, this cultural opposition goes far beyond modern times and dates back to the beginnings of Western civilization and literature. The demarcation between the Orient and the Occident was manifested in the *Iliad* of Homer, *The Persians* of Aeschylus, and *The Bacchae* of Euripides. In *The Politics*, Aristotle compared the people of the colder regions of Europe, the people of Asia, and the people of Greece. The peoples of northern Europe, he said, "are full of spirit, but deficient in skill and intelligence." The peoples of Asia are "peoples of subjects and slaves" because they "are endowed with skill and intelligence, but are deficient in spirit." However, he continued,

> The Greek stock, intermediate in geographical position, unites the qualities of both sets of peoples. It possesses both spirit and intelligence, for which reason it continues to be free, to have the highest political development, and to be capable of governing every other people—if only it could once achieve political unity. The same sort of difference is found among the Greek peoples themselves. Some of them are of a one-sided nature: others show a happy mixture of spirit and intelligence.
> (1327b18–35, Aristotle 1995: 266–67)

Implied here is that the non-Greek peoples are one-sided in nature and that any diversity among them can, by and large, be ignored. In relating to cultures different from one's own, this Aristotelian mode of thinking was popular among Westerners and Chinese alike in the modern period, and continues to be alive and well even in the new millennium.

For ethicists, Herodotus—the first great historian of the West as well as a pioneering anthropologist (for his detailed record of Eastern cultures)—is well-known for his descriptions of the disposal of the dead in different societies and the common tendency of human beings to view their own rites and customs as superior to those of other groups. Of relevance to our discussion, Greeks and non-Greeks are characterized in clearly dichotomizing terms, and his attitude towards Egypt in particular can be seen as modernist or even postmodernist. Having praised Egypt for having "more marvels and monuments that defy description than any other [nation]," he immediately adds a rider: "Together with the *contrary* nature of Egypt's climate and its unique river, the manner and customs established by the Egyptians are at least in most respects *completely opposite* to those of other people [i.e., Greeks first of all]." (Herodotus 2007: 133; emphasis added). Thus we are told that Egyptian women go to the market while the men stay at home; Egyptians eat out in the street; and over there "women urinate standing up, men sitting down."

The entire discipline of anthropology has for a long time regarded it as its basic mission to discover the peculiar features and determining patterns of non-Western cultures in terms of their differentiation from Western cultures. From the start, the fundamental difference between the West and the non-West has been assumed. A salient example is the classic study of young people in a Pacific island by Margaret Mead. In *Coming of Age in Samoa*, probably the most widely read anthropological book of all time, Mead (2001 [1928]) portrayed youth in Samoa as living a totally different lifestyle from their counterparts in the West, the United States in particular—a life free from restraint, frustration and crisis, especially in terms of sexuality. However, careful and sophisticated reassessment of her work demonstrated that Mead's carefree picture of the youth of Samoa was not only simplistic but seriously misleading (Freeman 1983). Apart from the influence of the doctrine of cultural determinism to which Mead was deeply committed, it seems to me that the entrenched dichotomizing way of thinking about Western and non-Western cultures played a crucial role in her distortion of the socio-cultural realities of Samoa.

Following the lead of first-generation anthropologists such as French Lucien Levy-Bruhl, who aimed to discover the *mentalité* of primitive societies and peoples, twentieth-century sinologists and scholars in other disciplines have sought to distinguish ways of seeing and acting in Chinese civilization that makes it unique. Many theories have been put forward to account for this perceived uniqueness of Chinese culture. They include holism, collectivism, categorical thinking, the system of correspondence, the organic worldview (correlative thinking), the philosophy of the organism, the theory of synchronicity (*Synchroniziät*), the "Asiatic way," oriental despotism, and so on.

Two academic works—one in comparative sociology and the other in comparative psychology—offer further examples of the popularity and persistence of this oppositional habit of thought. In his book *Americans and Chinese*, the Chinese-American scholar Francis Hsu (1970 [1953]) argued that the American way of life is "individual-centered" (emphasizing the predilections of the individual), in contrast to the "situation-centered" Chinese way of life (emphasizing the individual's appropriate place and behavior in his or her social context). More recently, social psychologist Richard Nisbett (2003) has sought to show how East Asians, Chinese included, and Westerners (or Anglo-Americans) think and see differently, and why. Nisbett argues that East Asian thought contrasts strikingly with Western thought: the former is holistic and dialectic, seeking a middle way between opposing concepts, and focusing on the perceptual field as a whole and relationships between the objects and events within that field; the latter is analytic, applying rules of formal logic, focusing on salient individual objects or people. The differences between these modes of reasoning and thinking—observable in fields as diverse as medicine, law, science, human rights, and international relations—reflect the influence of specific environmental settings, social structures, philosophical traditions and educational systems that date back to ancient Greece and China and have survived into the modern world. For Nisbett, collectivist Asians and individualistic Westerners have maintained very different systems of thought over thousands of years.

The myth in China

Dichotomizing is not just a Western sin. The perceived basic distinction between China and the West—the myth of a communitarian China versus the individualistic West—has been an essential part of academic, cultural and political discourse in China since the early 20th century in defining and addressing Chinese and Western cultural differences, medical ethics included.

Western, especially American, biomedical ethics began to enter China along with the policy of openness and reform in the late 1970s. A well-known Chinese text on the subject is a book entitled *Shengming Lunlixue* (Bioethics), written by Qiu Renzong (1987) and published in the influential "New Disciplines Book Series." In this work Qiu, one of the leading bioethicists and philosophers of science in contemporary China, introduced the emerging field known as bioethics in the West, and especially in the United States, to a large and very curious Chinese audience. The book covered some major bioethical topics and the debates that have grown up around them: reproductive technologies, birth control, genetics and eugenics, impaired new-borns, euthanasia, organ transplantation, behavioral control, and social policy and ethics.

In response to this newly imported Western bioethics, two opposing positions—acceptance and refusal—can be discerned among Chinese scholars. While Fox and Swazey had criticized the culture of American bioethics by emphasizing that "medical morality is not bioethics," the Chinese who favor American bioethics have used the same statement to critique Chinese medical morality and to stress the importance of learning from the developed Western countries. For these Chinese medical ethicists, concepts such as individualism and human rights—seen by Fox and Swazey and their followers as negative elements—provide an effective medicine for the perceived illness of Chinese medical morality, infected as it is by the tyranny of nation and community, authoritarianism, and the lack of a language of individual rights. While Fox and Swazey resented the dominance of law in American bioethics—seeing America as "a society under law, rather than under men"—the "Chinese Voltaires" use the West as an example of the necessity of establishing and amplifying the legal system in order to build a society subject to the rule of law, rather than the will of one man or a few. Few people in China today would deny the necessity for the modernization of medical science and technology, even if they reject Western moral values in general and American bioethics in particular. They understand that bioethics deals with moral issues in modern medical science and technology, areas in which America, the West in general, is well advanced. Learning from the West is widely regarded as an important way of reforming Chinese society, culture and medical morality.

From the time of the introduction and expansion of Western culture in China, there has always been anti-Western sentiment and discourse in the country. During the Cultural Revolution, ideas imported from the West—Marxism excepted—were censured as "bourgeois fallacies," at the same time as traditional Chinese moral norms were under official attack as showing the "pernicious influence of feudalism." As a result, for some Chinese scholars, adherence to the fundamental principles of Marxism and the construction of an ethic consistent with the social and cultural values of Chinese socialism is the legitimate path to follow. But traditional Chinese values never completely disappeared. With the increasing influence of Western bioethics and the advent of new policies of openness and reform, traditional medical ethics began to revive. While very few Chinese scholars would insist that China has nothing to learn from the West, some other Chinese scholars consider the Westernization of Chinese medical morality is not only impossible to achieve in practice, but also dangerous in theory. The proper way proposed to advance Chinese medical ethics is, on the one hand, to rejuvenate traditional Chinese ethical ideals, especially by rebuilding what may be called the Confucian moral order; and on the other, to resist the imposition of Western or American ideological frameworks and such "Western" values as liberty, democracy and human rights.

Most contemporary Chinese medical ethicists, however, eschew both of these extreme positions—either total acceptance or complete rejection of American-style bioethics (see, e.g., Du 1985, 2009). Whether the subject is Western bioethics or traditional Chinese medical ethics, the most widely accepted approach is "to discard the dross and select the essence." Efforts have been made to integrate both Western and Chinese medical moralities into medical practice in order to create a new medical ethics with Chinese characteristics. This model of thinking represents the Chinese type of pragmatism, which always seeks to organize things, however foreign they may be to one another, together in a peculiarly Chinese manner. However, a key problem with this particular orientation is the impossibility of gaining an impartial perspective from which to discard the dross and select the essence; in other words, there is never a nonpartisan point of view. Hence, in practice, practitioners in this middle group inevitably incline to one or the other of the above positions. In principle, they agree that the best way forward for Chinese medical ethics is to absorb and combine the advantages of both cultures, but they disagree on the specifics of what to preserve and what to reject.

These varied responses—acceptance, refusal, and integration—not only reflect the different attitudes of twentieth-century Chinese toward Western civilization, but also are consistent with modern Chinese responses to the challenge of Western biomedicine. In modern and contemporary China, responses to the issue of competing medical systems from medical professionals, intellectuals, policymakers, and ordinary people alike have tended to fall into three basic categories: (1) the wholesale adoption of modern Western medicine and the abolition of traditional Chinese medicine once and for all; (2) the retention of traditional medicine as the dominant modality and the rejection of foreign biomedicine, at most retaining Western medicine as a supplement to Chinese medicine; and (3) the integration of the two medical systems to create a "new Chinese medicine" that would be seen as the normative approach to the advancement of health care in China.

The admittedly sketchy materials presented in this and the first section are not intended to constitute a cultural-historical inquiry into the reception of Chinese medical ethics in the West or into Western or American bioethics in China (although these are fascinating topics that call for in-depth investigation), but to make a rather different point. No matter how dissimilar these various evaluations of and attitudes toward Chinese medical ethics or Western bioethics may be, and regardless of whether one takes a position for or against either of the two traditions, there exists a shared, underlying assumption that there is a Western bioethics and a Chinese medical ethics per se. As a result, like their Western counterparts, for the most part Chinese scholars also tend to think about the characteristics of Chinese medical ethics and Western bioethics as a set of general contrasts—in particular, in terms of a communitarian or collectivist China versus the individualistic West.

In one of his English-language publications, Qiu Renzong provides a clear summary of the popular Chinese view of the culture of Chinese medical ethics:

> A quasi-holistic socio-political philosophy has been developed from Chinese cultural tradition. It is based on two thousand years of power-centralized, autocratic monarchy—one that has lacked any rights-oriented, individualistic, liberal democratic tradition. In recent decades, Marxism—rather, a mixture of Russian and Chinese versions of Marxism—has become the dominant ideology. The historicism and social holism of this system, interwoven with traditional ideas, puts the greatest emphasis on nation, society, and country rather than on individuals.
>
> (Qiu 1992: 170–72)

For Qiu, and for many other Chinese scholars, Chinese culture and medical ethics give priority to country, community, and authority. More basically, in contrast to the West, there exists a characteristic Chinese way of thinking about and acting in public and private life, interpersonal interactions, and moral issues in medical practice.

Regardless of their philosophical orientation, the intellectual elite in twentieth-century and contemporary China have habitually based their arguments on cultural questions on the assumption—the myth—that Western and Chinese ways of living and thinking stand in sharp contrast to each other. As a dramatically intensified version of the old debate on the cultural differences between Chinese and foreigners and how to deal with them (*huayi zhi bian*), the controversy over Chinese versus Western culture was a salient theme in the cultural and political life of twentieth-century China, and continues into the twenty-first. Some commentators, such as Hu Shi, are advocates of radical anti-traditionalism, "Down with Confucianism" and wholesale Westernization; they offer a radical critique of Chinese Confucian values and promote Western democracy and science. Others, such as Liang Shuming, are advocates of cultural conservatism and criticize Western materialism and individualism while promoting socio-cultural reconstruction on the basis of traditional Chinese values (Deng 1994). But, whatever their attitude to Chinese and Western culture, almost all modern Chinese commentators agree that there is a fundamental difference between the two cultures and that this difference can be summarized as "collectivist China versus the individualistic West." This was true not only of the New Culture Movement in the first decades of the twentieth century and the Cultural Revolution of the 1960s and 1970s, but also of the post-Mao reform era starting with the "Cultural Craze" (*wenhua re*) of the 1980s.

Moreover, the myth constitutes a fundamental part of the official ideology of the Chinese state, so that Chinese ethicists regularly define Chinese and Western morality in these terms. For example, in officially-endorsed standard and influential textbooks on ethics for students in higher education (e.g. Luo 2002 [1989]; Zhou 2004; Luo, Ma, and Yu 2004 [1986]), high praise is awarded to socialist collectivism as representing the essence of Chinese morality, in radical opposition to a faulty Western bourgeois ideology characterized by individualism and egoism. Politically, of course, the stance taken here is hardly surprising, as it serves the ruling ideology by promoting the viewpoint of a single, homogenous and unified moral system. In order to legitimize its dominance and to maintain its own interests and power base, China's ruling ideology often depreciates and frequently suppresses minority voices, local perspectives, and the uniqueness of individual experience. It constantly urges Chinese to prioritize the officially defined collective or national interests over individual interests. Nevertheless, it is important to emphasize that the popular myth is not merely the reflection of a political ideology. Rather, it has deep roots in the universal habit of thinking about cultural differences in terms of "us" and "them."

How individualistic is the West?

It is needed to point out, albeit very briefly, how the myth of the individualistic West has distorted the socio-cultural realties in the West. A striking example is that Canada, New Zealand, most European countries and in particular Scandinavian countries are far more "socialist" than China, even more so than in Mao's China. Bioethics in Europe and the United States can have very different features.

Let me focus on the United States, often perceived as the most individualistic country in the West. It is obvious that the myth of the "individualistic United States" distorts the complexity of American cultures, just as the communitarian myth distorts the complexity of Chinese culture. My experience of living in the United States has taught me that Americans' respect for family and family values, pursuit for the common good, the concerns for the community, and love for the country are no less strong than those of Chinese people—perhaps even stronger. In fact, a survey conducted in the late 1980s by a group of

American and Chinese scholars on Chinese and American people's values indicates that a large number of American respondents, more than contemporary Chinese, held traditional Confucian values (such as family values) and that there are more similarities between the two cultures than often perceived (Pan et al. 1994). In Chapters 7 and 8, I have given a further Chinese-Western cross-cultural discussion about the role of family in such bioethical issues as medical truth-telling and informed consent.

The persistent internal critique of extreme versions of individualism indicates that the United States is not as individualistic as usually assumed. Besides the "first language" of individualism, there persists a strong "second language" articulated in American "habits of the heart"—the language of community, of deeply rooted biblical and republican traditions (Bellah et al. 1985; see especially de Tocqueville's classic work *Democracy in America*). Among many important scholarships on the complexity of American cultures and history is the work by American historian Barry Shain. As Shain (1994) has carefully documented and convincingly argued, contrary to what the common myth of American individualism has suggested, as early as in the eighteenth century Americans did not think and debate about the essential political and moral issues in an individualistic manner, but in a framework of a reformed Protestant communalism.

To claim that Western, and even American, bioethics is dominated by individualism is problematic to say the least. Communitarianism has had a prominent place in Western political philosophy since classical times and has come into revival and prominence since the early 1980s. A communitarian or non-individualistic approach was present at the birth and development of bioethics in the United States (see, e.g., the works of the co-founder and current president of the Hastings Centre, Daniel Callahan and Thomas Murray; the former presidents of the US President's Council of Bioethics, Leo Kass and Edmond Pellegrino; Carl Elliott; Renée Fox I have already cited, and so on). And even a liberal communitarian vision of bioethics has been long offered by Ezekiel Emanuel (1991). From the very beginning of bioethics, the Christian theological approach (e.g., the works of Paul Ramsey, William May and Stanley Hauerwas) has been a major powerful force within bioethics as a discipline and as public discourse. This approach has greatly stressed family values and the importance of flourishing communities. Simplistic generalizations about American individualism have also ignored the contribution of feminism to bioethics (e.g., by Rosemary Tong, Hilde Lindemann and Canadian philosopher Susan Sherwin) which, if not always opposed to rugged individualism, can hardly be characterized as promoting it. Interestingly, it is the secular bioethics of Engelhardt (1996) that is both libertarian and highly individualistic, but his more recent work has emphasized the importance of the family as a social institution and a source of moral value for health care and bioethics.

A heatedly-debated bioethical issue in the public domain in the United States concerns abortion. The American abortion controversy or "war" as some scholars have called it—is often simplified as a debate over the woman's right to choice and the fetus's right to life. However, the activities of both pro-choice and pro-life activists in the local communities illustrates powerfully that Americans deeply and genuinely care about their country and communities, from both which they derive, in large part, their individuality. Fascinating sociological and ethnographic studies on grass-root activists in local communities by Kristin Luker (1984) and Faye Ginsburg (1989) have proven beyond doubt that, in reality, abortion itself is the "tip of the iceberg," reflecting people's different worldviews, religious beliefs, views on womanhood, life, individual liberty and the state. As I see it (Nie 2005: Chapter 8), the American abortion debate demonstrates not only the "clash of absolutes, of life against liberty" but also the shared concerns and efforts on how to develop and sustain a good community and a good society in the face of the fundamental fact of unavoidable plurality and individuality.

To claim that American society and cultures prioritize individual liberty and thus are highly individualistic is not wrong. But to believe that the communitarian way of thinking is alien to Americans and to discard the existence and persistence of the communitarian language in American socio-cultural, political and moral life is distorting, to say the least.

Individuality and individualism in China

In his brilliant essay *On Liberty* (first translated into elegant classic Chinese by Yan Fu and published in 1903, and since published in a number of Chinese translations), John Stuart Mill made two contradictory points which are germane to the present discussion. The first point is that, without nurturing individuality, a society or culture would be unable to survive, develop and progress. He then used China as a "warning example" against the failure to pursue individuality. Unreflectively following the mainstream view of his times on the subject, Mill—one of the greatest liberal thinkers in the West—portrayed China as the "radical other" of Europe. In contrast with the West, where progress had been continuously pursued and originality cherished, Chinese civilization had remained "stationary" for thousands of years—because conformity, collectivism, paternalism, repression and despotism are normative values in China. For Mill, and for many people even today, the Chinese "have succeeded beyond all hope in what English philanthropists are so industriously working at—in making a people all alike, all governing their thoughts and conduct by the same maxims and rules." He warned that, "unless individuality shall be able successfully to assert itself against this yoke, Europe, notwithstanding its noble antecedents and its professed Christianity, will tend to become another China." (Mill 1998: 79–90)

But we should not forget that China has not only had a long history of advanced civilization, with a long record of internal developments, even before encountering the West, but it also survived the impacts of ruthless Western and Japanese colonialism and Mao's Chinese totalitarianism. More impressively, after overcoming these enormous historical handicaps, over the past few decades China has once again been developing rapidly and reassuming its active role in world affairs.

Mill's two assertions—the crucial role of individuality for the survival and development of any society or culture, and China as the exemplar of a society that lacks individuality—cannot both be true. Logically, one way to avoid this contradiction is to argue that a society or culture can survive and develop without individuality or at least respect for it. But a more reasonable solution is to revise our conventional and stereotypical image of China and Chinese cultures and to acknowledge that individuality has indeed been nurtured there in a variety of ways, but perhaps rather differently from in the West.

Individualism in China is potentially a very large subject, and I have room here only for a few brief observations. Just as there is a strong communitarian tradition in Western civilization, an ancient and continuous tradition of individualism can be discerned in China (e.g. Munro 1985). Besides sources such as Buddhism, the core of this tradition has been Daoism (Taoism), a major moral-political school and religious system that developed in China from the Axial Age. Throughout the history of the country, it has had a competing and balancing role with regard to Confucianism. If Confucianism can be largely characterized as communitarian, familist, authoritarian or moralist, Daoism has been highly individualistic, anti-paternalist, anti-statist, and has set its face against worldly authorities and conventional morality. Even within Confucian tradition, there are some notable individualistic components (e.g. de Bary 1970). As in contemporary bioethics, a major concern of Daoist philosophy as well as Daoist religion has been the issue of death and dying. For Daoist philosophy, like Western Stoicism, emphasizes the importance of accepting death as a natural part of life, while Daoist religion has been strongly focused on longevity and even physical immortality and has devised many techniques to achieve them including alchemy, herbal remedies, breathing exercises, and the sexual arts (see Chapter 3 on this last subject).

Conclusions

The pervasive myth of a communitarian or collectivist China vs. the individualistic West dominates—often in a "taken-for-granted" manner—the ways in which both Chinese and Westerners perceive and interpret China and Chinese cultures, especially in comparison with the West. It likewise dominates today's cross-cultural discourses—both casual and serious—on medical ethics in China and the West. In this chapter, I have not only presented the popularity of the myth but also traced its intellectual and historical root, that is, how the dichotomous and dualistic habit of thinking about East and West, and cultural differences in general, is deeply embedded in both the West and China as well. Moreover, I have indicated how the myth has oversimplified the realities of cultures and medical ethics in the West and China.

In the next chapter, I will further discuss the fallacy of this popular myth and especially the age-old dichotomous way of thinking. As I will demonstrate in the next and other chapters in this book, cross-cultural bioethics will do much better without this popular myth and without the deep-rooted habit of dichotomizing different cultures as "radical others." One effective way to overcome this popular myth and the dominant way of dichotomizing cultures is to take China's internal plurality and pluralism seriously.

Chapter 2

The fallacy of dichotomizing cultures

In the last chapter we have seen that, while the proverbial "twain" of China and the West have long since met, many myths still prevail in the comparative discussions on cultures and medical ethics in China and the West, and the most persistent and widespread one is to characterize Chinese and Western cultural differences as collectivism, familism or communitarianism vs. individualism. The age-old dichotomizing way of thinking—about East and West, about "them" and "us," and about cultural differences in general—still pervades much of our cross-cultural understanding and discussions in both cultural domains. Indeed, the dichotomous way of thinking about cultural differences has been greatly reinforced by the sweeping currents of postmodernism that still command considerable influence.

In this chapter, I will further demonstrate how seriously this pernicious myth and especially the deep-rooted and dominant habit of dichotomizing cultures have distorted the realities of cultures and medical ethics in China and thus muddied the waters for effective cross-cultural discussion. As explored in the rest of the book, more appropriate ways to understand Chinese and Western cultures include focusing on both cross-cultural differences as well as shared grounds and acknowledging and cherishing the great internal diversity of cultures and medical moralities in China.

Chinese and Western bioethics dichotomized

The myth of a communitarian China vs. an individualistic West has considerable power because it offers simple and clear-cut explanations of how and why Chinese and Westerners are different. As a result, both outside and inside China, it still persists in casual conversation and serious discussions among the general public as well as scholars. We have become thoroughly accustomed to conceptualizing the civilizations and ethics of East and West in dualistic, contrasting and general terms reminiscent of modernist categories, even though popular evaluations of these sets of polarities may have reversed over time. The leading sets of oppositions can be characterized as:

- family decision-making vs. individual autonomy;
- family and filial piety vs. individual development and self-realization;
- the social or common good vs. individual liberty and interests;
- the family, collective, community or nation vs. the individual;
- personal virtues vs. individual rights;
- the concept of social duty and obligation vs. the notion of individual freedom;
- self-examination vs. self-determination;
- trust vs. contract.

The list goes on and on.

The myth and its underlying way of dichotomizing cultural differences as "radical others" have been most plainly manifested in the popular but specious idea of an "Asian communitarian bioethics" vs. a "Western individualist bioethics" (Nie 2007; see Hongladarom 2008 for a critical review of what can be called the "Asian bioethics debate").

In the area of palliative care, one Chinese-Canadian physician has contrasted Chinese ways of thinking with "Western bioethical ideologies" in a series of sweeping oppositions:

- Confucianism, Taoism (Daoism) and Buddhism vs. dualism, a mechanistic world view and positive empiricism;
- filial piety vs. egalitarianism and individualism;
- interdependence vs. consumerism, autonomy and freedom of choice;
- a hierarchical power structure vs. egalitarianism;
- harmony and conformity with nature vs. control and manipulation of nature;
- suppression of emotion vs. expressiveness;
- death as normal to the life cycle vs. death as personal failure;
- modesty and stoicism vs. pride and confrontation (Woo 1999: 71).

The author, as a physician rather than a China expert or bioethicist, indicates how the dichotomizing way of thinking about China and the West has become a part of our common knowledge and widely-shared habit of thought.

It is interesting to note that Woo lists "stoicism" as a feature of Asian communitarian bioethics, despite the Western origins and identity of Stoicism as a system of thought. While many Daoist precepts, especially the teachings of Zhuangzi, are distinctively Chinese, one should not conclude that they are thereby incompatible with the wisdom of the West. Daoism and Stoicism do share some ethical views and assumptions such as the importance of acting in harmony with nature, and even the idea of the world citizen. (This is not the place for a detailed comparison of the ethics of Chinese Daoism and Western Stoicism.) Another point is that, given its strong anti-paternalistic and profoundly individualistic spirit, it is odd to include Daoism as a part of an

Asian or Chinese communitarian worldview. However, in considering the problems created by conventional ways of characterizing cultural differences, these inconsistencies are merely the tiny tip of a very large iceberg.

The conventional understanding of medical truth-telling in China and the West offers a telling example of the extent to which the habit of dichotomization has distorted the cultural realities of both domains, especially in China, and has drastically oversimplified the complexity involved in drawing cross-cultural comparisons.

The open and honest disclosure by medical professionals to their patients about their medical conditions, including the diagnosis and prognosis of terminal illness, has long been standard practice. In sharp contrast to the West, however, in China (including Hong Kong and Taiwan) medical professionals routinely withhold information about terminal illness from patients, and usually inform family members only. It is not uncommon for Chinese medical professionals, along with family members, to lie to patients about the seriousness of their condition, especially in cases of terminal illness. Based on this undoubted contrast in attitudes and practices between contemporary China and the West, it has been widely assumed that medical truth-telling is culturally alien to China—indeed, a practice that was unknown in the Middle Kingdom until the recent influence of the West. Mainly due to the influence of the pervasive dichotomizing way of thinking about cultural differences, a widely accepted image has been developed by Chinese and non-Chinese alike, amounting to a clear-cut cultural contrast between China and the West regarding the communication of a negative prognosis—a crude opposition between nondisclosure or indirect disclosure vs. direct disclosure. Based on this perceived and apparently definitive "cultural difference," an argument against medical truth-telling in China has been mounted by some medical ethicists.

However, the cultural differences at stake here are far more complex and rich, and thus far more intriguing and fascinating than anything implied by this crude dualistic schema. By carefully comparing and contrasting the cultural attitudes involved, and drawing on detailed historical and sociological studies, a number of rarely acknowledged features come to light:

- Based on extensive primary historical materials, including the biographies of ancient medical sages and famous physicians from various dynasties, a long although forgotten Chinese tradition of truth-telling about terminal illness—a tradition dating back at least twenty-six centuries—can be recovered. Contrary to what has been universally assumed both inside and outside China, the traditional practice and norm of Chinese culture and medical ethics was for physicians to disclose their diagnosis and prognosis of terminal illness truthfully and directly to patients. They offered important ethical reasons for doing so.
- This long Chinese tradition is remarkable in itself. It is especially remarkable when compared to the situation in the West where,

historically, concealing the truth about terminal illness was the cultural norm—clearly stipulated in ancient medical writings and modern professional codes of medicine alike—and where direct disclosure did not become the standard procedure until the 1960s and 1970s, or even later.
- Interestingly and ironically, along with the establishment of Western biomedicine in China from the late nineteenth century, the development of the contemporary mainstream Chinese practice of nondisclosure was closely connected with the then dominant Western norm of concealment.
- Generalizations about concealing or even deceiving the patient as *the* representative Chinese approach to the moral difficulties surrounding terminal illness echo such deep-rooted cultural stereotypes as the "untruthfulness of the Oriental mind"—designations which were in wide circulation in the West not so long ago.
- Even if medical truth-telling were culturally alien to China, as is usually assumed, ethical imperatives exist to reform the contemporary mainstream Chinese practice of nondisclosure or indirect disclosure through family members, as this practice can cause serious harm to patients and their families.
- Numerous surveys conducted throughout mainland China, like others in Hong Kong and Taiwan, demonstrate that the great majority of Chinese patients want truthful information about their medical condition, even in terminal cases. Moreover, the great majority of medical professionals and family members themselves would prefer to know the medical truth when they were asked to imagine that they were patients.
- The Confucian moral outlook mandates truthfulness as a basic ethical principle and a cardinal social virtue which physicians ought to take as their guiding star.
- An historic shift from current practice of no direct disclosure toward honest and direct disclosure by physicians is now occurring in China. Culturally, this change is not so much an aping of Western (and thus foreign) ways, but a return to a long-neglected indigenous Chinese tradition.

These findings, mostly surprising, provide compelling evidence against the historical validity and cultural authenticity of nondisclosure or indirect disclosure as *the* representative Chinese cultural approach. Either of the two practices of direct and open disclosure and non-disclosure or indirect disclosure is as Chinese as the other one; just as either of the two is as Western as the other. Therefore, the clear-cut contrast on medical truth-telling in China and the West as non-disclosure or indirect disclosure vs. direct disclosure is not only descriptively wrong but normatively misleading.

All these issues will be discussed systematically in great detail in Chapters 6 and 7. My point here is about the misfortunes brought about by the age-old and still popular habit of dichotomizing cultures. Too often, the habit grossly distorts the historical and socio-cultural realities in both China and the West (and especially in China); rudely oversimplifies the otherwise fascinating similarities and differences (including differences in similarities and similarities in differences) in Chinese and Western cultures; callously deprives the openness and new possibilities of cultures concerned; and finally and most dangerously, obscures the real ethical predicaments at stake.

Chinese attitudes to fetal life: a case of internal plurality

The conventional understanding, in both the West and China, of Chinese approaches to fetal life and abortion offers another typical example of the pervasiveness of the popular cultural myth of a collectivist China vs. the individualistic West and the dichotomous worldview that underlies it. There is a modernist perception of the issue. Echoing (albeit unconsciously) the remarks of John Stuart Mill, Thomas Mann's humanist character Settembrini, and Karl Popper cited in the previous chapter, U.S. constitutional specialist Laurence Tribe characterized abortion in China in his best-selling book *Abortion: The Clash of Absolutes* (1992: 63) in strongly oppositional terms:

> As in Stalin's Russia and Nazi Germany, in the Chinese context neither those advocating abortion nor those opposing it use the language of "rights" that characterizes the abortion debate in the United States. Scant attention is paid either to the rights of the women to have her child or to her right to terminate her pregnancy—or to any right of the fetus to be born. Rather, the conflict is structured almost wholly in terms of corporate groups, like the state and the family, and centers on the needs of and the duties owed to such groups.

Tribe's words express a point of view much shared in the West.

Alongside this view we can set a counter perception, postmodernist in character, which has been largely developed by professional anthropologists. Based on their fieldwork in a Cantonese village, Sulamith and Jack Potter discovered that while villagers resisted pressure to have abortions, this was not for the reasons registered by anti-abortionists in the United States; and while they accepted the morality of abortion, it was for different reasons than those espoused by Western pro-choicers. In the words of the Potters (1990: 230), "Valuing a child as a 'human life,' in isolation from its significance to the family and to society, is a senseless abstraction when considered in terms of Chinese ideas about what it means to be a person." They warned that attempts to impose categories which reflect "specifically American cultural concerns" (such as "pro-choice" versus "pro-life") onto traditional Chinese birth-planning "leads only to misunderstanding" (231). To make sense of Chinese methods of family planning, it is crucial "to stand aside from the emotionally powerful connotations that abortion has in American society" (239) and to grasp the "culturally specific assumptions" relating to birth and abortion in China.

However opposing these two evaluative attitudes—modernist and postmodernist—may seem, they espouse a common myth. It holds that Chinese, in striking contrast with Westerners, have little if any concern with the morality of terminating pregnancy. In a comprehensive review of population policy and demographic developments in mainland China, German scholar Thomas Scharping (2003: 12) asserts:

> [B]ecause popular medical knowledge continuously pre-dating the beginning of life is unknown, because modern psychology bestowing a soul to infants has not entered the peasant mind and because basic religious ideas are different, the question of abortion in China does not lead to the passionate pro and con arguments we witness in the West.

Many Western scholars and commentators would support the general conclusion that the Chinese do not consider abortion ethically problematic because they believe that human life does not begin until birth (Luk 1977; Rigdon 1996; Jennings 1999).

This viewpoint is not restricted to the West. For example, in a review of bioethics in China written for a Western audience, leading Chinese medical ethicist Yali Cong states:

> The reality of abortion in China is that most people do not regard it as an ethical issue. This is related to the policy of family planning but also to the traditional idea a human being begins at birth.
>
> (Cong 2003: 252)

Thus, the argument goes, throughout the long history of China induced abortion was never treated as a serious ethical issue. Scholars have emphasized the permissive position of Confucianism on abortion. It is claimed that Confucianism not only permits almost any kind of abortion but even tolerates infanticide. The most important reason given for this permissiveness is that Chinese, Confucians included, believe that the unborn fetus does not constitute a human life. It has been suggested that most Chinese would agree with the view of the great Confucian master Xun Kuang (Xu Zi) (286–238 BCE) that "human life" begins at birth and ends with death (Qiu 1992).

Failing to question these claims, in an earlier study of coerced abortion in China, I made similar sweeping generalizations in the context of a Chinese-Western comparative discussion:

> Among ancient Chinese philosophers, doctors, and lay people, the practice of abortion evoked little explicit discussions (if any concern), not to

mention public debate, as is still the case in contemporary China. Even though no ancient Chinese thinker explicitly advocated that both abortion and infanticide are justifiable on utilitarian grounds as did Plato and Aristotle, neither was there a Chinese "Pythagoras" to hold that abortion is killing because of the belief that human life begins at conception. The Chinese did not consider abortion morally objectionable mainly because they, like Jewish law and Platonists in ancient Greece, maintain that human life does not begin until birth. Confucians and Daoists rarely treated the fetus as a human being. So neither the "Absolute Sincerity of Great Doctor" (the Chinese "Hippocratic Oath") by the "King of Medicine," Sun Simiao, nor any other premodern professional maxims written by medical doctors clearly claimed that physician should "not give to a woman abortion remedy" as does the well-known Hippocratic Oath.

(Nie 1999a: 469)

Despite noting that China's imported Buddhism teaches that the fetus is a form of life and therefore put limits on induced abortion, I failed to question the assumption that, radically different from Westerners, Chinese in general take a permissive attitude toward abortion because they have little moral concern for fetal life—and that this was as true in the past as it is today.

However, the in-depth empirical evidence presented in the book *Behind the Silence: Chinese Voices on Abortion* (Nie 2005), the first systematic sociological study of the subject in any language, has proven beyond reasonable doubt that this widespread view of abortion, held by Westerners and Chinese alike, is seriously misleading. The book includes a survey of 600 Chinese from different walks of life throughout the country, and interviews with 30 women and 30 doctors. Many diverse and compelling Chinese "voices" exist behind the apparent public and even private silence on the subject. As these voices have been given the freedom to speak in this, my first English-language book, I want here to do no more than sketch out the diverse and conflicting viewpoints held by Chinese on the subject of fetal life.

The first position to be considered is the official discourse, or the socialist/Communist Party perspective. It is true that in the contemporary official and public discourse no significant moral attention is given to fetal life in particular—indeed, human life in general is not always accorded the highest respect. A widely shared assumption in the official discourse seems to be that, even though the fetus is a human life and even though taking a human life is usually wrong, abortion is morally acceptable because the moral status of the fetus is outweighed by competing and more significant interests—those of the woman involved, her parents and family, and especially the claims of society and the state. This official perspective has been articulated and promoted in many contemporary textbooks of medical ethics published in mainland China.

It should be noted, however, that the official discourse in China has never been fixed, coherent and unified, but is always in flux. In the first decade (the 1950s) of the People's Republic, the official standpoint was antithetical to that advanced today—induced abortion was legally prohibited in order to ensure "the life of the next generation," among other reasons. In addition, diverse and even dissident views exist within this discourse, such as the moral sentiment favoring the interests of the unborn life among family-planning cadres at the local level.

More importantly, today's official perspective does not necessarily represent either the mainstream beliefs of contemporary Chinese people or the historical heritage of Chinese culture. Contrary to the widespread perception—a common stereotyping of Chinese people—that most Chinese accept the official position and consider abortion morally acceptable on the grounds that human life begins at birth, my own fieldwork demonstrates that, on the contrary, most Chinese believe that life begins at some point before birth and thus regard the fetus as a human life. In the survey results published in my 2005 book, nearly half (48%) of all respondents agreed that human life begins at conception; just over a quarter (28%) considered that life begins at birth. A sizeable majority (72% overall, nearly three-quarters) of my informants believed that life begins sometime before birth—whether at conception, or when the mother feels the first movement of the fetus ("quickening"), or when the fetus is able to survive outside the mother's womb ("viability"). A large majority (76%) settled on one of the two extremities of pregnancy—*either* conception *or* birth—as the point at which life begins, with significantly more informants choosing conception (48%) over birth (28%). Moreover, 84% of all respondents agreed with the statement that "A fetus is a life." And, overall, nearly half (46%) of the 600 subjects surveyed agreed with the statement that "A fetus is a human being."

The twelve groups questioned in the survey showed a diversity of viewpoints on fetal life. A large majority of Catholics believed that human life starts at conception, with much smaller numbers choosing viability and birth. And, while more than half of the Protestant, Buddhist, Chinese medical students, and respondents in the northern city samples opted for conception, medical humanities scholars and residents of Village B were more inclined to see birth as the starting point. While most informants believed that a human life started sometime before birth, rather than at birth itself, in these latter two sample groups—Village B and medical humanities scholars—fewer than half held that human life begins sometime before birth.

I still vividly remember one occasion in my fieldwork, where ten rural people—men and women, young and old—gathered in a village house to fill out the questionnaires I had given them. After completing the forms, several of them started to discuss—or, more accurately, debate—the items I had listed in the questionnaire. This fascinating exchange revealed that the two most divisive issues were whether aborting a fetus was equivalent to taking a life and the question of when human life begins. This small group of villagers showed a lively disagreement on the question of whether human life starts at conception, at birth, or at some time in between.

Personal stories of women who had had abortions and physicians who routinely performed the procedure, especially those of women, are often heartbreaking and heart-warming at the same time. These very rich personal narratives exhibit a number of shared experiences and viewpoints, such as concern for the families involved and support for China's national population policies. But they also show some radical moral disagreements, especially about the moral status of fetal life. For some, the interests of the fetus should be subject to the interests of the pregnant woman, the family and the nation. For others, their deep moral concern for fetal life resulted in puzzlement and even anguish over the ethical dilemmas caused by abortion. Whatever the precise nature of these differences, there are no grounds for claiming, as the popular myth does, that in China abortion is merely a "medical" procedure because Chinese have little moral concern for fetal life (for a marvellous anthropological study on abortion and fetal life in contemporary Taiwan, see Moskowitz 2001).

The myth is also misconceived historically. There were controversies over abortion in imperial China, although these have mostly been forgotten. In general, Buddhism took a rather conservative attitude toward the subject. Contrary to popular assumptions about Confucianism, the (albeit fragmentary) historical evidence points in the opposite direction: Confucianism has been far from permissive on abortion and some ancient Confucian physicians were flatly opposed to it. Thanks to William LaFleur's fine anthropological and historical study of abortion in Japan (1992), we have some indirect knowledge of Chinese Confucian and Neo-Confucian responses to abortion. During the late Edo period (between 1721 and 1846), Japanese Confucians voiced strong opposition to the then fashionable practice of *mabiki* (i.e., abortion and infanticide; literally, "thinning out seedlings").

Although physicians in imperial China lacked techniques such as B-ultrasound that allow us to monitor fetal development directly, this did not prevent both physicians and laypeople from knowing a great deal about what happens in the womb after conception. By the time of the Sui Dynasty (581–618) Chinese medicine, especially the gynecological and obstetrics literature, already possessed amazingly detailed knowledge of fetal development from conception to birth. First, this ancient medical knowledge distinguished between the embryo, the unformed and developing fetus, and the late and fully formed fetus. Second, Chinese medical beliefs about fetal life were a part of traditional knowledge about cosmology and human physiology. Third, it is evident that human life was regarded as beginning before birth, as early as the first month of pregnancy, and that the human being was physically formed at some time during pregnancy. Fourth, fetal development was seen as not merely a process of physical growth, but a spiritual component—named variously as "soul" or "spirit" (*hun, po, shen, ling*)—was added or "infused" at the various stages of pregnancy.

This sketch of the diversity, complexity and antiquity of Chinese views of fetal life should provide sufficient evidence to overturn the widespread belief that Chinese people and cultures held no ethical concern on the subject. The general and straightforward lesson I want to draw here is that, rather than providing us with new insights and enhanced understanding, the dichotomization of Chinese and Western cultures can have profoundly negative effects. It has so often rudely distorted the cultural and moral realities of China. And it has often served to reinforce stereotypes and prejudices against Chinese people, embodied in slogans such as—in the case of fetal life and abortion—"life is cheap in the East" and "in China the individual is insignificant."

The fallacy of dichotomizing cultures

Dichotomizing cultures is a fallacy because, on both descriptive and normative levels, it commits a series of intellectual mistakes and promotes many problematic assumptions. Moreover, it vocally advances or tacitly accepts some politically dangerous theses.

First, the image of a fundamentally (or at least largely) homogeneous, single, unified Chinese or Western culture has to be posited in an attempt to define the entire sweep of Chinese civilization in contrast to the civilizations of the West. The main problem with this image is that the great internal plurality *within* every culture or society has been downplayed, if not totally ignored. This approach can be called the "*assumed homogeneity*" and the problem involved is the "downplaying the internal plurality."

Second, when the homogeneity of a given culture or social group has been accepted, the dominant practice or official position of a given culture or social group on a particular issue is then logically deemed to be the authentic representative of the culture or social group concerned. Other viewpoints, other discourses, other voices, especially dissident and marginalized ones, are generally dismissed as irrelevant or even outside the group concerned ("un-Chinese" in the context of China). For Western scholars and observers, those aspects of Chinese cultures that differ from the West have always been treated as more interesting and have thus been defined as "more Chinese" than other dimensions and discourses. As the issue at stake here is about whose viewpoints should be most representative of a given culture or social group, we can call it the "*problematic representative*".

Third, to define the overarching and dominant features of a given culture or society, it has been assumed that every culture or society has its peculiar "mentality" (for a critical examination and decisive refutation of this approach, see Lloyd 1990). As mentioned in the preceding chapter, enormous intellectual efforts in various academic disciplines—anthropology, sociology, social psychology, philosophy, history, economics, and politics—have been made to discover the assumed unique way of seeing and acting in Chinese civilization. Moreover, many grand theories have been formulated in this intellectual search by modern and contemporary scholars in the West and China to account for this perceived uniqueness of Chinese culture and mentality. But the crucial question is: Does a unique and uniform Chinese mentality really exist? This general approach can be named the *"grand hypothesis of a peculiar mentality."*

For the American philosopher Richard Bernstein, what is involved here is a "false essentialism" in thinking about different cultures, especially non-Western ones. This false essentialism and its popular dualistic and dichotomous classification of cultures have seduced many contributors to the debate "into thinking there are essential determinate characteristics that distinguish the Western and Eastern 'mind'." In consequence, it "violently distorts the sheer complexity of overlapping traditions that cut across these artificial, simplistic global notions" (Bernstein 1992: 66). In terms of the myth under discussion, the particular essential qualities which are perceived to distinguish China from the West are communitarianism, collectivism and familism on the one hand, and individualism on the other.

Fourth, dichotomizing cultures has suggested and promoted that culture is an iron cage or entirely rigid structure in which we are born, in which we grow up, and cannot change in any way. However, culture—Chinese culture included—is always an open system, changeable and changing. Every society and culture accepts, absorbs, and integrates elements from foreign cultures. Viable moral ideas and ideals, no matter which place or historical period they originate in, belong to the whole of humankind. The nation's history has proven that Chinese have always been very active in learning from other cultures. (Of course, resisting foreign ideas has always been an essential ingredient of learning.) Lu Xun, arguably the greatest Chinese thinker and writer of the twentieth century, coined the well-known aphorism *"nalai zhuyi"* (grabbism), emphasizing the importance of appropriating from foreign cultures anything useful to the Chinese. The problem here involved with dichotomizing culture can thus be called "the culture defined as an iron cage" or the *"denial of every culture as an open system."*

Fifth, to view and define culture as a closed system with fixed categories denies the openness of the culture concerned in an even more serious sense, that is, to deny that culture constantly reforms itself not just by learning from foreign cultures but also by following the imperatives of morality. Through dichotomizing cultures, the moral dilemmas or difficulties involved are often bypassed by substituting statements about cultural practices for serious ethical examination. In other words, it endorses the "tyranny of cultural practices over ethics." However, in Chinese culture, as in many other societies, following whatever is morally right and good has always been seen as an important virtue for individuals and the most fundamental value for societies. The Chinese proverb *"congshan ruliu"* has encouraged people to follow the good as naturally as a river follows its course. In other words, an uncritical reverence for cultural norms and practices can actually work against the most fundamental values of a given culture and society. As discussed in the introduction, the issues involved here are: endorsing the *"tyranny of cultural practices over ethics"* vs. upholding the "primacy of morality."

Sixth, dichotomization creates a severe barrier to cross-cultural understanding through the "assumption of radical differences" or the *"assumption of incommensurability"*. As I have shown, although the postmodernist attitude to other cultures has reversed polarities from the negative modernist assessment, like the modernist discourse, the postmodernist viewpoint is nevertheless based on a fundamental assumption that the differences between and among different worldviews, discourses, paradigms, and cultures are radical, incomparable and incommensurable. Indeed, this is one of the central themes of the various postmodernist movements—it is postmodernism that has popularized the very term "incommensurable" or "incommensurability."

Seventh, a salient problem with the popular thesis of cultural incommensurability, as already touched on in the introduction, is to repudiate the existence of many striking similar or shared features between and among different cultures as well as the common humanity and the common human morality. Cultural differences are often over-exaggerated. This belief can be called the *"rejection of cross-cultural similarities or commonalities"* or the "rejection of common humanity."

Eighth, politically speaking, the popular thesis of cultural incommensurability rooted in the habit of dichotomizing cultures leads to another popular belief that the clash, especially the violent clash, of the cultures of China and the West—or of different civilizations in general, as has repeatedly occurred throughout history—is conceived and accepted as to be inevitable. The clash of cultures and civilizations is defined as a matter of our destiny, not human choice. But history has also taught us that, so long as we are willing, genuine dialogue between and among different cultures—like those that take place between diverse moral traditions and viewpoints *within* every culture—is not only necessary but also possible, however difficult its realization may be in practice. The grave political danger cultivated by dichotomizing cultures can be named the *"self-defeating prophecy of the clash of cultures."*

Ninth, there are other political dangers, especially for non-Western societies. Let me focus on China specifically. While dichotomizing cultures may promote cultural pluralism in the West, the age-old and still powerful habit of homogenizing, totalizing, essentializing and radicalizing China not only distorts our descriptive knowledge about China and Chinese-Western cultural differences, but has severe perils for formulating social policies. In the preceding chapter I have shown that official Chinese ideology has readily subscribed and promoted the myth of a collectivist China vs. the individualistic West and the dichotomous way of presenting Chinese and Western culture because they serve well the official ideology. When coming to the issue of social policies, the dichotomization of cultures has nurtured the specious idea that promotes a *single* and homogenous Chinese culture and treats the collectivism or authoritarianism as the only authentic Chinese option. As a result, it helps to reinforce the status quo of existing political and cultural power. In particular, it dismisses the significance of an ever-present diversity and pluralism in China and renounces a series of universal human values (such as human rights) as being culturally incomparable to China. These political perils that dichotomization has caused can be called "*generating contentious and harmful social policies.*"

Another indicator of the political dangers of dichotomizing cultures is that this way of thinking about Eastern and Western cultural differences has cultivated the famous, or, in the eyes of its critics, infamous "Asian Values" thesis. It asserts that, as Eastern culture is essentially authoritarian and familist and thus radically different from the individualistic Western culture (note the singular nature of the term "culture"), such values as democracy and human rights are not applicable in Asian societies. The thesis was put forward most prominently by Lee Kuan Yew, the former authoritarian leader of Singapore, and greatly supported by many officials of other authoritarian Asian and even some African countries (see Chapter 9 for a critical discussion of this thesis). As a matter of fact, this dichotomizing way of thinking about Chinese and Western cultural differences is the major epistemological reason for the "cultural differences" argument against the applicability of a series of universal values in medical ethics such as medical truth-telling—especially those with a clear Western origin, such as informed consent, human rights, and women's rights—in China or other non-Western societies (see Chapters 6, 7, 8, 9, and 10).

All of these intellectual and political problems—the assumption of internal homogeneity, the question of representation, the grand hypothesis of a peculiar mentality, false essentialism, the denial of every culture as an open system, the endorsement of the tyranny of cultural practices over ethics, the misconception of cultural incommensurability, the rejection of cross-cultural similarities or common humanity, the self-defeating prophecy of the clash of cultures as inevitable, and the generation of contentious and harmful social policies—are directly associated with the dualistic and dichotomizing way of thinking about cultures and their differences. I thus group them all into a single all-encompassing category: the *fallacy of dichotomization* or the *fallacy of dichotomizing cultures*.

Conclusions

It is mainly due to the influence of this dichotomization that the myth of a communitarian China vs. the individualistic West has been so widely circulated. Dichotomizing cultural differences is a fallacy because it has been based on and led to a great many unfounded and specious assumptions being taken for settled matters of fact. Using medical truth-telling in China and Chinese views on fetal life as examples, in this chapter I have identified a series of grave intellectual and political problems involved with dichotomization. One of the most unfortunate consequences of this habit of thought is that the richness and internal plurality of a given culture, as well as the complexity of cultural differences within and between different groups, are oversimplified.

The common habit of dichotomizing cultural differences in the dualistic terms has underestimated the great variations in the fields within Chinese and Western societies, and especially in China. The plain matter of fact is that neither Western nor Chinese medical ethics is dominated by a single mentality or perspective. It is long overdue to put this way of dichotomizing cultures in its appropriate domain or even better, to a complete rest. Through careful examinations of a series of different topics from a Chinese-Western comparative perspective, one of the main tasks of this book is to demonstrate not only the fallacy of dichotomization and other stereotypes as manifested in our understanding or misunderstandings of medical ethics in the Chinese cultural context, but also the possibility to overcome the age-old Western and Chinese habit of thought by a transcultural or interpretative approach.

I want to make one final critique to the habit of dichotomizing cultures before bringing this chapter to an end, with a point I had just touched upon above. Just as the dichotomization of cultures has nurtured the specious idea of an Asian bioethics—an Eastern communitarian bioethics vs. an individualistic Western bioethics—it also fosters a specious idea of a *single* Asian or Chinese bioethics (Nie 2007; see also De Castro 1999; De Castro et al. 2004). This has been done by homogenizing bioethics in the region by latching onto one particular moral outlook—namely, authoritarianism or communitarianism or familism. According to this perspective, a multicultural Asia, with its attendant wonders, challenges and frictions, is treated as a problem and a curse, rather than a potential blessing (for a criticism of this view, see Nie and Campbell 2007). Other medical ethics traditions and alternative moral viewpoints, which have long been a part of Asian or Chinese civilizations or have recently developed there, are rejected and suppressed.

The kind of transcultural or interpretative bioethics I advocate in this book offers a different vision of how medical ethics in China and in Asia might be developed. Bioethics in China should resemble what Zhuang Zi (Chuang Tzu), a founder of Daoism, called the music of Heaven (*tianlai*): "Blowing on the ten thousand things in a different way, so that each can be itself—all take what they want for themselves" (Watson 1968, 37). Zhuang Zi, like John Stuart Mill and Karl Popper, believed in pluralism and considered a spurious unity of ideas and the rejection of different ways of living and thinking as contrary to the Dao, and indeed the worst nightmare that human beings could experience (Nie 2007: 150; see the epilogue for more on Zhuang Zi).

Chapter 3

China as the radical other of the West, or a misconstruction of Foucault

Sexual excess as a cause of disease in China and the United States

China characterized as the radical other of the West

Sexuality has been a major aspect of Western curiosity about China. The French theorist Roland Barthes (1987: 116) listed it as the first of "a thousand urgent questions, urgent and seemingly natural ones" that Westerners carry with them in their baggage when visiting China. After sexuality comes "women, the family, morality," and then "the situation in the humanities, in linguistics, in psychiatry." Barthes made these remarks as he reflected on his visit to China in the early 1970s when the Communist regime was reopening the country's doors to the West. However, rather than arriving home with "a secret deciphered," Barthes returned with "*nothing*" in his baggage (original emphasis). China, "bland, flat and colorless," seemed to resist yielding any "meaning" that Western intellectuals might set out to discover, "not because it hides it, but more subversively, because (in this respect very un-Confucian) it defeats the constitution of concepts, themes, and names" (117). As the "radical other" of the West, and of the French in particular, for Barthes all things Chinese—including sexuality—remained "eminently prosaic."

That of course was Mao's China. Today, Barthes would need to stand his judgment on its head. In the course of a few decades, China has become one of the most dynamic places on earth, economically, socially and sexually. Twentieth-century China experienced many revolutions and the last major revolution has turned out to be a sexual one. Divorce rates are soaring; premarital sex has become the norm and teenage abortion is commonplace; one-night stands have become almost fashionable; homosexual bars and clubs have sprouted; and numerous proposals to legalize prostitution and establish official red-light districts have been put forward. In response, the official ideology of the state puts the blame on the influence of "decadent and philistine Western bourgeois lifestyles." Westerners and Chinese alike are quick to explain that China's sexual revolution is simply a matter of catching up with the West in sexual mores, as in so many other areas of social life. However, few are aware that this apparently brand new revolution is also stimulating the revival of many traditional Chinese norms on sex. As in the West, there have always existed both repressive and self-indulgent forces in Chinese culture.

Underlying this popular explanation of China's sexual revolution is the belief that China has always been treated as the radical other of the West. In the past, foot-binding and concubine-taking were cited as evidence of China's otherness in the area of sexual mores. China has consistently been portrayed as a deeply repressive society, not only politically but also sexually. The most thorough exploration of China as the radical other of the West was developed by Barthes' countryman, the genuinely subversive thinker Michel Foucault. The fact that Foucault was not a China specialist is an advantage here, as his intellectual articulation of China is more representative of the common Western approach.

Foucault is fond of citing China as an illustration of the strangeness of the other, in terms of social and cultural discourse and its incommensurability with the West. In an attempt to shatter the familiarity of the conventional Western thought system, he began his magnificent work on the modern Western human sciences, *The Order of Things*, by citing a risible passage from a "certain Chinese encyclopedia" in which animals are classified in a way that makes no sense for the Western mind (Foucault 1994, 1). In his provocative series of studies on sexuality, power and "the techniques of self," Foucault once again evoked, repeatedly, China as the prime example of the radical other of the West. Radically different in character from the *scientia sexualis* of modern Western civilization where sexuality became a subject of scientific discourse, the other "great procedure for producing the truth of sex" has been the *ars erotica*, where pleasure is considered "first and foremost in relation to itself," as in "China, Japan, India, Rome, and the Arabo-Moslem societies" (Foucault 1990a, 57). On the one hand, possessing no *ars erotica*, modern Western civilization is "undoubtedly the only civilization to practice *scientia sexualis*," in which "strong pleasure, it warned, would eventually result in nothing short of death: that of individuals, generations, and species itself" (Ibid, 58, 54). In the Eastern tradition on the other hand, as in the Chinese discourse of sexuality, what is distinctive is "an absolute mastery of the body, a singular bliss, obliviousness to time and limits, the elixir of life, the exile of death and its threats" (Ibid, 58).

In an interview, Foucault regretted that he had not contrasted Western and Chinese sexualities even more strongly: "The Greek and Romans did not have any *ars erotica* to be compared with the Chinese *ars erotica*" (Foucault 1983, 234–5). According to Foucault, there are different representative "formulas" corresponding to the three poles of sexual behavior: act, pleasure, and desire. Whilst the Greek formula underscores acts, the Christian and modern formulas stress desire—the former to suppress and eradicate it and the latter to accept and liberate it. Different from either of the Western formulas, the Chinese "formula," on the other hand, "would be *plaisir—désir—(acte)*. ... Acts are put aside because you have to restrain acts in order to get maximum duration and intensity of pleasure." (Ibid, 243)

In comparing and contrasting sexuality in classical Greece and ancient China, Foucault (1990b, 137) noted "the presence of this same thematic complex: fear of the irrepressible and costly act, dread of its harmful consequences for the body and health, representation of the man-woman relationship in the form of contest, preoccupation with obtaining descendants of good quality by means of a well-regulated sexual activity." Despite this, he immediately went on to draw a strong contrast between the two approaches:

> But the ancient Chinese "bedroom" treatises responded to the anxiety in a manner completely different from what one finds in classical Greece. The dread one felt when faced with the violence of the act and the fear of losing one's semen were answered by methods of retention; the encounter with the other sex was perceived as a way to come into contact with the vital principle the latter held in her possession and, by absorbing it, to internalize it for one's own benefit. So that a well-managed sexual activity not only precluded any danger, it could also result in a strengthening of one's existence and it could be a means of restoring one's youthfulness. ... In this "erotic art," which sought, with pronounced ethical concerns, to intensify insofar as possible the positive effects of a controlled, deliberate, multifarious, and prolonged sexual activity, time—a time that terminated the act, aged the body, and brought death—was exorcised.
>
> (Ibid)

It turned out that the obscure passage from the "Chinese encyclopedia" Foucault cited at the beginning of *The Order of Things* was simply a fiction perpetrated by a Western scholar (Zhang 1998, 21–4). As a creation of the Western imagination, this passage has really nothing to say about the Chinese system of thought. Foucault's articulation of the features of Chinese sexuality is certainly based on a much more credible source, the monumental study by the Dutch sinologist R. H. van Gulik of sexual life in ancient China (2003 [1961]). Interestingly, one of van Gulik's primary aims was to demonstrate that China was not as alien or exotic as appearances might suggest so far as sexuality is concerned. However, basing his thinking on the materials presented by van Gulik, Foucault reached—and, indeed, wanted to promote—the opposite conclusion.

In this chapter, my aim is not to provide a systematic comparative account of Chinese and Western sexuality, as Foucault attempted. In other words, I will not discuss Foucault's treatment of the similarities and differences of the sexualities of China and the West. Rather, what I am seeking to achieve is a more general and indeed more modest aim—to show that treating China as the radical other of the West is not only misleading but also absurd. I will do so by presenting, through a sustained historical cross-cultural comparison, some surprising similarities and also some subtle differences between the understanding of sexual excess as a disease and a debilitating factor in nineteenth-century America and ancient China. In both cultures, great physiological and pathological significance was attributed to semen and its loss. Both medical systems considered the principle of "the less, the better" to be the golden rule of any sexual regimen. But while, for the Chinese, the rule actually meant "the fewer ejaculations—but the more sexual intercourse with many partners—the better," American doctors claimed that sexual stimulation or excitement in itself could induce disease.

Sexual excess as a cause of disease and death: cross-cultural similarities

It was a widespread medical belief in both nineteenth-century America and ancient China that sexual overindulgence—even in marriage—constituted a significant cause of many serious health problems including various functional disorders, physical and mental debility, somatic pain, and even premature death. Physicians and hygienists stressed the adverse consequences of any kind of sexual excess, including sex within marriage.

Since case histories written by medical doctors provide direct access to the prevailing view of sexual behavior in a given culture, I begin by citing two historical cases. One is drawn from the section on marital excess in the book *Chastity* by Dio Lewis, a doctor and prolific writer on many topics in nineteenth-century America; the second comes from the chapter on sexual hygiene in the seventh-century Chinese medical classic *Qianjing Yaofang* (The Thousand Golden Prescriptions) by Sun Simiao, the so-called "king of medicine" in China.

Lewis's account deals with a middle-aged American farmer (Lewis 1874, 74–6. References to Lewis in the first person have been changed to the third person for convenience.)

> One day, a farmer, with his wife, came to see Dr. Lewis. He had had problems with his stomach, back and nerves for about eight years and was in a sadly nervous and despondent condition. He had been married for nine years. By the time the patient finished his story, Dr. Lewis had seen the "source of his trouble."
> "Have you been temperate in your sexual indulgences?" the doctor asked.
> The farmer said that he was a Christian. "I have never touched any woman except my wife. I am all right in those things."
> "You misunderstood me," the doctor explained, "What I meant to ask was, whether with your wife you have been temperate." He said further, "I think you are suffering from sexual exhaustion, and I asked about your habits in order to discover, if possible, what the source of your unhappy conditions is."
> After a little hesitation, with his wife's urging, the patient told the doctor that he "usually indulged each night during three weeks of the

month." His wife added that they sometimes "have intercourse three or four times during the twenty-four hours." She had thought it might hurt her husband, but he insisted that married people could "indulge themselves as much as they please" and that "the sin and wrong was in going out of one's family among strange women."

Then, Dr. Lewis told the patient that "he had well-nigh ruined himself, and that entire abstinence for half a year was absolutely indispensable to begin his restoration, and that even after that he must limit himself to a monthly indulgence at most." For Dr. Lewis, the patient "is a good citizen and a professing Christian." The only problem is that he "had never had the slightest suspicion that a sexual indulgence which had been 'sanctified' by the minister could be wrong."

The second case, described 1200 years earlier and on the other side of the Pacific Ocean, concerns an elderly man in rural China:

In the early period of Zhenguan there lived an intemperate man in his seventies. He visited Dr. Sun and consulted him about his sexual activities. The old man told the physician that his yang-qi (male energy) had increased in recent days so that he wanted to sleep with his wife at night and make love to her. The patient asked whether this phenomenon was good or not.

Dr. Sun replied: "This is a great ill omen. Don't you know about what happens to an oil lamp? When the lamp is going out, its light flares up briefly—then it dies out completely. Now you are in your seventies you should be restraining your desire and holding back your $jing$ (essence, literally, semen). But all of a sudden, you have violently aroused your sexual desire. Isn't this abnormal? I'm really worried for you. Please take care of yourself."

Sun Simiao related further that the old man died from a relapse of his illness forty days later. He attributed his patient's death to his sexual indiscretion and stressed that this case was far from unique. "I describe merely one case out of many in order to warn people in the future."

Then Dr. Sun concluded: "People who want to look after themselves properly must carefully control their sexual desire whenever it is aroused. Having sex anytime one wishes is equivalent to self-destruction. ... Unfortunately, people are ignorant of the Dao of sexual hygiene when they are young. Even if it is known about, the Dao is still not followed in practice. As a result, when someone comes to appreciate the importance of the Dao of sexual hygiene, it is often too late. For, as he realizes only too well, his disease—the result of sexual overindulgence—is usually incurable."

Despite the apparent historical and socio-cultural differences between nineteenth-century America and imperial China, these two case histories vividly show how sexual overindulgence has been perceived as the cause of a number of health problems identified in everyday medical practice, and how physicians have invoked it to explain the illness and even premature deaths of their patients.

For nineteenth-century American doctors and health reformers, sexual overindulgence, even in a "natural" and legal way—sex in the "kingdom of wedlock"—was thought to be no less harmful to an individual's health than "self-pollution" (masturbation). Like masturbation, sexual excess was seen as a form of disease. Dio Lewis and Sylvester Graham, the great health reformer and theorist, were representative of American doctors and hygienists who condemned the disastrous results of sexual excess, even that occurring between husband and wife. Graham's *A Lecture to Young Men*—the nineteenth-century classic of sexual abstinence—was filled with stern admonitions about the horrible consequences of both sexual excess in marriage and masturbation in young people. According to Graham, it was beyond all question that "sexual excess within the precincts of wedlock" created "an immeasurable amount of evil results to the human family." The health problems caused included:

> Languor, lassitude, muscular relaxation, general debility and heaviness, depression of spirits, loss of appetite, indigestion, faintness, and sinking at the pit of the stomach, increased susceptibilities of the skin and lungs to all the atmospheric changes, feebleness of circulation, chilliness, headache, melancholy, hypochondria, hysterics, feebleness of all the senses, impaired vision, loss of sight, weakness of the lungs, nervous cough, pulmonary consumption, disorders of the liver and kidneys, urinary difficulties, disorders of the genital organs, weakness of the brain, loss of memory, epilepsy, insanity, apoplexy,—and extreme feebleness and early death of offspring,—are among the too common evils which are caused by sexual excesses between husband and wife.
>
> (Graham 1834, 35)

Graham even considered that many of the terrible plagues that had ravaged the earth "have been connected with such excesses" (Ibid, 29). "Dyspepsia" and "venery" were simply two modes of diseased action in the organic system of life. As Stephen Nissenbaum succinctly put it, Graham "associated sex itself with pain and disease." Venery or the pursuit of sexual pleasure "does not merely *produce* disease; it *is* itself a form of disease" (Nissenbaum 1980, 111, 109). In similar vein, in his *Chastity* Lewis listed the most common effects of sexual excess:

> backache, lassitude, giddiness, dimness of sight, noises in the ears, numbness of the fingers and paralysis. The drain is universal, but more sensitive organs and tissues suffer most. So the nervous system gives way, and continues the principal sufferer throughout. A very large part of the

premature loss of sight and hearing, dizziness, numbness and pricking in the hands and feet, and other kindred developments, are justly chargeable to unbridled venery. Not unfrequently I see in a single hour more than one man whose head or back or nerve testifies of such reckless expenditure.
(Lewis 1874, 58–9, 11)

For Lewis, people "perish for lack of knowledge" and they "exhaust themselves and fail in life" because of sexual overindulgence. Even the influential sexual radical and advocate of free love Thomas Nicholas (1853) believed that nervous exhaustion induced by sexual overindulgence was the direct cause of "two-thirds of all the diseases of mankind" including dyspepsia, rheumatism, palsy, epilepsy, apoplexy, and the nervous and uterine diseases of women.

For traditional Chinese physicians, the role of sexual hygiene in keeping good health was no less important than that of diet. Early deaths as well as many diseases were attributed to sexual excess. Moderation of sexual activity both within and outside marriage was considered one of the most fundamental principles for promoting health and longevity. According to the etiological theories of Chinese medicine, sexual over-strain is one of the crucial pathogenic factors related to the maladjustment of the rhythms of activity and rest. In Chinese medicine, the various kinds of pathogenic factors include the six exogenous causes of disease—excessive or untimely atmospheric influences, internal injury caused by "the seven emotions" (i.e., sudden, violent or persistent emotional stimuli), improper diet, the maladjustment of work and rest, and surgical trauma. Traditional Chinese medicine teaches that overindulgence in sexual activity can exhaust or impair the human vital essence, lower the body's resistance to disease, and produce an imbalance both in *qi* (the body's vital energy) and in the blood. Sexual excess causes a variety of disorders including lethargy in the loins and knees; dizziness, tinnitus and listlessness; sleeping disorders; and impotence, spermatorrhea or failure of ejaculation in males, and menoxenia and leukorrhagia in females. Almost all the ancient medical works dealing with this subject emphasize that intemperance in sexual life often produces a variety of diseases, and especially the relapse of past ailments.

Chinese doctors, like Sun Simiao, considered sexual excess to be one of the most significant causes of death. The idea of sexual excess as fatal was not peculiar to the Chinese; as the American doctor Augustus Gardner (1974 [1870], 84) expressed it, "Excess is too much. ... [E]xcess is premature death." Yet the Chinese tradition maintained, more explicitly than American physicians, that sexual overindulgence constituted a major factor in premature death. This difference might be explained by the observation that the desire for longevity played a more active role in Chinese culture than was the case in nineteenth-century America. Chinese people saw longevity as an important sign of individual virtue, and indeed the word *shou* (longevity) was traditionally the commonest term for a blessing. The opening chapter of the most important

Chinese medical classic, the *Huangdi Neijing* (The Yellow Emperor's Classic of Medicine), had argued that "entering the chamber of love in an intoxicated condition" not only produced a variety of diseases and the relapse of existing conditions, but also shortened one's life as sexual passion exhausted the vital force. For Xu Dachun, a well-known eighteenth-century scholar-physician, unrestrained sex was thought to be a cause of sudden death (Unschuld 1990, 127). One popular Chinese poem spoke about the dangers of sex for males: "A sixteen-year-old girl's body is like soft, sweet candy, but the sword between her thighs can kill foolish men. Although no one sees human heads falling off, dear gentlemen, it drains the marrow from your bones in secret." The female vaginal orifice—known as the "door of life"—was also dubbed the "entrance of death."

Nineteenth-century American and ancient Chinese physicians were likewise united in regarding orgasm as a serious evil. Graham described the effects of orgasm in rather alarming terms: "The convulsive paroxysms attending venereal indulgence, are connected with the most intensive excitement, and cause the most powerful agitation to the whole system that it is ever subject to." He continued:

> All the organs including brain, stomach, heart, lungs, liver, and skin, feel it sweeping over them with the tremendous violence of a tornado. The powerfully excited and convulsed heart drives the blood, in fearful congestion, to the principal viscera,—producing oppression, irritation, debility, rupture, inflammation, and sometimes disorganization;—and this violent paroxysm is generally succeeded by great exhaustion, relaxation, lassitude and even protraction.
>
> (Graham 1834, 40–50)

The author(s) of the *Yi Xin Fang* (Prescriptions of the Medical Mind) used similar language: "Indeed after the emission the man's body is tired, his ears are buzzing, his eyes are heavy with sleep, his throat is parched and his limbs inert. Although he has experienced a brief moment of joy, it is not really a pleasurable feeling" (cited in van Gulik 2003, 145). One of the many ills caused by sexual intercourse is "obstruction of the organs":

> This ailment is caused by a man's overindulgence in sexual intercourse and failure to regulate his copulation. If he repeatedly misses the right rhythm during the coitus, he will drain his vital essence. He has to force emissions and in the end his semen will be exhausted and will not come forth any more. As a result the hundred diseases will arise.
>
> (Ibid, 144)

In consequence, Chinese doctors admonished that, even though the orgasm was the culminating pleasure of the sexual act, it was not something to be enjoyed. One must curtail this brief and dangerous pleasure for the sake of longevity, health, and happiness.

There are, however, some tensions or ambivalences regarding the advantages and disadvantages of expressing human sexuality apparent in both the American and Chinese authors. *The Works of Aristotle*, a popular American sex and midwifery manual of the eighteenth and early nineteenth centuries that went under the name of the famous Greek philosopher, viewed sex as both a pleasurable activity and excellent general therapy. Sex "eases and lightens the body, clears the mind, comforts the head and face, and expels melancholy." Total sexual abstinence could actually do serious harm to a person's health. Naturally, it was emphasized that sexual activity was beneficial and good only for those people who used it "lawfully and moderately." Immoderate carnal copulation was harmful because it "destroys the sight, dries the body, and impairs the brain; often cause fevers, as Avicine [Avicenna] and experience shew." It even "shortens life too as is evident in the sparrow, which by reason of its often coupling, lives but three years" ("Aristotle" 1974, 195).

Chinese physicians likewise held that a normal sex life does no harm to health and, indeed, is essential to maintain it. In its well-known chapter on human sexuality, the *Yi Xin Fang* listed eight benefits of sexual intercourse: concentrating the vital essence, resting the spirit, nourishing the internal organs, strengthening the bones, harmonizing the circulation of the blood, increasing the blood supply, benefiting the humors, and adjusting the physique. Of course, these benefits could be attained only by healthy or proper methods of sexual intercourse. The *Yi Xin Fang* further claimed that intercourse undertaken with restraint could cure diseases. "Indeed sexual extravagance and debauch will result in diseases that harm one's system, a fact that will become evident during the sexual act itself. But the diseases caused by the sexual act can also be cured thereby" (Quoted in van Gulik, 2003, 148). In order for a person to remain healthy, sex was both a necessity and a danger at the same time, like water and fire. Ge Hong—the Daoist and medical scholar of the fourth century—argued that, although sexual overindulgence "diminished one's life," giving up sexual activity entirely could cause one to "die prematurely through the many illnesses resulting from depression and celibacy." He compared sexual intercourse with water and fire and pointed out that either element could "kill people or bring them life, solely depending on their ability to deal with them." The key to avoiding harm was "harmonizing the two extremes."

Cross-cultural differences in similarities

So far we have seen that both American and Chinese doctors clearly connected a series of functional disorders of both body and mind, as well as premature death, with sexual excess. However, there were also some subtle and fundamental differences.

The prevailing belief that sexual excess produced harmful and lasting effects of the kind described above led physicians and other medical advisors to suggest guidelines—or more accurately, rules—for the frequency of sexual intercourse in order to control lust in the marriage bed. A crucial question here was how much intercourse was considered excessive. Although a number of authors on sexual hygiene in both nineteenth-century America and ancient China urged the principle of "the less indulgence the better" as the "golden rule," they did not agree on a general standard for the frequency of healthy sexual intercourse.

Dr. Graham had firm ideas on the permissible frequency of "connubial commerce." He warned that there was a common error of opinion that "health requires an emission of semen at stated periods" and that "frequent nocturnal emissions in sleep" are not injurious to health. "All this is wrong,—entirely, dangerously wrong!" Though Graham realized that it was impossible to prescribe a single rule that would cover all cases, he maintained that frequency of intercourse should not exceed the "number of months in the year," and "cannot exceed the number of weeks in the year" (1834, 37). Otherwise, a man would impair his "constitutional power," shorten his life, and increase his susceptibility to disease and suffering. Many nineteenth-century American authors on the subject repeated Graham's prescriptions. Attempting to reach a compromise between absolute continence and promiscuity, following Graham's proposals, Eliza Duffy suggested coition once every month (cited in Haller, Jr. and Haller 1974, 131). In his famous sex manual *Sexual Physiology and Hygiene*, R. T. Trall pointed out that, even though the frequency of sexual activity depends on a variety of individual circumstances—stamina, temperament, occupation, habits of exercise, period of life, and so on—"few should exceed the limit of once a week and many cannot safely indulge oftener than once a month." Moreover, "as temperance is always the safer rule of conduct, if there must be any deviation from the strictest law of physiology, let the error be on that side." In matters of sexual hygiene, "no better rule can be given than the less indulgence the better." (Trall 1908 [1886], 233–4).

Even the advocates of "free love" emphasized temperance as emphatically as sexual conservatives like Graham. E. H. Heywood summarized the nineteenth-century American radical perspective on sexuality. In the minds of many people, he noted, "Free Love tends to unrestrained licentiousness, to open the flood-gates of passion and remove all barriers in its desolating course." However, "it means just the opposite; it means the *civilization of animalism*, and the triumph of Reason, Knowledge, and Continence" (Heywood 1877, italics in original). Thomas Nicholas also saw both sides of the issue. On the one hand, he regarded "the expression of love" as "beautiful" and called sexual orgasm the "most exquisite enjoyment of which the human senses are capable." On the other hand, like any advocate of chastity, he believed that overindulgence could lead to exhaustion and leave a variety of physical ailments and moral consequences in its wake. On the one hand, Nicholas insisted that "human passion must have freedom for development, freedom of action, freedom of enjoyment," and, of course, freedom for love as well. On the other hand, he stressed that there is no passion so exhausting as love. "Amative excesses, even at a proper age, and under the proper circumstances, produce exhaustion, and so cause disease." He proposed, just as Graham had done, that intercourse be performed no more often than once every month; he allowed weekly intercourse as the absolute maximum frequency, and only assuming that all other indications were positive. He warned that married couples ought not to violate this rule, even on their honeymoon. "Amative excess" at this time might well mean that "permanent happiness is sacrificed to a few days of delirious and not very satisfying enjoyment." (Nicholas 1853, 256, 200, 268–358, 419). He repeatedly emphasized that "free love" would result in a more healthy moderation of sexual activity.

For Chinese doctors, the key issue was not sexual intercourse itself, but the loss of semen. What one should regulate was the frequency of ejaculation. Although several ancient Chinese physicians discussed the proper frequency of seminal emission, their advice differed. Sun Simiao advocated reducing sexual activity with advancing age: "In one's twenties, one can cope with the emission of semen once every four days; in one's thirties, once every eight days; in one's forties, once every sixteen days; in one's fifties, once every twenty days; in one's sixties, one should refrain from this indulgence—but a maximum of once a month if one is still strong." The most important general principle advocated by all these writers was moderation and eschewing mere carnal desire. The *Yi Xin Fang* urged that "every man must regulate his emissions according to the condition of his vital essence." A man should never force himself to achieve orgasm as this would harm his system. The recommended frequency of sexual activity was laid down as follows:

> [S]trongly-built men of fifteen years can afford to emit semen twice a day; thin ones once a day and the same applies to men of twenty years. Strongly built men of thirty may ejaculate once a day, weaker men once in two days. Strong men of forty may emit semen once in three days, weaker men once in four days. Strong men of fifty can ejaculate once in five days, weaker men once in ten days. Strong men of sixty many ejaculate once in ten days, weaker men once in twenty days. Strong men of seventy may emit semen once a month, weak ones should not ejaculate anymore at that age.
>
> (cited in van Gulik 2003, 146)

The frequency of ejaculation sanctioned in the *Yi Xin Fang* was much higher than Sun Simiao proposed and not particularly moderate.

Traditional Chinese physicians stressed the special relationship between the human body and the natural environment. Just as the natural world was marked by the rhythm of the seasons, so one should regulate the frequency of sexual activity according to the seasons. According to the *Yi Xin Fang,* in order to attain longevity, "in spring a man can allow himself to emit semen once every three days, in summer and autumn twice a month. During winter one should save one's semen and not ejaculate at all" (Ibid). The natural or "heavenly" character of winter was thought to promote the accumulation of *yang* essence and, thus, one should correspondingly reduce sexual activity during winter. It was said that the loss of *yang* energy caused by a single emission in winter was a hundred times greater than that caused by one emission in spring.

In summary, although both American and Chinese doctors supported the rule of "the less the better" in principle, their recommended frequency of sexual activity varied widely. Moreover, for Chinese physicians, it was not sexual intercourse per se but the emission of semen that should be restrained. In fact, many Chinese medical professionals, especially religious adherents of Daoism, claimed that the more frequent sexual intercourse was, the fewer ejaculations; and the more intercourse with a variety of partners, the better.

China produced some of the world's earliest sex manuals and specialized texts on sexology. They include texts produced no later than in the second century B.C., unearthed in 1973 at the Mawangtui Tomb of the Han Dynasty, Changsha, along with the oldest systematic medical works in Chinese. In the official dynastic histories of the first century, texts dealing with the "art of the bedchamber" were listed side by side with medical bibliographies.

Daoist adepts and physicians developed a theoretical system as well as concrete techniques to achieve health, longevity, and even physical "immortality" through the art of the bedchamber—one of the most important Chinese prescriptions for longevity. One major method followed by this sexual practice was known as *tuojiao shuaoxie* (frequent coitus reservatus and few ejaculations). It was believed that this sexual "art" could make a man's body light, and would expel all disease and even make him an immortal like the Yellow Emperor, who was said to have had sexual intercourse with twelve hundred women. According to Ge Hong, the sexual art "is based on the theory that the more women a man copulates with, the greater benefit he derives from the act; and that for a man who is ignorant of this art, copulation with only one or two women suffices to bring about his untimely death" (in Ge 1967, 123). And the *Yi Xing Fang* stated succinctly: "The principle of this method is to have frequent intercourse with young girls, but emit semen only on rare occasions" (cited in van Gulik 2003, 136). Even Sun Simiao advocated that having sex only with the same partner was greatly harmful to a man's health.

By the standards of the nineteenth century, and even by today's American sexual regimen, the Chinese theory would have been condemned as overindulgence. However, from the Chinese perspective, what must be rigorously restricted is not the act itself but the frequency of ejaculation. In this sense, the Chinese art of the bedchamber by no means endorsed sexual intemperance, but subscribed to the same philosophy of moderation endorsed by nineteenth-century American commentators on sexual hygiene. Although the methods recommended by American and Chinese physicians and hygienists were completely different, their serious purpose remained the same: to keep oneself healthy and prolong one's life by controlling the loss of semen or increasing the amount of *jing* (the vital essence). It is interesting to note that the same philosophy of sexual moderation meant very different things to people in two different cultures.

Why was sexual overindulgence viewed as harmful and dangerous by nineteenth-century Americans and ancient Chinese alike? Why should the golden rule of sexuality be "the less the better"? Why were Chinese doctors more concerned with emissions than sexual intercourse? The answers to all these questions are to be found in the deep-rooted conception that semen was an essential vital substance.

In the ancient Chinese language, the character *jing* stands for both semen, including male and female ejaculate, and the fundamental substance of life that builds up the physical structure of the body and maintains its functions. A modern Chinese medical text summarizes the importance of *jing* to human health:

> The *jing* is the foundation of life; it is a fundamental substance that shapes the human body and maintains every kind of vital activity, directly affecting growth, development, aging, and death. If it is at capacity, it is possible for the body to be strong, vitality high, and the resistance of the organism powerful; if it is debilitated, the body may be weakened, the vitality inadequate, development retarded, aging accelerated, and the power of resistance weakened.
>
> (Sivin 1987, 242)

According to Chinese medicine, *jing*, *qi* (the energy in all life and in the universe) and *sheng* (spirit) constitute the three essential "treasures" found in the human body. *Jing* and *xue* (blood) have a common source and both belong to the *yin*. So how does this explain how sexual excess could result in major health problems? The fourteenth-century physician Zhu Zhenheng founded a well-known school of medical thought that emphasized the value of nourishing the *yin-jing*. It was believed that in the human body the *yin* (substance) was often in deficit and readily debilitated, while the *yang* (passions and desires) was always present in excess. Any form of indulgence, especially sexual excess and an unbalanced diet, was seen as lying at the root of all health problems and troubles in life. Thus, Zhu repeatedly emphasized the dangers of sexual desire and activity and devoted several chapters of his medical works to discussing the topic in detail. Xu Dachun compared the kidney-*jing* (referring here specifically to the male semen) to water in a well. Excessive use of *jing* leads to weakness and exhaustion. Following one's passions without moderation was as if "one drew water from a shallow, narrow well without any restraint. It would dry up and be exhausted" (in Unschuld 1990, 75–6).

In the West, sexual excess generally had been seen as debilitating since the ancient Greeks. In his essay "The Seed," Hippocrates stated that men are "weakened" by the loss of semen, even though the "actual amount we emit in intercourse is very small." For the father of medicine in the West, semen constituted the "most potent part" of all the fluids in the body (in Hippocrates 1986, 317). In later centuries, many authors and doctors emphasized the importance of semen and the debilitating consequences of its loss. In the eighteenth century, the French physician Simon-Andre Tissot developed this theory in his work on masturbation. In the anonymous English translation of Tissot's *Onanism*, which appeared in the United States in 1832, the writer asserted that the seminal fluid "has so much influence on the strength of the body and on the perfection of digestion which restores it, that physicians of every age have unanimously admitted, that the loss of one ounce of it, enfeebles more than forty ounces of blood" (Tissot 1832, v–vi). Another French doctor, Eugene Beckland, whose book was published in English translation in the United States in 1959, argued in similar vein that "the seminal fluid requires more blood for its concoction than any other secretion in similar quantity, of the body" (Beckland 1859, 14).

Nineteenth-century American doctors, like those in the ancient and modern West, also attributed great importance to the seminal fluid and its preservation. For example, Graham saw the semen as "the essential oil of animal liquors," the purest of the body's humors, or the most "spiritual part of the animal frame" (1834, 51). Alice B. Stockham claimed that "[t]he seminal secretion has a wonderful imminent value, and if retained is absorbed into the system and adds enormously to a man's magnetic, mental and spiritual force." Unfortunately, "this force is constantly being wasted" in ordinary life (Stockham 1896, 43). In a word, the reason sexual excess was so exhausting was the loss of this vital seminal fluid.

Seeking to explain further why sexual excess was such a powerful debilitating agent or cause of disease, Graham offered a new explanation, very different from conventional notions. For him, the importance of semen to the human organism and the negative consequences resulting from its loss "have been exceedingly overrated." "It is not the mere loss of semen, but the peculiar excitement, and the violence of the convulsive paroxysms, which produce the mischief." When an individual is sexually excited, Graham wrote, "something very analogous to electricity and galvanism, diffuse a peculiar and powerful excitement throughout the whole nervous system" (Graham 1834, 21, 32, 57). In other words, it is not only sexual activity and loss of semen that induce disease, but the sexual desire and excitement that accompanies it. Stimulation, rather than merely orgasm, brought on debility and ill health. Furthermore, desire itself was a form of irritation, and irritation was a symptom of debility and disease.

All extraordinary and undue excitements, however, whether caused by mental, moral or physical stimuli, increase the excitability and unhealthy activity of the nerves of organic life; and tend to induce diseased irritability and sensibility in them, which is more or less diffused over the whole domain; and affects all the particular organs and functions. A frequent repetition of these excitements, always induces a greater or less degree of debility and diseased irritability in the nerves of organic life;—disordering and deranging the functions, and often causing excessive morbid irritability and sensibility and inflammation, and even disorganization or change of structure in the viscera—such as the brain, stomach, lungs, liver, kidneys, heart, etc.

(Ibid 17–18)

Thus human passions—anger, fear, grief, etc.—when violent and frequent or prolonged, "irritate and debilitate the nerves of organic life, and induce in them, a state of morbid irritability, and thereby disorder all the organic functions of the system, and lead to the most painful and often the most fatal disease." Sexual desire, by throwing its influence over the whole domain of "the nerves of organic life" and all the other organs of the body, could "kindle into a passion" and disturb and disorder "all the functions of the system" (Ibid, 17–19).

Even though Zhu Zhenheng might agree with Graham that sexual stimulation—and not the loss of semen alone—is harmful to human health, it seemed that many Chinese doctors held the contrary theory. As we have seen, sexual stimulation and frequent intercourse (but not emissions) with as many partners as possible was thought necessary to maintain the body in a healthy and strong condition. This notion reflects a key feature of traditional Chinese thought—the interdependence of *yin* (female) and *yang* (male). According to the doctrine of *yin-yang*, neither *yin* nor *yang* alone can develop on its own (see Chapter 14 for more about this theory). The implanting and development of the life-giving *jing* in the human body needed sexual intercourse to occur. It was thought necessary to increase the amount of *jing* as much as possible by sexual stimulus, and at the same time to avoid as far as possible the loss of it. Because the *yin-jing* (the female fluid essence, i.e. vaginal secretions) was assumed to be reabsorbed by the male and therefore able to contribute to nourishing the *yang*, it was recommended that the (male) adept of the art of the bedchamber have numerous sexual partners—ten, one hundred or more. As female orgasms could strengthen a man's vital energy, the male act was required to be prolonged as much as possible.

From repression to freedom?

Since the 1920s, Americans' attitudes toward sex and sexual behavior have undergone dramatic changes. The sexual revolution of the 1960s and 1970s has brought about a "sexualized" society in which sex is identified as a crucial factor in individual happiness. Not only has premarital sex become socially acceptable, the "demedicalization" of homosexuality and masturbation has made these so-called "abnormal" or "unnatural" sexual behaviors morally tolerable or unproblematic. More frequent and less inhibited sexual intercourse has been widely commended as an important, even necessary, part of the make-up and growth of healthier women and men. For instance, in *The Joy of Sex*, a popular 1970s sex manual, Alex Comfort (1972, 65, 231–2) proclaimed: "The right frequency for sex is as often as you both enjoy it. You can no more 'have too much' sex than you can over-empty a toilet cistern." Quantitatively, excess is a misnomer in the case of sex. On the contrary, sex is "in fact the least tiring physical recreation for the amount of energy expended." Far from being debilitating, sexual overactivity is a kind of medicine. In the words of Comfort, "At night there is no sleeping pill as good as violent and shared orgasm—active lovers don't need barbiturates."

In contrast with the principle advocated by doctors and health reformers in the nineteenth century—the doctrine of moderation—today's dominant sexual philosophy is the philosophy of indulgence. Any profound historical change is extraordinarily difficult to explain convincingly, and almost impossible to understand fully. In discussing why TB and cancer emerged as the dominant metaphors in health care in the nineteenth and twentieth century respectively, Susan Sontag sought to explain this conceptual shift by examining broader social, political, economic and cultural changes. For her, early capitalism produced an economy that "depends on the rational limitation of desire" and assumes the "necessity of regulated spending, saving, accounting, discipline." By contrast, advanced capitalism depends on the "irrational indulgence of desire" and thus requires "expansion, speculation, the creation of new needs (the problem of satisfaction); buying on credit; mobility." TB and cancer represent two images that, respectively, sum up the negative behavior of two kinds of *homo economicus*: "consumption; wasting; squandering of vitality," and "repression of energy, that is, refusal to consume or spend" (Sontag 1990, 63).

Clearly, Sontag's argument can be logically extended to cover the two different sexual ideologies at issue here, and indeed some historians of sexuality in America have developed historical explanations along these lines. John D'Emilio and Estelle B. Freedman (1998 [1988], 234, 166–7) have argued that "an ethic that encourages the purchase of consumer products" that fosters an "acceptance of pleasure, self-gratification, and personal satisfactions" can easily be translated to the province of sex. Such notions have gradually replaced the nineteenth-century preoccupation with the individual management of sexual impulses, a perspective founded on the thrifty economy.

Over the past three decades, China has experienced a comparable change from a planned, thrifty economy to a consumer model. It is thus not surprising that China has similarly undergone a sexual revolution over the same period. To my knowledge, however, no systematic cross-cultural comparative studies have been conducted on the sexual revolutions in America and China—studies which would need to include a focus on the role of economic models, sociopolitical change, cultural norms, and the contribution made by medical professionals to these large-scale cultural metamorphoses.

A couple of preliminary observations can be made here. First, just as the history of sexuality in America should not be seen as a linear movement from repression to freedom (D'Emilio and Freedman 1998/1988), the Chinese story is hardly just a simple progression from suppression to liberation. Both the American and Chinese sexual landscapes are marked by great diversity. Traditional and conservative approaches to sexuality are still alive and well in both societies, where they coexist with, conflict and complement in various degrees the emergent contemporary ideology of indulgence. Second, the popular but contradictory stereotypes of sexuality in China as either "prosaic or repressive" on the one hand or "exotic or somehow liberal" on the other, views expressed respectively by Barthes and Foucault, share a common feature—the tendency to treat China and the West as radically different from each other. These stereotypes, and the ways of thinking and characterizing Chinese and Western sexuality underlying them, are serious obstacles to a mature cross-cultural understanding—they have grossly simplified and distorted the complexity of not only Chinese, but Western realities.

Ironically, I believe that Foucault's extremely insightful analysis of sexuality, power and morality in Western culture can be used to give us a better understanding of sexuality in Chinese culture—something that would be impossible if China is simply regarded as the radical other of the West. However, the usefulness and limits of Foucault's historical and social theories, including those on sexuality, in the Chinese context is a subject that will have to be left for another occasion.

A concluding observation

Studying history, especially cross-cultural comparative history, is a fascinating adventure because our experience of history and of foreign cultural practices exists both within and outside us at the same time. A major enjoyment of studying past eras and cultures lies in experiencing two paradoxical feelings simultaneously: it is both *buke siyi* (unimaginable), because what we learn from the human experience of other times and places may be so different from what we presently take for granted that it hardly makes any sense to us; and *sichen xiangshi* (déjà vu), because the human story we encounter may be so familiar, so similar to our own life-experience, that we often ignore the distance involved. As I mulled over the works on sexual hygiene by the nineteenth-century American commentators and the traditional Chinese authors discussed here, the similarities and differences in their ideas often provoked these two seemingly contradictory feelings and clarified for me my own enjoyment in studying comparative history.

The idea of sexual excess as an illness and a significant cause of disease in nineteenth-century America is, on the one hand, remarkably different from contemporary attitudes in America, and, on the other, remarkably, even inexplicably, close to the perspective of traditional Chinese medicine on the issue. At the same time, the subtle differences between American and Chinese views of sexual overindulgence and its consequences are no less striking than their similarities. Both are different, but there are similarities in their differences and differences among the similarities. In order for us to better understand both the differences and the similarities, we must first of all resist the temptation to treat either one as the "radical other," incompatible or incommensurable with its apparent opposite number.

Chapter 4

Excursion: "false friends" in cross-cultural understanding, or a misjudgement of Needham

Refuting the claim that the ancient Chinese discovered the circulation of the blood

Learning to identify the differences concealed by the apparent similarities or commonalities exhibited by different cultures is always a challenging task. One of the many difficulties in learning a foreign language (or a dialect of the same language) is the problem of "false friends"—words or phrases that sound or look similar but differ significantly in their meanings and connotations. Far from being limited to linguistics, false friends constitute another commonly encountered challenge to cross-cultural understanding.

Among the many obstacles to effective cross-cultural understanding are two common vices, each located at an opposing pole: "false opposites" (the assumed cross-cultural differences are not as dramatic as they appear to be) at one pole and "false friends" (the perceived similarities are not as real as they appear to be) at the other. The former, as illustrated by Foucault's fallacious notions regarding sexuality in China in the previous chapter, is grounded in the understanding of different cultures as radical others, incommensurable with each other. The latter is rooted in the treatment of cultural differences—as found for example in China and the West—as only superficial, never fundamental and significant. Often, Western standards are used to measure the value (or lack of it) of particular cultural achievements and practices found in China or other "alien" cultural domains.

The oft-repeated claim that the Chinese discovered the circulation of the blood is a striking example of this phenomenon—the problem of false friends in Chinese-Western cross-cultural understanding. Many scholars and historians of Chinese medicine and science in China as well as in the West—including the British historian of Chinese science and civilization Joseph Needham, arguably the greatest China scholar in the West, and his collaborators—have claimed that the ancient Chinese, in particular the unknown authors of the medical classic *Huangdi Neijing* (The Yellow Emperor's Classic of Medicine or The Yellow Emperor's Manual of Corporeal Medicine), anticipated William Harvey's monumental discovery of the circulation of the blood by more than two thousand years. However, despite the popularity and persistence of this claim, a careful examination of the historical evidence on which it is based and the general intellectual environment of Chinese medicine leads one to conclude that the "circulation" described in Chinese texts and the phenomenon discovered by Harvey are very different things—indeed, they are false friends.

The origin and development of a historical claim

Nowadays it is widely accepted, both inside and outside China, that the circulation of the blood was explicitly described in traditional Chinese medical literature—more precisely, in the *Huangdi Neijing*. In *The Genius of China: 3,000 Years of Science, Discovery, and Invention*—a popular distillation of the historic multi-volume work *Science and Civilization in China* by Joseph Needham and his collaborators—Robert Temple states that, although it is widely believed that William Harvey discovered the circulation of the corporeal blood in 1628, he was "not even the first European to recognize the concept, and the Chinese had made the discovery two thousand years before" (1986, 123). He continues (Ibid):

> In China, indisputable and voluminous textual evidence exists to prove that the circulation of the blood was an established doctrine by the second century BC at the latest. For the idea to have become elaborated by this time, however, into the full and complex doctrine that appears in *The Yellow Emperor's Manual of Corporeal Medicine* (China's equivalent of the Hippocratic writings of Greece), the original notion must have appeared a very long time previously. It is safe to say that the idea occurred in China about two thousand years before it found acceptance in the West.

The point of view expressed here originated in seventeenth-century Europe not long after Harvey announced his revolutionary theory of the movement of the heart and blood. As the history of Chinese science and medicine became an academic discipline in the twentieth century, mainly due to the efforts of a number of outstanding Chinese and Western scholars including K. Chimin Wong, Long Bojian, Joseph Needham, and Lu Gwei-Djen, the claim has been repeatedly "documented" and widely accepted as an "indisputable" historical fact.

As early as 1685, sixty years after the publication of Harvey's *Exercitatio Anatomica de Motu Cordis et Sanguinis in Animalibus* (An Anatomical Disquisition on the Motion of the Heart and Blood in Animals), the Dutch East India physician Willem ten Rhijne claimed in his *Mantissa Schematica de Accupunctura*—the work that introduced acupuncture to the West—that the ancient Chinese had established the notion of the circulation of the blood before Harvey.

> Although the Chinese physicians ... are ignorant in anatomy, they have nevertheless perhaps devoted more effort over centuries to learning and

teaching with very great care the circulation of the blood, than have European physicians, individually or as a group. They base the foundation of their entire medicine upon the rules of this circulation, as if they were oracles of Apollo at Delphi.

(cited in Lu and Needham 1980, 37)

In the same year, Issac Vossius, by mistaking the legendary emperor Huangdi as the genuine author of the *Neijing*, asserted that the circulation of the blood had been known in China for more than 4,000 years. Other seventeenth-century scholars like Thomas Baker and Benito Geronimo Fejoo Montenegro agreed with this view that the Chinese had understood that the blood circulated in the body for thousands of years (Ibid, 36–7).

In the twentieth century, many scholars of the history of Chinese medicine and science, both Chinese and Western, espoused the view that the ancient Chinese, and the authors of the *Neijing* in particular, had described the circulation of the blood. In 1928, three centuries after the publication of Harvey's *De Motu Cordis*, K. Chimin Wong described the circulation of the blood as discussed in the *Neijing* as one of the great scientific innovations of the ancient Chinese. In an article entitled "The Inventions of Ancient Chinese Medicine," he concluded that many of the discoveries and inventions of modern Western medicine had already been made far earlier in ancient China. Later, in his *History of Chinese Medicine,* a foundational work of the twentieth-century historiography of Chinese medicine, first published in English, Wong again argued, with his co-author Wu Lien-Tieh, that the *Neijing* had described the circulation of the blood. Wong and Wu, who were both trained in modern Western biomedicine, stated that the relevant passages from the *Neijing* were "very significant" and proved that "the ancients had made a very near guess at the facts" (1936, 35). At the same time, they acknowledged that it was difficult to prove the claim convincingly, admitting that the statement that Harvey's discovery had been anticipated in China by about two thousand years "is based on rather scanty evidence." They noted that there was no evidence that any further investigations had been made in China into the subject and that the systematic and pulmonary circulation systems were not understood. They also conceded that the *Neijing* failed to make a proper distinction between arteries and veins. However, in spite of these difficulties, Wong and Wu maintained that "the ancient Chinese had indeed grasped part of the truth concerning the circulation of blood" (Ibid, 35).

In the 1960s, the Chinese scholar-physician Long Bojian complained that Wong and Wu had failed to make their case in sufficient detail. In response, in his *Huangdi Neijing Gailun* (Introduction to the *Huangdi Neijing*), Long attempted to prove their claim using several lines of enquiry. He regarded the *Neijing* as explicitly recording the notion of the circulation of the blood, asserting that the ancient medical classic contained "a fairly detailed explanation of the circulation of the blood—a great discovery in the history of medicine in our country" (Long 1985 [1963]). In the 1980s, two other scholars, Liu Xueli and Zhao Yunfeng, affirmed that the ancient Chinese not only had a comparatively complete knowledge of the anatomical layout of the heart and vessels, but had also formulated the "brilliant hypothesis" of the circulation of the blood. Their historical evidence, again, was mainly drawn from the relevant texts in the *Neijing* (Liu and Zhao 1986, 35).

In their widely acclaimed work *Celestial Lancet: A History and Rationale of Acupuncture and Moxa* (1980), Lu Gwei-Djen and Joseph Needham included a special section on ancient Chinese knowledge of the circulation of the blood. They asserted: "Clearly the circulation of the blood and *chhi* [i.e., *qi*] was standard doctrine in the 2nd century, a situation contrasting rather remarkably with the long uncertainty in the Western World, with its idea of air in the arteries, or a tidal ebb and flow of the blood" (Lu and Needham 1980, 29). They cited a number of passages from ancient texts, mostly from the *Neijing*, to show that the ancient Chinese had not only formulated the primary concept but had also developed the "more detailed theory" of circulation. Moreover, Lu and Needham discussed several related questions: the quantitative approach to blood supply and the estimation of the rate of blood circulation in the *Neijing*; the Chinese metaphor of the heart as a pump or forge bellows; and the role of the macrocosm-microcosm analogy in the Chinese world-view. They even raised the possibility of the transmission of this knowledge and its influence on Harvey (Ibid, 32–6). Temple's assertion that the ancient Chinese had established the doctrine of the circulation of the blood thousands of years ago, quoted at the beginning of this section, was wholly based on this section of the *Celestial Lancet*. Temple (1986, 123) summarized the thesis in this way:

> The ancient Chinese conceived of two separate circulations of fluids in the body. Blood, pumped by the heart, flowed through the arteries, veins, and capillaries. Ch'i [*qi*], an ethereal, rarefied form of energy, was pumped by the lungs to circulate through the body in invisible tracts. The concept of this dual circulation of fluids was central to the practice of acupuncture.

This view has also been widely disseminated in China, and has appeared in many popular science publications. For example, it was included in *Ancient China's Technology and Science*, compiled by the prestigious Institute for the History of Natural Sciences, Chinese Academy of Science, and published by the Foreign Languages Press in Beijing in 1980. Parts of this work were reprinted from *Achievements of Science and Technology in Ancient China*, a popular book on the history of science first published in Chinese by the China Youth Press in 1978. The book claims that the explanation of the general and pulmonary circulation systems in the *Neijing* "is substantially correct," and that the *Neijing* also contains a passage that "affirmed the relationship between the heart and the blood and its circulation" (Yu 1983, 339). These claims found their way into the standard textbooks on the history of Chinese medicine and science for medical and other tertiary-level students (e.g., Zhen 2001 [1997], 38).

Despite the popularity of such views, it would be totally wrong to conclude, as my argument so far may appear to suggest, that no scholar has ever challenged these claims. In his influential book *Medicine in China: A History of Ideas*, the prominent German historian of Chinese medicine Paul Unschuld (1985, 75–6) argued that while Chinese medicine had developed "a straightforward concept of circulation in the organism," this concept "*differs from contemporary Western ideas in various respects*. It is not clear exactly what kinds of substances were thought to circulate and where exactly they were thought to flow." (My emphasis). Unschuld's evaluation of the subject, like his approach to the history of medicine in China in general, is complex and nuanced. He hypothesized the existence of four schools of medical thought in ancient China, with differing views on the movement of the blood and the role of the vessels. The first school advocated "the circulation of subtle influences [*qi*] in the vessels;" the second maintained "a belief in the flow of blood;" the third held "the simultaneous circulation of both ch'i [*qi*] and blood in identical vessels;" and the fourth plumped for "two simultaneous system of circulation, in separate vessels." For Unschuld, the *Neijing* texts "contain passages that may be interpreted as traces of all four of these differing perspectives." Moreover, disagreeing with Needham and Lu and previous Chinese scholars, he pointed out that "no force or 'motor' responsible for the ongoing circulatory movement in the body was mentioned in the *Neijing*." The ancient medical classic contains "absolutely no indication as to a conceptualization of either the heart or the lung as fulfilling any kind of a pumplike or bellowlike function" (Ibid).

Refuting the historical claim

Did the ancient Chinese, specifically the anonymous authors of the *Neijing*, actually discover or at least describe the circulation of the blood—a fundamental achievement in modern medicine and the life sciences? Is there really, in Temple's words, "indisputable and voluminous textual evidence" to prove that the circulation of the blood was an established doctrine by the second century BC at the latest in China? My own answer is: definitely not. There are at least four major reasons to refute this claim. First, the circulation described in the *Neijing* is not the circulation of blood, but of various forms of *qi* (the body's vital energy)—constructive *qi*, defending *qi*, and the channel *qi*—whose courses in the body have nothing to do with the circulatory pathways of the blood as advanced by Harvey. Second, Chinese physicians never took the words in the *Neijing* as an empirical or scientific starting point for the investigation of the structure and function of the heart, vessels, and blood. Third, the authors of the *Neijing* lacked the intellectual foundations and a grasp of the necessary empirical facts to make a discovery as sophisticated as the circulation of the blood. Fourth, intellectually speaking, in order to discover the circulation of blood as Harvey did, the theory of the movement of the heart and blood formulated by the ancient Roman physician Galen, although mistaken, provides a better foundation than the *Neijing*'s speculative ideas.

The circulation described in the Neijing is not the circulation of the blood

It is true that the *Neijing*—which consists of two parts, *Suwen* (Plain Questions) and *Lingshu* (The Miraculous Pivot)—contains some material that at first sight appears to refer to the circulation of the blood. A number of quotations from the *Neijing*, translated and interpreted quite differently by different authors, have been used again and again as the core evidence for the claim that the ancient Chinese had discovered the circulation of the blood at an early period.[1] I set out below the chief passages in question (for convenience of discussion, I have numbered them 1–5):

Quotation 1:
[The matter in] the channels flows constantly and never stops; it moves ceaselessly in circles.
(*Suwen*, Chapter 39: Differentiation of Pain)

Quotation 2:
The most fundamental activity of the *yingqi* (constructive *qi*) is the ingesting of food as a "treasure." Food enters the stomach and is transferred to the lungs. It [the essence derived from food] flows through the internal parts of the body and spreads over the external parts. The essential nourishment derived from food moves through the tunnels [i.e., channels]. [The constructive *qi*] travels in and nourishes the body. It begins again as soon as it ends. This is the law of Heaven and Earth [i.e., nature].
(*Lingshu*, Chapter 16: The Constructive *Qi*)

Quotation 3:
The *qi* [Wong and Wu (1936, 35) mistakenly translated it as "the blood"] is compelled to move continuously. It resembles the current in water, and also the sun or the moon that move ceaselessly in their orbits. ... [The movement of *qi*] can be compared to a circle without an end. It is impossible to count its revolutions because it begins again as soon as it ends.
(*Lingshu*, Chapter 17: The Measures of the Channels)

---

1 There are numerous ancient and modern editions of the *Neijing*. The original texts of the medical classics cited in this book are mainly taken from two contemporary volumes published by the Nanjing College of Chinese Medicine (1981, 1986). (For the English translations of the first part of this Chinese medical classic, *Suwen*, see Ni 1995; especially Unschuld 2011).

Quotation 4:
The human being receives *qi* from food. Food enters the stomach and is transferred to the lungs. As a result, the Five Viscera [i.e., the heart, the lungs, the liver, and the kidney] and the Six Bowels receive the *qi*. The lighter substance is the constructive *qi* and the heavier the defending *qi*. The former moves inside the vessels and the latter outside them. It circulates endlessly and never ceases. When both have made a circuit of fifty revolutions, they meet each other. This is known as "the Great Convention." As twin forces, *yin* and *yang* run through each other, just like a circle without an end.

(*Lingshu*, Chapter 18: The Birth and Meeting of the Constructive and the Defending *Qi*)

Quotation 5:
The floating *qi*, which does not move along the channels, is called the defending *qi*; the essential *qi*, which moves along and within them, is called the constructive *qi*. *Yin* and *yang* follow each other in a continuous line; the outside and the inside are linked up with each other. All this is like a circle without an end. They move long and far. Who is able to know their bounds?

(*Lingshu*, Chapter 52: The Defending *Qi*)

The crucial question here is not whether the *Neijing* mentions circulation, but rather *whether the circulation described in the* Neijing *is the circulation of the blood in the modern sense or in the sense Harvey used it*. Undoubtedly, there is much discussion of circulation in the *Neijing*. This is not unexpected, as the conception or metaphor of the circle (circulation) plays a fundamental role in the traditional Chinese worldview. Nevertheless, a careful reading of the original Chinese texts within their proper cultural context, comparing the various pathways for circulation described in the *Neijing* with the modern understanding of the circulation of the blood, reveals that what is described in the *Neijing* cannot be the latter.

It is necessary to bear in mind that, as a theory in early modern physiology and biology, the circulation of the blood involved more than the merely speculative notion that the blood circulates around the body. Among other things, it was necessary to demonstrate the course or pathway along which the blood moves. According to Harvey, the circulation of the blood was understood as the following process:

> the left ventricle——> the arteries ——> the veins——> the right auricle——> the right ventricle——> the pulmonary artery——> air intake and outlet in the lungs——> the pulmonary veins——> the right auricle——> the left ventricle.
>
> (Harvey 1952)

Taken together, the five passages cited above indicate that the circulation described in the *Neijing* mainly deals with the movement of the *qi* in the "channels," and with the notions of *ying* (nourishment or construction), and *wei* (defense). I want now to examine what the *Neijing* states about the pathways of these three elements in order to establish their connection with the circulation of the blood as advanced by Harvey. According to the *Neijing*, the movement of the *qi* in the channels is identical to the motion of the constructive *qi*. The authors describe the circular motion of the constructive *qi* in detail in *Lingshu*:

> Therefore, the *qi* starts from the Hand-Greater-Yin Lung Channel. It transfers to the Hand-Yang-Brightness Large Intestine Channel, ascends to be linked up with the Foot-Yang-Brightness Channel, descends to the upper surface of the foot, and flows to the great toe where it connects with the Foot-Greater-Yin Spleen Channel. It then ascends to the abdomen and transfers from the spleen to the heart. Along with the Hand-Lesser-Yin Heart Channel, it exits from the armpit, moves down the arm, and is transferred to the tip of the little finger where it connects with the Hand-Greater-Yang Small Intestine Channel. It then moves upward through the armpits, reaches the inner part of the eye-sac, transfers to the cantus of the eye, ascends to the top of the head, and descends to the nape of the neck where it connects with the Foot-Yang-Brightness Urinary Bladder Channel. It travels along the vertebral column, reaches the coccyx, descends to the tip of the little toe, and transfers to the middle of the foot where it connects with the Foot-Lesser-Yin Kidney Channel. It ascends to the kidney, transfers to the heart from the kidney, extends outside to the chest, travels along the Hand-Reverting-Yin Pericardium Channel, leaves the armpit, goes down the arm, runs between the two sinews, enters the middle of the palm, reaches the tip of the middle finger, and transfers again to the tip of the little finger where it connects with the Hand-Lesser-Yang Triple Burner Channel. It ascends to the mid-point between the two breasts, distributes itself in the Triple Burner, transfers to the gallbladder from the Triple Burner, exits from the rib-side, and transfers to the Foot-Lesser-Yang Gallbladder Channel. It descends to the upper surface of the foot, and transfers from the upper surface of the foot to the great toe where it connects with the Foot-Reverting-Yin Liver Channel. It ascends to the liver, transfers upward to the lung from the liver, moves upwards further along the throat, infiltrates the area of the nasopharynx, and enters the "door to the brain." One of the branches ascends to the forehead, travels along the top of the head, descends to the nape, and goes down the coccyx along the vertebral column; this is the Governing Channel. It encircles the genitals, ascends across the pubisure part, enters the centre of the navel, travels further upwards to the inner part

of the abdomen, enters the "Empty Basin" (the supraclavicular fossa), connects with the lung, and returns to the Hand-Greater-Yin Lung Channel. This is the complete and regular course of the constructive *qi*.
(*Lingshu*, Chapter 16: The Constructive *Qi*)

This passage immediately follows Quotation 2, cited at the beginning of this section. This long quotation thus should be seen as the *Neijing*'s explanation of the circulation mentioned in Quotation 2. Clearly, no further explication is needed for us to conclude that, in regard to its various pathways, the circulation of the constructive *qi* discussed here is totally unrelated to the modern understanding of the circulation of the blood. Because the circulation of the materials (*qi* and "blood") in the channels by and large corresponds to the pathway of the constructive *qi*, the movement of *qi* and "blood" in the channels is thus totally unrelated to the circular movement of the blood. Moreover, in the circulation of the constructive *qi*, the role of *fei* (the lungs) is much more significant than that of the heart—whereas in the circulation of the blood, the heart is the most crucial organ.

Is the movement of the defending *qi* closer to the circulation of the blood? The *Neijing* describes the movement of the defending *qi* in the human body in detail:

The defending *qi* circulates around the whole body fifty times in one day and one night. It moves in the *yang* twenty-five times during the day, and in the *yin* twenty-five times in the night. It also circulates around the Five Viscera. In the early morning, the *yang-qi* starts from the eyes when the *yin-qi* finishes. The defending *qi* ascends to the head, as the eyes are open. It travels along the nape, descends to the Foot-Greater-Yang Urinary Bladder Channel, and goes down further to the tip of the little toe. A tributary portion leaves from the point of the Inner Canthus, descends to the Hand-Greater-Yang Small Intestine Channel, and moves further down to the outer side of the tip of the little finger. Another tributary stream also leaves from the point of the Inner Canthus, descends to the Foot-Lesser-Yang Gallbladder Channel, and transfers to the mid-point between the little and the second toes. It ascends along the line of the Hand-Lesser-Yang Triple Burner Channel, and then descends to the mid-point between the little finger and the forefinger. One branch ascends to the area in front of the ear, connects with the channels in the area under the chin, transfers to the Foot-Yang-Brightness Stomach, descends to the upper surface of the foot, and enters the mid-point of the five toes [i.e., the point between the second and the third toes]. Another tributary stream leaves from the ear, descends to the Hand-Yang-Brightness Large Intestine Channel, enters the point between the thumb and the forefinger, and then proceeds to the middle of the palm. The defending *qi*, which reaches the foot [from the Foot-Yang-Brightness Channel], enters the middle of the foot, exits from the lower part of the inner ankle bone, moves in the *yin*, and returns to the eyes. This completes the circle.

(*Lingshu*, Chapter 52: The Defending *Qi*)

Once again, no further explanation is needed to conclude that the circulatory path of the defending *qi* described in traditional Chinese medicine and the circulation process as understood in modern physiology are totally different. By citing relevant passages from the *Neijing* at length, I believe that I have demonstrated that its detailed descriptions of the circulation of the two kinds of *qi*, and the channels through which they move, have nothing whatsoever to do with the circulatory paths of the blood as advanced by Harvey. Wong and Wu (1936, 39) noted that, from the viewpoint of modern physiology, the *Neijing* was "incorrect" in its detailed account of the bloodstream, the whole circular process of which in fact starts from the foot, travels to the kidneys, the heart, the lungs, the liver, the spleen, in that order, and then moves from the spleen back to the kidneys, thus making a complete circuit. In fact, it is not the unknown authors of *Neijing* who are mistaken here, but Wong and Wu themselves. The *Neijing* was not discussing the circulation of the blood at all, but a quite different process.

Chinese interpretations of the Neijing

Although many people would not argue that the *Neijing* describes the circulation of blood as explicitly as Harvey did, they believe that its material on circulation constitutes the seeds of the modern physiological theory. In other words, like the sprout to the plant or tree, the *Neijing* represents the embryonic stage of a great discovery. If this is the case, then the *Neijing* should have represented the starting point for later Chinese doctors to investigate the structure of the heart and vessel system and the movement of the blood. However, despite the fact that throughout history hundreds of scholars have written numerous notes and commentaries on this medical classic, the notion of circulation found in the *Neijing* was never developed into a systematic doctrine of the circulation of the blood.

In fact, although the *Neijing* remains the most authoritative work in the whole history of traditional Chinese medicine, the question of how the blood moves in the body was never really raised by ancient Chinese physicians. The greatest Chinese anatomist, Wang Qingren, provides powerful testimony to this omission. In his *Yilin Gaicuo* (Errors in Medicine Corrected), published in 1831, Wang (1976 [1893]) charged that the lack of detailed knowledge about the structure of the human body had resulted in many errors and contradictions in the ancient Chinese medical literature. Even though *Yilin Gaicuo* seems primitive when compared to *De Humani Corporis Fabrica Libri Septem* (On the Fabric of the Human Body in Seven Books), to a large extent Wang can be called the "Andreas Vesalius of China" (Nie 1989a, 1990b). He is the Chinese physician whose conceptual framework, logical thinking and methodological approach come closest to modern Western medicine. Moreover, Wang is even better known for his distinctive theory of *qi* and blood. He invented the method (and devised several recipes) for activating blood movement and removing blood stasis, which are still of great clinical value in contemporary Chinese medical practice. However, there is not one word in *Yilin Gaicuo* about how the blood circulates in the body. In addition, Wang himself made many mistakes with regard to the anatomical and physiological aspects of the heart, vessels and blood, even as he attempted to correct the errors of previous generations. For example, based on empirical "facts" he had gathered from observing children's corpses buried in shallow graves in a public cemetery, Wang claimed that the heart contains no blood. He called the arteries the "vessels of *qi* (air)" because he thought there was no blood in them either. When he referred in his anatomical dictionary to "vessels of blood," he meant only the veins.

No Chinese physician was prompted to investigate the structure and functions of the system of the heart and blood (in the modern sense) after reading the *Neijing*. Similarly, no traditional scholar of the medical classics interpreted the texts in this way. The great seventeenth-century physician and expert on the *Neijing*, Zhang Jiebin, is a telling example of the way in which traditional medical scholars understood the very passages which modern historians have taken as evidence for their claim that the circulation of the blood was explicitly described in the *Neijing*. After working on his project for forty-five years, Zhang published his *Leijing* (A Systematic Study of the *Neijing*) in 1624, only four years before the publication of Harvey's *De Motus Cordis*. The *Leijing* is usually considered one of the most important sources for the study of the *Neijing* and Chinese medical theories in general. With regard to the section listed above as Quotation 4, Zhang states:

> The constructive *qi* circulates ceaselessly in the body. It circulates fifty times in the whole body over the course of a day and a night and then returns for the "Great Convention." It moves in *the order of the Twelve Channels*. One travels by *yin* and the other by *yang*; one travels via the exterior [of the body] and the other by the interior. They move in a continuous line and run through each other. It begins as it ends; this is why it is described as "like a circle without an end." "The Great Convention" refers to the meeting of the constructive [*qi*], the defending [*qi*], *yin* and *yang*.
> (*Leijing*, Vol. 8: The Constructive, The Defending and the Triple Burner. Emphasis added)

In response to the passage listed above as Quotation 2, Zhang's annotations read:

> The food enters the stomach and is transferred to the lungs. The lighter the constructive becomes, the heavier becomes the defending. Therefore,

the heavier essence moves in the tunnels [i.e., channels]. It is constantly moving and starts again as soon as it ends. It *flows and circulates in the Twelve Channels*

(*Leijing*, Vol. 8: The Order of the Movement of Construction and Defense. Emphasis added)

Here, Zhang makes it very clear that the phenomenon discussed in the *Neijing* is the circulation of the constructive *qi* in the Twelve Channels whose course, as I have shown above, has nothing to do with the circulation of the blood as understood in the modern life sciences.

Neither Zhang nor any other traditional *Neijing* scholar ever interpreted the relevant texts as implying that the blood moves from the heart to the whole body by way of the arteries, and then back to the heart through the veins. Was the scholarship of traditional physicians insufficient to decipher the *Neijing*'s sublime words and their profound meanings? Or have the imaginations of modern historians run so wild that they have distorted the meaning of the *Neijing* by imposing what they already knew onto the classical text? Clearly, the latter occurred. In fact, the origins and development of this specious claim show that reading the relevant passages in the *Neijing* as a description of the circulation of the blood is very much a post-Harvey phenomenon. Its twentieth-century promoters mentioned in the first section of this chapter (Wang, Wu, Lu, Needham, Liu and Zhao) were all familiar with Harvey's theory of the circulation of the blood before they read the *Neijing*.

A lack of empirical and intellectual foundations

No scientific discovery can be made without certain empirical knowledge located within an existing intellectual tradition. According to the extant historical records, there existed neither the intellectual tradition nor the empirical foundations necessary for discovering the circulation of the blood in China at the time the *Neijing* was compiled. It was not until the introduction and spread of Western medicine that this occurred. At the time that the *Neijing* was compiled, the Chinese were ignorant of the fundamental empirical facts necessary to understand the circulation of the blood. These facts included: the distinction between arteries and veins; the distinction between the blood in the arteries and that in the veins; the anatomical structure of the heart (the two ventricles and two auricles); the contraction of the heart as the cause of the movement of the blood; and the existence of the cardiac and vessel valves and their basic function of making the blood move in one direction. The ancient Chinese were unfamiliar with—and indifferent to—the principles of anatomical and physiological science in the modern Western sense, since Chinese medicine has its own unique understandings of the human body and the causes of illness. The internal organs in the "Viscera and Bowels" theory of traditional Chinese medicine, the understanding of which is mainly based on the *Neijing*, do not even correspond to the organs as described in Western medicine.

It is well known that in traditional Chinese medicine no great emphasis is placed on the anatomical structure of an organ. The viscera and bowels in the medical system of the *Neijing* should be viewed as units of physiological function, rather than as anatomical entities. Although there are some passages in the *Neijing* which emphasize the possibility and significance of dissecting the human body and measuring its parts, anatomy never formed the intellectual basis of classical Chinese medicine. Despite the survival of a few records of anatomical interest, no *systematic* anatomy was developed in China until Western medicine was introduced (Nie 1986).

The Neijing in contrast to Galen and Harvey

Even if we assume that the phenomenon described in the *Neijing* actually refers to the circulation of the blood, its achievements remain fragmented and speculative in comparison with the discovery of Harvey. As historians of Western medicine have pointed out, the real importance of Harvey's work for the history of medicine and science is "not so much the discovery of the circulation of the blood as its quantitative or mathematical demonstration. With this start, physiology became a dynamic science" (Garrison 1929, 247). Harvey did not "merely put forward" the circulation of the blood as a theory; through his efforts, the concept "was proved by morphological, mathematical, and experimental arguments" (Ackerknecht 1982, 113).

It has been often noted that, although the *Neijing* may not describe the circulation of the blood in the complete manner that Harvey did, its theory of the blood's motion is still superior to that of the great Roman physician Galen. For Galen, the principal movement of blood was forward, like the ebb and flow of the tide. Galen's concept dominated the Western medical world for more than fourteen centuries and was still the standard theory in Harvey's time. However, it seems to me that, intellectually speaking, Galen's theory of the blood in particular, and his medical system in general, formed a better foundation for the eventual discovery of the circulation of the blood than anything found in the *Neijing*. The intellectual connections between Galen and Harvey cannot be explored in detail here, but it is important to point out that Harvey's discovery owed a considerable amount to Galen's medical achievements (Nie 1989b). First, Galen discovered some fundamental facts of the movement of the blood, such as the presence of blood in arteries and the different character of blood in arteries and veins. Second, Galen's model of the blood's movement, although mistaken in the general sense, provided an object for later physicians to criticize and correct. Third, some experiments conducted by Galen (e.g., on the way in which the valves of the heart determined the direction of the blood's motion) prepared the way for discovering the circulation of the blood. Fourth, and most significant, Galen established the foundations for the experimental methods of modern Western medicine, experimental physiology in particular. As George Sarton (1954, 48) put it, Galen not only "understood the need for experiments" but also "justified it in saying that the experimental path is long and arduous but leads to the truth, while the short and easy way (uncontrollable assertion) leads away from it." As Charles Singer (1957, 175) concluded, "Harvey took up his theme practically where Galen had left it." Without the heritage of Galen, it would have been difficult, if not impossible, for Harvey to develop his theory of the movement of the blood.

Much contemporary research on Chinese medicine, as it developed from the *Neijing*, has concluded that it is markedly different from Western medicine, as the latter developed from the work of Galen, Vesalius and Harvey. This has in turn led to the conclusion that the two medical systems should be seen as fundamentally different, representing two incompatible ways of seeing and thinking (Porket 1974; Liu 1982). The fundamental methodology of the *Neijing* and later Chinese medicine has been described as a "system of correspondence" or a "holistic methodology." The physiological doctrines in the *Neijing* are certainly different from the physiological theories and approaches of Galen and Harvey. The medical works of the two great second-century physicians, Zhang Zhongjing and Galen, display this fundamental difference vividly and powerfully (Nie 1990a). In other words, the analytic and experimental medical tradition had been relatively weak throughout China until modern Western biomedicine was introduced.

In conclusion, not only did the *Neijing* fail to describe the circulation of the blood, according to the historical logic of both the Chinese medical tradition and the scientific tradition, it was simply not possible for the authors of the *Neijing* to have made such a discovery.

The sources of an historical misjudgement: scientism and other ideologies

The above discussion has, I trust, proven that interpreting various statements and passages in the *Neijing* as early descriptions of the circulation of the blood is wholly without foundation. The speciousness of the claim is so obvious that one cannot help wondering why so many scholars have advocated it and why it has been so widely accepted. Exposing the epistemological and contextual reasons for this popular historical fallacy is a helpful exercise, insofar as it helps us to understand some of the reasons why we so often fail to recognize such "false friends" in cross-cultural understanding.

First of all, there are undoubtedly some technical or scholarly reasons for the dissemination of this fallacy. Technically speaking, it results from the habit of abstracting a statement or passage from the historical literature and interpreting it out of context. This tendency is one of the most persistent problems in the study and writing of history—the Chinese have a special phrase for it: *duanzhang quyi* (to garble a statement or quote out of context). In a footnote to his refutation of Lu and Needham's claim that the heart was understood as a set of bellows in the *Neijing*, Unschuld pointed out that their argument represents:

> an example of the approach not unfrequently employed by these authors when they cut out short statements with a particular meaning from longer passages conveying, as a whole, a rather different meaning, and also when they confuse the ideas conveyed by commentaries added many centuries later with the concepts conveyed by an original source.
>
> (Unschuld 1985, 371)

Of course, readings that distort the original meaning of historical texts cannot always be easily distinguished from attempts to interpret these same texts imaginatively and creatively. While the latter is an essential element of any good historical study, it should never present simple error as plain truth.

However, the specious claim that the Chinese discovered the circulation of the blood represents more than simply a technical error in the modern historiography of Chinese medicine and science. In fact, the origin, spread and wide acceptance of this specious claim in the historiography of Chinese medicine constitutes a glaring example of how what people *want* to see influences and even determines what they *actually* see. Socio-cultural discourse can often define or influence our perceptions of the past. For example, from a socio-political and cultural perspective, the popularity of China's prior claim for this epoch-making discovery is closely related to the prevalence of nationalism in the social and academic life of twentieth-century China. In other words, many Chinese, both scholars and laypeople, motivated by a sense of pride in China and its cultural heritage, want almost by "instinct" to believe in the validity of the claim. Patriotism and nationalism have had a powerful influence over the study of the history of Chinese science and medicine. To a great extent, "academic nationalism" has been a determining ideological force not only in the natural and medical sciences, but also in the social sciences and humanities in twentieth-century and contemporary China (Sleeboom 2004; Sleeboom-Faulkner 2007). Ironically, in acting and thinking this way, Chinese people are using modern Western medicine and science as the standard by which to measure, understand, and interpret the achievements of the Chinese medical tradition.

Furthermore, if nationalism is the most significant political factor in the popularity of this historical fallacy in China, scientism is the most significant epistemological reason for its perpetuation. Scientism has been, and remains, the dominant intellectual discourse in the twentieth-century historiography of Chinese medicine and science, and promotes itself as the sole standard of truth. It provides the foundation for the evaluation of all other systems of knowledge, including traditional Chinese systems.

The definition of the term is elusive, but it can be usefully considered under two heads. First, scientism can be understood as a conscious and identifiable philosophy or set of philosophical assumptions. According to John Wellmuth (1944, 1–2), scientism involves "the belief that science, in the modern sense of that term, and the scientific method as described by modern scientists, afford the only reliable means of acquiring such knowledge as may be available about whatever is real." According to Jurgen Habermas, scientism is the basic orientation prevailing in analytic philosophy. He views it as "science's belief in itself," that is, "the conviction that we can no longer understand science as *one* form of possible knowledge, but rather must identify knowledge with science" (Habermas 1972, 4). Secondly, scientism is not only a general metaphysical scheme, but is also a cultural phenomenon with the kind of emotional attributes of a substitute religion. R. G. Owen has attacked scientism as a form of idolatry, which he terms "scientolatry." As a result of this exalted status, science has, he remarks, "come to be worshipped as omniscient, omnipotent and the bearer of man's [sic] salvation" (Owen 1952, 20). For Owen, the result of this "scientolatry" is the widespread view that all problems can be solved scientifically, and that science can even examine questions of spirit, values, and freedom. D. W. Y. Kwok points out that these two characterizations of scientism, philosophical and cultural, complement one another. He considers scientism in general as "a form of belief arising from a tradition or heritage in which the limiting principles of science itself have found general application and have become the cultural assumptions and axioms of that culture" (Kwok 1965, 21).

Despite the difficulties in formulating an adequate definition of scientism, there is no doubt that it was one of the most influential modes of thought throughout the world during the twentieth century. It became a strongly held paradigm in the social sciences (taking the form of positivism) and permeated almost every aspect of social life in the Western world (taking the form of the near worship of science and technology). Along with the global movement for industrialization and modernization, this uncritical belief in science and the worship of modern technology was transported to and took root in non-Western societies, including China. Scientism exists both within and outside philosophy. Tom Sorell (1991) has offered a systematic analysis of scientism in Western philosophy. Although he does not deny that scientistic ways of thinking can be found elsewhere, Sorell is much less keen to criticize scientism outside philosophy than scientism within philosophy, because he holds that "outside philosophy, scientism sometimes has the useful effect of bolstering up an appreciation of, and respect for, science in the face of anti-scientific and pseudo-scientific ideas" (1991, 2). While I appreciate his point, this belief system can also inhibit genuine understanding—as is the case with assessments of Chinese medicine.

Lest I be accused of being somehow opposed to science, I want to emphasize that I believe scientism to be a kind of misinterpretation of the social and cultural functions of the modern sciences and their methods. Thus, my criticism of scientism is not intended to attack modern science and its methods, but rather to question the attitude which places too high a value on science in comparison with other branches of learning or culture, even to the extent of seeing scientific truth as the only reliable kind of truth. In his *Knowledge and Human Interests*, Habermas made it very clear that a critique of scientism did not constitute an attack on science per se, but an attack rather upon an arrogant and mistaken understanding of science that reduces all knowledge to some expression of a natural science.

In the social and cultural life of twentieth-century China, science replaced Confucianism and became the highest standard of value. Traditional Chinese medicine also succumbed to the disease of scientism. As a dominant discourse, scientism came to permeate almost all modern studies of Chinese medicine. Modern science and "scientific" philosophies, like dialectical materialism, were adopted to interpret traditional Chinese medicine and the Chinese medical system. Scientism was so pervasive that the statement "Chinese medicine is a science" has been accepted as a kind of truism in contemporary China (Nie 1995). Ironically, even though conservatives and iconoclasts held attitudes to traditional medicine that were as different as black from white, both parties defended or rejected traditional medicine in the name of the same values—science and progress. On the one hand, medical traditionalists have been at pains to prove that not only had China developed a completely scientific medicine, but that this was even more scientific than Western medicine. On the other hand, the attacks of modern Chinese medical iconoclasts on traditional medicine derive from a deep respect for modern biomedicine as representing the values of science, the enlightenment and modernity, coupled with the belief that traditional medicine is primitive (the polar opposite of modernity), non-scientific and even anti-scientific (Croizier 1968).

Thus, due to the influence of scientism, Chinese medicine is seen either as unscientific (even anti-scientific) or as proto-scientific (and pre-scientific). In the former case, the differences between Chinese medicine and the sciences have been exaggerated to the extent that the former is seen as mere hocus-pocus. In the latter case, concepts, theories, methods and procedures drawn from the modern sciences have been applied to the study of Chinese medicine, and considerable efforts have been made to discover the consistencies and convergences between the two systems. It is emphasized that traditional Chinese medicine is fundamentally compatible with the modern sciences and, moreover, that its holistic orientation provides a sort of spiritual guide for biomedicine. As a result, the great differences between the two systems have been minimized.

A concluding remark

Under the influence of scientism, in the twentieth-century historiography of Chinese science and medicine as exemplified in the monumental works by Needham and his colleagues, the two most important questions were: How many modern scientific achievements were anticipated in Chinese medicine, and why did the scientific and medical revolutions not occur in China? The latter question is one aspect of what has been widely known as the "Needham Puzzle" on the history of modern science and civilization: Why did the industrial revolution and modern science not originate in China? However, in the context of this chapter the crucial question should have been rather: *How and why is it possible for traditional Chinese medicine to remain effective in practice and challenging in theory, even though it possessed no knowledge of the circulation of the blood or modern anatomy and scientific physiology?*

The central point of this chapter is about the importance of acknowledging the differences between traditional Chinese medicine and modern Western biomedicine. However, to highlight the differences, one should not simultaneously fall into the opposite common intellectual trap: that is, to dichotomize China and the West as radical others. Historically and philosophically speaking, medicine in both China and the West consists of many different and diverse traditions and methodologies. Beside apparent and fundamental differences between the twain, some intriguing similarities can be identified as well. The Hippocratic medicine and the *Neijing* share many similar holistic medical theories and philosophical orientations. There exists a holistic tradition even in modern biomedicine as exemplified in social medicine and public health and, in the recent decades, the rise of the socio-psycho-biomedical model. In the Chinese history of medicine, a persistent quasi experimental and analytic tradition can be discerned long before biomedicine was imported. Therefore, it is highly problematic to conclude that traditional Chinese medicine is radically incompatible or fundamentally incommensurable with medicine in the West, modern Western biomedicine in particular. If this would be the case, the Chinese practice of "integrated Chinese-Western medicine" (a new form of medicine that has been developing in China since the nineteenth century) would be unimaginable.

Throughout this book, a series of "false opposites" and "false friends"—especially the former—are encountered in order to gain a better understanding of the nature of medical ethics in China from a cross-cultural comparison with the West. In this chapter, through a refutation of the widely accepted view that the ancient Chinese discovered the circulation of the blood, I have illustrated some issues linked to the challenges posed by false friends in cross-cultural understanding. The major task involved in enhancing such understanding is not merely to avoid these two too-common vices, but to learn to appreciate not only commonalities and similarities but all that seems alien and different—especially the differences in similarities and the commonalities in differences.

Part II
Truths of cultures

Chapter 5
Taking China's internal plurality seriously

In the preceding four chapters we have encountered a series of myths and stereotypes on China and Chinese-Western cultural differences, such as that of a collectivist or communitarian China vs. the individualistic West. In particular, I have shown that the epistemological root of such myths lies in the persistent and pervasive way of dichotomizing cultures, and discussed the fallacy and perils of dichotomization. The key question that should be posed then is: Can we overcome those popular myths and stereotypes that are often associated with the way of dichotomizing China and the West as radical others? My short answer is: "Yes, we can." The approach proposed in this chapter and the entire book is: to take seriously China's great internal heterogeneity and pluralism—social, political, economic, cultural, religious, and moral.

Moral diversity and pluralism have been widely acknowledged as a fundamental condition of today's Western societies, bioethics included. In one of the most influential works of contemporary Western moral philosophy, Alasdair MacIntyre (2007 [1984]) has eloquently described the deeply fragmented and divided character of the contemporary moral landscape and proposed an Aristotelian and communitarian version of ethics to restore the "lost paradise" of Western moral life, the perceived moral consensus of the distant past. Similarly, in a major work of contemporary bioethics, Tristram Engelhardt, Jr. (1996 [1986]) launched his project to develop a libertarian bioethical theory by singling out moral pluralism as the basic reality, "in fact and in principle," of the postmodern age and by proclaiming the impossibility of recovering what he calls "a canonical, contentful morality."

I have no reason to call into question this diagnosis of contemporary Western moral life. Nevertheless, the diagnosis offered us by thinkers like MacIntyre and Engelhardt implies a *mis*diagnosis of collective morality in the past, and especially in non-Western societies such as China. Indeed, this popular prescription displays a certain modern and Western arrogance in its insistence that moral diversity and pluralism constitute the *unique* feature of postmodern Western morality and the suggestion that this does *not* apply to the past or to non-Western societies. In this chapter, I will demonstrate that great internal plurality has been an essential condition of Chinese moral and cultural life, today as well as in the past. Indeed, the most persistent practical challenge faced by Chinese civilization, in the past as well as the present, is to find a means of unifying China politically and culturally without undermining the nation's vast internal diversity.

China's internal plurality

The discussions in preceding chapters have left us with no other choice but to search alternatives to the pernicious habit of dichotomizing cultures and resisting the comforting but fallacious categories it offers us. The only way I know to achieve this is by taking seriously the great internal cultural and moral pluralism of China, indeed by recognizing the diversity in all cultures. This approach sets its face against the age-old and still powerful habit of homogenizing, totalizing, essentializing and radicalizing Chinese culture(s). Indeed, it would be difficult to overestimate the nation's enormous sociocultural, economic, political, moral, religious, and spiritual diversity—including the fields of medical ethics and medical morality.

In this book, I sometimes use the term "medical morality" to refer both to the ethical theories and the moral practices involved in health care, especially the pluralism of moral experience, found in a particular community or society. Even though the contemporary Chinese term *yide* ("medical morality") refers primarily to the "professional and personal virtues of the health professional," throughout this book I use the term with a wider social reference. Philosophical analysis of medical practice and its ethical principles constitutes only a part of medical morality. In a more comprehensive understanding of the concept, practice always should be perceived as theory-laden, and theories as rooted in practice—i.e., there should be no sharp distinctions between ethical theories and moral practice. Moreover, the term "medical morality" emphasizes such characteristics of moral experience as flux, chaos, discontinuity, diversity, nontransparency, resistance to systematical explanations and clear analysis, and so forth. In this sense, medical morality is not coterminous with the structure of any given ethical system of health care or something underlying moral experience, but rather is—or ought to be—the moral experience itself.

Recognizing the enormous diversity of Chinese cultures is only common sense. It would be hard to draw any other reasonable conclusion, given such basic facts as China's great geographical variation, long and turbulent history, great linguistic diversity, huge economic variation, and diverse political systems (in mainland China, Hong Kong and Taiwan), as well as the variety of social customs and cultural norms and the ethnic diversity of the population (there are more than fifty nationalities in China)—not to mention the great local complexities encountered, and the richness of the lived experience of the nation's "silent majority" and of the numberless people living on the sociocultural margins.

It is difficult, if not impossible, to offer adequate definitions of the fundamental terms "China" and "Chinese." China as a political and cultural entity has never been a homogeneous whole. Historically speaking, it is a mistake to view China as continuously unified and united. China consisted of many separate states in the Axial Period, when the paradigmatic Chinese spiritual and intellectual contributions to science and culture originated. China did not become a fully united country until the establishment of the Qin Dynasty in 221 BCE. Since the Qin Dynasty, China has been united and fragmented over and over again—a phenomenon generalized as a rule of history in popular culture. As the first sentence of the popular classical historical novel *Sanguo Yanyi* (The Romance of the Three Kingdoms), which appeared in the fourteenth century and which is still widely read today, proclaims: "States cleave asunder and coalesce in turns. This is the general historical trend of the world [i.e., China]."

Traditional China

Many people today view contemporary China as a pluralistic nation. However, even a large proportion of this growing group believe that China was at best monolithic in pre-modern times, that is, before the mid-nineteenth century. To many people in both the West and China (myself included some years ago), China, especially pre-modern China, was like the unexplored Middle Ages in the West before the advent of the detailed and systematic discipline of medieval studies in the twentieth century. As the French historian Jacques Gernet (1982: 21) said of the monolithic view of the European Middle Ages, "the repeated accusations of stagnation, periodical return to a previous condition, and permanence of the same social structure and the same political ideology are so many value judgements on a history that is still unknown."

Therefore, in one of my contributions to the first comprehensive study of international medical ethics—*The Cambridge World History of Medical Ethics*— on the moral discourses of medical practitioners in China (Nie 2009), my first task was to justify my focus on Confucian physicians in traditional China, and socialist or communist health care providers in contemporary China. With regard to the diversity of ethics, healing systems and healers, an overview of the moral discourses of medical practitioners in China should ideally address the characteristics, and compare and contrast the various healing traditions over the full range of moral and religious systems and specific types of therapy over the full sweep of Chinese history. Unfortunately, the lack of systematic and detailed research in contemporary scholarship precluded the discussion of other Chinese medico-moral traditions, such as the moral discourses of itinerant healers, sorcerer-healers, and practitioners from various ethnic minorities. There were no doubt many shared values among these different discourses, partly because eclecticism was commonplace. However, it is misleading to assume that the moral discourse of orthodox Confucian practitioners or socialist health care providers represents the definitive Chinese discourse, or even the only legitimate Chinese discourse, of medical ethics.

Let me briefly mention some basic facts about the great diversity of morality and medicine in imperial China. Like religion, in traditional China morality had never been conceived of as a singular entity. Although traditional China is usually viewed as a Confucian society, Confucianism was just one of its major ideologies and moral systems. Indigenous Daoism and imported but gradually sinolized Buddhism, as more institutionalized religions, have exerted an extremely strong and enduring influence on Chinese socio-cultural and moral life. The conventional term, "Three Teachings," indicates the importance, co-existence, competition, complementarity, and sometime integration of these three major Chinese ways of thinking and living. All Three Teachings provided medical practitioners with different but not necessarily incommensurable values and ethical frameworks for considering moral issues in health care. While there are significant differences between Daoism and Chinese Buddhism, Daoist and Buddhist understandings of birth, life, illness, suffering, healing, dying, and death often differ significantly from Confucian views of the same subjects.

In traditional China, healing systems were also diverse. The German historian of medicine, Paul Unschuld (2010 [1985]), has identified seven medical systems incorporating concepts that either originated in China or were adapted from foreign cultures: oracular therapy, demonic medicine, religious healing, pragmatic drug therapy, Buddhist medicine, the medicine of systematic correspondence and, ultimately, modern Western medicine.

> The history of these seven major conceptual systems is not characterized by simply linear succession, in which practitioners exchange each old system for a new one. Instead, the evidence reveals a diversity of concepts extending for more than two thousand years. New ideas were developed or introduced from outside and adopted by authors of medical texts, while at the same time older views continued to have their practitioners and clients.
>
> (Unschuld 2010 [1985]: 5–6)

Thus, to describe Chinese medicine as unified and coherent seriously distorts the historical reality of medical practice in China. Traditional Chinese medicine as we are familiar with it today, the so-called medicine of systematic correspondence, is merely one of several systems of therapy. These healing systems were not always exclusive. Borrowing such elements as drugs, methods of treatment, and medical concepts and even whole theories from other modalities was commonplace. Followers of these different healing systems competed for clients, resources and legitimacy and, as part of this process, borrowed popular elements from other systems. For example, the more rational medicine of systematic correspondence incorporated some features of *zhoujin* or *zhuyou* (magic healing).

The historical evidence indicates that different groups of healers with distinctive moral worldviews and medical paradigms emerged and often co-existed at various periods. For example, the *Jinpingmei* (The Golden Lotus), a realistic novel of the sixteenth century, vividly describes the daily lives as well as the medical activities of a variety of healers in late imperial China. The largest group are literate male healers recognizable as practitioners of classical Chinese medicine. Among this group are physicians of general medicine, specialists in children's and women's disorders, and medical officials. Male religious specialists include foreign monks, Daoist priests, and the "Immortals," who mainly practiced divination. Other male healers described in the novel include the "Starmasters," specialists in "lesion poison" and pious practitioners. Female medical practitioners include midwives as well as "Old Women" and Buddhist nuns who performed healing activities (See Cullen 1993: 108–10). For pragmatic reasons, some practitioners embraced two or three (or even more) paradigms and employed therapies from more than one medical system. Wu the Immortal in the *Jinpingmei* not only told fortunes and practiced divination, but also treated the sick with empirical remedies such as herbs. As Unschuld has succinctly observed:

> Well beyond the end of the Confucian era, traditional physicians remained a non-homogeneous group which included practitioners of the most diverse training and skills. ... *The* Chinese physician as a definable entity did not exist...Up to this [i.e. the twentieth] century these have included shamans, Buddhist priests, Taoist hermits, Confucian scholars, itinerant physicians, established physicians, "laymen" with medical knowledge (gained from experiences or obtained through family tradition), midwives, and many others.
> (Unschuld 1979: 112–13, 118; emphasis original)

These people all were "Chinese physicians" when engaged in the practice of medicine.

Based on the ethical discussions found in traditional Chinese medical texts, mostly by orthodox Confucian physicians, it is commonly acknowledged that Confucianism dominated medical ethics in pre-modern China. Yet the contribution made by the great Confucian physicians is far from being the whole story. Indeed, a crucial question that has not hitherto been seriously raised is: To what degree do the ethical teachings and biographies of a small number of distinguished Confucian medical scholars represent the reality of traditional Chinese medical morality? Or, in what way do they offer us clues about the everyday medical practices of ordinary people? As expressed through the collective and individual behaviors involved in seeking and providing health care, traditional Chinese medical ethics must have been much richer and more complex than the evidence provided by the surviving medical literature indicates. In order to appreciate the historical realities of traditional

Chinese medical morality, one must take into account the influence of Taoism and Buddhism, as well as Confucianism, in any assessment of Chinese approaches to moral issues in medicine. For example, the concepts of individual freedom and spiritual liberation are of central importance, although Taoism defines and articulates these values in ways that differ from the Western philosophical-political and Judeo-Christian traditions. Moreover, and more importantly, medical ethical issues were not addressed solely in the ancient medical and philosophical literature. Without careful historical research into the manifold contributions of patients and laypeople to moral problems in health care—as recorded, for example, in pre-modern literature, folklore, the arts, unofficial historical works, and the enormous storehouse of historical records relating to localities, clans and families—the all-too-familiar claim that traditional Chinese medical morality was mostly shaped by Confucianism will remain unquestioned (even though it may still turn out to be correct).

The contemporary situation

It is far easier to make the point about the great pluralism of cultures and medical morality as manifested in China in various and obvious ways since the early twentieth century.

The revolution of 1911 brought about the fall of the imperial political system, the collapse of China's traditional social structure and the founding of a Western-style political system. The establishment of the People's Republic in 1949 laid the foundations for a Chinese socialist or communist society. The state policies introduced to promote economic reform and "openness" since the late 1970s have transformed China into a capitalist society with Chinese and "socialist" characteristics in a world capitalist order. Certainly, despite some shared cultural elements, the moral discourses of medical practitioners in particular (and medical moralities in general) in mainland China, Hong Kong, and Taiwan, as well as among the international Chinese diaspora, can in no way be regarded as homogeneous.

In contemporary mainland China, three legitimate medical systems—traditional Chinese medicine, modern Western biomedicine, and Chinese and Western medicine in various combinations—co-exist and compete with each other. In addition, many other forms of healing—from folk medicine to religious methods of healing and witchcraft—that are officially proscribed as "superstitious" are often practiced, both publicly and clandestinely. Chinese culture today is a mix of many diverse values and beliefs—ancient and modern, Western and Eastern. In today's China, despite the resistance of the official state ideology to cultural and moral pluralism, examples of the co-existence of sinolized Western Marxism and communism, traditional Confucianism, Daoism, and Buddhism, and Christianity and Islam are not hard to find, in the ways people actually live and even in official pronouncements. The result is a melting pot of concepts including socialism, collectivism, filial piety, mixed in with the ideals of individual happiness, self-realization, and self-perfection.

A few additional words are needed on the contribution made by Christianity. A history of medicine in China since the sixteenth century would not be adequate without acknowledging the significant contributions made by Christianity and its missionaries—medical missionaries in particular—as well as by Chinese Christians and Christian medical professionals. Christianity has played an essential role in the introduction of Western biomedicine and the establishment of modern hospitals, clinics, medical schools and professional associations. Moreover, although a Christian medical ethics tradition has long taken root in Chinese soil, few studies exist of Christianity's contribution to the development of Chinese medical ethics and medical moralities over the past four centuries or so, and especially today. After being ruthlessly persecuted and banished for more than three decades from 1949, Christianity has undergone a striking revival over the past few decades. This remarkable fact in itself upsets the familiar thesis that Christianity and Chinese culture(s) are antagonistic and incommensurable and that Chinese civilization is an homogenous entity, impervious to external influences.

Comparisons with the West

However marked the diversity of Chinese cultures and medical moralities, both historically and today, one may insist that it pales in comparison with the West, especially the United States. But this sweeping generalization needs to be put in perspective. To answer the question on whether or not the West, the United States for instance, is more culturally, morally and politically diverse, it all depends on which aspect of moral and cultural life we wish to discuss. If we are considering the contemporary debate on the (im)morality of abortion, in China the airing of this issue in the public domain is certainly far less intense than is the case in the West, the United States in particular. But this is not always or necessarily the case in coming to other dimensions of cultural and moral life. Two scenarios immediately come to mind.

As non-Western cultural traditions have attained greater visibility in the West over the past few decades, the issue of multiculturalism has been at the forefront of heated public debate in the political and moral arena. A central theme of Chinese history, especially since the later nineteenth century, has been the encounter of Chinese and Western civilizations, in both large-scale and intimate contexts. On the one hand, Western technology, science, institutions and values have injected many alternative and fresh ideas, perspectives and ways of thinking and living into Chinese cultures. At the same time, the aggressive expansion of Western civilization, Christianity included, has posed a series of challenges. Perhaps the most pressing of these is how China can assimilate the positive elements of Western civilization without jeopardizing its own identity and cultural traditions. The resulting conflicts in cultural and moral life within China may well become even more intense than the tensions between and among Western and non-Western value systems in the West, which have only recently been acknowledged and debated there. In China, the debate has been going on for several centuries and is still continuing on both the intellectual and, more acutely and even at times violently, the practical level.

The second scenario concerns the moral implications of the large-scale inequalities afflicting China today. They include regional imbalances between coastal areas and the inland, especially the vast Western region of China and, most strikingly, the social and economic divide between rural and urban China. A caste-like system of social stratification—the *fukou* (household registration) system—was introduced immediately following the establishment of the People's Republic of China in 1949 and has existed as a basic social institution in China ever since (for an historical and sociological study of this system, see Wang 2005). While it has become increasingly easier in the past few decades for rural people, known as *nongmin* (peasants), to work and live in the cities, Chinese people are still categorized into two civil status groups ascribed at birth: rural (with lower status) and urban. The level of social, economic, and cultural inequality between these two groups is so vast that stripping an urban-dweller of his or her residency status constitutes one of the most serious civil punishments. Rural people—the majority of the population—also suffer a shocking degree of health care inequality. As a result, the life expectancy of rural residents is several years less than that of their urban counterparts. Death rates due to infectious diseases, respiratory diseases, pregnancy and childbirth, injuries and poisoning, and even suicide (female suicides in particular, see Chapter 10 for more discussion on this issue) are much higher in rural areas. While mortality patterns in urban China are similar to those in developed countries, in rural areas they are often more typical of those of the developing world. With the collapse of the traditional three-tier health care system (county-township-village) and the disappearance of "barefoot doctors" in the wake of national economic reform, structural inequality in health care has only worsened.

Discrimination and injustice against rural people is widespread and pervasive in China. The problem resembles racism in the West, but is more serious. While racism as a major social problem has long affected Western countries, overt forms of racism are by and large illegal. But China's unique rural–urban divide has been not only socially accepted but legally endorsed as a fundamental social institution in mainland Chinese society. The question I want to raise in the present context—the internal moral pluralism of China—is to what extent this major social and geographical divide, and the inequality and injustice that accompany it, have impacted on Chinese morality and medical moralities in particular. If economic and social conditions indeed play an active role in people's moral worldviews—an essential role in Marxist terms, and common Chinese wisdom (in such ancient sayings as *canglin shi er zhi lijie*, "when the granaries are full, people appreciate rites and their moral obligations")—then there will very likely be significant differences between rural and urban people over various issues in medical ethics, although all are Chinese nationals and citizens of the People's Republic. Unfortunately, I am not aware of any systematic and in-depth investigations in either Chinese or English of the bioethical implications of this massive rural-urban divide and legalized structural inequality in China.

Therefore, I would argue that China's internal moral and cultural pluralism is not necessarily less complex than that evident in the West, depending on which dimension of moral and socio-cultural life is being discussed. However, there does exist a significant cultural difference on a closely related matter—while moral and cultural pluralism is widely acknowledged and debated in the contemporary West, the issue is yet to enter the public domain in China.

Conclusions

As outlined in the introduction, the two major tasks of an interpretative or transcultural bioethics are, first of all, to expose the many deeply rooted stereotypes and myths regarding cultures and medical ethics in both Western and non-Western societies, especially the latter, and then to acknowledge the internal moral pluralism that flourishes within every culture. In this chapter, along with the rest of the book, I hope that I have presented sufficient evidence and arguments to convince even the most skeptical reader that there is no such entity as a single and homogenous Chinese culture. Of course, Chinese medical morality cannot remain exempt from this general cultural diversity and be treated as a field with a single unified discourse. Just as there is no single and homogenous Chinese culture or morality, there is no single and homogenous Chinese medical morality. Great internal diversity has always been an essential feature of Chinese civilizations and cultures.

As a result, great care must therefore be taken when formulating any statement about the over-arching characteristics of Chinese cultures and Chinese medical ethics. When generalizing about China, we must acknowledge the sense and degree to which the generalization is valid, and we must always be acutely aware of the great internal socio-cultural and moral diversity of the nation we are attempting to encapsulate. We should always try to be as clear and specific as possible about what we mean when discussing Chinese cultures and medical ethics: *Which China? Whose China? Which Chinese culture? Whose Chinese culture? Which Chinese medical ethics? Whose Chinese medical ethics? Which historical period? Which region? Which groups? Which social milieu?* so on and so forth.

As for the politics of China, taking its internal diversity and pluralism seriously is an urgent task, not so much in intellectual but in practical terms. Indeed, the future of China very much depends on how well placed it is to meet the most persistent challenge that it has always faced: to unify the nation politically and culturally while maintaining due respect for its great internal pluralism and heterogeneity (see also "Conclusions: ways toward the uncertain future").

Chapter 6

The complexity of cultural differences
The forgotten Chinese tradition of medical truth-telling

While cultural differences are real and arresting, they can be very tricky to interpret accurately and insightfully. Their factual status, moral meanings and political implications are rarely, if ever, as straightforward as they appear. Cultural differences can be seriously misconceived, misrepresented and misused in various ways. Empirically problematic perceptions, ethically dubious judgments, and practically contentious resolutions can easily become entangled when considering matters of cultural difference. In this and the next chapter, focusing on the disclosure of information (or the contemporary practice of nondisclosure or indirect disclosure) by medical professionals in China from a Chinese-Western comparative perspective, I not only expose some of these confusions but also illustrate some appropriate methods to help us better appreciate and more adequately address cultural differences in bioethics.

Cultural differences oversimplified

In most Western countries, informing patients truthfully and directly about their medical condition, including the diagnosis and prognosis of incurable disease, is firmly established, both socially and institutionally, as an essential element of good medical practice. Contemporary bioethics in the West, both as an academic discipline and also in the public domain, is a vigorous advocate for truth-telling and informed consent and choice. In sharp contrast to the West, however, in China, including Hong Kong and Taiwan, medical professionals routinely withhold information about terminal illness from patients, and usually inform family members only, often in an overtly paternalist manner (e.g., Kleinman 1988, 152; Li and Chou 1997; Pang 1998, 1999; Tse, Chong and Fok 2003; Fan and Li 2004; Tang and Lee 2004; Zhu 2005; Zeng, Li, Chen and Fang 2007; Tang et al. 2008).

Based on this undoubted contrast in attitudes and practices between contemporary China and the West, it has been widely assumed that medical truth-telling is culturally alien to China—indeed, a practice that was unknown in China until the recent influence of the West. In case I should be accused of fighting a straw man or tilting at windmills (however fun this might be), let me cite a few examples in the English-language bioethical and medical literature where indirect disclosure or even deception is claimed as the Chinese cultural and moral norm. The first is from an article in an international bioethical journal by two Chinese physician-bioethicists seeking to justify the contemporary Chinese practice of nondisclosure (or indirect disclosure to family members) from a cultural and Confucian familial perspective: "In contrast [to the contemporary West], Chinese medical ethics, *even today*, in theory and in practice remains committed to hiding the truth as well as to lying when necessary" (Fan and Li 2004, 180; emphasis added). Again, to quote the words of a group of Taiwanese physicians, from a medical journal in English specializing in palliative care, truth-telling about terminal illness is "unfamiliar to the Oriental people" (Cheng, Hu, Liu Yao, Chen and Chiu 2008, 631). Finally, for an American bioethicist with extensive international experience who is strongly critical of the norm of nondisclosure from a universalist ethical standpoint—and who no doubt eschews the dichotomizing of East and West—withholding unpalatable truths has been "a nearly universal customary practice dictated by medical professionals throughout the world" (Macklin 1999, 99). China is not excluded in this observation.

In recent years, medical professionals, lawyers, scholars, and the general public in China have been engaged in a debate over whether terminally ill patients should be truthfully and directly told about their condition. More and more medical professionals, along with patients, are adopting a critical stance toward the dominant Chinese practice and advocating reform. Nevertheless, however opposed participants' normative positions may be in the debate—for or against truth-telling—one belief that the opposing camps share is that, whilst open and direct disclosure is the Western way, nondisclosure (or indirect disclosure through family members) is *the* authentic and representative norm of Chinese culture and medical ethics. In fact, this perceived cultural difference is cited by some Chinese medical professionals and scholars as grounds to oppose medical truth telling in the Chinese context because of its presumed "foreignness" and incompatibility with China's cultural and moral traditions.

However, as this chapter will demonstrate, utterly contrary to what has been universally assumed and presented both inside and outside China, the traditional practice and norm of Chinese culture and medical ethics was for physicians to disclose the diagnosis and prognosis of incurable illnesses truthfully and directly to patients. At the same time, far from being the venerable Western cultural and medical tradition regularly portrayed in discussions of cross-cultural medical ethics, open and direct disclosure about terminal illness is, historically, a very recent phenomenon in the West.

A new phenomenon in the West

It was not until the 1970s that the truthful disclosure of information to patients became standard procedure in the West. In the United States, for instance, 90%

of physicians surveyed in the early 1960s favored concealing the truth about a dire medical diagnosis and prognosis from cancer patients (Oken 1961). However, by the late 1970s this attitude had been completely reversed. In a survey which posed a questionnaire almost identical to that used in the 1961 study just cited, 97% of physicians said that they would prefer to inform cancer patients of their diagnosis (Novack et al. 1979; see also Glaser and Strauss 1965).

For centuries, in sharp contrast to medical practice in China (as presented below) and against the wider cultural emphasis on truthfulness, Western physicians regularly withheld medical information about terminal illness from their patients, a practice apparently tacitly accepted by laypeople. In fact, the history of the patient–physician relationship in the West has been summarized as a "history of silence," a tradition that goes back to ancient Greece (Katz 2002 [1984]). In the *Decorum*, Hippocrates, the father of medicine in the West, admonished physicians not to practice disclosure, but to "conceal most things from the patient while you are attending to him" and to "reveal nothing of the patient's future or present condition."

These attitudes were carried forward into modern times. The influential nineteenth-century Code of the American Medical Association (1847; section 4 of Article I) stipulated that physicians should "not be forward to make gloomy prognostications." Only "on proper occasions" should the physician "give to the friends of the patient timely notice of danger, when it really occurs;" and only "if absolutely necessary" should the physician disclose the information to the patient himself. The Code gives further advice on the conduct proper to the attending physician:

> This office, however, is so peculiarly alarming when executed by him, that it ought to be declined whenever it can be assigned to any other person of sufficient judgment and delicacy. For, the physician should be the minister of hope and comfort to the sick: that, by such cordials to the drooping spirit, he may smooth the bed of death, revive expiring life, and counteract the depressing influence of those maladies which often disturb the tranquillity of the most resigned, in their last moments. The life of the sick person can be shortened not only by the acts, but also by the words or the manner of a physician. It is, therefore, *a sacred duty* to guard himself carefully in this respect, and to avoid all things which have a tendency to discourage the patient and to depress his spirits.
> (in Katz 2002 [1984]: 231; emphasis added)

While the Code states that the doctor should not exaggerate the role he plays in treating and curing disease, it fails to acknowledge the place of honesty or veracity in the relationship between physician and patient. Rather, based on the paternalistic presumption that a terminal patient is in too frail a state to receive the facts about their medical condition, the physician has a "sacred duty" *not* to speak truthfully and directly.

In New Zealand, one of the most progressive Western countries, the practices of direct disclosure, informed consent and acknowledging patients' rights did not become the ethical and legal standard until the later 1980s and early 1990s. The Code of the American Medical Association was adopted by the New Zealand branch of the British Medical Association as a "Code of Medical Ethics for New Zealand" no later than 1887. Following the adoption of the Medical Ethics Guidelines of the British Medical Association, the 1963–64 Handbook of the New Zealand Medical Association stated that, although "the patient has a right to know the facts and the opinions about his case," "[i]n the face of serious illness or where there is little or no chance of recovery, it calls for particular discretion as to what is said and how it is said." The handbook points up an important role for family members in meeting "the best interests of the patient."

> When an opinion is demanded by the patient, the doctor may deem it wise to discuss the situation with the relatives on the matter of how far he should go in this direction. At any rate, a responsible relative should be informed of the true state of affairs. In any circumstances the doctor must act in what he believes to be the best interests of the patient.
> (British Medical Association NZ Branch 1964, 23; cited in Nie and Anderson 2003: 247)

Even in the late 1980s, in the well-known Cartwright Inquiry (1987–88) into the "unfortunate experiment" involving women with cervical abnormalities, several doctors who served as expert witnesses objected to the necessity (and even possibility) of truth-telling and informed consent in such circumstances. Dr. Graeme Duncan, then president of the Royal New Zealand College of Obstetricians and Gynaecologists, testified that telling patients the truth about their complications "would frighten a very large number of people from having necessary treatment, and it would also be beyond the intellectual comprehension of a considerable proportion of the population." (Coney 1988, 143; cited in Ibid)

The overt practice of deception by physicans is all the more surprising, given that it stands in total opposition to a strong and essential element in Western religious, literary and philosophical traditions which opposes lying and pursues truth and truthfulness even to the edge of absurdity. From the Old and New Testaments of Judeo-Christianity and the works of Augustine onwards, the West has adopted an uncompromising position on the wrongfulness of lying and deception. Greek tragedies like *Oedipus the King* clearly emphasize the importance of truth (however hurtful or destructive it may be) and reject the false comfort to be found in ignorance or concealment of the truth. As another play by Sophocles, *Antigone* (one of the most profound works on the fundamental moral conficts in human social life), puts it: "Why should I comfort and then tomorrow/ be proven a liar? The truth is always best" (in Grene and Lattimore 1991, 227). The virtues of truthfulness, sincerity and authenticity form part of the backbone of modern Western literature and culture from Shakespeare to Joyce, from Rousseau to Goethe, and from Hegel to Freud (Trilling 1971). In his ethical works, Immanuel Kant set out the philosophical justification for the absolute wrongfulness of lying, even to save human life (Kant 1996). And in the field of medicine, throughout history there have been exceptional physicians who have emphasized the importance of veracity in their professional practice. The personal oath of Amatus Lusitaus, a Jewish physician in the sixteenth century, contains the words: "If I lie, may I incur the eternal wrath of God and of His angel Raphael, and may nothing in the medical art succeed for me according to my desires" (cited in Bok 1978, 224; see also Appendix of Bok 1978, 250–88, for excerpts from works by Augustine, Aquinas, Bacon, Gratius, Kant, and BonHoeffer).

Despite this richly truth-affirming cultural context, and despite such heartfelt protestations from some physicians, the virtue of honesty to patients was rarely, if at all, mentioned in Western medical ethics documents such as the Hippocratic Oath or the 1847 Code of the American Medical Association (Ibid, 223–4). While today medical truth-telling is firmly established as the norm of good medical practice in most Western countries, this has not always been the case. In the West, telling terminally ill patients the truth about their condition and prospects as a standard practice has a history of only a few decades.

A long but forgotten tradition in China

However little known inside and outside China today, and however rarely acknowledged even by Chinese medical ethicists and historians of medicine ethics, a well-established tradition of medical disclosure existed in China—a tradition initiated by great physicians 2,600 years ago.

Primary sources

To my knowledge, there is no systematic historical study, in Chinese or English, of the diagnosis and prognosis of incurable disease in Chinese medical tradition. To avoid what the Chinese call *yi e chuan e* (incorrectly relaying a message so that it becomes increasingly distorted) or what Westerners call "Chinese whispers," a survey of the related primary historical data is an essential prerequisite. Also, when investigating a vast, ancient and culturally diverse nation such as China, it is always possible to find some kind of evidence for particular ideas or practices. However, in order to confirm the existence of a genuine tradition, one needs to bring to light far more extensive and reliable evidence than a few isolated historical cases could provide.

The major source for my investigations is the section on general issues in medicine in the medical classic, *Gujin Tushu Jicheng Yibu Quanlu* (A Collection

The forgotten Chinese tradition of medical truth-telling 103

of Ancient and Modern Books, The Part on Medicine). With imperial support and endorsement, *A Collection of Ancient and Modern Books* was published in 1726 after nearly three decades of editorial work by a large team of scholars. As one of the most comprehensive edited collections in Chinese publishing history, it comprised ten thousand volumes in the traditional Chinese printing format. The part on medicine contained five hundred volumes—ten large volumes in today's printing format. The last twenty volumes of the medical section gather up general commentary on the art of medicine from both medical and non-medical works. Among other things, they include numerous statements and treatises by both physicians and laypeople on professional and ethical matters relating to medicine. In particular, they include the biographies of nearly 1,400 well-known physicians dating from legendary times and antiquity up to the seventeenth century. These biographies were gathered from a very wide range of sources in official, unofficial, national, local, historical and non-historical works. The various accounts of the treatment of terminal illness in these extensive biographies of physicians from different dynasties offer an unparalleled window on the diagnosis and prognosis of incurable disease in China.

Other primary sources consulted include relevant accounts in a few classic literary works and the first modern book-length treatment of professional ethics authored by a Chinese physician trained in Western biomedicine.

The way of the medical sages

In the beginning, as Confucianism, Daoism and traditional Chinese medicine all agree, were the great sages who founded long-revered pathways of living, thinking and morality, as well as healing. Anticipating contemporary Western practice by more than two and half millennia, the Chinese medical sages took truthful and direct disclosure about terminal illness for granted.

Bing ru gaohuang ("the disease has attacked the vital area between *gao* and *huang*"), the phrase commonly used to refer to terminal illness (*jiezheng*) in both classical and contemporary Chinese, was coined by the great healer Yi Huan in the Spring and Autumn Period (770–476 BCE). The story surrounding the origin of this Chinese idiom indicates that the diagnosis of terminal illness and the necessity of informing the patient about it directly were inherently connected from the very beginning.

According to the *Zuozhuan* (The Chronology of the State of Lu), one of the earliest surviving Chinese historical works, in the tenth year of Duke Cheng (579 BCE), Yi Huan ("the physician named Huan") was called in to treat the duke of the state of Jin. After examining him, the physician told Duke Jin in straightforward terms: "The disease is beyond a cure. It is above *gao* and below *huang* [unknown or controversial anatomical locations in traditional Chinese medicine]. ... No medicine can reach the diseased place, so it is beyond curing." The duke replied: "An excellent doctor indeed (*liangyi ye*)!" The physician was rewarded by the patient and sent away with "generous gifts" after a grand ceremony (*houweizi li er guizhi*). Duke Jin died from a diarrhea-related illness shortly afterwards. Interestingly, in the same story, a *wu* (sorcerer) who also foretold the duke's imminent death was executed because his prediction was regarded as false. Duke Jin died immediately after the execution was carried out, and the prognosis of the physician and the sorcerer's prophecy were both fulfilled.

In classical Chinese in particular, the expression *He-Huan*, a conflation of the names Yi He and Yi Huan, denotes a healer, especially an admirable or model healer. According to the *Zuozhuan* and another very early Chinese historical work, *Guoyu*, Yi He ("the physician named He"), a near contemporary of Yi Huan, had informed a government minister directly of his diagnosis of terminal illness. Yi He, too, was praised by the patient as an excellent doctor and rewarded with generous gifts after a grand ritual.

Besides Yi He and Yi Huan, other founding figures of Chinese medicine include Qin Yueren (fl. c. 500 BCE, popularly known as Bian Que, dubbed the "father of medicine" by some historians), Zhang Zhongjing (c. second century AD, renowned as the "sage of medicine") and Hua Tuo (c. second century AD, known as the "father of surgery"). Without exception, their practice was to tell their patients the truth when their illness was diagnosed as terminal. There are no records of any of these great Chinese physicians ever recommending that a doctor should conceal such information from his patients. Zhang Zhongjian once predicted that a patient would die in twenty years' time, and prescribed medicine to prevent it. However, despite the doctor's warning, the patient refused to take the prescribed medication and died exactly as Zhang had foretold (Ibid, 73). Ten cases of terminal illness were recorded in the various biographies of Hua Tuo in the *Sanguozhi* (Records of Three Kingdoms), the *Weizhi* (Records of the State of Wei) and other historical works. In each instance, he is portrayed as directly informing his patients—whatever their social status—about the time of their death, varying from ten years to three days. In one case, he assured his patient, a traveler, that he would have been able to cure him had he seen him earlier. As it was, Hua Tuo told the traveler that his disease was incurable, and urged him: "Hurry back home so that you may see your family." The patient died five days later (Ibid, 97–102).

A number of cases reported by Chunyu Yi (popularly known as Cang Gong or Lord Cong, c. second century BCE), another well-known physician of the Western Han Dynasty, were documented in the *Shiji* (Records of the Grand Historian). For Cang Gong, telling the truth about terminal illness was also the norm, although marked by a certain ambivalence (Ibid, 82–90). In one case, he is recorded as delivering his diagnosis in unequivocal terms: "Death [is imminent]. [The disease is] incurable. ... This is a hopeless case." The patient died five days later, as the physician had predicted. In another case, Cang Gong's language was evasive. He first told his patient: "You are suffering from such a grave illness that I should not speak about it (*Jun zi bing'e, buke yan ye*)." He then disclosed some further medical information and told the patient's brother that he had just eight days to live.[1] In another case, although the truth about a terminal illness was delivered in straightforward terms, it is unclear whether this information was given to the patient or to a third party. In two other cases where the patients were respectively a maid and a male servant, it was their masters, not the patients themselves, who were directly informed.

Other celebrated doctors in history

The biographies of famous physicians recorded in *A Collection of Ancient and Modern Books* illustrate time and again that the physician's duty is to inform patients truthfully of the diagnosis and prognosis in cases of terminal disease, however unfavorable the outlook. Surveying additional biographies recorded in various official and unofficial sources, I have noted around fifty cases involving the diagnosis of incurable diseases, in addition to those involving the medical sages discussed above. As with the early sages, in these additional cases, physicians from different dynasties and places throughout China almost without exception were portrayed as informing their patients about their medical condition directly and truthfully. In the few cases where such information was not passed on directly, the patients were either children, women or servants. In several cases, these physicians anticipated the dates of their own deaths—one physician even invited all his relatives and friends to a big drinking party the day before his death.

Laypeople's expectations

The fact that these early texts depict physicians as often receiving financial rewards from patients or family members for their candidness indicates that laypeople expected doctors to disclose medical information, including the unwelcome truth, directly to their patients. Further evidence for this attitude is found in literary sources. According to the famous (or infamous, due to its many pornographic passages) sixteenth-century realist novel *Jingpingmei* (*The Golden Lotus*, literally, *The Gold, the Plum and the Verse*), ordinary people endorsed the practice of direct disclosure. The protagonist of *Jingpingmei* probably suffered from a sexually transmitted disease. Because taking the medicine prescribed for

---

1 Advocates of nondisclosure and indirect disclosure as the authentic Chinese practice have cited the biography of Cang Gong in support of their views. Furthermore, they claim, "this has become a medical-ethics rule for all traditional Chinese physicians" (Fan and Li 2004, 184). However, the biography contains no statement supporting this position, and his recorded medical cases indicate that Cang Gong did not practice indirect and partial disclosure as the norm. In fact, I have never encountered an unequivocal statement to this effect in any premodern Chinese historical or medical text.

him by several physicians was like "throwing stones into the sea," his wife finally called in a fortune teller who also practiced medicine. After taking his pulse, the fortune teller–physician informed the patient bluntly: "Sir, you are ill because you have taken too much wine and had too much to do with women. Now your vital fluid is exhausted and a furious fever has taken hold of the instrument of your passion. I fear I can do nothing for you. Your case is hopeless." Afterwards, acting on a request from the wife, he added the following words in the patient's presence: "It [the patient's coming death] is the will of Heaven, and neither god nor spirit can alter it." He was rewarded with "a roll of cloth" for his services. The patient, convinced of his imminent death, died shortly afterwards (Xiaoxiao Sheng, Chapter 79).

Liaozhai Zhiyi (Strange Stories from a Chinese Studio), a literary classic based on supernatural folktales and first published posthumously in the seventeenth century, contains a similar story. A man falls in love at first sight with a male fox spirit transformed into a young teenage boy, and suffers badly from lovesickness—especially after having sex with the beautiful creature. After examining the patient and taking his pulse, a physician detects the root of the problem—having relations with a ghost. After rejecting this diagnosis and dismissing the physician's advice, the lovesick protagonist becomes seriously ill. The same doctor is called in once again. After a further examination, the doctor tells the patient directly: "Your soul has wandered away into a vast wilderness. Even a great physician like Yi Huan could not do anything to cure your illness." The patient died soon afterwards, but was later reincarnated in the body of another man (Pu, Huangjiu Lang).

Ethical rationales for truth-telling

There are important ethical grounds for Chinese physicians to practice truth-telling about terminal illness. One argument, often mentioned by the medical sages and celebrated physicians discussed above, is based on pragmatic or consequentialist considerations. It holds that disclosure helps patients and their families prepare for death and dying as well as posthumous duties such as funerals. In other words, truth-telling has practical benefits for patients and their families, whilst withdrawing critical medical information can harm them.

A second, quasi-deontological, reason for direct disclosure is that truth-telling is an essential personal, professional and social virtue. The concept of *cheng* (honesty, truthfulness and sincerity) is fundamental in Confucianism, especially Neo-Confucianism. In his "Regulations on Practicing Medicine," the sixteenth-century Confucian physician Li Yan stipulated: "If I were asked for one word to summarize [how to practice medicine], my answer in a single phrase would be 'no deception'" (in Chen 1991 [1723], 56). Li went on:

> If one is practicing deception, one's conscience will be closed up and the way of medicine will be lost. If one is not practicing deception, one's

conscience will expand every day and the way of medicine will develop. [What happens] between "deception" and "no deception" is beyond the power of humans to bestow.

Included among the various kinds of medical deceit is the physician's failure to "honestly inform patients about their condition after taking the pulse [i.e., making a diagnosis]."

Western influence and its limits

It is a puzzle why such a venerable tradition of open and direct disclosure as I have sketched above has been so totally forgotten in China. Ironically, the traditional ethos from which modern Western biomedicine emerged may well have played a significant role in the development of the contemporary Chinese practice of nondisclosure. In other words, the "authentic" and "representative" Chinese practices of nondisclosure and indirect disclosure regarding terminal illness are highly influenced by the outdated Western norm and not at all as authentic or representative Chinese as has been so widely assumed.

One might lament, as Confucius and the ancient Chinese liked to do, that the glorious way of the sages is continually falling into decay, rather than being upheld, with the passing of time. It seems that, the closer to modernity, the more customary the practices of nondisclosure and indirect disclosure became in China. For example, in chapter nine of the great eighteenth-century realist novel *Hongloumeng* (Dream of the Red Chamber) or *Shituoji* (Story of the Stone), the wife of a member of the royal family was not told of her imminent death by her physician, even though she was very much aware of the prospect. Even family members received only hints about her true medical condition. The context suggests that this practice of veiled disclosure was tacitly accepted at the time.

Over the past two centuries or so, the norm of nondisclosure or indirect disclosure has become increasingly widespread. From the late nineteenth century, it developed as the dominant Chinese practice and remains so today. This was precisely the period in which Western civilization began to exert a profound impact on Chinese society and culture. This was also the period in which Western biomedicine began replacing traditional Chinese medicine as the primary medical system in China. To my knowledge, the first clear statement of the ethical acceptability of nondisclosure in the literature of medical ethics in China was made in 1933 in *Yiye Lunlixue* (The Ethics of the Medical Profession) by Song Guobing, a physician who was trained in Western biomedicine and who even visited Paris. In terms reminiscent of the codes of the American and British medical associations cited above, Song stated that "Physicians ought not to deceive, but may conceal the truth" in order to shield patients from psychological suffering, physical harm and unnecessary panic over their condition (Song 1933, 28–30).

Nevertheless, this Chinese document on the sanctions underlying nondisclosure differs in some important repects from Western documents such as the historic 1847 Code of the American Medical Association. Firstly, Song clearly acknowledged the importance of truthfulness for medical practice in particular and human social life in general. He recognized that the physician faces a serious ethical dilemma when a patient is diagnosed with terminal illness, a conflict of two moral obligations: openness and honesty versus the need to protect the patient from any possible harm. "Honesty is the indispensable virtue for physicians, as we all know." To deceive or mislead the patient violates the principle of honesty and faithfulness (*chengxin*) so valued by physicians. Furthermore, nondisclosure will not allow the patient to make funeral and other postmortem arrangements. On the other hand, "to speak truthfully will increase the suffering of the patient." As a result, to tell or not to tell is a question for the physician involved, one that needs careful consideration.

Secondly, in an attempt to clarify the moral issues at stake, Song made a distinction between lying or deceiving (*kuangyu*) and concealing the truth (*huiyan zhenshi*). These acts differ in their moral force because of the different intentions of the physician that they reveal. The first approach is unacceptable, just as any act of cheating for personal gain is wrong, whoever commits it. Here Song cites two well-known sayings of Confucius on the importance of *xin* (trust, confidence, faithfulness, honesty, truthfulness): "People cannot stand without truthfulness" and "Social relationships depend on truthfulness." He then poses a rhetorical but crucial question: "How can the physician set aside this age-old maxim?" However, Song reasoned, concealing the truth is not the same thing as lying or deceiving. "Concealing the truth has the form of deception, but lacks the substance. For the intention is to comfort, not to cheat [the patient]." Therefore, Song concluded, "physicians ought not to deceive, but may conceal the truth" in circumstances that will substantially benefit their patients.

Thirdly and most importantly, Song's approach differed from the American Code insofar as he never formulated the concept of a fundamental or "sacred duty" to withhold the truth about their condition from terminally ill patients. Rather, he suggested that physicians *may* conceal the truth, using the Chinese verb *keyi* which means "may, might or can," but not "should" or "ought." Song noted two situations in which a physician may conceal the truth: 1) if the illness is severe but a cure is anticipated; and 2) if the illness is incurable but death is not imminent. However, Song immediately qualified these remarks by stating that the physician should conceal the truth only "temporarily" in these circumstances and that the physician "should tell," rather than conceal, the truth if death is imminent (*wei zai danxi*) or if the patient's condition might deteriorate at any time. He retreated somewhat from this position by listing four circumstances in which the physician "may" still conceal the truth even if death is imminent: if the patient has set their affairs in order; if the patient does not want a religious funeral ceremony; if there are signs that learning the truth might induce the patient to commit suicide; or if direct disclosure will place the physician at significant risk. However, changing tack once again Song was quick to point out that, even in these circumstances, it is still "not permissible" (*buke*) "to practice deception (*she guici*, to indulge in verbal trickery) by telling the patient that there is some hope of recovery." Here Song's main rationale is pragmatic or consequentialistic: offering false hope or withholding crucial information will deprive the patient of their last opportunity to "make the necessary physical and spiritual preparations to set their affairs in order before death."

From this summary of Song's views, it is clear that the position taken by the Chinese physician on the sanctions surrounding nondisclosure is far less paternalistic than that expressed by the nineteenth-century American Code. In the case of Song, the Western norm of nondisclosure was significantly modified as a result of the influence of Chinese moral and medical ethics traditions (including Confucianism and Confucian medical ethics). Yet, while he cited the teachings of Confucius on the importance of truthfulness and mutual trust, it is unclear whether Song himself consciously appropriated this cultural and medical heritage that lay at his doorstep—the long tradition of medical truth-telling practiced by the medical sages and celebrated physicians of China.

Another significant point of difference between Song's position and the American and British codes relates to the role of the family. By delegating the task of breaking bad news to family members or friends of the patient, and stressing the necessity of discussing the patient's condition and outlook with the relatives, the Western codes display a stronger familism—or lay a greater emphasis on family autonomy, in today's terms—than the Chinese document. For Song, it is not imperative for relatives to be involved in this way. He said only: "In order to prevent patients from experiencing avoidable panic, the physician may (*keyi*) disclose the truth to the relatives." However, Song immediately retreated even from this moderate stance, stating that the relatives should not be informed if the physician suspects that they cannot keep a confidence (Ibid, 30). While elsewhere he suggests that the physician inform the family if the patient has an incurable illness, it comes with the proviso that, being so advised, the physician should be paid for his services whether or not the patient dies (Ibid, 115). In yet another place, Song stipulates that "in every case the physician *should* inform the patient and the family of the prognosis" (Ibid, 112)—but here the context is a discussion of the methods by which the physician can avoid liability.

Pointing to possible Western influence on the development of medical nondisclosure in China is not to say that contemporary Chinese practice is merely aping the West, and is thus not culturally authentic. In the same way, acknowledging the obvious Western origins of Chinese socialism does not mean that Chinese socialist practice is not genuinely Chinese. There are cultural roots for the norm of nondisclosure in China—the duty to help and not to harm the patient—just as there is Chinese soil for the development of socialism—such as the pursuit of equality in social and economic life. The point—one too often ignored in debating cross-cultural matters—is that no culture has ever been homogenous, static, and immune from foreign influences. The various cultures that go to make up "Chinese culture," as in all other human societies, contain many elements drawn from foreign sources—near and far, East and West, South and North. Another point—almost a cliché—is that, like people in any other society, Chinese have never passively accepted whatever has been borrowed and imported from other cultures, but have consistently transformed it into something new.

There are now many signs suggesting that, partly due to the influence of contemporary Western practice, a historic change from medical nondisclosure to direct disclosure is occurring in China. This transformation in attitudes, however, should not be treated as a slavish following of the Western model. It is, to a large degree, a return—albeit an unintentional one—to the long-forgotten Chinese tradition of open and direct medical disclosure, a tradition which is rarely referred to in the current Chinese debate on the subject, whether in the academy or the public square.

The mendacious Oriental vs. the truthful Occidental

The historical evidence presented here has, I trust, refuted the widespread notion of a clear-cut cultural contrast between China and the West regarding the communication of an unfavorable medical prognosis—a simple opposition of nondisclosure or indirect disclosure vs. direct disclosure. The cultural realities of both China and the West are far more complex than any stereotyped image can portray. The question now is: Why are so many intelligent people inside and outside China so ready to subscribe to such a groundless dichotomy?

The reason lies not merely in the unavailability of the historical data, especially material relating to China. While further historical studies are needed to recover the long-neglected Chinese tradition, our knowledge of direct disclosure as a new phenomenon in the West and the practice of the ancient Chinese sages is comparatively straightforward. Rather, the explanation for the persistence of the unambiguous image of medical truth-telling in the West vs. its total absence in China lies in a pervasive habit of thought about Eastern and Western cultures—dichotomizing them as "radical others" (see Chapters 1 and 2 for the discussion on the fallacy of dichotomization). Given this dichotomizing habit of thought, nondisclosure or hiding the truth about terminal illness has naturally enough been portrayed as the representative "Chinese way," whether in relation to the past, present or future. By the same token, direct disclosure is identified as the standard "Western norm." This perceived cultural opposition is believed to hold true not only for the present, but also for the past. Consequently, as I have demonstrated above, the complexity of the various Chinese and Western approaches to truth-telling and the diverse medical ethics that underlie them, especially the richness of the Chinese tradition, has never been adequately acknowledged.

This penchant for dichotomizing has deeper roots. The characterization of China as a place where open and direct disclosure about terminal illness is culturally alien is merely a contemporary version of a much older Western stereotype—or simple prejudice—that regards "untruthfulness" as an essential attribute of the Chinese or Oriental character. As we saw in Chapter 1, for the social and literary critic Edward Said (1994 [1979]), the ontological and epistemological distinction between "the Orient" and "the Occident" provides the intellectual foundation for the entire discourse of Orientalism as a style of thought, and for the geopolitical and cultural hegemony resulting from it. One of the main examples Said used to illustrate Oriental ways of knowing is the work of Evelyn Baring, Lord Cromer, the well-known nineteenth-century British colonial administrator in Egypt. In his book *Modern Egypt*, Cromer asserted that "[w]ant of accuracy, which easily degenerates into untruthfulness, is, in fact, the main characteristic of the Oriental mind." He continued:

> The European is a close reasoner; his statements of fact are devoid of ambiguity; he is a natural logician, albeit he may not have studied logic; he loves symmetry in all things; he is by nature sceptical and requires proof before he can accept the truth of any proposition; his trained intelligence works like a piece of mechanism. The mind of the Oriental, on the other hand, like his picturesque streets, is eminently wanting in symmetry. His reasoning is of the most slip-shod description.
> (cited in Ibid, 38)

"[T]he Oriental generally acts, speaks, and thinks in a manner *exactly opposite* to the European." (Ibid 39; emphasis added) According to Said, Cromer believed that "Orientals are inveterate liars, they are 'lethargic and suspicious,' and in everything oppose the clarity, directness, and nobility of the Anglo-Saxon race." And again: "any deviation from what were considered the norms of Oriental behavior was believed to be unnatural." (Ibid, 38)

In the discourse of Orientalism, China offers another salient illustration of the fundamental "untruthfulness" of the Oriental mind. Written by Arthur Smith, an American missionary who with his wife lived in a north Chinese village for several decades in the late nineteenth century, *Chinese Characteristics* was one of the most widely read Western works on China. Originally serialized in a Shanghai newspaper, its various Chinese-language versions, including editions published in the 1990s and 2000s, have attracted a large Chinese readership and fueled a significant debate about the national characteristics of the Chinese people (*guomin xin*). *Chinese Characteristics* includes chapters with titles such as "Face," "The disregard of accuracy," "The talent for misunderstanding,"

"Intellectual turbidity," "The absence of nerves," "Conservatism," "The absence of sympathy," and predictably, "The absence of sincerity."

Mendacity was believed to be institutionalized in Chinese life. According to an Austrian scholar favorably cited by Smith, one of "the surprisingly contradictory elements which make up the character of the Chinese as a people … contrasts their strict truthfulness in recording historical events and their earnestness in the search for correct knowledge, whenever statistical facts are concerned, with that absolute and generally sanctioned license in lying and dissimulation which prevails everywhere in China, in popular intercourse and in diplomatic negotiations." (Smith 2002 [1894], 268) For Smith, "the standard of the Chinese and the present standard of Western nations as to what ought to be called sincerity differ widely." (267) While there are social evils common to China and the West, it is of "the utmost importance clearly to perceive the points of essential contrast," One of them is the Chinese trait of insincerity. "Much of the incomprehensibility of the Chinese, so far as foreigners are concerned, is due to their insincerity." (273) Smith had a great deal to say on this subject:

> It is of course impossible to prove that every Chinese will lie, and we have no wish to do so if it were possible. (270)
>
> The ordinary speech of the Chinese is so full of insincerity, which yet does not rise to the dignity of falsehood, that it is very difficult to learn the truth in almost any case. In China it is literally true that a fact is the hardest thing in the world to get. One never feels sure that he has been told the whole of anything. (271)
>
> We by no means intend to affirm such a proposition as that there is no honesty to be found in China, but only that, so far as our experience and observation go, it is literally impossible to be sure of finding it anywhere. How can it be otherwise with a people who have so little regard for truth? (281)
>
> The needs of China, let us repeat, are few. They are only Character and Conscience. Nay, they are but one, for Conscience *is* Character. It was said of a famous maker of pianos that he was "like his own instrument—square, upright, and grand." Does one ever meet any such characters in China? (320)

Smith also tried to frame his thesis in positive terms:

> There is wealth enough in China to develop the resources of the Empire, if there were but the confidence, without which timid capital will not emerge from its hiding-place. There is learning enough in China for all its needs. There is no lack of talent of every description. But without mutual confidence, based upon real sincerity of purpose, all these are insufficient for the regeneration of the Empire. (285)

After citing the Victorian cultural critic Matthew Arnold, Smith ended his book with the hope that China would experience a spiritual transformation:

> What China needs is righteousness, and in order to attain it, it is absolutely necessary that she has a knowledge of God and a new conception of man, as well as of the relation of man to God. She needs a new life in every individual soul, in the family, and in society. The manifold needs of China we find, then, to be a single imperative need. It will be met permanently, completely, only by Christian civilization. (330)

In one way or another, cross-cultural bioethics is still in the shadow of Orientalism and has not sufficiently distanced itself from its insidious spell. The fact that, in contemporary China, medical professionals routinely conceal the truth about terminal illness would offer Smith one more piece of "evidence" of the absence of sincerity and truthfulness in China. Certainly, those who subscribe to the notion of a thoroughgoing cultural dichotomy over medical disclosure have a much more positive attitude to Chinese people and cultures. Indeed, they have been at pains to defend the "authentic Chinese way," a way perceived to be radically different from that of the West. But however well-intentioned and even apparently innocent such efforts may be, the old stereotypes and prejudices can very easily infiltrate our cross-cultural discussions—even those conducted in the rarefied intellectual atmosphere of the academy. Old stereotypes, as always, die hard.

Conclusions

In his *History of the Peloponnesian War* (Book I. 19), Thucydides, the great ancient Greek historian and an insightful observer of human nature, noted that a great many unfounded ideas were circulating among his fellow Hellenes, "even on matters of contemporary history which have not been obscured by time." He added that human beings were very prone to accepting the traditions of their own country, "without applying any critical test whatever."

In this chapter I have identified a widely assumed but unfounded idea—that honest and direct disclosure in medical matters is a Western value and one that is culturally alien to China. The historical evidence I have adduced, however, tells a very different story. Medical truth-telling is far from a Western invention; it has a history of at least twenty-six centuries in China. The norm of direct and truthful disclosure is at least as Chinese—as culturally authentic and representative—as the norm of nondisclosure or indirect disclosure as widely practiced today. In fact, taking into account Western influence in the development of the norm of secrecy and lying to the sick and dying in China, claims about the cultural authenticity of non-disclosure as the Chinese norm become very problematic, to say the least. It is totally false to treat the standard practice of medical nondisclosure in contemporary China as an intrinsic part of the logical development of traditional Chinese culture and medical morality.

In challenging the historical validity and cultural authenticity of this practice, in this chapter I have also sought to expose some serious problems associated with the pervasive and popular mental habits involved in characterizing, and often oversimplifying, cultural differences—especially those responsible for dichotomizing Chinese and Western cultures as "radical others" and also for regarding the current mainstream practice or official position as the characteristic norm of the culture concerned (see Chapter 2). On both the intellectual and social levels, the old prejudice of the untruthful Orient vs. the truthful Occident can be seen as providing the groundwork for the emergence and spread of this unfounded dichotomy.

Some important general lessons for enhanced cross-cultural understanding can be drawn from this (albeit sketchy) comparative historical study of medical truth-telling in China and the West. As in this case, Chinese and Western cultural differences in bioethics and other areas are far more complicated than they appear on the surface. Rather than uncritically accepting ready-made, if apparently plausible, generalizations, we must investigate apparent differences and similarities with care. A more adequate cross-cultural medical ethics must first of all avoid these common intellectual pitfalls, be alert for disguised prejudices and pay serious attention to the fascinating complexity of cultural differences.

In this chapter, I have compared the long Chinese tradition of medical truth-telling to contemporary practice. In so doing, I am keen to avoid commiting a widespread sin in Chinese culture—the vice of claiming that whatever is new and foreign was already known in ancient China (*guoyi youzhi*) (cf. the wisdom of Ecclesiastes, that there is "nothing new under the sun"). There are significant differences between the old tradition and the contemporary norm. One obvious feature which informs the broad sociopolitical context of the contemporary discourse of medical truth-telling—patients' rights as an aspect of civil and human rights—was unknown in China until recently. This is not to say of course that the language of human rights, including the right of informed consent, patients' rights and women's rights, is culturally incompatible and thus inapplicable to China (see Chapters 7, 8 and 9).

In addition, in many countries the values of truthfulness and informed consent in contemporary medical practice rest on the foundation provided by national medical ethics and legal documents as well as a variety of international declarations on matters relating to bioethics. We should not assume that any firm principles regarding truth-telling about terminal illness were explicitly formulated in the literature of traditional Chinese medical ethics. To some degree, the kind of disclosure known in the Chinese tradition was not so much a deliberate professional requirement as a custom honored by practitioners. Furthermore, while in general traditional Chinese medical ethics, following

Confucianism, underscores *cheng* as a primary value (see Chapter 8), in traditional Chinese medicine it is nevertheless ethically acceptable in certain cases for physicians to practice deception—assuming that this is in the best interests of the patient. In fact, there has never been an indigenous moral tradition in China which advocates truth and truthfulness as an absolute value and treats lying or evasion as an absolute wrong, as some Western theologians and philosophers have argued. However, these caveats regarding this venerable Chinese tradition and its cultural context are by no means intended to undermine its remarkable character and worth, especially when viewed from a Chinese-Western comparative perspective.

The Chinese tradition of medical truth-telling, pioneered by the ancient sages, is returning in China today. In the next chapter, I critically examine the normative dimensions of what can be called "the cultural differences" argument against open and direct disclosure in the Chinese context. I argue that, even if medical truth-telling were culturally alien to China as is often assumed, there are significant ethical imperatives to reform the current dominant practice of concealing crucial medical information from terminally ill patients. In addition, the Confucian moral outlook mandates truth-telling as a basic ethical principle and a cardinal social virtue which physicians ought to take as their guiding star.

Chapter 7

The "cultural differences" argument and its misconceptions

The return of medical truth-telling in China

In bioethics and politics today, in the West and China, cultural differences have often been presented as an ethical justification for rejecting those norms perceived as originating in the West and strongly advocated there—such as truth-telling by medical professionals, informed consent, patients' rights, women's rights and human rights in general. It has been argued and believed that such values are inapplicable and thus irrelevant to non-Western societies and cultures.

In this chapter, I will critically examine the "cultural differences" argument as it has been formulated against medical truth-telling in the Chinese context. I will demonstrate that, despite its popularity and apparent plausibility, the argument is seriously flawed both descriptively and normatively. Through comparisons between China and the West and supported by extensive primary Chinese materials, in the last chapter I have shown that direct disclosure is far from culturally alien to China and that, on the contrary, there was a long, though forgotten, tradition of medical truth-telling in China. Here, I argue that, even if medical truth-telling were culturally alien to China, as is usually assumed, ethical imperatives exist to reform the contemporary mainstream Chinese practice of nondisclosure or indirect disclosure through family members. The results of surveys conducted throughout China indicate that the great majority of Chinese patients want to know about their medical conditions, even with terminal cases. Moreover, I will offer a Confucian defense of truth-telling as a fundamental ethical principle and a cardinal personal and social virtue which physicians would do well to take seriously. In the process, I will expose some common intellectual flaws in the "cultural differences" argument—such as the fallacy of dichotomizing and distorting cultural differences, obscuring the real ethical issues at stake, and promoting the tyranny of existing cultural practices.

The "cultural differences" argument

As we saw in the previous chapter, it is well known in contemporary China (including Hong Kong and Taiwan) that medical professionals customarily withhold from patients crucial information about terminal illnesses such as cancer. This Chinese practice is in sharp contrast to that seen in most Western countries where, in a wider cultural context of respect for patients' rights and individual autonomy, truthfulness and informed consent constitute an essential, often legally required, element of good medical practice.

The practice of nondisclosure is not restricted to China. Nondisclosure or indirect disclosure through family members is the mainstream practice in other Asian countries such as Japan and Nepal, as well as in other parts of the world such as the Middle East and eastern and southern Europe (e.g. Surbone 1992; Mitsuya 1997; Gongal et al. 2006; Mobeireek et al. 2008). In different countries or within different ethnic groups within the same country, patients suffering from cancers and other terminal illnesses receive very different levels of information about their diagnosis, prognosis, and therapeutic options (e.g. Macklin 1999; Mitchell 1998; Mystakidou et al. 2004; Tuckett 2004; Jotkowitz, Click and Gezundheit 2006; Hancock et al. 2007; Surbone 2006, 2008).

According to one recent investigator, although "there is a shift in truth-telling attitudes and practice toward greater disclosure of diagnosis to cancer patients worldwide ... partial and nondisclosure is still common in many cultures that are centered on family and community values" (Surbone 2008, 237). It is remarkable that such a striking cultural difference is still prevalent in the twenty-first century. As the title of an editorial by an Italian physician in the journal *Support Care Cancer* characterizes the situation, there is a "persisting difference in truth telling throughout the world" (Surbone 2004).

It is from acknowledging the existence of this cultural divide that the "cultural differences" approach—cited in opposition to medical truth-telling in non-Western societies like China—has taken root. Two Chinese medical ethicists put the issue succinctly: "In contrast [to the West], Chinese medical ethics, even today, in theory and in practice remains committed to hiding the truth as well as to lying when necessary to achieve the family's view of the best interests of the patient" (Fan and Li 2004, 180). Moreover, direct truth-telling—the so-called "Western individualistic mode"—is defined as culturally alien to China and therefore morally flawed because it violates so-called "Chinese familial values."

In Japan, similar arguments have been put forward to reject Western-style medical truth-telling and replace it by a family-centered Japanese style of informed consent. A major rationale behind the distinction holds that the construal of the self in Japanese and Western culture is to be defined as "interdependent vs. independent" respectively, or, to put it another way, in terms of the family vs. the individual (Akabayashi and Slingsby 2006).

The cultural differences argument against medical truth-telling can take a number of different forms. In the Chinese context, one common argument, phrased in the form of a syllogism, goes like this:

> *Major premise*: Different cultural norms and practices ought to be respected and maintained;
> *Minor premise*: In contrast to the Western practice of direct disclosure regarding terminal illness, the cultural norm in China is nondisclosure or indirect disclosure through family members;
> *Conclusion*: Therefore, medical professionals should refrain from telling Chinese patients the truth about their terminal illness.

A more sophistic version of the argument goes thus:

> *First premise*: Different cultural norms and practices ought to be respected and maintained;
> *Second premise*: Chinese and Western cultures are fundamentally and radically different from each other;
> *Third premise*: Truth-telling is the Western cultural norm and is founded on individualistic Western culture;
> *Fourth premise*: Nondisclosure or indirect disclosure through family members is the Chinese cultural norm and is founded on family-oriented Chinese culture;
> *Conclusion*: Therefore, nondisclosure or indirect disclosure through family members should be maintained and the practice of medical truth-telling rejected in China.

Whatever form it takes, the cultural differences argument consists of two core claims—one descriptive and the other normative. The empirical or descriptive claim generalizes secrecy and lying to the sick and dying as the representative and authentic cultural norm for Chinese. The normative claim insists the practice of nondisclosure should be maintained in order to respect perceived cultural differences. The descriptive claim is more widely held than the normative one: those who subscribe to the normative claim always found their position on the descriptive claim. Yet, those who accept the descriptive claim do not necessarily agree with the normative claim; they are thus free to take an ethical position against nondisclosure or indirect disclosure.

The current debate in China

Defying its stereotype as a monolithic, changeless nation or (in the famous metaphor of Napoleon) a "sleeping lion," China has always been in a state of flux. In the past three or so decades—a period designated by the Chinese authorities as one of "reform and openness"—the enormous social and economic transformations undergone by China have had a profound impact on both China and the world. On the medical front, the patient–physician relationship, including the handling of medical information relating to incurable and terminal diseases, has undergone a comparable "revolution." In the 1980s when I was a medical student and intern in China, it was standard practice that patients were never told directly about their terminal illness. We were instructed to conceal such a diagnosis and even lie to the sick and dying—for instance, not to write the Chinese character for cancer, *ai*, on the patient's card, but the English abbreviation *Ca*. This cloak of secrecy surrounding the terminally ill was (and still is) referred to by a special quasi-medical term—"protective medical treatment" (*baohuxing yiliao*).

Since the 1990s and especially the early 2000s, however, the practice of withholding crucial medical information has been challenged by patients, medical professionals, and the general public. An historic change is happening in China, a shift from secrecy and lying toward honest and direct disclosure. In 2008, thirteen hospitals throughout China and the premier Chinese journal *Medicine and Philosophy* jointly issued a series of documents on informed consent (*Yixue Yu Zhexu* 2008, 1–12). One of them is entitled "Guiding Principles on Truth-telling to and Consent from Cancer Patients." The underlying ethical concern of these guidelines is to minimize the harm and maximize the benefits to patients. While it promotes only partial disclosure and insists on the necessity of "appropriate concealment of the truth" (ibid, 7–8), this document indicates that the Chinese debate on the issue has subtly shifted from *whether* patients should be told about their condition to *when* and *how* they should be best informed.

In many ways, the Chinese debate closely resembles the Western debate of the 1960s and 1970s. As a matter of course, advocates of honest and direct disclosure take up the language of rights—the right of the patient to know and decide. They also call attention to the damage done by secrecy and concealing the truth from patients, as well as the benefits of honest communication for both patients and physicians. On the other side of the debate, defenders of nondisclosure, especially medical professionals and family members, emphasize the duty to protect patients and, at least, to avoid doing harm. It is assumed that the communication of complex and negative medical information is bad for patients' morale, if not beyond their intelligence. It has often been asserted—not only in the mass media but also in the medical and academic literature—that telling the truth about terminal illness frightens and depresses patients, deprives them of hope, and may even shorten their lives. It has been alleged that young women are more vulnerable than other groups and are more likely to commit suicide after learning of a negative prognosis.

The Chinese debate differs in one salient area from that conducted in the West several decades ago: the issue of cultural differences. A common argument invoked to oppose medical truth-telling in China lies in the appeal to cultural differences, in particular to Chinese values and cultural context. Indeed, the invoking of the cultural argument raises a number of questions regarding the current Chinese trend to honest and open disclosure. Is this new development merely an aping of the contemporary Western norm? Is it a consequence of Western cultural hegemony or even of bioethical imperialism? More fundamentally, is this current shift in attitudes merely a change of fashion or is it based on sound moral foundations? If the cultural differences argument against medical truth-telling in China is valid, then current Chinese efforts to reform the still widespread practice of secrecy and lying to the sick and dying are heading in the wrong direction.

But, however we look at it, the argument is seriously flawed. In what follows, I reveal and discuss a number of empirical and normative problems with this argument, however appealing it may be on the surface.

Chinese patients want to know the truth

Sociologically, the cultural differences view has assumed that Chinese patients are not only kept in ignorance of their condition, but even prefer things this way. However, in total contrast to this assumption, the great majority of Chinese people, like Westerners, want to know the truth about their medical condition if suffering from serious illness.

In a telephone survey of 2,674 Chinese households conducted in Hong Kong in 1995, 95% of 1,138 interviewees aged between 18 and 65 indicated that they would prefer knowing their medical diagnosis, even if the outlook was grave. The same proportion said they would object if their family only was informed, while they themselves were not told. And 97% of respondents would want to know their prognosis. The researchers concluded that the patterns of preference shown by Chinese people in Hong Kong were "very similar to those reported in studies on Western populations" (Fielding and Hung 1996). Taiwanese cancer patients also expressed a strong preference for medical professionals to tell them the truth, even before informing relatives (Tang and Lee 2004).

The same is true of mainland Chinese. In the early 2000s, speaking to a class of about 60 students, mostly postgraduates, in one of the leading ethics programs in China (in Hunan Normal University located in Changsha, a central southern Chinese city), I asked if they would like to know the truth if they were diagnosed with a terminal illness. A large majority responded "yes" (about 50), and only a handful said "no."

Many extensive surveys conducted throughout mainland China—despite some deficiencies in sample selections and research design—clearly indicate the preference of the great (or even overwhelming) majority of Chinese patients suffering from terminal illness to be fully apprised of the medical facts about their condition. A survey of 311 cancer patients in Guangzhou in southeast China found that 72.99% believed that patients should be fully informed; 24.12% responded that the decision should depend on the wishes of the patients themselves; and only 2.89% thought that patients should not be told about their cancer diagnosis (Huang, Wang, Zhang, Lü and Li 2001). In a survey conducted in Shenyang, northeast China, involving 198 hospitalized elderly cancer patients and 312 family members, 94% of patients and 82.7% of family members considered it essential for the truth to be told about their terminal illness, and 97% of patients and 90.4% of family members believed that the sharing of accurate medical information would improve treatment outcomes (Gao, Zou and Yang 2006). Another survey of 302 cancer patients in Wuhan, central south China, concluded that, in general, cancer patients are very keen to know the truth about their illness and that the practice of "protective treatment" had resulted in distrust of medical professionals and increased concerns about the seriousness of their condition (Zeng, Zhou, Hong, Xiang, and Fang 2008).

Despite these findings, the cultural differences view is painfully accurate on one point—in China, most medical professionals are unwilling to inform patients truthfully. Significantly, however, when asked whether or not they would like to learn the truth if diagnosed with terminal illness, the great majority of medical professionals would want to know. A survey conducted in 2004 among 180 nurses in Shandong in northeast coastal China showed that, when imagining themselves as patients, they would prefer to be informed even though, as medical professionals, they would hesitate to tell the truth to their own patients (Zhu 2005, 73). When the nurses were asked to put themselves in their patients' shoes, the overwhelming majority of them, 92.6%, preferred to know the diagnosis and prognosis of severe and terminal illness. However, when asked whether they as nurses should inform their patients about *their* adverse medical conditions, 71.6% said that they would withhold the truth. When asked to imagine themselves as patients' family members, only 2.5% would speak directly and immediately, 69.1% would choose to tell the truth after prevaricating for a time, and 28.4% would not disclose the condition in any circumstances (Ibid). A survey of 634 doctors and nurses, conducted in Wuhan, again illustrates the reluctance of medical professionals to speak candidly about cancer; patients' awareness that they have insufficient knowledge about their medical condition; and the tendency to let family members, rather than patients, make important decisions (Zeng, Li, Chen, and Fang 2007).

However, there are signs that the attitudes of mainland Chinese medical professionals are changing. Some hospitals in China have formulated policies designed to foster open and direct communication about terminal illness. As mentioned above, in 2008, thirteen hospitals throughout China joined forces with the premier Chinese journal *Medicine and Philosophy* to issue a series of documents on medical truth-telling and informed consent (*Yixue Yu Zhexu* 2008, 1–12). In 2009, lecturing to a class of 50 medical students at Peking University Health Science Centre, a leading medical school in China located in Beijing, I asked the class whether they would tell patients about their diagnosis and prognosis of terminal illness. The great majority answered "yes" by raising their hands.

The cultural differences argument is also painfully right about the reluctance of family members to tell the truth to their terminally ill relatives.

As with the medical professionals, the great majority would want to know the truth if they had themselves been diagnosed with a terminal illness. Survey results confirm the disparity between patients' wishes on the one hand and the reluctance of family members on the other. In a survey of 175 patients and 238 family members visiting a hospital clinic in Beijing (He, Wang, Tian, Zhou and Wang 2009), 42% of patients wanted to be told immediately after a diagnosis of cancer was confirmed, 31.4% wanted both patients and family members to be told together, and 26.3% preferred that only family members be informed. However, only 2.1% of family members wanted the diagnosis to be communicated directly to the patient—although 16.4% wanted both patients and family members to be told. The contrasts in this survey are stark: whereas nearly three quarters of patients wanted to be informed, either alone or with family members, more than three quarters of family members preferred that doctors inform them alone. In another survey of 194 family members of recently diagnosed and hospitalized cancer patients, 57.7% disagreed and 42.3% agreed that patients should be told (Sun, Li, Sun and Chang 2007). A further survey of 382 patients and 482 relatives in Chengdu, southwestern China, indicates that cancer patients were more likely than family members to believe that patients should be informed (early stage, 90.8% vs. 69.9%; terminal stage, 60.5% vs. 34.4%) and that most participants preferred being told immediately after the diagnosis (Jiang, Liu and Li et al. 2007).

These empirical studies reveal a radical level of disagreement between patients on the one hand and medical professionals and family members on the other. One ethical question that arises from this disagreement is—what should be done when patients want to know about their condition but medical professionals and relatives prefer to withhold information and even lie to them? Advocates of the cultural differences argument would insist that the family should be the ones to decide whether the truth should be told to the patient. But, as I argue below, this alleged Chinese or Asian "familist" approach to medical truth-telling is not ethically sound. Furthermore, although it appears to be culturally sensitive, it is in reality disrespectful of the fundamental moral norms and values of the cultures it seeks to privilege.

The harm done by secrecy and untruthfulness

As Tolstoy's *The Death of Ivan Ilyich* and Solzhenitsyn's *Cancer Ward* so vividly illustrate, patients can often sense the seriousness of their illness even though both medical professionals and relatives strive to keep the truth from them. My own experience as an intern at a Chinese county hospital in the 1980s confirms the reality of this instinctive awareness of their condition by patients. In fact, a major practical difficulty of hiding the truth in these circumstances is that it is almost impossible to carry out successfully. Humans communicate with each other not only through language, but also through their social context, body language, and by many other means. The specialized wards and hospitals in which patients find themselves, and the gestures of medical professionals, relatives and friends can easily reveal the truth, despite all efforts to hide it. For the patients concerned, whatever others may tell them, the secrecy surrounding their treatment reveals a truth of paramount importance—their illness is serious.

Even if it were feasible to hide the truth from patients, the practice of nondisclosure—the norm in China today—should be reversed because it is harmful to patients. On the one hand, the advocates of nondisclosure have offered no compelling evidence of its benefits for patients or their families. On the other hand, they often downplay or ignore the enormous harm that the practice of nondisclosure and evasion has caused to patients, families, the medical profession, and society at large. In addition to dismissing patients' wish to know, the practice of nondisclosure increases the feelings of abandonment of those suffering from terminal illness and undermines the bonds of social trust, in particular those between patients and medical professionals.

For the cultural differences argument, the ethical rationale for disclosure turns on the question of individual rights and personal autonomy. The norm of medical truth-telling is thus not applicable to those societies and cultures where the language of individual rights and autonomy is largely absent. It is true that, politically, the shift from nondisclosure to disclosure that occurred in most Western countries around the 1970s had a great deal to do with the patients' rights movement. And, in bioethics, disclosure and informed consent are often theoretically justified out of respect for the patient's autonomy, a leading principle in the discipline. However, it is a mistake to regard the ethical rationale for direct disclosure as wholly based on the notions of individual rights and autonomy. There are other significant ethical reasons for direct disclosure—for instance, the principle of beneficence, a fundamental value for almost every healing system and medical ethics tradition worldwide.

Although often overlooked in cross-cultural discussions of truth-telling and informed consent, a major factor in the historical shift toward disclosure in the West was the practical necessity for effective (but not overly aggressive) therapeutic intervention. Jay Katz's *The Silent World of Doctor and Patient* (2002), a classic of bioethics, has highlighted this crucial point. The practice of truth-telling and informed consent is grounded not only in the principle of autonomy or self-determination, but also in good therapeutic management in face of the problem of uncertainty in medicine and the new challenges that have arisen in caring for seriously ill and dying patients. Nondisclosure and untruthfulness are not ethically justifiable because "[t]he iatrogenic deprivation of information makes a powerful contribution to patients' sense of abandonment." (Ibid, 212)

> Doctors' ready retreat behind silence—apparent to patients by doctors' demeanor when they keep most of their thoughts to themselves, deprive

patients of vital information, or pat patients on the back and assure them that everything will be all right and they need not worry—makes patients feel disregarded, ignored, patronized, and dismissed.

(Ibid, 209–10)

In the words of two other commentators, "Tacitly to impose silence, denial, deception, and isolation upon the dying patient may itself cause suffering and bring about bereavement of the dying, a state of premortem loneliness, emotional abandonment, and withdrawn interest" (cited in Katz 2002: 222). The practice of nondisclosure thus serves medical professionals' interests more than those of patients. Disclosure and informed consent, on the other hand, "seek to protect patients from the ravages and pain of abandonment" (Ibid, 208).

In the late nineteenth century, Tolstoy imaginatively rendered the detrimental effects of lying to the patient with terminal illness:

> Ivan Ilyich suffered most of all from the lie, the lie, for some reason, everyone accepted, that he was not dying but was simply ill, and that if he stayed calm and underwent treatment he could expect good results. Yet he knew that regardless of what was done, all he could expect was more agonizing suffering and death. And he was tortured by this lie, tortured by the fact that they refused to acknowledge what he and everyone else knew, that they wanted to lie about his horrible condition and to force him to become a part of that lie. This lie, a lie perpetrated on the eve of his death, a lie that was bound to degrade the awesome, solemn act of his dying to the level of their social calls, their draperies, and the sturgeon they ate for dinner, was an excruciating torture for Ivan Ilyich. And, oddly enough, many times when they were going through their acts with him he came within a hairbreadth of shouting: "Stop your lying! You and I know that I'm dying, so at least stop lying!"
>
> (Tolstoy 1986: 102–3)

Acknowledging to patients the seriousness of their medical condition may not be caring or healing in itself (although one could argue that it is), but it is at least the starting point for any good caring and healing regime. Medical professionals and other caregivers may lack the power to truly relieve the suffering of gravely ill and dying patients, but, as Ivan Ilyich urged, they can "at least stop lying."

Those who defend the practice of nondisclosure in China may argue that Chinese patients do not feel the abandonment, loneliness and agony that Ivan Ilyich or Western patients' experience when deprived of critical medical information. But, unless convincing empirical evidence is provided for this imagined cultural difference, one must assume that Chinese patients do not differ radically from their counterparts in the West in this regard.

The major concern in contemporary China, as in the West a few decades ago, is that open and direct disclosure may harm patients. Yet, in Western countries where medical truth-telling has now become firmly established it has been proven that concerns over the presumed psychological and physical harms to patients are in most cases unfounded. And it need hardly be said that such paternalistic attitudes seriously underestimate the intelligence, resilience and resolve of patients suffering from terminal illness in dealing with the realities of death and dying.

Lying has a further serious detrimental effect—the harm done to the patient–physician relationship. Social trust is the foundation of any good communal life. Lying to patients undermines their trust in medical professionals, just as lying in public life does lethal damage to the sustaining and nourishing of social trust. So nondisclosure and untruthfulness can hardly be justified by an appeal to either "individualistic" or "communitarian" values.

The question of family

As we have seen, a key element of the cultural differences view that defends the Chinese practice of nondisclosure stems from a highly legitimate and important concern—the interests and integrity of the family. However, a number of the assumptions and assertions involved in defending this concern are empirically problematic and ethically misleading. Although detailed discussion of the role of the family in bioethics from a Chinese-Western comparative perspective needs much more space, I wish to at least raise a few questions on the subject here (for a discussion on the widespread Chinese practice of family consent, see Chapter 8).

Firstly, the argument from the family assumes that the practice of nondisclosure or indirect disclosure is more beneficial to family members than that of direct disclosure. However, there is no empirical evidence to support this. Secrecy and lying can be very harmful to family relationships—a situation vividly portrayed, once again, in Tolstoy's *Death of Ivan Ilyich*. On the contrary, a strong case can be made that direct disclosure will better serve the interests of the families affected, and family values in general, than nondisclosure and deceit.

Drawing on the classic work of Sissela Bok (1989 [1978]), who condemns deception in public life, including lying to dying patients, as both ethically unjustifiable and practically harmful, some Western scholars have challenged the "cultural difference" view of truth-telling to the sick and dying in the Chinese context (e.g. Wear 2007). Still, we are warned to "studiously avoid presuming to take a firm stand" on lobbying for truth-telling as a general rule in Chinese society because the available data allegedly do not give a clear picture on two crucial points at the heart of the ethical dilemma: what Chinese patients typically want, and whether medical truth-telling will undermine the traditional Chinese family (Ibid).

However, as discussed above, we do have reliable data on the preference of the majority of Chinese to know the truth about terminal illness. As for the relationship between truth-telling and the family, the practice of direct disclosure in the West over the past several decades suggests that disclosure in itself does not necessarily harm the family as a social institution or as a locus of moral value. Truth-telling can empower family members to better support dying patients, attend to the needs and wellbeing of their loved ones, and diminish the feelings of abandonment and loneliness experienced by their suffering relative. In such difficult times when, as a Chinese saying expresses it, the whole family suffers if a single member is in pain (*yiren xiangyu, mandang bule*), truth-telling can strengthen, rather than weaken, the bonds of love and interdependence among family members.

Secondly, based on the popular dichotomy of China and the West as "radical others," the cultural differences argument posits a cross-cultural distinction, asserting that the family is central or even unique in Chinese culture but not so in the West. Those who would make this assertion are very selective and arbitrary in their choice of cultural traditions. Several major Chinese schools of thought and socio-political movements such as Daoism, Moism, the New Culture Movement in the early twentieth century and Chinese socialism— both in its ideology and its political-economic system—have all challenged the primacy of the family. At the same time, the essential role of the family in Western civilization (e.g., in Judeo-Christian tradition) as well as in Western bioethics has very often been downplayed and even dismissed. The truth is that, both as an essential social institution and a cardinal moral value, the family has always been a vital element of any society or culture, whether in the East or West. In the area of palliative care in Western countries, the family plays an essential, active and important role.

Thirdly, the practice of nondisclosure in China has been attributed to the value placed by Confucianism on the primacy of the family. Yet, as I showed in the previous chapter, the well-established Chinese tradition of open and direct disclosure on medical matters was endorsed by one of the key Confucian moral ideals, that of *cheng* (truthfulness or sincerity). In addition, it was in response to the essential Confucian ethical notion of *xin* (faithfulness, honesty or trustworthiness) that in the first modern Chinese statement on nondisclosure Song Guobin, a Chinese physician trained in modern Western biomedicine, distanced himself from the older Western-style model with its overt paternalism. It is now time to consider the Confucian understanding of truthfulness and its implications for how medical professionals should deal with the diagnosis and prognosis of terminal illness.

The Confucian morality of truthfulness

For Confucianism, the highest moral ideals or principles are *ren* (humanity, humaneness), *yi* (righteousness) and *li* (the correct performance of rites), although scholars disagree about which has primacy (for a discussion of Confucian professional ethics of medicine, see Chapters 11 and 12). While *chengxin* (truthfulness, honesty, trustworthiness or sincerity), another virtue highly regarded in Confucianism, is often used as a single phrase in modern Chinese, in classical Chinese *cheng* and *xin* are two closely related but different concepts, especially in Confucian tradition. Confucius himself discussed *xin* frequently in the *Analects*. While it rarely appears in the *Analects*, *cheng* is a key term in Neo-Confucianism and in two other Confucian classics, *The Great Learning* and *The Doctrine of the Means*.

Influenced by the nineteenth-century stereotype of the mendacious Oriental (see Chapter 6), it has often been claimed that truthfulness was not a major concern for Confucius and Confucianism. A frequently cited example is the occasion when Confucius declined to receive a visitor by falsely claiming that he was sick. According to the *Analects* (XVII, 29), "Zû Pei [Ru Bei] wished to see Confucius, but Confucius declined, on the ground of being sick, to see him. When the bearer of this message went out at the door, (the Master) took his lute and sang to it, in order that Pei might hear him." (Legge 1971 [1893], 327) On the basis of this story, one Western observer commented: "That such laxity on the part of China's noblest Exemplar has fostered that disregard for truth for which this nation is so notorious, can hardly be denied" (cited in Waley 1992, 43). Arthur Waley tried to defend Confucius and Chinese culture by pointing out that this kind of lie is "ritually enjoined" and that its necessity is also "recognized by 'society' in Europe," although not by the Church. "In this instance a man of the world would have understood Confucius better than a clergyman has done." In general, he concluded, not all pre-modern peoples "regard telling the truth as good in itself." (Ibid)

However, the interpretation of the sage's actions as a further example of "China's notorious disregard for truth" is a gross misunderstanding of Confucius. This misreading indicates once again how easily contemporary stereotypes can contaminate our reading of classic texts, especially those from cultures foreign to us. The real issue at stake in the story was very different: How should an educator respond when an arrogant and ill-mannered young man shows a half-hearted interest in learning from him? One option was to decline on the pretense of illness, a common and acknowledged practice in ancient China for politely brushing off an unwelcome visitor. A straightforward "no" was not an option for Confucius, regardless of whether or not he personally endorsed the custom of lying about one's health. A negative answer was out of the question because the fundamental principle of Confucius's philosophy of education was "education for all without discrimination." Before he accepted Ru Bei as his student, however, he wanted the young man to become aware of the serious flaws in his character such as arrogance, bad manners and the lack of a "pure heart for learning." Because for Confucius actions spoke louder than words, by dismissing the messenger on the grounds of a feigned illness, and then immediately taking up his lute, he was delivering a message that even the rude young would-be scholar could not ignore. [Here I do not want to go into the question whether or not Confucius was indulging a kind of Liar's Paradox logicians are so fond of.] As a result, Ru Bei realized his character defects and made an effort to overcome them. Confucius went on to teach him the rituals which constitute the core of classic Confucianism.

Far from being seen as an example of deception, in the eyes of one ancient Chinese commentator, it was through this incident that the genuine truthfulness (*cheng*) of the sage was manifested (Cheng 1990 Vol. 4, 1231). If untruthfulness would be indeed one of the characteristics of Chinese people, then Confucius should not be blamed for having fostered it. A more pressing question would be to determine the intellectual and socio-cultural factors that gave rise to the gross misinterpretation of this story by Western critics.

The necessity of acquiring *xin* is a major theme in the *Analects*. According to a contemporary Chinese scholar, the term—meaning honesty, faithfulness and truthfulness—appears at least 24 times in the "Bible of China" (Yang 1980, 257). The other fundamental Confucian concepts of *ren*, *li* and *yi* appear 108, 74, and 24 times in the *Analects* respectively (Ibid, 221, 311, 291). Since the early Han Dynasty (c. the second century BCE) when Confucianism was established as the official ideology of the state, *xin* has been regarded as the fifth of the Five Cardinal Virtues (*wuchang*) of Confucianism. Confucius used the metaphor of the yoke or horse harness to illustrate the importance of honesty and truthfulness for both individuals and social life (II, 23):

> The Master said, "I do not know how a man without truthfulness is to get on. How can a large carriage be made to go without the cross-bar for yoking the oxen to, or a small carriage without the arrangement for yoking the horses?
>
> (Legge 1971 [1893], 153)

Confucius placed a very high value on *xin*, stating that "No human being can stand without truthfulness" (XII, 7) and, in *The Great Learning* (III, 3), "In communication with people, he [i.e., the truthful person] abides in faithfulness."

While the term *cheng* (sincerity, authenticity or truthfulness) is rarely mentioned in the *Analects*, it is a crucial concept in other Confucian classics and for Confucianism in general. The term embodies a complex nexus of metaphysical, ethical, psychological, and spiritual meanings, as the following quote from *The Doctrine of the Mean* (XX, 18) indicates:

> Sincerity [truthfulness] is the way of Heaven. The attainment of sincerity is the way of men. He who possesses sincerity, is he who, without an effort, hits what is right, and apprehends, without the exercise of thought;—he is the sage who naturally and easily embodies the *right* way.

He who attains to sincerity, is he who chooses what is good, and firmly holds it fast.

(Legge 1971 [1893], 413; emphasis in original)

Philosophically, this passage stands comparison with Kant's discussion of "the good will" (Kant 1996). However sophisticated the ramifications of the term may be, at the most basic level, like *xin*, *cheng* equate to a fundamental moral maxim endorsed by all human societies and ethical systems: be honest and, at the very least, do not deceive.

Despite this, different from Kant's ethics, while the ethical principle of truthfulness is essential for Confucianism, it is not an absolute. In certain situations concealing the truth is certainly an acceptable course, even a praiseworthy one. According to a story in the *Analects* (XIII, 18):

> The duke of Sheh [Ye], informed Confucius, saying, "Among us here there are those who may be styled upright [or just] in their conduct. If their father has stolen a sheep, they will bear witness to the fact".
>
> Confucius said, "Among us, in our part of the country, those who are upright are different from this. The father conceals that misconduct of the son, and the son conceals the misconduct of the father. Uprightness [or justice] is to be found in this."
>
> (Legge 1971 [1893], 270)

In one of the early dialogues of Plato, *Euthyphro*, Socrates challenged the similar belief that it is right to indict one's father for committing manslaughter. Many commentators, ancient, modern and contemporary, have debated the rationale behind the position taken by Confucius here. For the purposes of our discussion, the point is that, in striking contrast to Kant's deontological ethics, truthfulness is not an absolute value in Confucianism.

Ethical implications for medical practice

What are the implications of the Confucian morality of truthfulness and Confucius's discussion about sheep-stealing with the duke of Ye for health care and medicine? First and foremost, as a general maxim for medical practice, health care professionals should abide by truthfulness as strictly as they can, following the consensus established by traditional Chinese medical ethics over the centuries. To deceive patients for motives of personal gain is always absolutely wrong and morally corrupt. Even when delivering painful news, as in the diagnosis and prognosis of terminal illness, truthfulness should not be easily set aside and medical practitioners should practice open and direct disclosure as a general rule, following the practice of the ancient Chinese medical sages. However, following the example of Song Guobin, a careful distinction should be made between lying (or deception) and concealing the truth. Ethically, there is a subtle but significant difference between these two; in the words of a Chinese idiom, "an error the breadth of a single hair can lead someone astray by a thousand miles."

The principle of truthfulness should be breached only in exceptional circumstances, such as when complete candour would lead to serious dangers for the patient, such as real risk of suicide due to breaking bad news. For Confucian medical ethics the highest ideal is *ren*, as articulated in the ethical definition of healing: "medicine as the art of humanity or humaneness." Nevertheless, the burden of proof should fall on those who believe that the principle of open and direct disclosure should be breached in order to avoid perceived risks to the patient. I have presented overwhelming evidence in this chapter that the great majority of Chinese patients want information about their medical condition. And we have seen that a conspiracy of silence or outright deception by family members and medical professionals can do great harm to patients. So those cases in which the truth needs to be concealed are likely to be rare. Cases where patients need to be deceived should be even rarer.

Yet, while most Chinese patients would prefer to know the truth about their medical condition, there is still a significant proportion of patients who prefer to be kept in ignorance about their prognosis. This raises a moral question as well as a medical challenge. The short answer is that one should not impose the unpalatable truth upon this group. To ignore a patient's wish not to know is as wrong as dismissing their legitimate desire to know. Of course, patients who subscribe to the "ignorance is bliss" mentality can be found not only in China but also in the West. On this point, it is worth pointing out that, as far as Confucianism is concerned, the concept of *cheng* includes a condemnation of self-deception.

The radical level of disagreement revealed in the hospital survey results cited above provide evidence of a genuine moral dilemma for contemporary Chinese. What should be done when patients want to know the truth about their condition but medical professionals and relatives prefer to withhold information and even lie to them? In Chinese culture, the Golden Rule taught by Confucius is widely known and respected: "Do not impose on others what you do not wish for yourself" (*jishuo buyu, wushi yuren*). If the general preference of Chinese people for knowing the truth about terminal illness is interpreted as a wish *not* be lied to or to be kept in ignorance, then, according to this key moral precept of Confucianism, it is ethically unacceptable for others to impose on patients what they consider to be in the patient's best interests, regardless of what the patients themselves prefer.

Placing the onus of disclosure on family members in cases of terminal illness, a widespread practice favorably endorsed by the advocates of the cultural differences argument, raises additional ethical questions. Is this really in the patient's best interests, or for the convenience of medical professionals? Telling patients the truth about their serious condition is an art; however caring and experienced he or she may be, no physician will be perfect at this. As the 1947 Code of Ethics of the American Medical Association recommends, it is not ethically sound for physicians to delegate this difficult task wholly to family members. Apart from their obvious lack of systematic training in medicine and counselling, most importantly, lay relatives may lack the necessary professional and personal distance often critical for imparting sensitive information in a caring and humane way. Chinese medical professionals need to lift their game here. Shunning a professional duty merely because of its difficulty is unacceptable, ethically and professionally. If the real motivation for "familist" practice is simply the convenience of medical professionals, then the practice clearly needs reform. For Chinese medical practitioners, the basic requirement of the Confucian medical ideal, "medicine as the art of humanity," is to fullfil their professional duties, however challenging they may be.

Conclusions

Taking a universalist ethical position on human rights and patients' rights, some bioethicists have forcefully argued for the importance of truth-telling and informed consent anywhere on the globe, including China (Macklin 1999). Whereas this approach may be seen as stemming from an outside perspective, in this and the preceding chapter my view is from "the inside out."

My aim in this book is not to dispute the validity of the widely acknowledged cultural differences between China and the West on the issue of medical truth-telling. Rather, the key question for me is how this prima facie cultural difference *should be interpreted historically, sociologically and ethically*. I have attempted to show that the truth about cultures and cultural differences over medical truth-telling are far more complicated (and fascinating) than the dichotomizing overgeneralizations of popular mythology might suggest, however appealing they may be.

The cultural differences argument is directly based on a clear-cut cultural contrast between China and the West, in this case a crude opposition regarding the disclosure of terminal illness. The argument, along with the stereotyped image, is anchored in and perpetuates a deeply rooted and still prevalent habit of thought: the dichotomizing of the West and the non-West as "radical others" to one another. It thus commits what I have called the "fallacy of dichotomization" (see Chapter 2).

In particular, I have demonstrated that, despite its popularity and apparent plausibility, the argument has oversimplified and distorted both the historical and socio-cultural realities, including the role of family, in both China and the West. Historically, it has ignored the venerable Chinese tradition of direct truth-telling and, sociologically, it has dismissed the wishes of the great majority of Chinese patients who want to know the truth about their prospects. Ethically, it has obscured the critical moral problems involved in nondisclosure and deception by medical professionals, and promotes the tyranny of existing socio-cultural practices over ethics and morality.

The contemporary Chinese practice of concealing the truth and even lying to patients about their terminal illness, no matter how widespread, ought to be critically examined, vigorously challenged, and systematically reformed. Culturally, the shift toward honest and direct disclosure now occurring in China is not so much following a Western (and thus foreign) pathway, but constitutes a return to a neglected indigenous tradition. More importantly, even if it were proven to be culturally alien to China, as universally assumed, the norm of truth-telling should be instituted on the basis of the ethical imperatives presented here.

Respecting perceived cultural differences constitutes a major ethical stumbling block to implementing the practice of direct and truthful medical disclosure in non-Western societies (and non-European groups within Western countries). By this logic, the current mainstream cultural practice is proffered as a sufficient ethical rationale to reject medical truth-telling. In other words, the "cultural differences" proponents attempt to bypass the moral difficulties involved by substituting statements about cultural practices for serious ethical examination. Against this tyranny of cultural practice, a transcultural approach emphasizes the primacy of morality and ethics (see the introduction). When cultural practices and moral imperatives are in conflict, the primacy accorded to ethics and morality in Confucianism and Daoism provides a powerful rationale to seek reform of Chinese cultural practices, however deeply rooted and widespread, to meet the calling of ethics, rather than degrading ethics to suit socio-cultural realities. In the context of medical truth-telling, this means that, even if truth-telling about terminal illness were totally alien to Chinese culture, China would still need to reform its current approach to medical disclosure in order to meet the demands of a universal ethics.

As for cross-cultural bioethics, if I have appeared to argue that all cultures are fundamentally the same and that cultural differences do not matter, I would like to say that this is not my intention. My point is that Chinese and Western cultures *are* different, but not in the ways suggested by popular stereotypes, not in the sense of their being "radical others" to one another. As this study of medical truth-telling in China, other chapters of this book, and other research projects (Nie 2005, 2009) have I hope illustrated, Chinese-Western cultural differences are far more complicated, subtle, intriguing—and thus more difficult to grasp and articulate—than facile overgeneralizations.

May the forgotten way of truth-telling of the ancient Chinese medical sages return to China, and may the great Dao prevail in this world!

A personal note

I would like to end this study of medical truth-telling in China on a personal note. In the late 1980s, the father of a former medical school classmate and best friend of mine was suffering the final stages of lung cancer. A psychiatrist himself, without any knowledge of the new practice of disclosure in the West, my friend informed his father of the diagnosis and prognosis—something his father's doctors and nurses never did. In taking this step, my friend set out bravely in defiance of the dominant social and medical norm of nondisclosure, and unknowingly travelled a way that ancient Chinese medical sages had walked more than twenty centuries ago. At the time, I should have questioned him further about his courageous decision to choose this unorthodox route. But our discussions were kept brief—after all, it is never easy to talk about the death of a loved one. Now it has become impossible for me to continue the dialogue. Having just celebrated his 30th birthday, and when working as a visiting physician in Japan in 1994, my friend was hit by a car while riding a bicycle and died from his injuries.

This and the preceding chapter are humbly dedicated to Dr Zou Xinxing, a brilliant physician and friend. If only I could have had the benefit of his endorsement and criticism ...

Chapter 8

Is informed consent not applicable in China?: further intellectual flaws of the "cultural differences" argument

The "cultural differences" argument against informed consent

Bioethics is not only an academic discipline, but first of all a public discourse, a socio-cultural movement. This is the case not only in the United States (Jonsen 1998). The birth and development of bioethics in New Zealand constitute another typical example on how this new field has been shaped by the broad socio-cultural forces such as the women's rights and patients' rights movements and how it has significantly contributed to contemporary socio-cultural transformations (Nie and Anderson 2003). Bioethics in China, and indeed as a worldwide phenomenon, also manifests this striking feature.

Informed consent is probably the most influential concept in contemporary bioethics as an academic discipline and especially as a socio-cultural movement. The principle of informed consent has had a significant impact upon medical research involving human subjects and on health care practices since the 1970s, especially in Western countries. It has greatly facilitated the historic change from a physician-centered, professionalized and paternalistic mode of medical ethics to a patient-centered way of practicing medicine and conducting scientific research.

Informed consent as an essential ethical principle for medicine (and medical research in particular) was most prominently prescribed in the 1947 Nuremberg Code, although as a moral norm for medicine it had appeared before the Second World War. With informed consent as its conceptual cornerstone, the Nuremberg Code was part of the legacy of the highly publicized trial of the Nazi physicians and scientists who conducted a series of medical atrocities and unethical medical experiments on unwilling human subjects in the name of science and the interests of the state. The first and longest of the ten principles enshrined in the Code states clearly: "The voluntary consent of the human subject is absolutely essential." The Code also identifies four essential elements of valid consent: it must be voluntary (i.e. free from "force, fraud, deceit, duress, overreaching, or other ulterior forms of constraint or coercion"), legally valid, informed, and fully comprehended by the subject.

The ethical requirements of the Nuremberg Code did not immediately exert a direct and perceptible influence on medicine. This was partly because it was originally seen as irrelevant by medical professionals as it dealt with physicians and scientists who had been condemned as war criminals. The World Medical Association's famous Declaration of Helsinki was not formulated until 1964, nearly twenty years after the Nuremberg Code. Nevertheless, partly due to the civil rights and patients' rights movements of the 1960s, along with the birth and development of bioethics, since the 1970s "informed consent" has become an almost household word in the West. It now plays a central place in the ethics of medical research and health care, including the major question of the withdrawal of treatment.

The question I want to pose and address here is a basic one. Is the notion of informed consent, with its apparently Western origins, applicable to non-Western societies where cultural traditions and social contexts are often perceived to be very different? More specifically, is this moral concept and ideal applicable to China?

It is usually argued that, philosophically speaking, the doctrine of informed consent is based on the Western cultural tradition of liberal individualism, and especially the notion of personal autonomy. By contrast, Chinese cultural and moral traditions, represented by Confucianism, are customarily described as communitarian, i.e. emphasizing the importance of family, community and state, rather than the individual. As a result, serious doubts can be raised about informed consent in non-Western societies. Indeed, it is commonly believed in certain circles in China as well as in the West that, due to the perceived Chinese-Western cultural differences, informed consent is not applicable to China. The reasoning behind this view can be summarized in the following syllogism:

> *First premise:* Informed consent is a Western moral concept because, not only did it originate in the West, but its rationale is wholly based on the Western notion of individualism;
> *Second premise:* Chinese culture, represented by a communitarian Confucianism, is fundamentally different from Western culture with its individualistic orientation;
> *Conclusion:* Therefore, the doctrine of informed consent is neither relevant nor applicable to China.

This can be called the "cultural differences" argument against informed consent. Based on this argument, it has been suggested that, in China, an alternative moral concept such as family consent should be formulated to substitute for the principle of informed consent in medical practice.

In this chapter I set out a number of arguments to counter this opposition to the applicability of informed consent in China. Like the "cultural differences" argument against medical truth-telling in China, the similar argument against informed consent endorses the popular myth of a communitarian China vs. the individualistic West and thus committed the "fallacy of dichotomizing cultures" and its associated problems including the assumption of homogeneity, the problematic representation, false essentialism, the denial of the openness of cultures, and the thesis of cross-cultural incommensurability (see Chapter 1). While emphasizing the fundamental differences or incommensurability between Western and Chinese culture, it simplifies and even distorts the complexity and internal pluralities of both cultures, especially the Chinese one (see Chapter 2). In doing so, it fails to appreciate the reality of the integration or co-existence of a diversity of value systems within one cultural "region," thereby ignoring existing strategies and experiences in the field of normative cross-cultural communication.

Following my critical discussion on medical truth-telling in the preceding two chapters, here I expose some further intellectual shortcomings involved in the "cultural differences" argument against informed consent in China. First, according to the argument, informed consent is defined primarily as an issue of culture. However, in reality it is mainly concerned with the issue of power—balancing power relations between medical institutions and professionals on the one side and vulnerable patients on the other—a situation which exists in the West as well as in China. Second, the cultural difference thesis has confused the philosophical justification for informed consent, based on individualism and individual autonomy, with informed consent as a practical moral guide or principle for health care practice and medical research. There are communitarian reasons for the importance of informed consent or choice, and patients' rights in general. Furthermore, I will critically examine some ethical and cross-cultural issues related to the current dominant Chinese practice of family consent.

Empowering patients

The first intellectual flaw in the cultural differences argument as it relates to informed consent is to misconstrue the subject primarily as an issue of culture. But at the heart of the matter is the unbalanced power relationship between powerful medical institutions and professionals and vulnerable patients. Medical information and knowledge is power. The basic social function of the ethical principle of informed consent is to prevent the abuse of power by medical professionals, to limit the misplaced power of physicians over their patients, and to empower patients in decision-making related to their health care, including the major issues such as the withholding and withdrawing of medical treatments.

Here it is necessary to stress that informed consent is, as presented in the previous section, a very recent historical phenomenon even in the West. Historically, Western patients have basically been silent in medical decision-making; and informed consent has been more a fairy tale, myth or mirage than reality (Katz 2002 [1984]); Faden and Beauchamp 1986). Together with medical truth-telling, informed consent did not become a common ethical norm in medical research, health care, and social research in most Western countries until the 1970s and 1980s.

Many medical professionals in mainland China are opposed to truth-telling and informed consent, and to the patients' rights movement in general. Ruth Macklin (1999: 190–3) once reported that a mainland Chinese physician-researcher, who was participating in an international biomedical research project that included rural Chinese, had articulated two major reasons for opposing the introduction of informed consent to biomedical research in China. First, he claimed that it was a wholly alien concept in Chinese medical practice and would be unfamiliar to the study's participants; indeed, it would likely arouse suspicions about the intentions of the research project. Second, due to the complexity of biomedicine, it would be difficult—and perhaps impossible—for Chinese participants to understand any information passed onto them as part of the consent process.

This kind of opposition is not surprising, given that professional power is the real issue at stake. But the reasons given by the mainland Chinese physician-researcher do not stand up to scrutiny. First, the kind of biomedicine he was practicing was regarded as foreign well into the early twentieth century, and is still known as *xiyi* (Western medicine), by contrast with *zhongyi* (traditional Chinese medicine). Second, it may well be difficult for patients, especially poorly educated rural residents, to understand the technical terms used in biomedicine. But this does not mean that they are not capable of understanding and estimating the balance of risks and benefits that medical intervention may deliver them. In this instance, the Chinese physician-researcher was echoing the views of New Zealand obstretician/gynaecology doctors who in the late 1980s testified in the Cartwright Inquiries into an unethical medical experiment on the impossibility of informed consent and informed choice for the assumed reason that complicated medical knowledge was beyond the understanding of ordinary patients (see Chapter 5). Third, and most importantly, the preferences of Chinese patients were simply not taken into account by this physician-researcher. He seemed to assume that Chinese patients did not care whether they were informed or not. However, many patients *do* want to be informed and Chinese people do not trust medical professionals and hospitals as much as we are usually led to assume.

There has never been a Chinese culture that exists somewhere "out there." Chinese culture, as with any culture, exists in its various manifestations and interpretations. Interpretations of Chinese culture can never be homogenous, neutral or objective. Different individuals and groups will have different interpretations of, and ways of expressing, cultural forms. In the current discussions of informed consent and Chinese culture, the opinions of medical professionals and other dominant groups in the field are usually taken as the representative or even sole legitimate account. One crucial question has rarely been asked, let alone empirically and systematically researched: What are the attitudes of Chinese patients toward informed consent? Or is informed consent desirable for Chinese people? From my own experience, which includes growing up in a remote village in south-central China (the bottom rung of Chinese society), I have many reasons to believe it is desirable, at least for many people. As cited in Chapter 6, a large number of surveys conducted throughout China demonstrate that a great majority of Chinese patients who suffer from terminal illness do want to be informed about their medical condition. In order to adequately address the subject of informed consent in the Chinese socio-cultural context, listening to the voices of patients, especially those from underprivileged groups, is of the first importance.

Mao Zedong was the most powerful Chinese person in the twentieth century and Zhou Enlai, one of his comrades, probably the second most powerful. A few events related to the medical treatments Mao received for his own health problems and a critical surgery he refused for Zhou are illustrative of what informed consent is really about, that is, a matter of power. According to the well-known memoir of Mao's private physician Li Zhisui, in the 1950s Mao (who was not so much a communist but a Chinese emperor) had clearly requested his physician to practice what is today called "informed consent":

> If I have a disease, before treating me, you must discuss with me what the disease is and how it can be treated. If I've agreed with the treatment, I will not blame you even if your treatment fails. If you do not discuss with me beforehand, even if your treatment succeeds, you will not only gain no credit but should be blamed.
> (Li 1994, 77–8; My translation as available English version trans. by H. C. Tai 1994, 81 is not accurate about this passage.)

Moreover, Mao requested Dr. Li to explain to him the physiological and pathological changes, the aim the treatment is meant to achieve, and the possible effects as well as the possible consequences. Dr. Li knew that it would never be easy to persuade Mao to accept the best medical treatment according to the professional judgment of medicine and especially to explain related medical matters in plain language. But he also knew that he had to do it.

Dr. Li did very well in giving his patient informed consent and choice. The first success was to change Mao's medication to better treat his insomnia, a problem Mao had suffered almost his entire life, and to avoid the addiction of sleeping pills. In order not to overdose on barbital, a placebo was employed with Mao's consent. Afterwards, Mao joked to his physician several times about the use of placebo: "Your medicine bag is full of skimpy capsules, but they still work." (Li, trans. Thurston 1994, 109).

Other Chinese doctors also practiced very good informed consent and choice for Mao. According to an article published in one of the official magazines on the history of the Communist Party (Dou 2003), since the early 1970s Mao, in his late seventies, started to develop a number of health problems. One of them was cataracts caused by old age and he became almost totally blind in 1975. Two highly-regarded and politically reliable eye-doctors were called in. After careful examination and discussions, they concluded that two options—one Western biomedical and the other traditional Chinese medical—were available as the treatment: extracting cataract and dispelling cataract with the needle. First, doctors experimented upon 40 elderly patients with the same disease with these two methods. Both groups were successful. Physicians then reported the results to Mao and Mao approved the method of traditional Chinese medicine. His eyes could see again.

Unfortunately, Mao did not extend this practice of informed consent and choice to Zhou Enlai, formerly Prime Minister and a leader probably better loved by more Chinese but disliked by Mao. According to an authoritative (but, like the memoir of Dr. Li about Mao, banned in mainland China) biography of the late Zhou (Gao 2003, 509–19), Zhou was suffering from cancer of the bladder. However, from the very beginning, Mao—through other officials—denied the patient access to necessary medical information and appropriate treatment. The ordered principles for the medical matters related to Zhou were: "keeping secret [from the patient]" and "no surgery." Mao's given rationale was all too familiar: individuals should be subject to the overall situation (*fucong dajiu*). The surgery was not conducted until the cancer's final stages, much too late for successful treatment. Partly as a result of inadequate medical treatments, Zhou passed away in January 1976, quite a few months earlier than Mao who died in September of the same year.

The principle of informed consent and choice is first of all about balancing the unbalanced power relationship between medical professionals and patients and between patients and other concerned people. Without this principle, the appropriate medical information and treatment can be refused even to extremely powerful high officials like Zhou. In the same way, without due respect for fundamental human rights and the social institution of democracy, even Liu Shaoqi, the former Chairman of the People's Republic of China, could fall from his position in a single day, be beaten by the Red Guards, and die miserably and anonymously in prison.

The foremost social aim of informed consent is therefore to empower patients, especially those already socially, politically and economically disadvantaged, so that at least their rights and interests will be not neglected and violated by medical professionals and others in whatever apparently legitimate names.

Justifying informed consent from a communitarian angle

The second intellectual flaw in the cultural difference argument is that it confuses informed consent as a practical moral guide or procedure with the theories called upon to justify it. In other words, even if we assume that it is valid to characterize Chinese culture as basically communitarian and thus fundamentally different from the individualistic culture of the West, this does not necessarily result in the conclusion that informed consent is inapplicable to China, or incompatible with Chinese values.

It is important to distinguish the acceptance of informed consent as a practical ethical principle in health care and medical research from its theoretical justification(s). It is a common cross-cultural phenomenon that people in different cultures accept the same or similar moral norms for different ethical reasons. Even within the same culture, shared moral norms can be justified by different ethical worldviews. For instance, in the West the fundamental human rights of the individual can be justified by an appeal to divine ordinance, to natural law and reason, or to the concept of personhood as developed in modern moral philosophy; the reasons given by Christians, deontologists and utilitarians for why killing is wrong are markedly different from each other. For me, informed consent is not only compatible with the clear anti-paternalism in Daoist ethical and political philosophy, certain Confucian moral traditions, and traditional Chinese medical ethics, but also can be justified in terms of indigenous ethical concepts such as *ren* (humanity or humaneness), *yi nai renshu* (medicine as the art of humanity or humaneness), and *cheng* (sincerity and truthfulness) (see Chapters 10 and 11).

It is true that, in Western bioethics circles, the doctrine of informed consent has usually been seen as based on the notion of autonomy, the language of individual rights and the worldview of individualism (most notably, see Faden and Beauchamp 1986; Beauchamp and Childress 2009 [1979]; Katz 2002 [1984]; Veatch 1981, 2009). However, the principle of informed consent does not depend on this particular moral perspective for its justification. Even those commentators who emphasize the importance of informed consent mention other ethical reasons, such as the "necessity of good therapeutic management" (Katz 2002 [1984], Chapter 8). A number of Christian theologians have supported the concept from foundations in the Christian moral tradition. For example, Paul Ramsey (2002 [1970]) has powerfully defended the ethics of informed consent by drawing on the Christian theological concepts of loyalty, fidelity between persons and the "faithfulness claim" that individuals legitimately have on one another.

One can certainly justify the importance of informed consent from a communitarian perspective. In other words, one may argue that it is not a matter of individual autonomy only, but also of the common good. As a matter of fact, one of the most influential works in contemporary Western political, legal and ethical philosophy on the nature of individual freedom and political authority justifies freedom from an anti-individualistic or communitarian perspective (Raz 1988). British philosopher Joseph Raz clearly argues for a liberal morality or rights-based morality on non-individualistic grounds. For him, rights by definition mean to hold someone or certain authorities to be under a duty so that rights and duties are correlative and never separable. In other words, theoretically, rights-based morality does not have to be individualistic as widely assumed.

Informed consent can be viewed as the best way of promoting trust between patients (the public) and physicians (the medical profession). Without this trust, the medical profession would face increasing difficulties in gaining the necessary resources and the participation of patients for research projects. As a result, the common good of the whole society or community would be undermined.

It has been widely acknowledged in mass media and academic literature in China that the Chinese patient-physician relationship has been rapidly deteriorating. One indicator is the increasingly high rate of various types of violence and even murders against medical professionals by patients and their relatives. In some cases, as a result of patient-physician conflict, facilities of hospitals were damaged. The results of the First National Survey on the Practice and Attitudes of Medical Professionals conducted in 2008 indicate that the great majority (80%) of medical professionals consider the doctor-patient relationship poor or very poor, and that under half (49%) say that patients trust them (Zhang and Sleeboom-Faulkner 2011). One recommendation made by Chinese and Western researchers is to improve medical professionals' communication skills so that better patient-physician trust can be established (Ibid). This recommendation is definitely important. Nevertheless, two main suggestions of mine on this issue are to reform institutions and social policies. First, there are serious problems with the current health care system and many of the reforms with the health care system have made it worse. As a part of developing the market economy, most hospitals are now profit-driven. Second, it is necessary to formulate adequate social policies and implement them in practice to safeguard patients' rights—including the rights to truthful information and informed consent or choice.

The experience of New Zealand offers a positive example on how to establish and maintain social trust between the medical profession and the public. In general, social trust in New Zealand, particularly the trust patients have put on their medical professionals, is very high, certainly higher than in many other countries including China. According to a cross-country survey conducted in 2002 on health care in five major English-speaking countries (Australia, Canada, New Zealand, UK and the United States) (Blendon et al. 2003), while New Zealanders demonstrated the highest levels of dissatisfaction with the health care system overall, expressing concerns such as waiting times for hospital care and endorsing more public funding for health care, in comparison to people in the other four countries, New Zealand patients gave the highest rating on the quality of health care received from their physicians and reported fewer problems with accessing doctors' offices. It seems to me that, ethically and politically speaking, one of the main reasons for this positive outcome lies in a series of legislations and social institutions which have safeguarded patients' right to confidentiality and informed consent or choice. These include *The Code of the Health and Disability Consumers' Rights* and the Health and Disability Commission in dealing with patients' complaints (Nie and Anderson 2003).

Family consent

In striking contrast to the West, consent forms for medical procedures and treatments (such as surgeries) in China are often signed by relatives rather than patients themselves. Laws and social policies recognize the social practice. Family members seem to play a far more active role in the process of medical decision-making. There are many important ethical and cross-cultural issues arising from the Chinese practice of family consent. Following my brief discussion on the problem of family in medical truth-telling in the preceding chapter, my purpose here is to raise a few questions in the context of refuting the cultural differences argument against informed consent in China.

From a transcultural perspective, family as an essential social institution and an important moral value is vital in every society and culture. These are not merely Chinese values, alien to other cultures such as Western ones. Intellectually consistent with the postmodernist discourse, contemporary academic discussions of cultures have been fashionably focused on their differences, discontinuities and divergences. Yet, the fact that Chinese and Western cultures and moral traditions are "different" does not necessarily mean that they are inevitably incompatible or mutually exclusive. For example, in Confucianism, the concept of filial piety, the moral basis of Chinese family values, is so fundamental that it has been regarded as much more than a domestic virtue. It has been traditionally viewed as the foundation of morality, and in the words of *Xiao Jing* (The Classic of Filial Piety), "the root of virtue and the source of civilization" (in Ebrey 1993, 64). It seems that no moral tradition in the West has placed the same emphasis on filial piety as Confucianism. One eighteenth-century British philosopher even argued for the immorality of filial affection from the utilitarian perspective (Godwin 1972, 187–92). But it would be wrong if, based on these perceived differences, one were to claim that Chinese and Western moral traditions are incommensurable and that the concept of filial piety is totally alien to the West. A salient counter-example to this claim is the Fifth Commandment in the Old Testament and many passages in the New Testament on the importance of honoring parents—although the ethical justifications for respect for one's parents in Confucianism and Christianity are certainly different.

The results of available cross-cultural empirical comparative studies on values held by people indicate that cross-cultural differences are more complicated than what we usually assume and that the cross-cultural similarities are far more striking than what the dichotomization of cultures can imagine. For instance, a cross-country survey conducted in the late 1980s by a group of American and Chinese scholars on people's values in China and the United States shows that a large number of American respondents, more than contemporary Chinese, held traditional Confucian values and that there are more similarities between the two cultures than often perceived (Pan et al. 1994). As for family values, Americans have arguably shown a stronger adherence to them than Chinese. Many more Chinese than American respondents were permissive regarding divorce. More surprisingly, only slightly more Chinese than Americans agreed that aging parents should be cared for by their adult children; and far more Americans than Chinese endorsed extended family values such as "benevolent fathers and filial sons" and "a house full of children and grandchildren" (Ibid, 66–8). It is difficult to rightly interpret and explain these empirical findings. But one point is certain: Family values do not belong to Chinese and Chinese cultures alone; they are important values in the West as well.

Indeed, based on his visit to the United States, Fei Xiaotong, a founder of Chinese anthropology and sociology, had written from as early as 1948 pointing out a number of misgivings of the concept of "Chinese familism" invented by Western scholars and the popular myth that the Chinese culture is centered upon family (Fei 1999 [1948], 396). One point he made is that, compared with Americans, Chinese parents spent much less time with their children, and Chinese spouses much less time with each other. My own personal experiences of studying, working and living in Canada, the United States and New Zealand is consistent with Fei's observations. By all means, Westerners do not necessarily place lesser value on family values than the Chinese.

Western bioethics has been paying attention to the normative role of family in health care (e.g. Nelson and Nelson 1995). The essential role of family has been discussed in medical and bioethical literature on a number of ethical challenges related to genetic testing, palliative care, long-term care for chronic illness, and elderly care in increasingly aging societies. Difficult ethical dilemmas arise when individual family members disagree with each other. The heated debates go on—for instance, whether it is ethically sound for a family member to veto the wish of a deceased family member to donate organs to others for organ transplantation (a practice currently endorsed by laws in New Zealand)?

Just as there are difficult ethical issues involved in the individual consent model, there exist serious ethical problems with the family consent. Marxists and feminists have offered powerful warnings not to romanticize family as a social institution. Reflecting the ubiquitous issue of power in larger societies and in every form of interpersonal relationship, family as a social unit cannot avoid the issue of unbalanced power as manifested in the very deplorable fact that negligence and domestic violence physical, psychological and sexual—

against children, women and elders is a worldwide problem, a problem which persists in the West as well as in China. One scenario is that, as pointed out by Chinese-Canadian bioethicist Edwin Hui (2008), based on actual cases occurring in Hong Kong, Chinese familism faces serious ethical problems when parents refuse life-saving treatments for ill adolescents.

In a very perceptive legal and ethical review of the Chinese practice and related legislations of family consent for competent patients, Ding Chunyan (a Chinese PhD candidate at the Law Faculty at the University of Hong Kong) (2010) has identified that the real reason for the dominance of family consent in contemporary China is not so much a cultural concern as an economic or pragmatic one. Hospitals and medical professions seek for family members' consent to secure payment of medical expenses and to reduce the risk of medical malpractice liability against medical institutions and practitioners. Ding has identified some negative impacts of family consent upon the individual patient which include that family members may refute necessary medical treatments for various reasons, often economic ones; that patients' privacy may be breached; and that the judgments made by family members about the best interests may not accord to the genuine best interests in the views of patients themselves.

The last point of Ding, a point about a possible danger of paternalism in general and family consent in particular, has been vividly illustrated by a parable presented by Zhuang Zi, a Daoist founder, more than two thousand years ago.

> The emperor of the South Sea was called Shu [Brief], the emperor of the North Sea was called Hu [Sudden], and the emperor of the central region was called Hundun [Chaos]. Shu and Hu from time to time came together for a meeting in the territory of Hundun, and Hundun treated them very generously. Shu and Hu discussed how they could repay his kindness. "All men," they said, "have seven openings so that can see, hear, eat, and breathe. But Hundun alone doesn't have any. Let's try boring him some."
>
> Every day they bored another hole, and on the seventh day Hundun died.
>
> (Zhuang Zi trans. Watson 1968, 97)

Along with Zhuang Zi, Daoist ethical and political philosophy would endorse a more individualistic model of informed consent in medical decision-making for competent patients.

A caveat needs to be made to avoid a possible misunderstanding. Here I am not arguing against the importance of family values. The issue indeed constitutes a very weak and weakening point in contemporary bioethics and in our life in general, in the West as well China. I am acutely aware of the threats modernity, capitalism and nation-states have posed for the family as an essential social institution and a crucial moral value. However, in order to uphold and promote family values, one does not have to romanticize it and to cover up the ethical dilemmas and moral problems involved.

Conclusion

Informed consent—in both the individual and familist models—has been clearly enshrined in the *Law of the People's Republic of China on Medical Practitioners* (1998) and the State Council's *Code of Medical Malpractice* (2002). As cited in the preceding chapter, in 2008, thirteen hospitals, eight universities and six academic associations throughout China, organized by the premier Chinese journal *Medicine and Philosophy*, jointly issued a series of documents or guidelines on ethical and legal issues of informed consent in medical research and health care (*Yixue Yu Zhexu* 2008, 1–12). In these guidelines, informed consent, either by the patient or his or her relative, is treated as an essential moral requirement for medicine. A search for Chinese databases of academic articles published in Chinese indicates that there are at least hundreds of articles in Chinese which directly discuss the topic of informed consent in medicine. The first Chinese book focusing on this important topic in medical ethics by Zhu Wei, a bioethicist in Fudan University in Shanghai, appeared in 2009. The book takes an individualistic justification of informed consent and argues that individualism is not necessarily incompatible with Chinese cultural traditions (for a brief English discussion, see Zhu 2009b).

The remarkable fact that informed consent has come of age in China defeats the cultural differences argument more than any sophist theories. More significantly, the fact itself shows again how open Chinese cultures and medical ethics are to foreign ideas and new possibilities.

In this chapter I have drawn attention to some intellectual flaws in the view that informed consent is not applicable to China because the cultures of China and the West are fundamentally different. My conclusion is that the cultural differences argument is founded on serious misunderstandings of Chinese cultures and medical moralities as well as Western cultures, and of what informed consent is really about and how it can be theoretically justified. Furthermore there are serious ethical dilemmas and problems involved in the Chinese practice of family consent.

While I believe in the moral necessity of informed consent in China and its cultural compatibility with the Chinese moral and medical ethics traditions, I am aware that I have not argued directly for this point of view in this chapter. Neither have I discussed the socio-cultural obstacles to realizing the moral ideal of informed consent in the contemporary Chinese context. To reject the opposition to informed consent in China on the grounds of cultural differences does not mean that the question of the socio-cultural context is irrelevant with regard to informed consent. The question is: What kinds of cultural differences matter, and in what sense? But these issues need separate exploration.

Part III

Cultural norms embodying universal values

Chapter 9

Human rights as a Chinese value

A Chinese defense and critique of UNESCO's Universal Declaration on Bioethics

A specter—the specter of human rights—has been haunting the global village. China, a big family in this haunted village, is no exception.

Even during the darkest times, such as the decade of the Cultural Revolution, Zhang Zixin, Lin Zhao, and Yu Luoke—to mention only a few individual Chinese on a very extensive list—were willing to sacrifice their lives in order simply to live like a human being with dignity and freedom from serfdom. Although having been publicly exiled out of the Chinese political, social and cultural landscape for about three decades in Mao's regime, the language and visions of human rights have come into force again since the 1980s. Like a wild fire, the grass-roots movement of *weiquan*, "defending rights," has been spreading far and wide throughout China, from North to South, from East to West, from cities to villages. The revival of human rights in China has been transforming not only Chinese society and culture but also the history of human civilization in its ever-lasting struggle for dignity, liberty, justice, righteousness (*yi*), humanity (*ren*), and the realization of the Dao.

However, in Western and non-Western societies including China, it is widely believed that the concept of human rights is by and large a Western cultural norm, often at odds with non-Western cultures and, therefore, not applicable in non-Western societies such as China. Unfortunately, *The Universal Declaration on Bioethics and Human Rights* (UDBHR) adopted by the United Nations' Educational, Scientific and Cultural Organization (UNESCO) in 2005 reflects this deep-rooted and popular assumption. By using Chinese culture(s), a culture I belong to and treasure with my heart, as an illustration, in this chapter I will point out the problems of this widespread misconception and stereotypical view of cultures and human rights. I will highlight the often downplayed international nature of the human rights discourse and especially the often ignored positive elements in Chinese cultures that promote and embody universal human values such as human dignity and human rights. It concludes, accordingly, with three concrete suggestions on how to amend the UDBHR to address human rights and cultural issues more adequately.

A widely-held but flawed assumption

The UDBHR follows the tradition of the historic *Universal Declaration on Human Rights* of more than half a century ago, a series of other universal declarations of the United Nations on human rights and bioethical issues such as scientific research and human genome, and the declarations of other international and regional organizations such as the World Medical Association on medicine. As the first international effort and consensus formulated on the fundamental values in bioethics, UNESCO's UDBHR is bound to exert a significant impact on bioethics worldwide, as an academic discipline and, especially, as a social discourse or socio-cultural movement. In general, in the context of great socio-political and cultural diversity on the globe, the UDBHR is itself a remarkable achievement in promoting the universal norms of human dignity and freedom in the areas of medicine, life sciences and biotechnologies.

Nevertheless, as I see it, there is a serious flaw in the UDBHR's way of addressing the most essential tension of any international documents on bioethics and other topics, i.e. the relationship between universal human values and cultural differences. The UDBHR puts forward a number of principles including human dignity and human rights, non-discrimination, autonomy and individual responsibility, informed consent, respect for human vulnerability and personal integrity, equality and justice, solidarity and cooperation, and social responsibility to the common good and the biosphere. Article 12 clearly upholds "respect for cultural diversity and pluralism" as a major bioethical principle. It asserts:

> The importance of cultural diversity and pluralism should be given due regard. However, such considerations are not to be invoked to infringe upon human dignity, human rights and fundamental freedoms nor upon principles set out in this Declaration, nor to limit their scope.

This article is the only clause in the entire UDBHR that explicitly deals with cultural diversity.

The tone of Article 12 clearly reveals a basic assumption of the UDBHR, the assumption holding that such norms as human rights, human freedom and human dignity are basically Western ideas, have no grounds in other cultural traditions, and are therefore in contradiction with non-Western cultures. Here the UDBHR is not expressing an idiosyncratic position, but has taken for granted a widespread and stereotypical view of the relationship between human rights and non-Western cultures. For too long, non-Western cultures have been treated as the "radical other" of Western cultures. Among the many consequences of the mentality of dichotomizing Western and non-Western cultures in radical contrasting terms is this popular myth of cultures and human rights.

No matter how widespread and deep-rooted this assumption has been among people in both Western and non-Western societies, it is problematic and misleading at best, because it has seriously downplayed, if not totally ignored, the positive elements and traditions in non-Western cultures that maintain, favor, honor and advocate universal human values including the primacy of morality, respect for individual persons, human freedom and rights. Contrary to the assumption universally accepted and clearly reflected in the UDBHR, moral and cultural traditions in non-Western societies are often *for*, rather than against, such universal norms as human dignity and human rights.

The fallacy of the "Asian values" argument against human rights

The UDBHR, as Article 12 makes crystal clear, takes an obviously straightforward universalist stance against both cultural and moral relativism. On the one hand, the document, as stated by Article 12, disagrees radically with the major conclusion of cultural relativism on human dignity and human rights. On the other hand, the UDBHR ironically agrees almost fully with the fundamental premise from which the relativist conclusion is reached: that is, cultural values and practices in non-Western cultures often, if not always, conflict with universal ethical ideals such as human rights. Along with cultural relativists, these universalists who have drafted the UDBHR assume that, in general, universal ethical ideals such as human dignity and human rights are usually alien to, and incompatible and incommensurable with, non-Western cultures, moralities and traditions.

In the Asian context, there has been a famous, or, (in the eyes of its critics) infamous thesis that opposes human rights from the perspective of the perceived Eastern-Western cultural differences—that is, the "Asian values" thesis against human rights. The thesis asserts that Eastern culture is essentially authoritarian and familist, that it is radically different from the individualistic Western culture, and that such "Western" values as human rights, democracy, and liberty, therefore ought not to and cannot be applied in Asian societies. It was put forward most prominently and controversially by Lee Kuan Yew, the former leader of Singapore, in an interview with the influential magazine *Foreign Affairs* (Zakaria 1994). Despite enormous criticism, it has gained much currency and strong support among some high-ranking officials in some Asian and even certain African countries.

Obviously, the drafters of the UDBHR contest the "Asian values" thesis against human rights from a universalist moral and political stance. Ironically, just as they have agreed with relativists on the widely-held assumption on the incomparability of human rights with non-Western cultures, the drafters of the UDBHR also agreed, as indicated in the tone of Article 12, with the initiators and supporters of the "Asian values" thesis on the incomparability of human rights with Asian cultures.

Despite their totally opposing stances about human rights, both the "Asian values" advocates and the universalist drafters of the UDBHR have subscribed to the same myth of the collectivist or authoritarian East vs. the individualistic West and committed the same fallacy of dichotomizing cultures (see Chapters 1 and 2). As I have discussed in Chapter 2 and further demonstrated in other chapters on medical truth-telling, informed consent and women's rights in the Chinese context, the persistent and popular way of dichotomizing cultures has fostered many empirically problematic assumptions, normatively misleading conclusions, and politically contentious resolutions. Serious problems involved with dichotomizing cultures include the assumption of internal homogeneity, the problematic representation of the culture concerned, the grand hypothesis of a peculiar mentality omnipresent in the entire culture, false essentialism, denying every culture as an open system or treating culture as an iron cage, the endorsement of the tyranny of cultural practices over ethics, the misconception of cultural incommensurability, the rejection of common humanity and universal human values, the self-defeating prophecy of the clash of cultures as inevitable, and generating harmful social policies. Based on the habit of thought of dichotomizing cultures, the notorious "Asian values" thesis against human rights have all these problems in either hidden or noticeable forms.

As my topic here is about human rights as a Chinese value, I will focus on how the "Asian values" thesis has utterly misrepresented cultural traditions in Asia in the efforts of serving or self-serving the status quo of the existing socio-political power. To treat authoritarianism as the only authentic representative of Asian cultural traditions is a simple intellectual mistake and a reprehensible political insult. Taking into account the enormous cultural, religious, social and moral diversity in Asia, it is intellectually absurd to homogenize, totalize and essentialize Asian cultures as authoritarian in nature or Confucian on the one hand, and dismiss many other Asian traditions (such as Buddhism and Daoism) which nurture and promote individuality, self-cultivation, self-development, and the efforts to reform and even rebel against the un-ethical secular authorities. The "Asian values" thesis is a reprehensive political insult for all men and women in Asia, young and old, who have sacrificed so much—many even their lives—and are continuing to struggle courageously to uphold humanity, dignity and human rights in the face of social injustice, including those brought about by Western colonialism and imperialism and by the power abuse of the totalitarian, authoritarian or democratic state.

The interview with Lee Kuan Yew was entitled "Culture is Destiny." In an immediate response to the interview, Kim Dae Jung, former political dissident and later President of South Korea, entitled his robust criticism of Lee's thesis "Is Culture Destiny?: A myth of Asia's anti-Democratic Values." One of the main points made by Kim is that, long before Locke, there exists a rich heritage of democracy-oriented philosophies and tradition in Asia and that this Asian heritage can contribute significantly to the evolution of global democracy. An example he cited, very rightly, is the well-known political philosophy of Mencius (372–289 BCE), a founder of Confucianism. In a striking contrast to Plato, who vindicated the authoritarian or totalitarian government as the ideal state, Mencius justified that people can and should rebel and overthrow a government if the rulers and the state are not following the mandates of Heaven and not serving the people. Among three key factors in the political life, the order given by Mencius is: people first, the kingdom second, and the emperor or rulers third. This thought, the household Chinese thought of "people first" or "people-based polity," has greatly influenced Chinese for generations, as well as other East Asians such as Kim. For Kim (1994, 194), in Asia's great struggle to establish democracy and strengthen human rights, "the biggest obstacle is not its cultural heritage but the resistance of authoritarian rulers and their apologists." "Culture is not necessarily our destiny. Democracy is." Human rights certainly ought to be. If human rights are not our destiny, China, Asia, and humankind will be doomed.

It is very unfortunate that, under the spell of dichotomizing cultures, the advocates of human rights like the drafters of the UDBHR have subscribed to the same flawed assumption on the incomparability of human rights with Asian or other non-Western cultures that human rights opponents such as the "Asian values" holders and other cultural and moral relativists hold.

Human rights as a Chinese value

> It has been a long-cherished ideal of mankind to enjoy human rights in the full sense of the term. Since this great term—human rights—was coined centuries ago, people of all nations have achieved great results in their unremitting struggle for human rights for people with lofty ideals are still working determinedly for this cause. However, on a global scale, modern society has fallen short of the lofty goal of securing the full range of human rights for people the world over. And this is why numerous people with lofty ideas are still working determinedly for this cause.

Most readers will be surprised if I point out the original source of these marvellous words on human rights. They are articulated not by any international human rights organizations, or by any Western governments, or by any non-governmental organizations in the West or China, or by Chinese political dissidents. They are from the preface to the 1991 White Paper on Human Rights officially issued by the State Council of the People's Republic of China. The preface carries on:

> The issue of human rights had become one of great significance and common concern in the world community. The series of declarations and

conventions adopted by the UN have won the support and respect of many countries. The Chinese government has also highly appraised the Universal Declaration of Human Rights, considering it the first international human rights in the world arena.

Many people will dismiss this as merely lip service to achieve a certain purpose of propaganda. But, just as hypocrisy is the tribute that vice pays to virtue, this official lip service from a "Communist" government is still a formal acknowledgement of the greatness of human rights. At least, it does not state that human rights are alien to Chinese cultures as those drafters of the UDBHR have clearly assumed. On the contrary, it clearly states that human rights are a universal human value and that the Chinese government endorses it.

In order to appreciate Chinese cultural values of human dignity and human rights, one needs first of all to overcome some common mistakes in perceiving and understanding Chinese culture(s). For example, Chinese culture is too often portrayed as somewhat homogenous. According to this view—probably the principal modern myth surrounding Chinese culture—the great diversity and plurality, especially of those traditions counter to authoritarianism and collectivism, are far from significant if not ignorable. But the reality is that China, as powerfully demonstrated in Chinese people's views and experiences of abortion, is essentially and clearly plural (Nie 2005). And, like in the West, the internal cultural and moral plurality is an obvious and fundamental condition of life in China (see Chapter 5).

The contemporary official standpoints and mainstream practices are too often treated as being *wholly* representative of Chinese cultures. However, as the Chinese understandings of abortion and fetal life indicate, the reality is that not only do various un-official, dissident and underground discourses exist, but contemporary official standpoints and mainstream practice can differ from those in the history of China. As for the issue of human rights, we have seen that even the Chinese government has acknowledged the value, albeit as a lip service.

Moreover, the dominant interpretation of the nature of Chinese culture, as characterized by collectivism and authoritarianism (versus Western individualism and liberalism), has too frequently been accepted without the questioning of its validity (see Chapter 1). By characterizing Chinese cultures in this way, norms such as human dignity and human rights are thus believed to be against Chinese values.

However, the truth is the opposite. As a matter of fact, pursuing human dignity, human rights and individual freedom has long been an intrinsic and prominent part of Chinese cultures. First and foremost, the great struggle of the Chinese people in the past several decades has demonstrated to the world in a variety of sometimes heart-breaking ways that the Chinese, above and beyond simply *caring* about human dignity and human rights, are even willing to suffer persecution and die for them. Indeed, many Chinese have actually sacrificed their lives for human dignity and human rights, particularly during the last century. It would be an insult to those Chinese martyrs and the persecuted to claim that these are not "Chinese," but merely "Western" or "foreign" values. No one should be surprised that the whole history of China, as recorded in official and un-official historical works, has been a history of struggling for humanity (*ren*), righteousness (*yi*), freedom, equality, dignity, and justice.

Second, human rights have long been a Chinese value and the Chinese have significantly contributed to the international struggle for human dignity and rights. In the history of political and cultural life in twentieth-century China, individual freedom and human rights constitute a major leitmotiv, except in the three decades of Mao's era (1950s–1970s) (for a pioneering study, see Svensson 2002). It has been a significant theme in modern Chinese thoughts (Angle 2002). In fact, a Chinese participant played a significant role in the formation of the first *Universal Declaration of Human Rights* by bringing Chinese (and especially Confucian Chinese) moral and political ideals into the historic document. Indeed, the origins of human rights visions and the development of the international human rights discourse do *not* belong to any single society, political system, culture or region of the world (Lauren 2003).

Moreover, more and more contemporary scholarship is providing compelling evidence that human rights are not at all incompatible with indigenous Chinese moral-political-religious systems such as Confucianism (e.g. Xia 2007 [1995]; Xia 2004; de Bary 1998; de Bary and Tu 1998). It is one thing to say that Confucianism and traditional Chinese cultures have not generated a strong discourse for human rights. It is entirely another to claim that human rights are culturally incompatible to Confucianism and other Chinese political and moral traditions. Although Chinese cultures have never developed a distinctive school of thought similar to natural law in the West, both Confucianism and Daoism (Taoism) have their own traditions of individualism. A Confucian communitarian system of human rights is feasible not only theoretically, but also practically. As shown more than sufficiently in the Daoist classics by Lao Zi (Lao Tzu) and Zhuang Zi (Chuang Tzu), Daoism has been well-known and characterized by its treasuring and promoting of individual freedom, as well as its criticism of the suppressing and damaging aspects of state and other socio-political power. To understand Confucian and Daoist moral political-spiritual traditions properly, it is crucial not to confuse—as the authorities in China and some other Asian countries often do—the secondary values (such as respecting the authorities and harmony) with the fundamental or primary ideals (such as Dao, the mandate of Heaven, the primacy of morality, humanity, righteousness, and individuality) (about this point and for one of the most insightful works ever written on Chinese ethical thought in the first Axial Age, see Roetz 1993).

Critics often refute cultural relativism by emphasizing the importance of universal ethical norms, the existence of the common humanity and the shared human values as manifested in different cultures. Here I would like to point out a rarely noticed paradox (and a fallacy) with cultural relativism. Cultural relativism itself is alien to two fundamental moral commitments of Confucianism and Daoism. First, the ethical principles and ideals in Confucianism and Daoism are meant to be universal to all human beings, that is, applicable to Chinese and non-Chinese alike. Relativism, which advocates respecting cultural differences, itself disrespects this universalism of Confucian and Daoist moralities. Second, for Confucianism and Daoism, what should prevail is not any existent social order or cultural practice, but ethical imperatives. To critically engage with the reality one lives in, and reform it by the moral requirements, is far more important than anything else. In this sense, even though the conception of human dignity and human rights would be totally alien to, and incommensurable with, Chinese culture as assumed, this does not mean that it is not applicable in China. According to the most fundamental principle of Confucianism and Daoism on the primacy of morality, one should follow what is morally right and desirable, rather than merely his or her own cultural traditions. As outlined in the introduction to the book, upholding the primacy of morality and opposing the tyranny of cultural practices constitute the most important feature of a transcultural bioethics.

Human rights negligence and violations

Human rights absolutely matter in China. The most important reason lies, unfortunately, not in any theoretical account, but in the plain fact—that is, human rights negligence violations happen in China and everywhere in our global village. A striking irony here is that wherever the authorities claim that there are no serious human rights issues in the territories under their governance or that human rights are respected better than other parts of the world, one can almost warrant that it is there that human rights are often neglected and violated in a routine way.

In stark contrast to the tremendous progress achieved in science and technology, the dramatic increase in life expectancy, great improvements in living standards, and the unprecedented expansion of wealth, the twentieth century was an era of violence and man-made disasters. It witnessed the extremes of good and evil, impressive progress and shocking inhumanity. The First and Second World Wars, Dachau and Auschwitz, the Gulag and the Red Soviet Union, the Khmer Rouge of Cambodia, Japan's war in East Asia and the Pacific, Hiroshima and Nagasaki, the Korean war, the American's Vietnam war, the Chinese Cultural Revolution, the racial conflicts of Yugoslavia, the genocide of Rwanda, and the dictatorship of Saddam Hussein's Iraq all sit on the dark side of the ledger. Enormous advances in science and technology made the mass killing possible. Even medicine, the science and art of healing, was harnessed to the killing machine, as Nazi "racial hygiene" and Japan's biological warfare in China have demonstrated.

Chinese people suffered greatly in the twentieth century—despite remarkable progress in many areas of socio-cultural life and a life expectancy that more than doubled during the period. The major episodes of massive social violence and suffering that wracked China over the past century read like a history of the nation: the Boxer Rising of 1898–1901 that led to the looting of Beijing by an international army and a punitive protocol concluded with eleven foreign powers; the 1911 Republican Revolution that overthrew the Qing Dynasty and brought an end to imperial China; conflicts among local warlords from the late 1910s to 1949; Japan's invasion in 1931 and the war against the Japanese that engulfed the entire nation (1937–45); the three-year civil war between the Nationalist government and the Communist insurgents (1947–49); the war with the U.S. in Korea in 1950–53; the 1957 Anti-Rightist Campaign that banished millions of intellectuals to the countryside and silenced the whole nation; the Great Leap Forward that brought about a man-made famine in 1958–60 in which some twenty to forty million people, mostly peasants, died; the notorious Cultural Revolution of 1966–76; and the violent suppression of peacefully-protesting students and civilians throughout the century, from the May Fourth Movement in 1919 to the Tiananmen Square Massacre in 1989.

In his brilliant essay on Maoism as a source of massive social suffering in China, contemporary Confucian scholar Tu Wei-ming states,

> China has witnessed massive suffering in her modern transformation. Without exaggeration or a stretch of the imagination, an examination of the frequency and magnitude of destructiveness in China since the mid-nineteenth century may reveal it to have been one of the most violent countries in human history. A chronology of China's man-made disasters, generated by domestic conflicts as well as outside aggression, in the last 150 years makes it blatantly clear that *a defining characteristic of modern Chinese history is the destruction of lives, property, institutions, and values*.
>
> (Tu 1997, 149, emphasis added)

This massive destruction has not been limited to human lives, property, institutions, and values, but also includes nature and the environment. As the meticulous study of politics and environmental damage in Mao's China by Judith Shapiro (2001) has demonstrated, the abuse of people is often closely related to the abuse of nature. Since the 1980s, this multi-level campaign of destruction has manifested itself in, among many others, rapid economic development achieved at the cost of social justice and political reform and the construction of the Three Gorges Dam which will damage the entire ecological system of southern China. This systematic abuse of both people and nature is unprecedented in Chinese history, both in scale and degree.

Therefore, more than anything else, massive destruction of life, property, institutions and values in twentieth-century China has demonstrated what terrible things can befall when human rights and human dignity are ruthlessly trampled by ideologies, the hunger for power, the totalitarian state, the utopian zeal, various kinds of war, and other socio-political forces. This plain fact shows that the language and visions of human rights offer us an indispensable theoretical tool and some practical resolutions to prevent these massive human rights violations from occurring again, not only in China but in other parts of the world as well.

The language and visions of human rights can certainly offer us better ways to identify and address many issues related to medicine and health care. Two issues highly related to bioethics in China have been highlighted by two reports of Human Rights Watch (2003, 2011). The first one is about AIDS/HIV in China. One of the main public health disasters which occurred in contemporary China was that, during the 1990s, many local authorities were complicit in the transmission of HIV to hundreds of thousands or even millions of villagers through pursuing and encouraging an unsanitary but highly profitable blood collection industry (see also Gao 2005). Similarly, in the process of developing the economy, many highly polluted factories, such as lead smelters and battery factories, have been built usually in the countryside. One of the severe public health consequences of these lead smelters and battery factories is that hundreds of thousands of children in China are suffering permanent mental and physical disabilities caused by lead pollution and poisoning.

The international nature of human rights

According to the implied assumption in the UDBHR on the incomparability of non-Western cultures with human rights, human rights have been perceived to be by and large a Western invention rooted in Western religious and philosophical traditions such as natural law and the Enlightenment, and that Western cultures are the genuine advocates and fighters for human rights. This perception, however, overlooks the human rights abuse imposed by Western capitalism and imperialism upon many parts of the world and that the human rights discourse has always been international by nature. The Drafting Committee of the UDBHR exhibits this international nature by having representatives from many non-Western societies (including China).

There are many different visions in international human rights. As Paul Lauren, an American historian of worldwide human rights struggle, has well documented and beautifully written:

> The origins of these visions did not result from a single society, political system, culture, region, or manner. Some emerged out of religions belief, compassion, or a sense of duty to care for brothers and sisters suffering in

distress. Others grew from philosophical discourse about the nature of humankind itself, nature law, ethical limits on how individuals should treat one another, or the appropriate powers of government. Still others emerged not from quiet contemplation or careful reflection, but rather from violence and upheaval or the heart of anger generated by a passionate sense of injustice being inflicted upon innocent or defenseless victims. Over the centuries these cases have spanned the globe, involving brutal exploitation, slavery, racial segregation and apartheid, gender and class discrimination, persecution of minorities, violence against civilians in times of war; torture of political prisoners, forced conquest, and the mass exterminations of genocide or "ethnic cleansing." As one might expect, the responses to these wide-ranging abuses also have varied greatly depending on historical circumstances, with the result of not just one single school of thought or unified vision of human rights—but rather many visions.

(Lauren 2003, 1–2)

One should not downplay the leading role Western cultures have been playing in promoting human rights. But this leadership does not mean monopoly. Human rights are not the patent of the West. As from the very start, they belong to humankind.

Euro-centrism is a criticism human rights advocates in the West—including those representatives from the Western countries in the Drafting Committee of the UDBHR—often face. This is a criticism from human rights opponents who usually argue that human rights are a Western value and culturally alien to non-Western societies. While I am inclined to agree with these human rights opponents as to the Euro-centrism of the international human rights discourse, I do so for an entirely different reason. Through subscribing to the thesis of the cultural incomparability of human rights in the non-Western societies, many human rights advocates, as implied in the tone of Article 12 of the UDBHR, have tacitly accepted that somehow only people in the West aspire to and are capable of the pursuit of human rights. It is in this sense they are Euro-centrists.

Western scholars have begun to acknowledge the contributions, including those in the advancement of human rights, of non-Western cultures to Western cultures. For instance, in many of his publications, British anthropologist-historian Jack Goody (see 2006 in particular) has documented a pervasive Euro-centric process, what he has provokingly called the "theft of history." Through this process, allegedly modern values and institutions such as democracy, capitalism, individualism, and romantic love have been treated as though they were solely Western inventions, and the contributions of other cultures to the creation of the modern world have been dismissed as insignificant, if acknowledged at all. Another British historian, John Hobson (2004), has documented how the rise of the West would not have been possible without the assimilation of Eastern ideas, technologies and institutions and the appropriation of Eastern natural and human resources.

It is indeed long overdue to adequately acknowledge the positive contributions and enormous sacrifice people in non-Western societies have made to international human rights. Non-Western cultures have greatly enriched our understanding on why human rights matter and how they can be realized in reality.

Suggestions for amending the Declaration

From the above discussion, I would therefore conclude that the UDBHR, as it stands now, is inadequate in addressing cultural issues because the positive elements in non-Western cultures that promote and embody universal human values (such as human dignity and human rights) are not at all acknowledged and far from highlighted. Accordingly, to help overcome this inadequacy and to give a too-long-overdue recognition of non-Western cultures *for* human rights, I would like to make three concrete suggestions for amending the UDBHR.

Firstly, a statement would need to be added in the general introduction of the UDBHR regarding the international nature of human rights and the positive contributions from people around the world:

> Acknowledging the struggle for human rights and human dignity as a universal human pursuit, the international nature of the origin and development of human rights over the centuries, and the contributions and sacrifice made by people—men and women, old and young—from every part of the world for upholding human freedom, human rights and human dignity in midst of various kinds of violations of these values.

This added statement will follow immediately after the first four general statements on the shared human moral sense, the rapid developments in science and technology, the ethical challenges raised by these rapid scientific and technological advances, and the necessity for the international community to state universal principles respectively. It will be added before those statements on other related Universal Declarations issued by the United States and UNESCO.

Second, another major goal would need to be added in Article 2 on the aims of the UDBHR, something in the vein of:

> to promote cultural pluralism among different societies and internal plurality within every culture, the positive elements for human dignity and human rights as developed in each culture, and cross-cultural dialogue on individual freedom and human rights as well as common good.

Thirdly, Article 12 "Respect for Cultural Diversity and Pluralism," would need to be modified to something in the vein of:

> Any decision or practice should take into account cultural traditions and value systems, whether religious, spiritual or secular. They should develop the common moral grounds of different cultures, promote the elements in every culture that uphold human dignity and human rights, and foster cross-cultural dialogue based on common humanity and cultural differences. They should particularly respect internal diversity and plurality, especially those un-official and even dissident perspectives, within each and every culture. At the same time, no decision or practice which would infringe upon the fundamental moral values shared by all cultures, or upon human dignity and human rights, or upon the principles set out in this UDBHR, or which would limit their scope, should be carried out in the name of respecting cultural diversity and pluralism.

Conclusion

In emphasizing that cultural values promote and embody universal human values, I do not mean at all to suggest that all cultures are fundamentally the same and that we should all pursue human rights and dignity in the same way. No. Cultures are different, but *not* in the sense that Chinese cultures are authoritarian and thus fundamentally different from the individualistic Western ones, *not* in the sense that individual freedom matters in the West only, *not* in the sense that universal norms such as human dignity and human rights are alien to, and inapplicable in, China. Chinese-Western cultural differences are far more complicated, subtle, fascinating, and thus more difficult to discern and articulate than these clear-cut contrasts can indicate.

Also, the historical and socio-political contexts are always different. People in different societies should, and always do, pursue such fundamental and universal human rights in different ways due to the difference and uniqueness of their socio-political, religious, cultural and historical conditions. Actually, it is the different characteristics Chinese people have developed in their struggle for human dignity that not only display the Chineseness of a global human rights discourse, but also call for effective cross-cultural dialogue and cross-national engagements on these universal human norms.

One repeated skeptical claim (not a criticism) regarding all universal declarations issued by the United Nations and other international and regional organizations is that they can hardly be implemented in reality and thus cannot make any real difference. To this widespread skepticism on the actual effects of those universal declarations, I would like to emphasize that the real power of these declarations lies in helping to raise individual and collective moral consciousness in human hearts and that we should never underestimate the power of morality. David Hume, a famous skeptic on human knowledge and a major figure of the Scottish Enlightenment, was not skeptical about the power of human moral sentiments. In the conclusive chapter of *An Enquiry Concerning the Principles of Morals* which, like Emmanuel Kant's *Fundamental Principles of the Metaphysics of Morals*, is a masterpiece in Western moral philosophy, Hume tells us that we should not feel despair about the weakness of human morality:

> Let these generous sentiments be supposed ever so weak; let them be insufficient to move even a hand or finger of our body; they must still direct the determinations of our mind, and where every thing else is equal, produce a cool preference of what is useful and serviceable to mankind, above that is pernicious and dangerous.
> (Hume 1998, 147)

Though centuries apart and thousands of miles away, this confidence in the power of human hearts, morality and conscience (*liangzi*) would be endorsed by many Chinese thinkers, including the founders of Confucianism like Confucius and Mencius and Neo-Confucians like the idealist Wang Yangming (1472–1529). Human conscience and moral sentiments universal declarations such as UDBHR serve to raise and cultivate is the prerequisite for the realization of freedom, dignity and the Dao in this earthly world full of discrimination, inequality, injustice, abuse of power.

I started this chapter by paraphrasing the opening sentence of *The Communist Manifesto*, let me end it with paraphrasing the ending slogan of the revolutionary document:

"PEOPLE OF ALL COUNTRIES FOR HUMAN RIGHTS, UNITE!"

Chapter 10

Women's rights in the Chinese context
Toward a Chinese feminist bioethics

For many Chinese compatriots of mine, including well-educated and professional women, *nüquan zhuyi* (the Chinese translation of feminism; literally, the doctrine of women's power) has negative connotations. Chinese feminists who have invoked this term have been viewed as advocating too aggressively for the improvement of Chinese women's conditions, and as importing Western views about gender justice to China without recognizing that just because a certain type of feminism works in the West does not mean that it will work equally well in China. For this reason and others, Chinese—feminists and non-feminists—are increasingly using the phrase, *nüxing zhuyi*, the doctrine of the female gender, to refer to feminism. This phrase, which de-emphasizes the political dimensions of feminism, has the advantage of drawing attention to feminism's potential for re-conceiving and/or introducing new conceptual schemes through which to interpret male–female relationships and other relationships characterized by an inequitable distribution of power, opportunities, and resources.

Feminism has changed socio-cultural life as well as everyday interpersonal relations in the West. It has also challenged each discipline in the humanities, the social sciences, and even the natural sciences. In bioethics, for example, feminist approaches are altering the ways in which ethical issues in medicine and health care are perceived and handled (e.g. Sherwin 1992). Though feminist thought and feminist bioethics are characterized by a great variety of perspectives, there is considerable unity within their diversity. For example, according to Rosemarie Tong, "... all feminist approaches to bioethics seem interested in asking the so-called women or gender question, raising women's (and men's) consciousness about the subordinate status of women and eliminating gaps between feminist theory and feminist practice" (Tong 1997, 75). Importantly, feminist bioethics is not about only *women* "talk[ing] about *women's* issues in bioethics" (Little 1996, 1); rather, it is about men and women examining "all sorts of bioethical issues from the perspective of feminist *theory*" (Ibid 1996, 1). Because the primary contribution of feminist bioethics is "to note how imbalances of power in the sex-gender system play themselves out in medical practice and in the theory surrounding that practice" (Nelson

2000, 493), its essential goal is the "elimination of gender inequality" (Tong 1998, 268). Recently, many feminist bioethicists have been particularly concerned about the way in which the sex-gender system seems to value men's rights more than women's rights, as if women's rights were less fully "human" than men's rights. But this is decidedly not the case. Thus, it is crucial that both feminist theorists and activists use the language of rights to serve women's interests. For all its limitations, the language of right is one that the contemporary world acknowledges as worthy of its attention.

Although feminist approaches to bioethics largely remain a product of Western thought, they have attracted attention in many nations, including China. But because, despite the similarities such as both societies being patriarchal, there are apparent socio-cultural differences in politics and gender relationships in China and the West, it is not immediately clear that Western feminism in general, and Western feminist bioethics in particular, can and ought to be applied and taken seriously in Chinese contexts. Thus, the burden of this chapter is to establish that Western feminism, feminist bioethics and feminist human rights language are highly relevant and significant for China. Collectively, they provide both Chinese theorists and activists with useful conceptual lenses and powerful political strategies to better address bioethical issues in the Chinese context.

The condition of Chinese women: still oppressed, still not equal with men

Feminist perspectives, feminist human rights talk, and feminist activism can help the men and women in China better perceive social reality in general and instances of rights violation in particular. At present, many Chinese fail to see the ways in which Chinese women's status is not equal to men's. The Chinese have been indoctrinated to believe that, thanks to Marxist-Socialist efforts, they are the happiest, most fortunate, and most equal people in the whole world. I once believed this to be true. Specifically, I believed that Chinese men and women were equally free and well-off. As a result of being exposed to Western feminist thought, as well as studying and working abroad in several countries, however, I changed my belief. I now think that although Chinese women in the twentieth century are far less oppressed than they were, say, in imperial China, they are still not men's full equals.

Chinese women are using suicide as the ultimate way to say "no" to their oppressors and various old and new oppressing socio-cultural forces. According to recently available studies and statistics, China is the only country in the world that rural people have a higher suicide rate than urban residents and that women have a higher suicide rate than men. Young rural women are at particularly high risk because conditions in the rural outposts are very difficult for them. In the early 1990s, China accounted for 44 percent of all reported suicides and for 56 percent of all female suicides in the world, although its population constitutes only 21 percent of the world's population (Lee and Kleinman 2000, 221). In 1995–1999, rural suicide rates were three times higher than urban rates; the rate in women was 25 percent higher than in men mainly due to the extraordinarily high suicide rates in young rural women (Phillips, Li and Zhang 2002). In the Chinese context, suicide is a strong indicator of many political-social problems such as the rural and gender discrimination. For women in China, especially rural China, suicide has been taken as a desperate act of revenge and rebellion in a moral and spiritual sense (Meng 2002, 300–309). Suicide is a "strategy of resistance" "by women who feel powerless in situations of political and social domination" (Lee and Kleinman 2000, 221). The socio-cultural factors and forces they are resisting by sacrificing their lives include "long-term patriarchal influences, recent economic reforms and the adverse consequences for certain susceptible families, state-imposed birth control policy, preference for sons over daughters" (Ibid).

Gender inequality and injustice in China, as in other parts of the world, exist in both blatant and subtle forms, on both the macro and micro level, in both public and private life. When people live under certain conditions long enough, they often get used to them and even try to justify them, no matter how wrong they are. As the ancient Chinese saying goes, "one will not notice how bad-smelling it is, if one stays long in a market full of rotten fish; likewise, one will not notice how nice-smelling it is, if one stays long in a room full of fragrant flowers."[1] Thus, it is crucial to raise consciousness in men as well as women about all forms of sexual inequality and injustice, especially subtle and unnamed ones. The feminist lens can help Chinese men and women ask themselves why most abandoned babies are girls, why most abortions subsequent to prenatal sex diagnosis result in the elimination of *female* fetuses, and why the suicide rates of Chinese women, especially young rural women, are the highest in the world. In other words, the feminist lens of gender can help us Chinese acknowledge the degree to which our relationships smell of "rotten fish" (gender inequity) in China.

Ge Youli, a feminist activist in Beijing, has vividly expressed how Western feminist concepts helped her "see" her reality better. Although she always recognized that her parents treated her brother better than they treated her, for a long time she could not identify and articulate what was wrong about

---

1 This saying originated from *Kongzi Jiayu* (Confucius' Home Sayings). The original text read: "If one lives together with good people, one's character will become good without noticing it." This is as if to say that one will not notice how nice smelling a room full of *zhilan* (irises and orchids) is if they remain in that room for a period of time. On the other hand, if one lives with bad people, one's character will become bad without noticing it. Similarly, one will not notice how foul a market full of rotten fish smells if they remain too long in that market. All of these metaphors illustrate how people become assimilated to their environments. In classic Chinese, *zhilan* (irises and orchids) often symbolize good and noble characters, true friendship, and beautiful surroundings.

this situation. Western feminist thought gave Ge Youli the words and expressions needed to express her dissatisfaction with being treated less well than her brother simply because she was a girl and he a boy (Milwertz 2003, 58). She comments:

> I came to acquire words and concepts such as gender discrimination, gender stereotype, gender role and gendered structure. I began to put things in perspective, a gender perspective. I was amazed at *the effectiveness and forcefulness of these English words in describing and deconstructing {Chinese} women's secondary position in families and societies*.
>
> (cited in Milwertz 2003, 58)

Significance of human rights and women's rights for China

In order to eliminate gender inequalities in China, I contend that feminist human-rights language is useful, indeed essential. Admittedly, there are many arguments or theories to reject the relevance and applicability of the idea of human rights, including women's reproductive rights, in the Chinese context. One popular objection builds upon Chinese-Western cultural differences. In its typical form, the cultural difference argument runs as follows:

> *First premise:* The notion of human rights in general and women's rights in particular arose in and is a part of Western culture;
>
> *Second premise:* The cultural tradition of China is fundamentally different from that of the West;
>
> *Conclusion:* Therefore, the notion of human rights in general and women's rights in particular is neither relevant nor applicable to China.

A variation of the typical cultural difference argument runs as follows:

> *First premise:* The conception of human rights and women's rights is based on Western individualism;
>
> *Second premise:* Traditionally, Chinese culture is community-oriented;
>
> *Conclusion:* The notion of human rights and women's rights is neither relevant nor applicable to China.

Although the cultural difference argument contains a grain of truth, it has many serious problems (see Chapters 7, 8 and especially 9). As I see it, it relies on exaggerated assessments of the differences that exist between Western and Chinese cultures; on wrong assumptions about the existence of a unified communitarian Chinese culture; and on essentialist presuppositions which claim Chinese culture and norms are unchangeable. The cultural difference argument assumes that all those who engage in a given moral practice (such as informed consent) must justify that practice with the same arguments or theories. But, as Carol Gilligan has pointed out, one can use either the language of rights or the language of responsibilities to express the same moral reality (Gilligan 1982). Moreover, one can learn how to translate concepts from these two languages into each others' terms and to speak one or the other as the situation demands. Thus, just because the language of rights has not been spoken as frequently as the language of responsibilities, relationships, and duties in China, does not mean that the Chinese people lack a concept of rights or that women do not feel violated and wronged when, for example, their fetuses are coercively taken from their wombs.

The argument presented for refusing to engage in "rights talk," on the grounds that the idea of human rights is a strictly Western ideal with no place in the Chinese mentality or social reality, is intellectually flawed (see Chapter 9). Just because relationships, duties, and responsibilities are the preferred vocabulary for the Chinese does not mean the Chinese are "hardwired" to reject individual rights and to banish them from their conceptual scheme. As Kant's (as well as Gilligan's) ethics show, it is a mistake to assume that a moral tradition that emphasizes duty and responsibility will necessarily ignore individual rights and dignity (Kant 1996; Gilligan 1982). It is perfectly possible that a moral tradition, which stresses individuals' relationships to each other and to the community can treasure and promote individual autonomy at the same time.

Significantly, more and more evidence indicates that the notion of individual rights is at least compatible with many streams of Chinese thought (see, e.g. Xia 2007 [1995]; Xia 2004; de Bary and Tu 1998; and Angle 2002). In the words of the sinologist and philosopher Chad Hansen, the failure of traditional Chinese thought to find "the inherent dignity and worth of the rational individual to be a natural first principle of morality ... would not block any Chinese thinkers, ancient and modern, from adopting various kinds of posterior arguments for greater individual freedom" (Hansen 2000, 91). Rights-related concepts such as freedom, self-expression, and choice are quite easy to distill from ancient Daoist thought. Significantly, the works of Zhuang Zi (Chuang Tzu), a founder of Daoist philosophy, stress respecting individual dignity and difference; rebelling against paternalism, authoritarianism, and the constraints of conventional morality; and permitting individuals to "freely and easily wander" in this world, constructing their lives as they wish.

Moreover, even closer approximations of rights talk are present in some modern Chinese works. In her groundbreaking work on the human rights debate in China from 1898 to 1949, the Swedish scholar Marian Svensson discovered that in the late nineteenth and early twentieth century, many Chinese publications advocated that women and men were equal and should enjoy equal civil and political rights such as freedom of thought and speech. These rights were declared natural or heavenly (*tianfu zhi quanli*). The authoritarian and patriarchal elements in traditional Confucianism were seen as enemies of science, democracy, human rights, and the emancipation of all individuals, but particularly women whose subjection was epitomized in the notorious practice of foot-binding (see Svensson 2002). A noteworthy historical fact is that Chinese delegates were directly involved in writing the Universal Declaration of Human Rights, particularly Article One which is heavily influenced by Confucian moral–political ideals. Were it not for late twentieth-century developments such as the emergence of the Maoist cult in which (understandably) human rights were totally rejected as part of "capitalist" and "anti-revolutionary" theory, the Chinese may have learned to speak the language of rights as fluently as most Westerners do.

In discussing human rights and culture, it is crucial to notice to whom the language of human rights appeals. As Svensson has observed, rights "are called for by those who feel that they are being deprived of them, and those to whom they are directing their calls seldom regard them as legitimate or valid" (Svensson 2002, 16). It is usually those whose power has been undemocratically secured that reject the universality of human rights, or re-define the notion of human rights in a way that is favorable and convenient to themselves. And, not surprisingly, it is usually those who have been deprived of their freedom who know they have rights and want to assert them in order to empower themselves. In the words of Ruth Macklin, former president of the International Association of Bioethics:

> There is a disconnect between the statements of traditional leaders and the views of activists for social reform, academics and professionals and community leaders who know and care about individual rights, participatory institutions, and other so-called "Western" values. There is a disconnect between the statements of those who defend a status quo perpetuating an oppressive and hierarchical social system, and people from the same cultures who advocate social change based on ethical principles very much like the principles of humanity and humaneness. Can the beliefs and values of this latter group be explained only under the hypothesis that they are dupes of Western cultural imperialism? This supposition demeans advocates of reform by implying that they are not or cannot be independent thinkers, but are slavish adherents of the Western moral concepts with which they come into contact and seek to emulate.
>
> (Macklin 1999, 273)

A common criticism about importing so-called "Western values" into non-Western societies is that to do so fosters cultural imperialism. This criticism should be taken seriously when Western cultures *impose* values on non-Western cultures regardless of the wills and wishes of people in these societies. But it is an entirely different matter if people in non-Western societies *want* to use

"Western" values in their own struggles against injustice and inequality (see Xia 2009 [1995]). For example, Ren-Zhong Qiu, a prominent Chinese bioethicist, claims that the Chinese people are now *voluntarily* in the midst of "an awakening of the rights sense" (Qiu 1992, 172).

Although Qiu has reservations about rights-oriented individualism as a theory, like many Chinese he welcomes the practical consequences of rights talk. He views affirmatively the fact that "students and intellectuals are striving for civil rights, girls in villages are claiming the right to freely choose marriage (as opposed to accepting arranged marriages), and patients are asserting the right to self-determination" (Qiu 1992, 172). Moreover, the fact that the Chinese government signed the United Nations International Covenant on Civil and Political Rights is not only the result of *external* pressure from the international community, but also the consequence of *internal* demands from the Chinese citizenry. The 1989 Chinese democratic movement proved to the world that Chinese men and women are willing to die for personal freedom and social democracy. Clearly, within the spirit of the Chinese people there is present a deep sense of their individual worth and value as human persons. In view of the Chinese who died fighting for their rights and individual dignity, how can anyone claim that the Chinese do not treasure their human rights?

Within China, one of the main objections to encouraging the use of the language of human rights is that China cannot afford to spend time worrying about civil, political, and reproductive rights when its population lacks adequate food, clothing and shelter, employment, education, and basic health care. Indeed, not only Chinese state authorities but the bulk of the Chinese people believe that economic interests or rights must take priority over civil and political rights, and that population control is more important than reproductive rights. In particular, it is the view of the Chinese people as a whole that especially in rural areas where living standards are very low and illiteracy rates are very high, talk about civil and political rights, particularly reproductive rights, is not only inappropriate but destructive. Specifically, letting illiterate rural people, who believe that one can never have too many children, make their own reproductive choices is to court disaster and to retard the development of China's economy which cannot afford yet more mouths to feed. In all fairness, I am somewhat sympathetic towards this view, though I think that there are ways to nurture the growth of political, civil, and reproductive rights that do not jeopardize economic rights. Indeed, to claim that for the Chinese people only the right to survival matters assumes that the Chinese people, especially rural folks, are not capable of active political participation and a decent civil life. Clearly, this view is wrongheaded if my fellow Chinese peasants' participation and enthusiasm in elections for local officials is any sign. Chinese people are not simply animals for whom food is the be-all and the end-all. Like all other human beings, they are completely capable of decent political and civil life.

Chinese women's reproductive rights as human rights

Western academics and political leaders decry the lack of human rights, particularly reproductive rights in China. Yet, as a result of interviewing both many Chinese women who have had abortions and many Chinese female physicians who have performed them, I am convinced that simply because Chinese women do not ordinarily use the language of rights to express or defend their reproductive choices does not mean that Chinese women are not concerned about controlling their reproductive destiny. On the contrary, Chinese women want to have more of a say in Chinese family planning policies than they have previously had.

Although most Chinese obstetricians and gynaecologists (OB/GYNs) realize that the size of China's population needs to be controlled if China is to prosper, a growing number of them have serious reservations about the *means* government authorities have used and still use to achieve this goal. For example, in my fieldwork on Chinese views and experiences of abortion conducted in China in 1997, Dr. Zhang, a middle-aged OB/GYN physician, admitted to me that she has had second thoughts about some of the "family planning" operations she performed in the past. Like most Chinese, she does not question the necessity of controlling China's population or the legitimacy of the state family planning program. In fact, she considers limitations on people's procreative choices the business of the state and not, in her own terms, that of an "ordinary OB/GYN doctor" like her. Nevertheless, she is not entirely comfortable with the methods the state employs to achieve its goals. In particular, she is uncomfortable with the role she has played and is asked to play in controlling other women's bodies. For example, she related the following situation to me:

> Some time ago, women in the countryside were compelled to be sent group by group by automobile to the hospital at the city for IUD insertion, abortion and sterilization. The family planning cadres surrounded them. They guarded the gate out of the ward. They even watched them when they went to the restroom because they were afraid [the] women would run away. Then, I performed many "family planning" operations [that is, abortions and sterilizations].
>
> (Nie 2005)

In retrospect what bothered Dr. Zhang the most about the operations she performed was that no attempt was made to secure the women's informed consent to sterilization or abortion. She was particularly troubled by her participation in a coercive late abortion in which the pregnant woman had no say, commenting that:

The reality is that the pregnant woman had no right if the family planning official required her to have late abortion. The woman cannot say whether she wants to or not. She cannot demand or do anything but accept. However, I felt, . . . I do not know how to say it. In present and new-fashioned terms, you should at least get consent from the woman herself (*zhengde benren tongyi*), let her know beforehand (*geita dage zhaohu*). Yet, in that situation [in which the pregnant woman was required by the family planning official to have the abortion], no one got consent from her.

(Ibid)

Fortunately, for Dr. Zhang, the particular women she aborted/sterilized, and Chinese women in general, local and state authorities have begun to give Chinese women more say in the kind of birth control methods they use. Since the 1990s, some social experiments have been carried out giving rural women more freedom to choose the method of birth control most congenial to them, a phenomenon called *"zhiqing xuanze cun"* (the village of informed choice). Dr. Zhang has applauded these experiments, hoping to see them expand:

Now there have been some experiments regarding informed choice in some villages where people choose their methods of birth control. After bearing a [first] child, people are allowed to choose for themselves what they think is the best method. Even after the second child, sterilization is not forced on people. This practice gives people some degree of freedom of choice (*"yiding de xuanze ziyou"*). While some experiments have been conducted in some villages, unfortunately, this practice [of informed choice] is not fully under way yet.

(Ibid)

Although Chinese women do not have much choice about participating in the effort to control China's population, it is encouraging to know that local and state authorities are beginning to recognize people's need to have as much freedom as the constraints of necessity permit. Even if the urgent need to control China's population demands that all Chinese exhibit reproductive restraint, that does not mean that women should have no choice about how they exercise reproductive restraint. Sex control, long-term or short-term contraception, sterilization, and early abortion are all reasonable birth control options, provided that women get to choose which method they prefer.

In her important study on how Chinese urban women with one child only view China's birth planning program, the Danish sociologist Cecilia N. Milwertz discovered that most of these women complied with the program despite their wish to have more than one child (Milwertz 1997).² Their compliance was a result not so much of fear or coercion as of "conscientious acceptance" (*zijue jieshou*). Still, many Chinese urban women with one child sense that their "conscientious acceptance" is not entirely free. In particular, they "experience a violation of their reproductive self-determination, but they do not have a concept with which to label the experience" (Milwertz 1997, 198).

The Western feminist language of human rights can help these and other Chinese women label their so-far nameless problem, to express their sense of reproductive loss and possibility. Consider the practice of forced abortion in China, including forced partial-birth abortion, as an example. Examined through the perspective of Chinese state authorities, coerced abortion, for whatever reason, is not a serious problem. Indeed, Chinese state authorities often regard Westerners who oppose such abortions as *dajing xiaoguai* (being surprised or alarmed by the normal things) or *bieyou yongxin* (having ulterior motives, i.e., hostile to China and Chinese people). Through the lenses of human rights' theorists and activists, however, forced abortions become abnormal; indeed, immoral. They become something to protest as violations of women's human rights to personal privacy and bodily integrity (for a discussion of the ethical issues related to coerced abortion in China, see Nie 2005, Chapter 7).

Toward a Chinese feminist bioethics: importance of native concerns and language

Even as Chinese and Western academics continue to debate whether or not the language of human rights and the concepts of Western feminism are helpful for China, feminist bioethics has started to take root in practice in China. Among others, Ren-Zhong Qiu has organized a series of activities to promote feminist perspectives on bioethics.³ From its inception, Chinese feminist bioethics has been a part of the international bioethics community.

---

2 The results of my survey of twelve different population groups throughout China, conducted in 1997, also shows that a great majority of Chinese men and women in urban and rural areas genuinely support the national birth planning policies (Nie 2005).

3 As part of a research project on reproductive health and ethics chaired by Ren-Zhong Qiu, a symposium entitled "Reproduction, Sexuality, Ethics and Women's Rights: Feminist Perspectives," was held in Beijing 25 February–1 March 1994. Sixty-six physicians, sexologists, sociologists, demographers, philosophers, bioethicists, lawyers, experts in women's work and women's studies, and administrators of birth control attended the conference. They discussed a variety of issues related to women's sexual and reproductive rights. The Symposium papers, together with papers presented at two other conferences held in China, were published in 1996 (Qiu 1996). From November 1–3 2001, yet another international conference on feminist bioethics was held in Beijing. More than fifty scholars from a wide variety of disciplines attended the meeting. The activities organized by Qiu can be regarded as the birth of feminist bioethics in China.

Qiu's projects, including two international conferences on feminism and bioethics in Beijing in 1996 and 2001, were attended by scholars from such countries as the UK, USA, India, Australia and New Zealand. At the same time, Chinese scholars have been eager to participate in international discussions elsewhere (e.g. Wang 2001; Nie 2010b).

Whether feminist bioethics will continue to survive and thrive in Chinese soil is hard to predict. I have so far argued that, in spite of the great sociocultural differences between China and the West, Western feminism, feminist bioethics, and feminist human rights language are relevant to China. They provide the Chinese people with useful lenses to understand the Chinese experience. Thus, it is vital that Chinese thinkers and activists learn from Western feminism and feminist bioethics, and that they import to China not only Anglo-American bioethics but all kinds of foreign bioethics.

Yet, no matter how important it is for Chinese bioethicists to learn from the bioethicists of other countries, it is even more important for them to, 1) focus on native problems and concerns, and, 2) create a Chinese feminist language rooted in indigenous Chinese moral and political traditions. It is imperative for Chinese feminist bioethics to integrate academic bioethics with the grass-root activities of Chinese women struggling to make the health care system sensitive to their interests, respectful of their rights and dignity, and appreciative of their labors and bodies. A Chinese feminist bioethics must above all be a bioethics for Chinese women. It must be attentive to, and grounded in, the personal experiences and voices of individual women. Western feminism can help expose the oppressive and unjust nature of Chinese women's individual experiences and collective conditions. Equally as important, Chinese women's experiences and conditions can enrich Western feminism by challenging strictly Western interpretations of them.

The narratives of Chinese OB/GYNs (almost all are female) who perform abortions and women who have had abortions offer a good example of the ways in which individuals' lived experiences can be an effective antidote against the simplifying and over-generalizing tendency in current understandings of this topic. According to the official Chinese standpoint, Chinese women support the national birth control program because it is beneficial to both country and the women as individuals. In contrast, according to the dominant Western feminist view, the Chinese national population policy is a serious violation of women's reproductive rights and Chinese women are opposed to it. But the reality of the situation is somewhere between these two extreme perspectives. Most Chinese women, as well as Chinese men, support the policy, but not without some reservations and, in particular cases, resistance.

Clearly, Chinese feminist bioethics must resist the impulse to identify as normative for all Chinese women the perspectives and experiences of urban, well-educated, professional Chinese women. Instead, it should closely attend to the lived-experiences, concerns and voices of all types of Chinese women:

urban and rural, Han and minority nationalities, educated and uneducated, rich and poor, university professors and *sanpeinu* (female sex workers), white-collar professionals and *dagongmei* (countryside women working in the cities). Most importantly, Chinese feminist bioethics should be centered on and oriented to underprivileged and marginalized groups such as the millions of increasingly illiterate or half-illiterate women in rural China. The concerns and problems of underprivileged groups and individuals—the exploited, the oppressed, the silenced, and the deprived—should always be the focus of the medical social sciences, humanities, and bioethics, be they Chinese or non-Chinese (Nie 2000).

In the West, the lenses of gender, no matter how powerful, are never sufficient to analyze issues; one must always look at reality through the lenses of race and class at the same time. In the Chinese context, the rural–urban residency as a category of analysis is essential. There exists a caste-like, institutional social stratification in China in which people are divided into two birth-ascribed civil status groups: rural as the lower and urban as the higher. In spite of some recent improvements, social, economic, and cultural inequality between these two groups is so enormous that depriving an urban person of his or her urban-residence status constitutes one of the most serious civil punishments inflicted in China.

Rural–urban injustice in China is a form of discrimination that is more serious but much less acknowledged and addressed than, say, racism. Although discussion of rural discrimination in China is beyond the scope of this chapter, I feel compelled to stress that 0.8 billion rural Chinese—the great majority of the total Chinese population—lack adequate primary health care. While the cause-of-death patterns in urban China are similar to those in developed countries, cause-of-death patterns in rural areas are much more typical of those in developing countries. Death rates due to infectious diseases, respiratory diseases, pregnancy and childbirth, injuries and poisoning, and even suicide are much higher in rural areas than in urban areas. The life expectancy of rural residents is several years shorter than that of urban residents. As the county-township-village three-tier health care system collapses, and as the "barefoot doctors" (the primary health care givers who provided basic free services in the countryside in the 1960s and 1970s) are transformed into physician entrepreneurs, rural–urban inequalities are worsening. Rural girls and women suffer the most. In the same way that it is regarded a misfortune to be born a woman in China—"*tuocuo le tai*" (being conceived in the wrong womb)—it is regarded a misfortune to be born in the countryside. But the double "misfortune" of being born a rural woman need not be a misfortune at all—not if the Chinese people as a whole decide to improve the situation of women in the rural outposts.

At present, Chinese feminist bioethics remains overly dependent on Western feminist bioethics. In addition to focusing on and addressing specifically Chinese problems, Chinese bioethics also needs to explore indigenous moral and ethical traditions for new insights to stimulate the development of Chinese feminist bioethics in particular and bioethics in general. Chinese feminist bioethicists must overcome the radical anti-traditionalism that grounded the "New Culture" movement of the 1920s, the Cultural Revolution of the 1960s and 1970s, and the "New Era" of the 1980s. The twentieth century in China is a century of revolutions, which have destroyed not only millions of lives and a great amount of material civilization but also traditional institutions and values, including those important or even essential for a good society.

All of these losses are sad, but as an intellectual, it disturbs me in particular that often Confucianism, Taoism, and Buddhism are dismissed as entirely retrograde and repressive systems of thought that oppress women in particular. But this is not an accurate evaluation of traditional Chinese thought. Within it are several revolutionary perspectives for Chinese feminists to use. The concept of yin-yang is a good example here. Admittedly, since the Han Dynasty (205 BCE–221 ACE), the yin-yang concept has been used by Confucians to justify men's power and dominance over women and women's inferior status in socio-cultural life. However, according to the original yin-yang concept, yin and yang (symbolizing the female and the male) are not only fundamentally different but also completely equal. They originate in each other, depend on each other, nourish each other, and struggle with each other. One cannot exist without the other. One is neither superior nor inferior to the other. In Daoist theories and practice, yin, being often associated with water, plays an even more critical role than yang in the everlasting metamorphoses of nature. Early Daoist ethical theories, as articulated by Lao Zi and Zhuang Zi, imply and encourage that one begins explanations of difference from a female perspective rather than a male perspective (see Watson 1968; for an English translation of Lao Zi, see Chan 1963). Certainly, properly interpreted, the yin-yang concept and ancient Daoism can help Chinese feminist bioethicists articulate ways in which the two sexes, though different, are nonetheless equal. Old Chinese wisdom can serve today's Chinese women well, provided that it is continually reinterpreted in the context within which it finds itself situated.

Even Confucianism, which in the twentieth century has been blamed as the major ideology responsible for the oppression and subordination of women in China, has significant common ground with contemporary feminism from ethics of care to ecofeminism as the essays in a volume on Confucianism, gender and feminist ethics have demonstrated (Li 2000). In other words, there is basis for allying Confucian moral and social philosophy with feminist concerns and gender equality. It is not true that Confucianism has nothing to do with long-rooted sexism in Chinese history and socio-cultural life and that the founders and leading thinkers of Confucianism have often addressed sex inequality. Nevertheless, Confucian attitudes toward women are far from always degrading and repressive as usually described. In fact, historically speaking, women in Confucian China are far from universally victimized as the common wisdom has presented (Ko 1994; Bray 1997; Raphals 1998; Forth 1999). In this sense, the relationship between Confucianism and feminism is more like that between Christianity and feminism rather than that between an exclusively anti-women ideology and feminism.

To explore how to develop a Chinese feminist bioethics by re-visiting Chinese traditions is not the subject of this chapter. My point is this: it is not only desperately needed but definitely possible to create a Chinese feminist language rooted in indigenous Chinese moral-political traditions and to develop not only a Daoist feminist bioethics but also a Confucian feminist bioethics. A new China cannot and should not be built from scratch and free from its ancient traditions, and Chinese feminist bioethics should not fall into the black hole of a totally anti-traditionist and abstract way of thinking.

Conclusions

Western feminism has great intellectual and moral charm for me academically and personally. Because I am a Chinese male, I cannot experience the injustices Chinese women experience as women. However, growing up at the bottom of Chinese society, I witnessed and experienced many instances of social injustice, political discrimination, economic inequality and cultural prejudice, most notably, the uniquely Chinese rural–urban split. Because feminism is deeply and passionately concerned about gender-based discrimination, prejudice, and inequality, it has been a powerful intellectual tool for me to make better sense of my experiences, concerns and pains of living with a wide range of social injustice in China, especially the reality of rural–urban injustice. In this sense, feminist theory is *my theory* or *a theory for me*. It helped me understand the ways in which all forms of discrimination are interrelated.[4]

A global feminist bioethics without Chinese voices is not truly international. In this chapter, I have argued that Western feminism and feminist bioethics provide Chinese women and men with useful perspectives to identify and

---

4 Moreover, through challenging a number of "common sense" beliefs, feminism has helped me become aware of some of my own biases against and misconceptions about women. For example, until knowing feminism, I assumed that women were biologically or naturally ill-suited for higher learning. I thoughtlessly accepted the view that while girls may do better in elementary school or junior high school than boys, due to "biological" reasons they could not, as a group, compete with boys in and beyond the university level. This belief is to some extent based on the historical fact that great writers, thinkers and scientists in China as elsewhere have been mostly men. But, as feminism has firmly established, the fact that there have been relatively few great female philosophers is not the result of women's inability to reason and create but instead the result of gender discrimination; that is, women have not had the same intellectual opportunities and resources that men have had until relatively recently. Increasingly provided with the same education as men, women are proving to have as much natural talent to excel intellectually, including in abstract thinking, as men have.

highlight gender inequality issues and to face squarely the "rotten fish" in everyday Chinese life. Specifically, they give the Chinese people the hope and inspiration, vocabulary and language, practical strategies and political means to overcome patterns of subordination and domination that block the growth of gender freedom and justice in China. I have also pointed out the importance of the Chinese context—focusing on native concerns of Chinese women and developing a feminist language rooted in indigenous Chinese culture. China is ready to incorporate feminist bioethics into its bioethics development. I urge its theorists and practitioners to grow Chinese feminist bioethics from the grassroots. To participate in this cause of advancing Chinese feminist bioethics, elsewhere I have attempted to employ the feminist lenses to make a better sense of abortion in China (Nie 2005) and to critically analyse China's ambitious and intrusive birth planning program (Nie 2010b).

May a Chinese feminist bioethics grow well in China—my motherland! May Chinese feminist bioethics play a positive role in reforming China into a society with less gender inequality and other forms of social injustice! May all men and women in China and other parts of the world live together fully equally and with mutual respect and dignity, as the ancient Chinese wisdom has dreamed of, yin and yang in a true harmony!

Part IV

Chinese wisdom for today

Chapter 11

After *cheng* (sincerity or truthfulness)

The professional ethics of traditional Chinese medicine

A simple listing of some of the distinctive concepts, theories, procedures, techniques, and treatments developed by traditional Chinese medicine (TCM) over many centuries indicates the apparently unbridgeable gap between this ancient medical system and modern biomedicine originating in the West: yin-yang; the five phases or agents; *qi*; essence; the five viscera and the six bowels; channels and points; tongue-observing; moxibustion; "damp heat affecting the spleen"; "the exhausted fire of the middle burners"; "extinguishing wind by nourishing yin"; "treating cold with cold and treating heat with heat"; "white tiger decoction"; and "cockcrow powder." To modern sensibilities—with the exception of a handful of individuals who have consistently romanticized foreign ideas and practices—these terms sound primitive, unscientific, exotic, or even laughable. Even many contemporary Chinese do not feel at home with these "old-fashioned" concepts.

Nevertheless, TCM undeniably works in practice for at least some illness or diseases—e.g., the use of acupuncture to relieve certain kinds of chronic pain—despite the inability of modern science to explain adequately the nature of the "channels" and "points" involved. It works—regardless of the foreign character of its concepts and theories for patients, just as contemporary biomedicine "works," even though those who are sick have no real knowledge of anatomy, physiology, or pathology. Other ancient medical traditions, like those of Greece and Rome, are today merely part of history, supplanted by more effective treatments. Yet TCM is still alive today as one of the main healing systems practiced extensively in East Asia, side by side with modern biomedicine. Even in the West, the techniques of TCM—a cornerstone of the developing field of complementary and alternative medicine—are increasingly accepted as a fresh approach to treatment.

As TCM evolved in China, its practitioners formulated a series of pragmatic rules governing the physician's conduct. Moreover, in an effort to systematize their occupational morality according to the key concepts of Chinese ethical–social worldviews, they developed some core principles of professional ethics including the concepts of the virtuous physician (*liangyi*), medicine as the art of humanity or humaneness (*yi nai renshu*), sincerity or moral excellence (*cheng*), and compassion (*ci*). Although these Chinese concepts of professional ethics may not seem as strange as some of the corresponding medical terms, it is far from clear that they will be able to continue to serve as guides for practice today. In this age of globalization and Western hegemony, it is far from certain whether the professional ethics of TCM can still serve as a source of inspiration for promoting a more ethically-rooted practice of medicine and a more robust concept of professionalism—or even if they can survive as the moral foundation for practitioners of TCM in China and elsewhere. At a time when TCM continues to be a major medical system in the East and is serving more people in the West, the vitality of traditional Chinese medical ethics is under threat, if not completely lost.

There are complex socio-cultural and intellectual obstacles that prevent us from taking seriously the professional ethics of TCM and recognizing its contemporary significance. Three factors stand out. The first is the Western habit of treating Chinese traditions as exotic, unscientific and parochial. The second is the trend in both contemporary Chinese and Western scholarship which equates traditional Chinese medical ethics merely with decorum, a set of good behaviors displayed by the individual physician and nothing more. A third factor, and one with particular significance in the Chinese context, is a nihilistic modernist perspective which categorizes the past as backward, primitive, an obstacle to progress, and something that should be discarded. In the twentieth century, China developed a radical anti-traditionalism that first became prominent in the May Fourth movement and reached its peak in the notorious Cultural Revolution. Just as Chinese traditions like Confucianism were viewed as an obstacle to modernization, and, at best, irrelevant to modern China's search for national strength, wealth and power, traditional Chinese medical ethics were—and still are—regarded as having, at best, only a very limited or supplementary role in contemporary health care practice.

This and the following chapters will introduce some fundamental concepts or principles of the professional ethics of TCM and discuss their contemporary relevance. In this chapter, I offer a study of the most influential text of Chinese medical ethics, the *Lun Dayi Jingcheng* (On the Proficiency and Sincerity of the Master Physician) of the great seventh-century physician Sun Simaio (Sun Szu-miao). To better explain the professional ethics of TCM as articulated by Sun, I will also sketch out some of the metaphysical and spiritual dimensions of Chinese medical professionalism through a discussion of the complex and multi-layered Confucian understandings of *cheng*, often but inadequately translated as "sincerity," but also carrying connotations of truth, truthfulness, authenticity, purity, honesty, genuineness, reality, self-realization, and moral excellence.

Both contemporary Chinese and Western scholars (e.g., Unschuld 1979; Qiu 1988; Lee 1999; Jonsen 2000, 36–41; Zhang and Cheng 2000) have treated humanity or humaneness (*ren*, often perceived as the foundational notion of Confucian ethics and politics) and/or compassion (*ci*, a key ethical concept derived from Buddhism) as *the* fundamental principle of traditional Chinese medical ethics. In this chapter, I focus on the norm and ideal of *cheng* rooted in Confucianism and influenced by Buddhism. Along with the principles of humanity or compassion, *cheng* constitutes the core doctrine of the professionalism espoused by adherents of TCM, especially when seen in the context of the personal morality of practitioners.

The medical profession and professional ethics in China

For sociologists, the concept of profession implies far more than an ordinary occupation. According to Eliot Freidson (1988), an occupation becomes a formal profession only when it obtains legitimate and organized autonomy, that is, the right to control its own work in an exclusive way and freedom from supervision by society. Medicine in the United States since the Flexner Report, and especially since World War II, constitutes the archetype of professionalism in this sociological perspective. Under the criteria for professions developed in the United States, the process of the professionalization of medicine in China did not truly begin until the twentieth century when modern Western biomedicine took root and began to marginalize TCM and other traditional healing systems. Under the threefold spell of scientism, modernism and radical anti-traditionalism, proposals were made and action taken to abolish TCM in the first half of the twentieth century in China (see Croizier 1968; Zhao 1989). Thus in the case of TCM, the beginnings of professionalization can be viewed as a response to a threat to its survival. In fact, as a result of its specific socio-political contexts, even in contemporary China, medicine—whether TCM or biomedicine—hardly enjoys the kind of autonomy that marks the American medical profession.

Despite the very recent professionalization of TCM, some elements necessary for the development of a profession are detectable in early Chinese civilization. First among these elements is the development of a systematized body of knowledge, with foundations reaching back to the Han Dynasty (205 BCE to 220 AD) or even earlier. These foundations include the appearance of the so-called "four classics" of TCM in this period, comprising two theoretical volumes, *Huangdi Neijing* (The Yellow Emperor's Classic of Medicine, which consists of two parts, *Suwen* and *Lingxu*) and *Nan Jing* (The Classic of Difficult Issues), as well as the major clinical works known as *Shanghan Zabing Lun* (On Various Fevers and Internal Diseases) and *Shennong Bencao Jing* (The Legendary Farmer's Classic of Materia Medica). According to the *Huangdi Neijing*, in remote and supposedly "golden" antiquity, physicians were obliged to participate in a set of rituals and take an oath sworn in blood before beginning the study and practice of acupuncture (see *Lingshu*, chapters 9 and 48). Unfortunately, there is no surviving evidence relating to the performance of these rituals or the content of the oath.

The second element of a growing profession to be observed in Chinese antiquity was the division of labor and specialization, which occurred as early as the third century BCE when the imperial palace was equipped with specialists in medical administration, nutrition, internal medicine, and surgery (Chen 1991, 2–4).

Third, the governance and regulation of practitioners within a national system of medical education and qualifying examinations began, at least for physicians in the Imperial Court, over 1,500 years ago. State-sponsored medical services and state-controlled medical education evolved together early in the history of China (Needham 2000).

The fourth and most telling aspect of the development of professionalism was the creation of a distinctive professional ethics for TCM. As a rule, a given medical system will develop its own professional morality or ethics. Rooted in the socio-cultural and historical context in which a particular medical system originates and grows, the resulting professional ethics can vary from rules of thumb based on practitioners' customs to a highly systematic professionalism. Although professional medical ethics usually develop alongside the process of professionalizing the services of healers, a formal profession is not required for the existence of a professional ethics. And while professional ethics may not be the crucial and necessary attribute of a formal profession, as medical sociologists have argued, they are essential for the mature development of any profession.

Let me here recapitulate some basic historical facts and major themes in the professional ethics of TCM (for more information see Unschuld 1979; Qiu 1988; Nie 2009). Since antiquity, discussions of moral issues in medicine, including the professional behavior of practitioners, have appeared in a variety of genres including works by physicians such as Zhang Zhongjing, philosophers like Confucius and Lie Zi, and historians like Sima Qian. One of the most notable of these treatises is the essay "Lun Yi" (On the Physician) from the *Wuli Lun* (A Treatise on the Nature of Things) by Yang Quan, a fourth-century scholar. For Yang, to practice medicine requires not only talent, intelligence, knowledge and the requisite skills, but above all virtue and moral character. One should not seek medical help from those lacking in humanity and universal love (*boai*), and should not entrust oneself to practitioners who are deficient in wisdom and a well-cultivated morality. He distinguishes the "good" or excellent physician (*liangyi*) from the "celebrated" one (*mingyi*), and points out that the latter does not necessarily imply the former, while even a nameless doctor can be excellent. Yang gives high praise to the ancient tradition by which only those who displayed both natural talent and excellent moral character were selected by the community to study and practice the art of medicine (in Chen 1991, 16–17).

The morals and virtues of the good physician constitute the most salient theme in traditional Chinese medical ethics. In orthodox medical literature, *yongyi* (common physicians) were often described critically and in a derogatory tone. In contrast, there were *dayi* (Great Physicians), *ruyi* (Confucian physicians), *mingyi* (enlightened physicians), *deyi* (virtuous physicians), and *liangyi* (good physicians). According to Xu Chunfu in the twelfth century, "Learners of medicine differ greatly in their degree of excellence in mastering the art of medicine. They thus have different names" (in Chen 1991, 50–52). Xu distinguished the five types of practitioners: 1) *mingyi* (enlightened physicians), "those who practice medicine excellently"; 2) *liangyi* (good physicians), "those who are good at medicine"; 3) *guoyi* (state or court physicians), "those who bring a long life to the emperor and protect the ministers from diseases"; 4) *yongyi* (common physicians), "those who perform their work in an unskilled manner and to whom the principles of medicine remain hidden"; and 5) *wuyi* (sorcerer-physicians), "those who beat the drum and perform dances, who recite prayers and prepare sacrifices to [ward off] sufferings and diseases. They are merely followers of witchcraft and have no knowledge of medicine" (in Ibid; Unschuld 1979, 40–41). "Common physicians," as perceived by orthodox Confucian practitioners, were neither morally virtuous nor technically competent. Some practiced medicine just to make a living, with no noble moral ideals.

The insistence on a high standard of both technical expertise and morality has dominated the paradigmatic seventh-century writings of Sun Simaio on professional ethics (see next section). In fact, this emphasis on excellence in both the professional skills and moral character of the physician constitutes the basis of the professional ethics of TCM. Following Sun, many writers added to the discussion on professional conduct and ethical practice, contributing material that may still be relevant to practitioners in the twenty-first century. Zhang Gao (about 1149–1227), a Confucian physician heavily influenced by Buddhism, expressed his ethical views on good medical practice and good physicians in the section, "Retribution for Medical Services," of his *Yishuo* (Teachings on Medicine). Using the common device of telling stories to promote morality, Zhang related twelve detailed anecdotes. In these he discussed some central themes of traditional Chinese medical ethics. Selfless practice will bring rewards in this world and beyond, while bad or greedy practice will result in punishment and death. Conscientious practice requires a physician not to have sex with patients or their family members. The physician should not use fraudulent methods. The practitioner should refuse to sell abortitifacients for the sake of the aborted fetus (child). In the sixteenth century, Zhu Huiming devoted special sections to ethical discussion, including "Physician Should Preserve Humaneness," "Good Conduct Brings Rewards," and "A Warning to Determine the Prospect for a Good or Bad Cure Early Enough." In the seventeenth century, Gong Tingxian, a prolific medical writer who from time to time was employed in the imperial office for medicine, offered "Ten Maxims for Physicians" and "Ten Maxims for Patients." In the same century, Chen Shigong put forward the "Five Admonitions to Physicians" and "Ten Maxims for Physicians" in his classic work *Waike Zhengzong* (Orthodox Manual of Surgery).

A few caveats are required at this point. First, although a cursory glance at the works of the classical medical authors of China might suggest a unified system, the diversity of medical practice in China cannot be overemphasized (see Chapter 5). It is important to notice that there is no single Chinese culture, moral code, system of healing, no definitive Chinese medical ethics, archetypical Chinese medical practitioner or singular moral discourse that could embrace the wide range of practitioners in antiquity.

Second, it must be emphasized that no one can be certain about the actual influence of these maxims and admonitions on daily medical practice and about the character assumed by medical practitioners. In reality, as a classic realistic novel, *Jinpingmei*, vividly illustrates, most physicians were "common," rather than truly "good" or "enlightened" or "great."

Third, these ethical rules were offered in the form of moral advice and suggestions, and so were not professional codes in the modern Western sense or duties as stated in the Hippocratic Oath. Although the *Yellow Emperor's Classic of Medicine* does mention that the physician should participate in rituals and take a blood oath before learning and practicing acupuncture (*Lingshu*, Chapters 9 and 48), the rite and the content of the oath(s) are not recorded and the practice of taking a blood oath was not continued after antiquity.

Pursuing both proficiency and sincerity: the idea of technical and moral excellence

The *Lun Dayi Jingcheng* (On the Proficiency and Sincerity of the Master Physician),[1] one chapter of the monumental medical work *Qianjin Yaofang* (Prescriptions Worth More Than a Thousand Pieces of Gold), was written by the medical master Sun Simiao (c. 581–682) in the early Tang Dynasty. It is considered to be the most important document of medical ethics in Chinese history and has had an enormous influence, with a status similar to that of the Hippocratic Oath in the West. Sun brought together various medical practices and techniques known prior to the seventh century, and his work served as a guide for practitioners in later centuries in China, Japan, Korea, and elsewhere in East Asia. He is still popularly known as "the King of Medicine." His life and achievements have made him a paradigm of ethical practice and elevated

---

1 Paul Unschuld translated *dayi jingcheng* as "the absolute sincerity of great physicians" (1979, 29). In classic and modern Chinese, *jing cheng* usually means "absolute or total sincerity," with *jing* as an adjective, as in the proverb *jingcheng suo zhi, jingshi wei kai* (total sincerity can affect even metal and stone). An alternative reading is possible here. The word *jing* can be read as a noun parallel to *cheng*, rather than as an adjective qualifying *cheng*. The term *jing cheng* first appeared in "The Old Fisherman," chapter 32 of *Zhuang Zi (Chuang Tzu)*, the ancient Daoist classic. The text, translated by Burton Watson (1968, 349), reads: "By the 'Truth' I mean purity and sincerity in their highest degree. He who lacks purity and sincerity cannot move others."

him to the position of the ideal physician, not only because of the high standard of morality advocated in his medical ethics writings but also because he was known to have met these exacting standards in his own medical practice. Even his longevity (Sun lived to 101) is treated as a symbol of his great virtue and humaneness—Confucianism considers longevity to be the crowning fruit of a virtuous life.

The key tenet of Sun's ethics, as the title of this important text indicates, is that a physician must be simultaneously *jing* (proficient, or at least competent, in the study and practice of medicine) and *cheng* (sincere in one's moral commitment, honest and virtuous). Sun Simaio was the first to put forward the ideal of *dayi* (the Master Physician) and to articulate the ethical principles and conduct appropriate to the role. Beginning with a series of insightful discussions on learning and mastering the art of medicine, the *Lun Dayi Jingcheng* focuses on the professional ethics of medical practice.[2]

Like other classic medical authors such as the compilers of the *Huangdi Neijing*, Sun first emphasizes the difficulty of learning medicine. The study of medicine requires devotion and tenacity. It is dangerous "to pursue the most subtle matters by means of careless and superficial studies." "Only those who learn with the heart and study meticulously" can begin to understand the complexity and subtlety of medicine. Sun strongly opposes the habit of satisfying oneself with a mere smattering of knowledge on a particular subject (*qianchang jizhi*, stopping after gaining a little knowledge of something). Any true student of medicine must "master all the sources of medical knowledge and study them diligently and constantly" (*boji yiyuan, jingqing buzhuan*). Even those who study in this way may not achieve excellence in medicine, as the task requires more than human insight. For Sun, medicine, like divination, involves grasping the finest subtleties with the help of "divine revelation"—something beyond purely human talents and powers.

In the *Lun Dayi Xiye* (On the Master Physician's Way of Learning Medicine), another chapter from his masterwork *Qianjin Yaofang*, Sun discusses in detail the proper course of study entailed in becoming a physician. To be competent in the art of medicine one must first have a substantial general education. A thorough knowledge of the ancient classics and of history, literature, and philosophy is essential. Thus Confucianism, Daoism and other traditional schools of thought, as well as astrology and divination, are appropriate premedical subjects. One must also study the classic works of medicine, acupuncture, and materia medica. Finally, learning must not only come from books. One must practice the arts one studies and acquire personal experience as a physician because the knowledge derived from books is never sufficient in itself.

---

2 Chinese version in Chen 1991, 18–19 and Zhou 1983, 98–103; for a complete English translation, see Unschuld 1979, 29–33. The translations of the text below are based on that of Unschuld.

The notion of *jing* refers to excellence not only in medical skills but also in personal morality. In the *Lun Dayi Jingcheng*, Sun formulates the fundamental ethical principles of healing and elaborates on the moral excellence of the Master Physician. A good physician must first of all cultivate a heart of genuine and deep compassion for human pain, suffering, and distress:

> When a Master Physician practices medicine, he must calm his mind ... develop a heart of great mercy and compassion, and solemnly pledge to relieve without any discrimination the pains from which the souls of all existences (*hanling*)—human beings—suffer.

Sun promotes a universal medical humanism and maintains that a doctor should treat all patients equally:

> When the ill come for help, whether they are noble or lowly, rich or poor, old or young, handsome or homely, enemies or good friends, Chinese or foreigners, intelligent or simple-minded, the Master Physician should pay no attention to any of these things but rather should treat all his patients equally, as if they were his closest relatives.

For Sun, a morally excellent physician takes an "heroic" attitude to medicine. He stresses that a physician should not shrink back from his work because of unfavorable or even dangerous circumstances, but, instead, should always involve himself wholeheartedly in the situation that presents itself.

> A physician should not be overcautious and indecisive, should not worry about good or bad luck, and should not be concerned about his own body and life. Seeing the patient unwell, a physician should feel as if he himself had been struck down. With deep sympathy welling up from the bottom of his heart, a physician should not merely appear to have done his best, but get involved wholeheartedly—not worrying whether the location is dangerous and precipitous, the time is day or night, the weather cold or hot, or whether he himself is hungry, thirsty and exhausted. Whoever practices medicine in this way is a Master Physician to all human beings. Whoever practices medicine in a contrary way is the worst enemy of humankind.

As a result, a good doctor should never shrink from treating a patient who suffers from a loathsome illness like skin ulcers:

> Among the patients will be those suffering from skin ulcers and foul-smelling dysentery whom no one wants to examine, and others hate to visit. A physician should not show even a small amount of unwillingness, but treat the sick with compassion, sympathy and pity. This is my commitment.

Most notably, Sun's view of professional ethics requires a physician to treat all forms of life—animals and human alike—equally. This is a very radical viewpoint in Chinese medicine and clearly derived from Sun's Buddhist beliefs. In the materia medica of TCM, a large number of drugs are derived from animal body parts. Standing alone among his peers, Sun strongly opposes this practice:

> Although animals are usually devalued and humans valued, animals and humans are the same in loving their own lives. To damage others for the benefit of oneself goes against the nature of even physical things—let alone the feelings of us human beings.

Sun's principle here is that "To kill one life to save another life takes us further away from life." This is the reason that living creatures are never used to make drugs in the prescriptions in his medical book.

Sun then outlines how a virtuous doctor should behave as an individual, and especially how he should treat his patients:

> The manner of a Master Physician should be concentrated on his inner self, appearing composed to others, carrying himself with ease and confidence, and behaving in neither an overbearing nor servile manner. When examining the patient and diagnosing the disease, he should pay the closest attention. He should scrutinize all the symptoms in great detail and should not err by a hair's-breadth. In prescribing acupuncture or herbs, he should not be in any kind of doubt. Even though the disease should be treated as soon as possible, the physician should not be rushed in dealing with a case, but should investigate it carefully and reflect on it deeply. If, to show off and gain a reputation for making a speedy diagnosis, a physician acts carelessly over matters of life and death, this is contrary to the way of humanity. (*buren*)

As the major location for treatment was the patient's home before the advent of modern clinics and hospitals, Sun emphasizes that a physician should behave with decorum—even a degree of asceticism—when attending his patients in their own homes:

> After arriving at the patient's home, the physician should not look around even though his eyes are dazzled with silks and satins. He is not distracted at all, although his ears are filled with beautiful music from string and bamboo instruments. When delicious food is presented to him, one course after another, he eats as if the food had no taste. When various fine wines are offered him, he treats them as if they did not exist. The physician is to behave in this way because, when one of its members is distressed due to illness, the whole family will be unhappy—not to mention the fact that

pain and suffering never leave the patient even for a moment. For the physician to simply enjoy everything and take a professional pride in himself in the patient's home shames both humans and gods (deities), and is something the Perfect Man should never do. All this points to the true meaning of medicine.

In addition, Sun strongly advises that a good physician should not talk too much, never boast about his own achievements and virtues, and never belittle his colleagues:

> Regarding the way of practicing medicine, the physician should not be talkative, nor tease people, raise his voice, gossip, judge others, parade his fame, belittle his fellow physicians, nor be conceited over his own virtue. Whenever he has treated a case successfully—perhaps by chance rather than skill—he should not put his nose in the air, puff himself up and claim that no physician under heaven could measure up to him. That kind of behavior is the terminal illness of medical practitioners.

Citing Lao Zi (Lao Tzu), the founder of Daoism (Taoism), Sun held that visible virtuous conduct will be rewarded by humans and invisible good deeds by the spirits, while immoral behavior—even that hidden from human eyes—will be punished supernaturally. If the medical practitioner refrains from using his skills for gaining material reward, but is rather determined to relieve suffering, "he will be happy on the way to the underworld."

For Sun, a doctor should not take advantage of the vulnerability of any patient, rich or poor, in any situation:

> To take another example—noticing that the patient is rich and enjoys noble status, in order to show off his rare abilities the physician then prescribes precious and expensive drugs and intentionally makes it hard for the patient to get the medicine. This is not the way of conscientiousness and altruism. (*zhongxu*)

In summary, in the *Lun Dayi Jingcheng* Sun Simiao stipulates the moral requirements for the practice of medicine as well as making practical suggestions for the everyday conduct of physicians. He ends this powerful and eloquent work with an apology:

> As my aim is to cure and relieve sickness, I have not refrained from discussing these apparently trivial matters. Whoever studies medicine should not treat them as something vulgar and be ashamed of talking about them.

In a second major medical work, the *Qianjin Yifan* (Supplement to Prescriptions Worth More Than a Thousand Pieces of Gold), published when he was about 100 years old, Sun further prescribes ten types of good conduct in medical practice: 1) assist those in need or experiencing difficulties; 2) respect demons and celestial beings; 3) do not kill or injure anyone; 4) develop an attitude of compassion; 5) do not envy the rich or despise the poor; 6) cultivate a temperate disposition; 7) avoid valuing luxurious items and despising ordinary ones; 8) seek moderation in diet including avoiding wine, meat, and rich food; 9) seek moderation in life and avoid indulging oneself with women and music; 10) maintain a well-balanced disposition and character (cited in Unschuld 1979, 33–4).

In general, Sun emphasizes that the purpose of medical practice is to help others, rather than gain material wealth and fame. Influenced as he was by the moral and spiritual traditions of Confucianism and Buddhism, he would have considered healing as a vocation or calling. At the heart of his maxims and instructions on learning and practicing medicine, *cheng* (sincerity of moral commitment or moral excellence in general) is the foundation and first principle of Sun's professionalism. *Cheng* is the starting point of medical practice, for only those who are sincere in their moral commitment will study medicine diligently and tirelessly, move the presiding divinities and thus master the art. Here, the notion of *cheng*, as understood in the Confucian tradition, is not only a psychological concept, implying a unity between actions and beliefs, but has metaphysical, religious and spiritual ramifications as well.

Cheng in Confucianism: the philosophical and spiritual basis of traditional Chinese professional ethics

While traditional Chinese medical ethics have been influenced most heavily by Confucianism, there are also significant elements derived from Buddhism and Daoism. Indeed, Sun Simaio's *Lun Dayi Jingcheng* is an eclectic product of elements drawn from Confucianism, Buddhism and Daoism. All three of these major social and ethical traditions of imperial China emphasize the importance of sincerity in moral life. The classic Confucian discussion of *cheng* comes from the *Zhongyong*, often translated as "The Doctrine of the Mean," which is one of the canonical "Four Books" of Confucianism. According to historians of Chinese philosophy, the teachings of the *Zhongyong* attracted both Buddhists and Daoists even before Neo-Confucianism categorized it as one of the handful of fundamental Confucian works (Chan 1963, 95). Scholars from these differing, and sometimes conflicting, traditions wrote their own commentaries on the *Zhongyong* from early times. The idea of sincerity as the heart of the moral life had an appeal to both Buddhist and Daoist traditions, despite their divergence from Confucian thought in other areas.

In the eleventh century, the Neo-Confucian philosopher Zhou Dengyi (Chou Tun-i) considered *cheng* as the foundation of all the virtues:

> Sagehood is nothing but sincerity. It is the foundation of the Five Constant Virtues (humanity, righteousness, propriety, wisdom, and faithfulness) and the source of all activities ... Without sincerity, the Five Constant Virtues and all activities will be wrong. They will be depraved and obstructed. Therefore with sincerity very little effort is needed [to achieve the Mean]. [In itself] it is perfectly easy but it is difficult to put into practice. But with determination and firmness, there will be no difficulty ... It is [a] subtle, incipient, activating force giving rise to good and evil.
>
> (Chan 1963, 466)

For Sun Simiao, sincerity is the foundation of the other virtues needed for learning and practicing medicine including persistence, medical humanism, heroic self-abnegation, the need to treat all patients equally, and respect for all forms of life.

Psychologically, sincerity entails both avoiding cheating others and not indulging in self-deception. It means behaving honestly with others and being honest with one's self. The *Daxue* (The Great Learning), the first of the "Four Books" of Confucianism, defines "making the will sincere" as one of the eight steps toward the acquisition of wisdom and becoming a sage:

> What is meant by "making the will sincere" is allowing no self-deception, as when we hate a bad smell or love a beautiful color ... For other people see him as if they see his very heart. This is what is meant by saying that what is true in a man's heart will be shown in his outward appearance. Therefore the superior man will always be watchful with himself when alone ... Wealth makes a house shine and virtue makes a person shine. When one's mind is broad and one's heart generous, one's body becomes big and is at ease. Therefore the superior man will always make his will sincere.
>
> (Chan 1963, 90)

For Sun Simiao, those who believe that they can achieve technical and moral excellence in medicine without sincerity of the heart are deceiving themselves regarding both the nature of the art of medicine and their own character.

The notion that sincerity is concerned with how one behaves even when unobserved, and with a unity of knowing and acting, suggests a psychological aspect to this concept. But sincerity is not just a state of mind; it also implies a state of being and thus has a metaphysical and religious character. The *Zhongyong* itself links sincerity not only with growth in virtue and personal responsibility, but with spirituality (*tian* or "heaven") and Dao (the Way):

Sincerity is the Way of Heaven. To think how to be sincere is the way of man. He who is sincere is one who hits upon what is right without effort and apprehends without thinking. He is naturally and easily in harmony with the Way. Such a man is a sage. He who tries to be sincere is one who chooses the good and holds fast to it ... Study it (the way to be sincere) extensively, inquire into it accurately, think over it carefully, sift it clearly, and practice earnestly. When there is anything not yet studied, or studied but not yet understood, do not give up ... If another man succeeds by one effort, you will use a hundred efforts. If another man succeeds by ten efforts, you will use a thousand efforts. If one really follows this course, though stupid, he will surely become intelligent, and, though weak, will surely become strong.

(Chan 1963, 107)

The key insight of the Confucian moral understanding and vision of *cheng* is that only those who are absolutely sincere can fully develop their inner nature. The infinite purity of sincerity cannot but reveal itself in such people. Interestingly, according to a modern compiler and commentator on Chinese philosophical texts, the five steps involved in following the way of sincerity set out in the passage cited above—study, inquiry, thinking, sifting, and practice—closely resemble the educational philosophy of John Dewey (Chan 1963, 107).

Moreover, *cheng* is not only a state of being but also a process of becoming and self-completion. As Tu Wei-ming, a brilliant contemporary Confucian scholar, argues, "*Ch'eng* as a state of being signifies the ultimate reality of human nature and, as a process of becoming, the necessary way of actualizing that reality in concrete, ordinary human affairs. Therefore, *ch'eng* symbolizes not only what a person in an ultimate sense ought to be but also what a person in a concrete way can eventually become" (Tu 1989, 80). In the case of medicine, the figure of the Master Physician embodies this state of being and this process of becoming.

In his ground-breaking study of medical ethics in Imperial China, Paul Unschuld has explored the role of ethics in the way practitioners develop their profession. Unschuld defines professionalization as "the process by which one group (or a number of them) endeavors to expand its possession of the medically related resources available in a culture, until it exercises exclusive control over those resources." From Unschuld's sociological perspective the development of professional ethics, even those based on sincerity and authenticity, is still a manifestation of self-interest. Unschuld's insightful thesis on the origins of professional ethics in China echoes the remark of the fourth-century BCE philosopher and social thinker Hanfei Zi. "Physicians are good at sucking human sores and drawing in the diseased blood with their mouth. They do so not because they see their patients as their close family members but because this is where their profits lie and self-interest can be achieved" (Chen 1991, 490). His thesis also echoes the well-known remark of Adam Smith (1991) on the human pursuit of self-interest: "It is not from the benevolence of the butcher, the brewer, or the baker, that we expect our dinner but from their regard to their own interest. We address ourselves, not to their humanity but to their self-love" (*Wealth of Nations*, Book I, Chapter II). It even perhaps recalls the extreme cynicism of the ancient Greek comic writer who, according to de Montaigne (1965, 77), claimed that "no doctor takes pleasure in the health even of his friends."

Yet Montaigne's point is to reveal the absurdity of the suggestion that making profit out of another's misfortune is morally wrong, because no profit can be made except at the expense of others. Pursuing a legitimate self-interest does not contradict a sincere and authentic concern for the welfare of others. Adam Smith also acknowledges that self-interest exists alongside the beneficent aspects of human nature. In *The Theory of Moral Sentiments*, Smith (2000) states that the sentiment of "pity or compassion" exists "evidently" in all humanity, not only in the "virtuous and humane" but even in "the great ruffian," albeit in different degrees.

Confucianism anticipated a similar perspective centuries earlier than Smith, although even among Confucians the question of whether human nature is intrinsically good or evil has been a controversial one. Mencius, one of the central sages of Confucianism, stated unequivocally: "Man's nature is naturally good just as water naturally flows downward. There is no man without this good nature" (in Chan 1963, 52). Humanity comes from within the heart of each individual. The Confucian roots of traditional Chinese professional ethics provide a broad platform for the notion of building on the inherent goodness of human nature.

Conclusion

In the West, there is a recognition that the Hippocratic Oath already exists to provide a source of inspiration for medical professionalism today (see Kass 1985 and Miles 2004). Traditional Chinese morality likewise has a contemporary relevance and, potentially, a deeper significance (given some of the problems that afflict the medical profession) in its emphasis on sincerity, personal growth, and enlightened care of the other. A medical ethic and an ethics of professionalism based on sincerity and truthfulness creates a vision of a profession that allows for transparency of relationships, a dedication to the other as a recognition of enlightened self-interest, and a mode of being that has the potential to transform medical practice from a technical craft into a spiritual pathway.

In striking contrast with the Chinese concept of *cheng* is the almost exclusive stress on external standards in contemporary medical professionalism, both Eastern and Western—its distinguishing feature and guiding spirit is an "ethics of rules," rather than the traditional "ethics of character or virtue."

Contemporary ethical codes of medicine—such as the series of international declarations on medical ethics, especially research ethics, put out by the World Association of Medical Associations; the "Code of Medical Ethics" issued by the American Medical Association; and the "Regulations on Medical Ethics for Medical Professionals in the People's Republic of China" promulgated by the Chinese Ministry of Health—are all dominated by an ethics of rules. In both the East and the West today, the issue of a practitioner's sincerity or authenticity in their moral commitment—whether they are "a virtuous person"—is seemingly less important than following the rules listed in the professional codes. Rather, "acting in conformity with the rules" and "playing the role of a medical professional" are presented as far more important than the practitioner's individual moral formation.

Doubtlessly, rules are essential for the development of any ethically sound medical practice. And a medical ethics based on Confucianism can be compatible with contemporary bioethical principles, although the way of prioritizing these principles may differ significantly (Tsai 1999, 2005). Even for the professionalism of Sun Simiao, following the rules is extremely important. Nevertheless, from the perspective of the professional ethics developed by TCM and based on the concept of *cheng*, the contemporary theory and practice of medical professionalism has significantly neglected the central role not only of the inner disposition of the moral agent, but also of the metaphysical and spiritual dimensions of the moral life.

Chapter 12

"Medicine as the art of humanity" and the physician as a general

What should be the right model for the patient-physician relationship? Or what is, and what should be, the appropriate role of medical professionals in health care? What is the nature of medicine and what is the ultimate moral goal medicine should aim to achieve? There are a lot of discussions on these two sets of questions—one about the patient-physician relationship and the other on the moral goals of medicine—in contemporary bioethics. In this chapter, I introduce two concepts developed in the professional ethics of traditional Chinese medicine—the metaphor of the physician as a general and medicine as the art of humanity—and briefly discuss their contemporary significance.

The physician as a general

Let me start from a lesser-known Chinese image of the healer—namely, the notion of the physician as a general.

The physician may be broadly defined as a person skilled in the art of healing. Different cultures and historical ages can have very similar understandings on the appropriate role a healer should play in health care. They have also developed some very different answers to this basic question in medical ethics. The Western world features many images of the healer as parent, technician, teacher, fighter, and captain of the ship. All these images emphasize the authority of the physician as a main and final decision-maker in settings related to patient care. Such images, the physician as the captain of the ship for instance, have been critically examined and seriously challenged following the rise of the patient's rights movement in the contemporary West (King, Churchill and Cross 1988). Alternative models based on Judeo-Christianity tradition on the professional ethics of medicine—the covenant model—was proposed (May 1983). Robert Veatch, a founder of contemporary bioethics in the West, once outlined four main models available for the physician-patient relationship in what he called "a revolutionary age." They are the engineering model, the priestly model, the collegial model, and the contractual model. Based on his distinctive medical ethics theory built on social contract tradition, Veatch (1981, 1987, 1991, 2009) proposed that, as medicine is transforming from modern to postmodern, the patient-physician relationship should be revolutionized accordingly. That is, there is a moral imperative to develop a model of the patient as a partner, and even putting the patient in charge.

An ancient Chinese metaphor unfamiliar to the West and indeed to contemporary China—that of the physician as a general—endorses the patient-physician model Veatch proposed, although the philosophical rationales between the two markedly differ.

Interestingly, traditional Chinese medicine and modern Western biomedicine can differ radically, not only in their methods of diagnosis and treatment, but also in the images of healers. The military metaphor in Chinese medicine goes back at least as far as the great classic *Huangdi Neijing* or *Neijing* (The Yellow Emperor's Classic of Medicine). The first theme in this metaphor concerns the importance of prevention. As the author(s) of *Neijing* have prescribed, just as a good general tries to avert war, a good doctor treats disease by preventing its occurrence. At the end of Chapter 2 in *Suwen* of *Neijing*, it reads:

> In the old days the sages treated disease by preventing illness before it began, just as a good government or emperor is able to take the necessary steps to avert war. Treating an illness after it has begun is like suppressing revolt after it has broken out. If someone digs a well when thirsty, or forges weapons after becoming engaged in battle, one cannot help but ask: Are not these actions too late?
>
> (Ni trans. 1995, 7)

In the eighteenth century, Xu Dachun—a great physician, scholar and civil officer—wrote an important essay discussing parallels in the art of medicine and the art of war and concluded that there is nothing in the treatment of illness that cannot be found in the *Sun Zi Binfa* (The Art of War), a military classic composed by General Sun Zi (Sun Tze) more than 2,000 years ago. Sun Zi notes, for instance, that there has never been protracted war from which a country has benefited. Therefore, the supreme art of war is "to subdue the enemy without fighting." Xu Dachun (Hsü Ta-ch'un) (Unschuld trans. 1990, 183) argues that this principle in warfare is also valid for medicine: "Those people of antiquity who liked to ingest [strong medicine] … were bound to be affected by extraordinary illness [just as] those who love to fight in wars … [are] bound to receive extraordinary injuries." Observing this rule, a good physician employs medical procedure only as a last resort and limits the use of pharmacology in order to minimize the detrimental side effects medicine always has.

Such attitudes are particularly critical in Chinese medicine since all medicinal substances, including tonic drugs like ginseng, are considered to be "toxic substances" because they may cause harm if not properly applied. Nowadays—when wholesale medicalization has become a basic fact of contemporary life in the West and in China—physician and laypeople alike can gain wisdom from the ancient Chinese military metaphor of healing in regards to the downside of medicine and war. It is always important to understand the limits of medicine and not to exaggerate the effectiveness of treatment or minimize potential harms.

A possible ethical objection to the metaphor of the physician as a general lies in its paternalistic or authoritarian tendencies. In *AIDS and Its Metaphor*, American critic Susan Sontag decisively attacks the military imagery in the Western characterization of disease because it "immobilizes," "overdescribes," and "powerfully contributes to the excommunicating and stigmatizing of the ill" (1990, 182). On this score, however, the Eastern metaphor of the physician as a general is innocent, notwithstanding similar problems in contemporary China of the excommunication and stigmatization of the ill.

According to the original version of the Chinese metaphor, the physician-patient relationship is not defined as that of general to soldier, but rather that of general to emperor. That is, the patient is the sovereign—and the physician is the general chosen by the sovereign to marshal the forces against disease. As the ancient physician Zhe Cheng remarked: "Using medicine is like employing troops and choosing the physician is like appointing a general ... Knowing the general's talents and intelligence, [the patient] gives him the army ... This is the Dao (way) of choosing a physician" (in Ma 1993, 787). Like the sovereign who chooses a wise general, the patient who has the right physician will prosper. But it is the patient who ultimately determines the lifelong strategies of health and, on occasions of medical intervention, oversees the physician's tactics in the battle against disease.

Despite obvious dissimilarities between the art of war and the art of medicine, the wisdom of ancient Chinese military philosophy, especially in its understanding of the good qualities of the general, is highly related to today's physicians and can be applied to contemporary health care in China as well as in the West. For Sun Zi, wisdom, sincerity, humanity, courage, and strictness constitute the five cardinal virtues of the general. An old Chinese saying has it that, although occupational distinction between different professions have a mountain dividing them, the passage of wisdom and good reasoning among them cannot be obstructed. [It seems to me that this Chinese saying can be applied in thinking about cross-cultural differences as well.] If this is true, then Chinese military classics like *The Art of War* (Sun 1963) may indeed help physicians act wisely, humanely, sincerely and courageously.

Medicine as the art of humanity

"Medicine as the art of humanity or humaneness" (*yi nai renshu*) has been widely acknowledged as *the* fundamental principle of traditional Chinese medical ethics by both contemporary Chinese and Western scholars (e.g., Unschuld 1979; Qiu 1988; Lee 1999; Jonsen 2000, 36–41; Zhang and Cheng 2000; Nie 2009). It is based on *ren*, often perceived as the core notion of Confucianism as an ethical, political and spiritual tradition.

For orthodox medical practitioners in traditional China, *The Yellow Emperor's Classic of Medicine* (*Neijing*) is "the unshakable originator" of the medical system they practiced. *Neijing*, mostly compiled during the first and second centuries, consists of two parts—*Suwen* and *Lingshu*—and 162 chapters (for an annotated new English translation of *Suwen*, see Unschuld 2011). The role of *Neijing* in the history of China has perhaps been even more significant than that of the Hippocratic Corpus in the history of Western medicine. *Neijing* defines medicine as "the Dao (way) of excellence and the business of great saints" (*Suwen*: Chapter 8). It calls medicine "the ultimate virtue" and acupuncture "the superb craftsmanship" (*Suwen*: Chapter 11). Thus, one should be very careful in selecting future physicians, for they must possess the requisite character and clinical skills. One must "pass on [medical knowledge and skills] to those who are truly appropriate and should not teach medicine to those who are not appropriate" (*Lingshu*: Chapter 73). *Neijing* mentions that the physician should participate in rituals and take a blood oath before learning and practicing acupuncture—that is, the art of medicine (*Lingshu*, Chapters 9 and 48). Unfortunately, the nature of these rites and the content of these oath(s) are not recorded and, to my knowledge, the practice of taking a blood oath was not continued after antiquity.

Healers in traditional Chinese society, even orthodox Confucian practitioners, never enjoyed the social and economic position that physicians occupy in the contemporary West, or today's China. This was mainly due to Confucianism, in which healing was treated as just a type of *ji* (technique or craftsmanship) or *shu* (art or craftsmanship). The Confucian tradition usually looked down on forms of craftsmanship, i.e., working with one's hands, and many Confucians were ashamed to learn or to practice medicine for this reason. In the household essay, "Discourse on Teachers," Han Yu (768–824), a celebrated literary figure of the Tang Dynasty, stated: "Sorcerers, doctors, musicians and various craftsmen are held in contempt by gentlemen." In the twelfth century, the prominent master of Neo-Confucianism, Zhu Xi, classified medicine as *xiaodao* (petty teaching, small way, little Dao), together with agriculture, horticulture, divination, and other specialized works. Zhu considered it extremely deplorable that Sun Simiao (581–682), one of the greatest physicians in Chinese history (see last chapter), in spite of being an extremely talented person, was relegated to the lower social category of artisan or technician in the official history because of his occupation. It was not uncommon that court physicians were persecuted and killed for treating the illness of emperors and high officials and their family members ineffectively (see Ma 1986, 8–9).

In traditional China, the social status of medicine as an occupation or profession was as low as that of other technical skills, certainly much lower than *rushu* (the art of Confucianism)—civil service and Confucian scholarship. In his essay, "On the Confucian Physician," the twelfth-century physician, Xu Chunfu, emphasized the dissimilarities between Confucianism and medicine, when he stated: "Compared to the art of Confucianism, the art of medicine is definitely secondary" (in Chen 1991, 52). The thirteenth-century physician Zhang Gao was frequently laughed at by people because he engaged in such technical skills as medicine. Before devoting himself to medicine, the scholar-physician Li Shizhen (1518–1593), one of the greatest figures in the history of medicine in China, attempted to become a civil official and did not give up until he had failed the official examination three times.

Understandably, many Confucian medical practitioners disagreed with this view. For Lai Fuyang (fl.1596 A.D.), whether medicine is mere craftsmanship or not depends on how it is practiced. He wrote:

> If medical practice is based on deception, it is to be considered low. If medicine is practiced on the principle of veracity (*cheng*), it is not to be considered low. If a person's knowledge of medicine is applied only to his own body, this is petty (*xiao*). If the application [of a person's medical knowledge] is extended over all mankind, this is not petty.
> (Cited in Unschuld 1979, 41)

In the seventeenth century, the great Ming Dynasty physician, Zhang Jiebin, wrote an essay, "Record [of an Instruction] that Medicine is Not a Petty Teaching." For Zhang, medicine demands considerable conscientiousness from the individual because its concern focuses on life. "Medicine is certainly difficult! Medicine is certainly sublime! It represents the earliest tradition of genuine supernatural and exemplary people, and the first duty of a people" (in Unschuld 1979, 83).

Partly in order to enhance the moral and social status of medicine in a Confucian society, orthodox practitioners promoted the idea "*yi nai renshu*" (medicine as the art of humaneness). The strategy was to connect medicine to Confucian moral ideals and principles, thus elevating it to the art of humaneness: "Confucianism and medicine are inseparable, complementary of each other, and medicine is an essential part of Confucianism" (Qiu 1988, 283). According to Huangfu Mi (214–282 A.D.), a literary man who compiled the famous text, *Zhenjiu Jiayi Jing* (Systematic Classic of Acupuncture and Moxibustion), "If a person is not good at medicine, he cannot help his emperor and parents when they are suffering from disease even though this person has a heart of loyalty and filial piety (*zhongxiao*) and the nature of humaneness and compassion (*renci*)" (Chen 1991, 109). The connection to Confucianism was further advanced by claiming that, because medicine undertakes to save lives as a duty, it is kindred to the way of Confucianism.

There is a widely known saying in China, attributed to the eleventh-century statesman, Fan Zhongyan, that "Whoever has no chance to work as a good prime minister, may work as a good physician." This saying suggests that both civil service and medicine, while the former is superior to the latter, serve the same Confucian moral ideals and that a good physician might even be comparable to a good prime minister.

Medicine as the art of humanity or humaneness requires the physician not only to master Confucian teachings but also to follow Confucian morals in medical practice. It was stressed that, before and during both learning and practicing medicine, one must study Confucian texts diligently. In the section entitled "Regulations of Practicing Medicine," the Ming Dynasty (1368–1644) physician, Li Yan, wrote that, because "medicine comes from Confucianism," a medical practitioner "should get up early in the morning to study one or two Confucian books every day. In this way he can purify the source of his thoughts" (in Chen 1991, 56). The most important ethical requirement of "medicine as the art of humaneness" is that practitioners must practice medicine from a humane heart and in accordance with Confucian moral principles and ideals. Another Ming Dynasty physician, Gong Tingxian, in his famous "Ten Maxims for Physicians," explains:

> In the first place physicians must adopt a disposition of humaneness [*renxin*, a heart of humanity or sympathy]. This is a necessary maxim. They should make special efforts to assist people at every walk of life so that their good deeds have far-reaching influence. Secondly they must master the Confucian teachings. As the precious treasures to the world, Confucian physicians should understand all the [Confucian] principles and consult all the [Confucian] works."
>
> (Cited in Chen 1991, 58–60)

Physicians as the agents of states and nationalism in medicine: A Confucian critique

Although the historical origin of the Confucian ideal of medicine as the art of medicine was not a particularly noble one, it has had significant impact upon the development of professional ethics of traditional Chinese medicine, and has often been mentioned in discussions of medical ethics in contemporary China. However, in general this notion has been interpreted as primarily or, indeed, solely concerning the personal moral characters or virtues of individual medical professionals.

As a core concept in Confucianism, *ren* has been translated variously as "humaneness," "benevolence," "perfect virtue," "goodness," "humanheartedness," "love," "altruism," or "humanity." Along with Confucianism as a whole, the ethical norm and ideal of medicine as an art of medicine offers a vision about the social ethics of medicine in general. In today's world, medical professionalism faces a number of serious threats originating from broad social, economic and political forces. One such threat is the commercialization of medicine and health care. Nevertheless, this is not a new problem for medicine. Even in traditional China, the tendency of some medical practitioners to use medicine for profit rather than employing it as an art of humanity or benevolence had been criticized. What is new about this alienation of medicine for profit in today's world is that large medical institutions (such as pharmaceutical companies) play the most active role in the profit-making machine (about this dark side of medicine in the United States, see the chilling account by Elliott 2010). The medicine driven by profits is obviously against the Confucian principle of medicine as the art of humanity.

One of the new problems modern and contemporary medical professionalism faces is directly related to nationalism in medicine and of physicians serving as the various types of state agents. Although the great majority of social thinkers in the nineteenth and the early twentieth centuries anticipated the significance of scientific advances for human life, few foresaw the massive expansion of nationalism and chauvinism or their deadly consequences during this period (Berlin 1998). In fact, most major modern social thinkers including Karl Marx anticipated the opposite: the decline and gradual death of nation-states and the shrinking power of nationalist ideology. Today, the study of nationalism has become a field with voluminous and continuing contributions from scholars from across the humanities and social sciences. On the one hand, it has been widely acknowledged that nations are socially and historically constructed, that they are "imagined communities" (Anderson 1991 [1983]), and that the ideology of nationalism has led to the foundation of nations and nation-states (Hobsbawm 1990), rather than the other way around as is commonly assumed. At the same time, the sweeping power of nationalism is a contemporary reality that continues to develop and is increasingly felt in every aspect of life, from sport and politics to science and medicine. Surprisingly, while such disciplines as the history and sociology of science have been institutionalized from the mid-twentieth century, the literature on the interaction of nationalism and science remains fragmentary (Crawford 1992). Surely, studies of such notorious subjects as Nazi medicine and Lysenkoism in the Soviet Union should at least touch on the role of the nation-state and nationalism. But the major focus of these investigations often lies elsewhere—e.g. on the impact of racism, particularly anti-Semitism, and totalitarian attitudes to science and medicine.

Nationalism as an ideology and physicians and scientists serving as the agents of nation-states can have a very dark side to show with respect to medicine and science. While nationalist sentiment has often stimulated the advance and positive social application of scientific and medical knowledge, nationalism can also turn science and medicine (scientists and physicians), whether voluntarily or involuntarily, into the handmaiden of the nation-state, including its expansionist (internationally) and suppressive (domestically) aims. Let me briefly mention three examples.

The first one is historical. It is a well-known fact that, without nationalist ideology, the Third Reich and its notorious Nazi medical killing (euthanasia, eugenics and inhuman experimentation) would not be possible. This is also true of Japan's wartime medical atrocities. Nationalism provided Japan with an ideological path to medical butchery and thus turned the art of healing into a vehicle for inhumanity. Nationalism has also played an active role in the international postwar responses (or the lack thereof) to these medical atrocities. The consideration for national interests and security has also served the United States as a justification for exploiting the fruits of such evils and making a deal with the war crime perpetrators. Moreover, the failure of the primary victim, China, to deal effectively with the "inhuman medicine" to which it was subjected and to pursue justice for victims is itself directly linked with nationalism. On the altar of the nation-state, all that is good and valuable may be sacrificed: not only human lives, but also (to use some potent Confucian terms) morality and justice, humanity and righteousness (Nie 2002, 2004, 2010a).

The second example occurred in the contemporary West, in the United States. To help the American war against terrorism and to serve the nation-state and the perceived national interests, American physicians and other medical professionals have participated in tortures, interrogations, and mistreatments of inmates at prisons at Guantanamo Bay and elsewhere. For the American medical ethicist Steve Miles, an expert of the Hippocratic Oath, this is clearly the betrayal of the age-old medical oath in the West (Miles 2006). According to Chinese professional ethics, this simply violates the principle of medicine as the art of humanity and alienates the Great Dao of healing into a means for advancing the interests of nation-states.

The third one concerns a problem in contemporary China, namely, physicians' participations in coerced abortions to carry out the ambitious national population control policies. For many doctors who have routinely performed abortions and with whom I interviewed in my study on abortion in China, they often felt very satisfied and proud about their work because they believed that they were not only helping other women—assisting their patients in solving their problems and relieving their pain and suffering—but serving the whole society by providing medical services that made the national birth control program possible (Nie 2005, Chapter 6). An attitude of quite a few doctors toward performing abortions can be summarized as "just doing it," that is, performing abortions was nothing more than a routine part of their professional life. Understandably, most of them have rarely raised any ethical concerns about the nature of their professional work. But a few were anguished because they considered the fetus an unborn child, had strong reservations on many methods employed in implementing the birth control policies, and deeply sympathized with the patients' various sufferings caused by forced abortions due to the national population policies. They felt that their professional duties to serve patients were in conflict with the required duties to serve the country by participating in coerced abortions.

Here the ethical question that should be raised is not about physicians' participation in performing abortions for patients who have *voluntarily* decided for such a choice, but about physicians' participation in *coerced abortions*. Like the official ideology, the socialist discourse of medical ethics in the People's Republic of China is statist and collectivist, i.e. emphasizing the almost absolute primacy of the interests of the state, the country, and the collective over those of individuals. As a result, medical professionals are morally obliged to be loyal to not only the individual patient but also the state. Indeed, many physicians and medical professionals, like professors in universities, belong to the political and economic category "cadre of the nation-state." Historically speaking, however, this statist and collectivist element in contemporary Chinese socialist medical morality is unprecedented because for centuries major Chinese medical ethics traditions rooted in Confucianism, Daoism and Buddhism respectively have always advocated the individual patient as the primary duty of healers. It seems to me that the active participation of Chinese physicians in coerced abortions violates the fundamental principle of Chinese medical ethics—medicine as the art of humanity.

The moral imperative of medicine as the art of humanity offers a counter thesis to the exaltation of nationalism in science and medicine. In general, the Confucian universalist ideal of "all people under heaven" as brothers, an ancient Eastern version of internationalism, runs counter to the sweeping tide of nationalism in the modern world. In particular, the old Confucian designation of medicine as a great Dao (Way), medicine as the art of humanity, defines the primary goal of medicine not as glorifying any particular nation-state or group but serving the general welfare of humanity. In light of this, scientific research and the social application of scientific knowledge must strive to adhere to moral norms. Science and medicine should ultimately be life affirming.

Confucianism has too often been misinterpreted as a moral and political philosophy which puts secular authorities (such as emperors or the state) with the highest ethical concern. However, the influential but oft-violated Confucian political principle of ethical governance (*renzheng*) as articulated by Mencius requires all social policies, including those related to science and medicine, to put people as the highest priority, the ruler as secondary, and the kingdom or nation as the least weighty entity of the three. This Confucian political ideal of the good governance as serving people first is parallel to the principle of medicine as the art of humanity—the same norm applying to different aspects of human life with the former in politics and the latter in health care. The principle of medicine as the art of humanity urges us to always keep a careful watch on nationalism in medicine and physicians as the agents of nation-states, which can so easily fall into the alienation of the ultimate moral aims of healing as a moral means to serve humanity.

Conclusion

In the preceding chapter, I have discussed the professional ethics of traditional Chinese medicine rooted in the Confucian notion of *cheng* (sincerity or truthfulness) and put forward by the great seventh-century physician Sun Simiao. In this chapter, I have briefly presented two other ideas in Chinese professional ethics: the image of physician as a general and the norm of medical as the art of humanity. I have argued that, along with the perspectives of Confucianism and even classic Chinese military philosophy, traditional Chinese medical ethics can provide valuable insights into the problems of contemporary health care.

At the end of my study on the international aftermaths (the lack of adequate responses) to Japan's wartime medical atrocities, I've appealed to the concept of medical as the art of humanity (Nie 2010a, 136):

> The old Confucian ideal of medicine as the art of humanity—rather than being merely a means of serving nationalist interests and the political tool of the state—has a renewed relevance for our so-called "postmodern" world. Resisting the abuse of science and medicine by the nation-state should be a priority, if not *the* priority, for contemporary medical ethics and medical professionalism. In the modern world, science and medicine can no longer develop—or even survive—without support from the state. But if they are totally subordinated to the interests and power of the nation-state, science and medicine erode their own moral grounds for existence as autonomous professions.

The rich sources in the traditional Chinese professional ethics of medicine have the potential to contribute more to the positive development of medical professionalism in both China and the West, so long as we are willing to heed carefully and interpret them in creative ways. They can help to guard medicine—the lofty art of humanity and the oldest and newest profession of humankind—so as not to be metamorphosed into a slave, serving merely the interest of profit-making and the claims of nation-states.

Chapter 13

Exploring the core of humanity

A Chinese-Western dialogue on personhood

French sociologist Marcel Mauss, Emile Durkheim's nephew and student, began the 1938 Huxley Memorial Lecture by telling his audience that the idea of the "person" (*personne*), the notion of self (*moi*), is one of the most significant categories of the human mind. Although the concept "originated and slowly developed over many centuries and through numerous vicissitudes," according to Mauss (1985, 1), "even today it is still imprecise, delicate and fragile, one requiring further elaboration." Although seven decades have passed, the notion of the person is still unsettled and requires further elaboration, as in Mauss' day. The subject of personhood—or the question of what makes a human being a special entity with dignity and fundamental moral rights that ought to be respected and protected—is one of the crucial and most controversial topics in contemporary bioethics and moral philosophy. It is not only theoretically important but practically significant, because any argument about personhood carries implications for contemporary academic and public debate on a series of moral dilemmas such as abortion, infanticide, the withdrawal of medical treatment, and euthanasia. Gerhold K. Becker (1998, 2), the well-known German philosopher and bioethicist who spent most of his professional life at Hong Kong Baptist University, has called these discussions on personhood "exploring the core of humanity."

The dominant perspective on personhood in contemporary bioethics, as exemplified in the theories of Michael Tooley, Joseph Fletcher, Mary Anne Warren, Joel Feinberg, H. Tristram Engelhardt, Jr., and Peter Singer, has been developed within a specifically modern Western philosophical framework and is rooted in the thought of Locke and Kant in particular. In this perspective, such words as autonomy or self-determination and reason or rationality are used as the key terms to define personhood. The knowledge, teachings and insights of Judeo-Christianity, non-English-speaking cultures in the West, and non-Western traditions, as well as other academic disciplines such as anthropology and sociology, are marginalized or remain in the background—if not totally banished from the picture—in mainstream bioethics.

The two volumes edited by Gerhold K. Becker—*The Moral Status of Persons* (Amsterdam and Atlanta: Rodopi, 2000) and a special issue of the *Kennedy*

Institute of Ethics Journal (Vol. 9, No. 4, 1999)—represent some successful steps beyond the prescriptions of this dominant bioethical discourse. The eighteen essays collected in these two volumes offer new and challenging perspectives on personhood. Not only do they critically analyze a number of accepted ideas in the bioethical discourse on personhood, but they also draw on the ethical legacies of Eastern cultures and Christianity, German theology in particular. Few volumes in bioethics can boast such a diverse international authorship. They suggest that no single intellectual tradition, no single culture, no single discipline, no single perspective, can fully explain the core of what makes us human. Since the contributors to these two volumes deal with a wide range of issues, I have no intention of reviewing all the essays and the arguments they contain. My focus here will be on the cross-cultural perspectives they embody, specifically their treatment of Eastern, especially Chinese, understandings of personhood.

First, though, I will mention a group of essays which address conceptual issues and practical concerns from within the Western philosophical tradition and which challenge many popular ideas on personhood both in bioethics and moral philosophy. For example, inspired by the work of Robert Spaemann, the Taiwanese philosopher Johannes H. C. Sun criticizes the liberal functionalist view in which some human beings are not regarded as persons, and offers a defense of the traditionalist view that all human beings are persons. Michael Quante, a German philosopher, disagrees that autonomy is the basis of personal identity and argues rather that personal identity is the sole basis for autonomy. He argues that personal identity has existential priority over autonomy and that, conceptually speaking, the ethically relevant meaning of autonomy is directly or indirectly based on personal identity. The British medical ethicist John Harris rejects both the potentiality argument and gradualism and defines a person as "a creature capable of valuing its own existence." The American bioethicist Tom Beauchamp thinks that modern and contemporary theories of personhood all fail to capture the depth of moral commitment embedded in the use of the term "person" and fail also to distinguish what he calls "metaphysical" from "moral" concepts of persons. Despite popular beliefs, Beauchamp argues that a unique moral status or concept cannot be derived from a description of some non-moral, usually cognitive, property of persons such as self-consciousness. Both volumes discuss a number of practical issues from the perspective of personhood and personal identity including gene therapy (the essay by the British philosopher Ruth Chadwick), human cloning (Jonathan Chan, a philosopher from Hong Kong), brain injury (Derrick Au, head of rehabilitation services at a hospital in Hong Kong), the status of animals (the Scottish philosopher Elizabeth Telfer), and advance directives (Michael Quante and Australian bioethicist Helga Kuhse).

Judeo-Christian theology was a vital force in the birth of bioethics in the West, particularly in the United States, and is still probably the most significant source for public debate on bioethical issues in Western countries. But in the dominant bioethical discourse on personhood, theological reflection has often been treated as irrelevant, if not downright harmful. In an attempt to remedy this deficiency, two essays in *The Moral Status of Persons* focus on Christian theological viewpoints of personhood. Dennis P. McCann, an American theologian, discusses the conception of personhood in Catholic social teaching as articulated by Pope John Paul II and its implications for health care policy. The German theologian Friedrich-Wilhelm Graf charges that current bioethical discussions, especially those framed in British utilitarianism, are reductionist because bioethical theorists define persons as a class of object with distinctive natural, physical, and psychic features. For Graf, in contrast to the status held by things and other living beings, the essential characteristic of a person in the Protestant tradition lies in the Christian idea of freedom; personhood "is not phasic in itself," but "has a life history."

The cross-cultural perspective is the most notable feature of both volumes, especially *The Moral Status of Persons*. This work is the 96th volume in the Value Inquiry Book Series edited by Robert Ginsberg and the first volume in a new series titled Studies in Applied Ethics under the general editorship of Gerhold Becker, both published by Rodopi. The general goal of Studies in Applied Ethics, as stated by Becker in the editorial foreword, is to publish scholarly works in the field with preference given "to comparative studies, ... to multicultural approaches, and to research that draws on and makes available for critical reflection and moral discourse the ethical resources of the East, particularly of China." For Becker, an "unbiased, critical exploration" of personhood from the vantage point of non-Western, particularly Eastern, cultures and intellectual traditions is a "genuine task."

In a sense, the two volumes reviewed here present a Hong Kong approach to bioethics. All the essays originated in an international symposium on bioethics and the concept of personhood held at the Centre for Applied Ethics, Hong Kong Baptist University, in May 1998 (for a detailed report about the symposium, see Becker 1998). Among the international team of authors, the editor Becker is the director of the Centre, and four other contributors are currently teaching in Hong Kong. More importantly, these two volumes reflect the role of Hong Kong as a meeting place of Western and Eastern traditions and as a bridge connecting different cultures. Hong Kong has proven to the world how fruitful the meeting of East and West can be. The experiences of Hong Kong—its successes, problems, and failures—can teach citizens of a globalized world how to think about and live with the civilizations of China and the West, their inevitable conflicts, their potentially harmonious co-existence, and even the seamless fusion of their cultural horizons. Hong Kong seems to be an ideal place to conduct Chinese-Western comparative studies in many fields including ethics. In 1996 Becker edited *Ethics in Business and Society: Chinese and Western Perspectives* (published by Springer).

Through the two volumes under discussion, he has provided readers with a further valuable and timely service in the field of cross-cultural applied ethics.

Five essays in *The Moral Status of Persons* and one article in the *Kennedy Institute of Ethics Journal* address the topic of personhood from a cross-cultural (Eastern) perspective. All are interesting and thought-provoking. Using as an example the practice of Japanese physicians of disclosing the diagnosis of a terminal illness to the patient's family first, the Japanese ethicist Shin Ohara reasserts the importance of "we-consciousness"—or "we"-dentity rather than "i"-dentity—and emphasizes the need for moving beyond the restricted "i-we" or family relationship to a more communal ethics. The Chinese bioethicist Ruiping Fan, editor of an anthology titled *Confucian Bioethics* published by Kluwer in 1999, outlines four international approaches to the issue of personhood. He characterizes the Confucian conception as an "appeal to rites," in contrast to what he calls the Judeo-Christian "appeal to creation," some contemporary Western authors' "appeal to rights," and Engelhardt's "transcendental" or "general" conception of personhood. Based on Herbert Fingarette's famous interpretation of Confucianism in *Confucius: Secular as Sacred*, Fan considers "participation in rites" as the essence of the Confucian conception of personhood.

Renzong Qiu, a leading bioethicist and philosopher of science in mainland China, argues for a holistic version of personhood that includes the biological, psychological, and social characteristics of being a person. For him, possessing the human genome with a human body and brain and possessing the potentiality for self-consciousness are *necessary* conditions for being a person, whereas being a social agent with the capacity to communicate and interact with other persons is the *sufficient* condition for personhood. Qiu also briefly discusses the implications of his conception of personhood for human cloning, abortion, infanticide, irreversible coma, brain transplantation, split brain, a human baby in E.T. society, and the "rights" approach in bioethics.

The sophisticated and seminal essays by Chad Hansen, Edwin Hui and Jiwei Ci challenge, explicitly and implicitly, some widely held but problematic (or at least insufficient) approaches to Chinese culture and Chinese-Western comparative ethics. For example, even though Western modernist and postmodernist attitudes toward Chinese culture appear totally opposite—one negative and the other positive—both have treated China as the other, the alternative, something fundamentally different. A number of generalized comparisons or dichotomous terms of the type "China vs. the West" have been formulated to indicate these supposed differences in cultural values and social mores: communitarianism vs. individualism; personal responsibility and duty vs. individual liberty and freedom; moral and spiritual vs. materialist; secular vs. religious and transcendental—to list only a few. Even the essays by Shin Ohara, Ruiping Fan and Renzong Qiu seem by and large to follow this model in their elaborations of Eastern and Western cultural differences regarding personhood. However, the serious problem with this deeply rooted and widespread way of thinking is that it usually simplifies and distorts the complex reality of both Chinese and Western cultures.

In his remarkable essay "*Jen* and *Perichoresis*: The Confucian and Christian Bases of the Relational Person," the Chinese-Canadian theologian and bioethicist Edwin Hui, who is currently teaching in Hong Kong, has put this "East vs. West" dichotomy far behind him. On the one hand, Hui shows how the foundational Confucian concept of *jen* (*ren* in the current *pinyin* system) stands in contrast to the modern Western Cartesian view of self and person, and emphasizes the dynamic process of "person-making" or the relational basis of personhood. On the other hand, he points to an alternative language in modern Western philosophical thought and shows that such thinkers as Gabriel Marcel, Martin Buber, and John MacMurray have given prime importance to the experience of the "other," relation, and community. For Hui, within Western culture Christianity has developed a relational conception of personhood as exemplified in the notion of *perichoresis* formulated in early Christian theology. Moreover, Hui interprets the Confucian teaching of the "person-in-relation" as deeply rooted in a religious system embodied in belief in "The Great Plan." He demonstrates that the Confucian concept of *jen*, like the Christian concept of *perichoresis*, possesses not only a relational but also a transcendental understanding of personhood. These insights make Hui's essay a model for the Chinese-Western comparative studies of ethics. Ideally, cross-cultural comparisons should avoid stereotypes, getting stuck at the level of "West vs. Non-West," but should rather explore pertinent differences and similarities at the same time.

It is widely held that the individual rights approach in the West and in Western bioethics is not applicable to non-Western societies, including China, because Chinese and most other non-Western cultures are not individualistic in nature. Interestingly, while Renzong Qiu is an enthusiastic advocate of patients' rights in China and co-author of the first book on the subject in mainland China, he seems unhappy with the rights approach in bioethics. Though he only touches on this topic in his essay, Qiu does claim that the rights approach, in contrast with the holistic Chinese perspective, has put too much emphasis on the individualistic and autonomous dimension of persons and failed to give sufficient attention to social, interpersonal relationships or to individual responsibilities and duties.

However, in his essay "Why Chinese Thought is not Individualistic: Answer 1 of N," the Hong Kong philosopher and Sinologist Chad Hansen presents a rather different argument. On the one hand, using Western "semantic individualism" as a reference point, Hansen elucidates why Chinese thought is non-individualist in its semantic theory, i.e., the ideographic nature of Chinese language. On the other hand, supplementary to his main thesis, he emphasizes that there are many types of "individualism" in both Western and Chinese cultures and that Chinese moral thought is not predominantly communitarian. He warns that the fact that Chinese thought did not find "the inherent dignity and worth of the rational individual to be a natural first principle of morality ... would not block any Chinese thinker, ancient or modern, from adopting various kinds of a posteriori arguments for greater individual freedom." Hansen provokingly concludes: "Individualism in China would merely sound more like John Stuart Mill than like Immanuel Kant."[1]

Jiwei Ci's marvelous essay, "The Confucian Relational Concept of the Person and its Modern Predicament," in the *Kennedy Institute of Ethics Journal*, critically examines the treatment of the Confucian communitarian view of personhood as an epistemically more cogent and ethically more attractive alternative to liberal individualism. Without defending liberal individualism, Ci argues against the proposed superiority of Confucianism due to its serious ethical and epistemic flaws. First, as both theory and practice Confucianism in its specific historical form is normatively unattractive—i.e., Confucian personhood, defined by hierarchical and unequal relationships within family and clan, is not able to provide an adequate ethical foundation for the modern understanding of relations among equals. Second, epistemically, Confucianism falls into the essentialist fallacy by presupposing that its theory of personhood reflects the "essence" or true nature of human relations. As a result, the Confucian relational concept of the person fails to provide a viable framework for dealing with contemporary social issues including those dealt with in bioethics.

It seems to me that Ci's theoretical and methodological approach is insightful. Of course, the fact that the Confucian relational view (or the perspectives on personhood held by other cultural and intellectual traditions) fails to provide a viable framework for contemporary social and bioethical issues does not necessarily—*should not* in my understanding—mean that we cannot develop a viable framework for today's social and bioethical issues from that standpoint. This conclusion does not necessarily—*should not*— mean that other aspects of Confucianism or theories derived from it cannot provide valuable insights for dealing with contemporary social and bioethical issues. Moreover, Ci's conclusion does not necessarily—*should not*—mean that the viewpoint in question cannot make significant contributions to the development of a viable framework for dealing with contemporary social and bioethical issues. In cross-cultural bioethics, a critical attitude toward the dominant Western discourse is certainly needed. However, the point I want to emphasize here is that a critical attitude toward cultural traditions and social practices in non-Western societies including China is *also* needed. This

---

1 Hansen does not focus on this topic in the essay reviewed here. For his views on human rights and traditional Chinese thought, see his other works (Hansen 1996, 1997). For a defense of the rights approach in international bioethics from a Western-style universalist perspective, see Macklin (1999). I myself have addressed such issues as informed consent and human rights in the Chinese context (see chapters 8, 9, and 10 of this book, also Nie 2005, Chapter 8).

critical attitude differs from the nihilist or "total anti-traditionalist" approach exemplified in the total dismissal of Confucianism and Chinese culture by the May Fourth New Cultural Movement in early twentieth-century China, and especially in the infamous Great Proletarian Cultural Revolution of the 1960s and 1970s. That is to say, while it is unhelpful to reject Chinese and other non-Western traditions out of hand, neither is it helpful to romanticize them. Genuine cross-cultural communication and exchange depends on a critical analysis, along with imaginative reading and creative interpretation, of Confucianism and other non-Western intellectual traditions.

Bioethics is a practical discipline and should ideally be a form of social and cultural criticism. From the outset, the bioethical discussion of personhood has never been a game played in an ivory tower or a diversion for armchair academics. There are many urgent practical issues and troubling social practices related to health care and medicine in the East including China, like anywhere else. These outstanding theoretical essays covering the Chinese situation are all most helpful and call for further research to enable us to discuss more directly, critically and cogently—from our knowledge of the various Chinese understandings of personhood—how China ought to deal with such thorny practical issues as organ transplantation, euthanasia, human experimentation, abortion, the extraordinary and increasing inequality in health care resource allocation, rural health care, *yousheng* (eugenics or "healthy birth"), and population control.

In his lecture devoted to a social history of the notion of the person, Marcel Mauss used China as evidence to illustrate his evolutionary theory in which the "Chinese" understanding of personhood represents a lower level in respect to the highest form—"a fundamental form of thought and action"—developed in the modern West. For him, through the modern Western view of the person as an individualistic and autonomous entity, the whole "course [of history] is accomplished." Mauss also equated "Confucian" (in fact, one of many Confucian viewpoints on the subject) with "Chinese." As a result of our greater knowledge and changed perspectives on both China and the West, it is clear now that, for many, most of what Mauss said about China is simply wrong. However, in spite of our enhanced knowledge and changed perspectives, some myths about Chinese culture still remain. As pointed out above, one of the most widespread myths depicts Chinese culture as a single, unified whole and assumes the existence of a distinctive Chinese mind or mentality. Yet, Chinese culture—indeed, any culture—is always plural and changing. To treat Confucianism as representative of the Chinese worldview is like treating Christianity or liberalism as representing the whole of Western culture. It goes without saying that, along with classical Confucianism, Daoism (both philosophical and religious), "Legalism," Neo-Confucianism, sinolized Buddhism and sinolized Marxism (socialism) have all greatly influenced Chinese history and culture. They all, among many other schools of thought in China such as Moism (universal love) and Yuangzhu (egoism), have their own distinguishable perspectives on the person and self.

In one of his characteristically thoughtful articles, Becker (1995) critically addresses the "Asian values" approach, reminding us of some "simple facts" and "real dangers" we often overlook in considering cross-cultural matters: the tendency to simplify the rich plurality of values in every culture, including Western cultures, and to deny the existence of a common humanity. These two fascinating volumes which Becker has generously put together illustrate these points and more.

In conclusion, *The Moral Status of Persons* and the fourth issue of the 1999 *Kennedy Institute of Ethics Journal* have significantly expanded our intellectual horizons regarding the conception of personhood and thus made a valuable contribution to applied ethics in general. Any future venture that sets out to explore the core of our humanity cannot afford to neglect them. In regard to cross-cultural conceptions of personhood and East–West comparative studies, these two volumes have given us reason to anticipate the appearance of even more stimulating and definitive studies. We can be sure that a steady flow of publications, focusing on Chinese and other Eastern perspectives on personhood and their implications for bioethics in China and the wider world, will appear as part of Becker's Studies in Applied Ethics series and elsewhere. Indeed, this is already happening. In his insightful book *Confucian Bioethics*, a systematic and in-depth study of the subject in the Chinese language, Taiwanese philosopher Lee Shui-chuen (1999) discusses the various perspectives of contemporary New-Confucianism on personhood and some of their implications for bioethics.

Becker has long been an internationally recognized doyen of Eastern/Chinese-Western comparative applied ethics. His dedication and work magnificently testify to the fact that effective cross-cultural dialogue can enrich not only "our" cultures, the cultures we are most familiar with, but also "their" cultures, the cultures we know little about, to such an extent that we all know ourselves, humankind, much better as a result. Mauss (1985, 21) ended his lecture by saying: "Let us labour to demonstrate how we must become aware of ourselves, in order to perfect our thought and to express it better." Let us continue the quest Becker has ably initiated. Let us, as he had done and continues to do, strive to take seriously our individual and communal responsibilities and commitments to our different cultures, and to our common human vocation of promoting cross-cultural dialogue in bioethics.

Chapter 14

Beyond individualism and communitarianism

A yin-yang model on the ethics of health promotion

with Kirk L. Smith

> The way to solve the problem you see in life is to live in a way that will make what is problematic disappear.
>
> Wittgenstein

There is an inherent and essential tension in human moral and political life—the individual vs. community and society. And, as a consequence, there are two conflicting versions of a great number of moral and political issues: individualism vs. communitarianism. This tension has been particularly manifested in the ethics of health promotion.

It has been often acknowledged that health promotion in the West, the U.S. in particular, has harbored a strong strain of individualism motivated by traditional American values of self-reliance and freedom of choice. Most health promotion programs are designed to change personal "lifestyles"; they encourage the public to modify personal "risk behaviors" such as obesity and cigarette smoking in order to prevent and control disease. At the same time, while these individual-oriented strategies have succeeded in reducing some health risks, they are at odds with a competing communitarian conception of the "common good." Communitarians applaud the good intentions of the lifestyles approach, but charge that it ignores important social, political, economic, and structural factors that powerfully affect personal and public well-being. They seek to reform the health promotion movement with a community-oriented approach that emphasizes the general welfare interests of society.

In this chapter, a cross-cultural perspective is employed to illuminate the tension between individualism and communitarianism and apply an Eastern-style remedy to relieve the conflict between them. Using traditional elements of Chinese wisdom—tact, moderation and diagnostic completeness—we translate health promotion into a yin-yang/dialectical model in which the seemingly opposed interests of the individual and of the community are weighed and reconciled and the essential identity of their health interests revealed, in effect making the problematic tension disappear.

Individualism and communitarianism in conflict

The modern health promotion movement emerged as part of the "limits of medicine" debate of the 1970s when critics drew attention to the discomforting fact that rising medical care expenditures did not correlate well with actual improvements in public health. They suggested that a greater health dividend could be achieved by persuading the public to adopt "healthy habits" of living—e.g. better diets, more exercise, safer driving practices—thus reducing the need for costly medical interventions.

As medical sociologist Marshall Becker (1992, 1–6) has observed, this personalized focus on health is consistent with a "Western ideology [that] has always placed great value on the individual, particularly with regard to the importance of personal responsibility for one's own successes or failures." As a consequence of this "self-help" philosophy, American health policy has for the most part been directed at educating the public about potential health risks, rather than passing legislation to regulate ill behavior—a "hands off" policy in keeping with the ethos of rugged individualism. In accordance with this ideology, individuals at risk (and given the prevalence of "risk factors," e.g., cholesterol and the like, this includes nearly everyone) are expected to seize control of their health destiny as an exercise in willpower and self-determination.

Because many risk factors are in fact matters of individual choice, but more perhaps because it supports cherished notions of liberty and self-expression, individualism has emerged as the dominant language of health promotion, used to articulate not only the benefits of personal well-being, but the larger claims of personal autonomy as well. However, as Robert Bellah and his colleagues (1985) discuss in *Habits of the Heart*, there are "second languages" of community that voice commitments substantially different from those of individual autonomy. In contrast to the individualistic ethic of the lifestyles approach, the language of community focuses on society's obligation to protect the welfare of its members; in particular, communitarians warn that introspective visions of well-being, by minimizing the value of social relations, threaten the "common good."

To enlarge the sense of social responsibility and emphasize the ties that bind, communitarians emphasize compassion and urge individuals to heed each other's needs in respect of a greater moral unity; they promote the view that communities have interests of their own which they may legitimately defend. Dan Beauchamp (1985, 29), for example, in an article defending public health paternalism, suggests that "the community itself has a reality apart from the citizens who comprise it" and argues that group interests "can transcend and take priority over private interests."

Unfortunately, such efforts to strengthen the status of community as an entity in itself heighten the tension between communitarianism and individualism, i.e. the conflict that arises when the interests of the community challenge those of individuals. To argue that a community is a free-standing subject whose interests are worthy of respect encourages social responsibility; it may also alienate those who view such talk as a totalitarian strategy to override individual rights.

This is not to say that individualists find all public health and safety measures objectionable. Laws that prohibit drunken driving or that enforce vaccination orders, for example, are widely accepted as legitimate ways to reduce harm. The rub comes when community interests are invoked to justify paternalistic intrusions into so-called "self-regarding" behaviors that individualists consider to be matters of private discretion, e.g. the use of safety belts or motorcycle helmets. In these areas, individualism and communitarianism often conflict, with advocates on either side raising competing ethical standards of autonomy on the one hand, social responsibility on the other.

While conflicts are not inevitable, disagreements are common enough to excite concern, especially since those who are most involved in health-related issues tend to express their views in two quite opposite ways: individualists condemning the erosion of privacy and communitarians lamenting the egocentrism of "lifestylers." Moreover, when opposing views grow sufficiently extreme, they are likely to pit the welfare interests of the community against the private interests of individuals. At such times, it is indeed as if the antagonists were speaking different languages, featuring two distinct sets of values and two mutually exclusive subjects—the autonomous "individual" and the socially responsible "community."

Ironically, conflicts arise precisely because the interests of the individual and of the community often overlap. The problem is thus one of setting boundaries. For example, the health problem posed by someone refusing to wear a motorcycle helmet can be represented either as a matter of private risk over which the individual exercises personal discretion, or as a community hazard into which the public may legitimately intrude in order to limit social service costs and insurance premiums, i.e. the public tab for treating head injuries. In this scenario, the overall setting of health promotion remains constant, but the subject changes: in the one case, risk is predicated on the individual; in the other, the community bears the brunt of the "misbehavior."

In areas of overlap the tendency is then for one subject to displace the other, since the "individual" and the "community" represent monolithic entities whose moral imperatives cannot be reconciled within a single vision of health promotion. Dan Callahan (1990, 28) illustrates the resulting tendency to take sides when he argues that we will not be able to "work out the problems of our health care system unless we shift our priorities and bias from an individual-centered to a community-centered view of health and human welfare" that puts "individual needs, rights and interests in the subordinate position."

This characterization of the polarization of individualism and communitarianism is admittedly overdrawn. In particular, it does not appear to appreciate recent attempts to incorporate individual- and community-oriented approaches in a single paradigm. Marion Danis and Larry Churchill (1991, 26), for example, propose that a truly effective health promotion strategy requires an "integrated moral framework, one that puts individual autonomy and social equity questions into focus simultaneously." In spite of the fact that this and similar proposals are appealing, they will eventually run afoul of an ideological predilection that resists compromise.

In particular, strategies to reconcile the ethics of individualism and communitarianism are destined to fail because these philosophies as presently conceived are burdened by a problem facing all moral talk in our times, a problem that moral philosopher Alasdair MacIntyre (2007 [1984]) identifies as one of "conceptual incommensurability." In *After Virtue*, MacIntyre offers the "disquieting suggestion" that Western ethics is in disarray. He describes contemporary ethics as a hodgepodge of moral theories, a patchwork whose fragments are "conceptually incommensurable," that is, irreconcilable because the concepts that various thinkers employ to promote their moral views cannot be fitted within a single ethical scheme. This incommensurability would explain why debates about ethics often break down. Rather than arriving at a negotiated synthesis or integration of alternative views, the antagonists are essentially "talking through each other." In analyzing individualism and communitarianism, a theorized discourse of health promotion which attempts to represent individual and community interests simultaneously may be a similar, unworkable hodgepodge, involving mutually exclusive claims that cannot be reconciled.

What then are we to do? If our efforts to promote good health are burdened by irreconcilable differences, are we doomed to unwinnable debates between the defenders of autonomy and the proponents of moral unity, whose arguments will grow ever more strident, but will never be resolved? Thankfully, we think not, although the remedy we propose is foreign to Western notions of health promotion, calling as it does for a dose of traditional Chinese medicine.

The yin-yang/dialectical approach

Drawing our inspiration from the traditional Chinese conception of yin-yang, the authors seek an alternative perspective on the ethics of health promotion. Specifically, our yin-yang model calls for shifting the focus of health promotion from questions about the priority of the individual or of the community to a deeper concern for the necessity of their relationship. In particular, we argue that these seemingly distinct entities are actually indistinguishable in virtue of their common health interests, thus dissolving the apparent problems posed by absolutist claims regarding the importance either of the individual or of the community.

We begin this section with an introduction to the concept of yin-yang. Yin-yang is far more than simply a theory of natural philosophy or a precept of Chinese thought. It is a unique way of seeing and thinking about the world. The dialectical logic of yin-yang—which seeks to discover truth through weighing and reconciling opposites—underlies all of Chinese culture and forms the basis, not only of ancient Chinese cosmology, science, and medicine, but also its ethics, and social and political philosophy. As a way of understanding reality, yin-yang so dominates Chinese thinking that it is often regarded as a quintessential expression of the Chinese mind, and worthy of comparison to the Western habit of abstraction and objectification.

The first question many Westerners ask about the yin-yang conception is, "What are yin and yang?" Like most fundamental concepts, it is difficult, if not impossible, to define yin and yang precisely. They are primitive explanatory concepts used to explicate basic phenomena; they resist explanation themselves. The problem is compounded when rendering their dialectical meaning in a Western language that is itself fundamentally different in its epistemological orientation, one bent on defining categories and identifying discrete entities. In the words of Nathan Sivin (1987, 64), "Although yin and yang classify, their point is not taxonomy." Indeed, the very question, "What are yin and yang?" insofar as it is a question about two specified entities—the yin and the yang (the reader should be aware that there is no definite article in Chinese)—is prima facie false, that is, unanswerable—because yin and yang are not specific categories. Rather, they are relational terms, a distinction that should grow clearer as the discussion progresses.

The terms yin and yang first appeared in Chinese texts sometime prior to the Zhou Dynasty (1066 BC–221 BC) and originally referred to the location of landmarks relative to the sun, e.g. the sunny side of a hill or riverbank is yang, while the side in shade is yin. From this original meaning, there evolved a generalized realization that all things in reality have two aspects or complementary components, symbolized as yin-yang. This understanding gradually developed into a cognitive technique for reasoning through, and analyzing, material phenomena and their underlying processes. All things in the world—both "natural" and "human"—were conceived to be an amalgam of yin and yang. Lao Zi, the paramount Chinese master of dialectics, summarized this worldview thus: "All things in the universe carry yin on their back and hold yang in their arms."

The yin-yang doctrine teaches that the true being of things—their essence in reality—lies in their relationship one to another. English speakers attempt to convey this doctrine through terms like "interdependence" or "interpenetration." But these locutions do not adequately capture the central idea, since the essence of yin-yang is not just that one aspect exists relative to the other in a complementary fashion. Ultimately, each exists as the other in a relational interplay that is key to yin-yang understanding. Yin and yang complete each other; each actively creates the other. In the end, there is no distinction. For example, just as there would not be a "sunny" side were it not for the recognition of a side in shadow, acknowledging yang necessarily involves the simultaneous recognition of its relationship to, and dependence on, yin. One defines the other; neither can thrive alone.

In contradistinction to the Western preoccupation with identifying and classifying discrete entities, the dialectic of yin-yang focuses, not on the discrete nature of things, but rather on the necessity of their interrelations. Consequently, the yin-yang idea is always focused on a relationship which is implied, even if not explicitly stated. Indeed, yin-yang is a discourse designed to elicit and describe relationships: relationships of opposition and cooperation, of interdependent growth and diminution, and of transformation. This focus on relationships is illustrated in the familiar figure of the Tai-Ji-Tu ("The Picture of the Supreme Ultimate"), a design formulated by eleventh-century Chinese philosophers.

In many ways, this diagram is the perfect symbol of Chinese wisdom, for it expresses well the dynamic and dialectical character of yin-yang. According to this dialectical way of thinking, nothing can exist in isolation in and of itself, just as yin and yang cannot exist apart from their relation to each other. They depend on each other, balance and control each other, and are transformed into each other.

Through their constant interaction, yin-yang promote the genesis, development, and transformation of all things. The primary correspondences of yin and yang are posed in numerous pairings: earth and heaven, moon and sun, female and male, night and day, and so on—with earth, moon, female, and night being of yin, and heaven, sun, male, and day belonging to yang. From their original phenomenal meanings, yin-yang have acquired additional qualitative meanings. All that is static, heavy, shady, weak, cold, down and downwards, in and inwards is yin; all that is active, light, bright, strong, hot, up and upwards, out and outwards is yang.

Now, it should be noted that these pairings are not mutually exclusive nor are the associated qualities simple opposites. Indeed, it is important to emphasize the non-dual nature of the yin-yang scheme. Although Western thinkers are tempted to see the qualities associated with yin-yang—e.g. the shady and the weak, or the bright and the cold—as having negative and positive connotations, these connotations are not part of the original scheme. Yin-yang is specifically non-dualistic in that it does not suppose one aspect to be superior to, or more important than, the other. Both are necessary for a full existence.

Second, yin and yang are not simple complements, that is, they do not represent distinct halves which are somehow pieced together to form reality. While reality requires the joining of yin and yang, their combination is more complicated than a mere fitting together of separate parts; the opposed aspects are so deeply involved in each other that they are fundamentally inseparable. Indeed, as illustrated in the diagram above, there is an element of yin within yang, and vice-versa, symbolizing the idea that each harbors the seed of the other.

The yin-yang perspective, while recognizing the appearance of opposites, employs its insight to transcend opposites and elicit the truth of their underlying union and shared identity; it emphasizes interconnection, dynamic process, change, and mutual transformation. In the words of the twelfth-century philosopher Zhu Xu:

> Yin and yang are one and the same qi [i.e. the primary creative force]. The retreat of yang is the birth of yin. It is not that once yang has retreated a yin separate from it is born. ... You can look at yin-yang as single or as twofold. Seen as twofold it divides into yin and yang; seen as single, it is simply a waxing and waning.
>
> (cited in Sivin 1987, 64)

Neglecting the comparative relationships of yin-yang renders the concept meaningless. For example, man is yang with respect to woman; the moon is yin to the sun. But with respect to a young man, an old man becomes yin; while the moon is yang to the stars. Consequently, statements such as "The moon is yin" and "The man is yang," if not simultaneously referring to their counterparts (i.e. the "sun" and "woman"), are devoid of meaning. Yin and yang have no significance apart from their relationship.

Practical implications

With this introduction to yin-yang in mind, let us employ a similar perspective to re-evaluate health promotion. According to the yin-yang conception of things, the individual and the community are deeply involved in each other. While in one sense they oppose each other, they also nourish and sustain each other. We are, after all, social beings; a life, if it is a fully human life, is a life lived in concert with others, and the majority of what people consider good—love and conviviality, as well as material abundance—are goods necessarily held in common. This apprehension of human existence is clearly stated in the Western tradition in seminal works such as Aristotle's *Nichomachean Ethics*, but the tradition of political individualism and contractarian doctrines of community have attenuated social relations in modern times.

Yin-yang suffers no such tradition, thus leaving room in the dialectic to maneuver around the obstacle posed by the intransigence of the individual and the community. On the contrary, just as yang is yin and yin is yang, the individual is the community, the community is the individual. And not simply because the community is comprised of individuals, but rather because these terms have no meaning apart from their dyadic relationship. In the same way that "sunny" implies the existence of "shade," to address the needs of the individual is automatically to invoke those of the community. Consequently, the problem of reconciling differences between personal and communal interests collapses with the realization of their common identity.

But it may be objected that yin and yang represent opposing qualities. Therefore, if the interests of the individual and the community are simultaneously invoked, they are nonetheless invoked in opposition. However, this is not the case. For while yin-yang was originally suggestive of opposition, the developed doctrine is far more elaborate in depicting the plasticity of relationships. Exponents of the doctrine often say that "yin is born of yang, and yang of yin" and that "yin alone cannot be born; yang alone cannot grow." While yin-yang are sometimes opposed, they also are interdependent, mutually focused, and supportive of each other; just as the actual relations between individuals and communities are also sometimes opposed, sometimes supportive. In this regard, it is not so much the nature of the relationship that matters in yin-yang as the *fact* of relationship—its central place in the dialectic.

In this regard, it is appropriate to render "individual" and "community" with diacritical marks to indicate that, relative to a yin-yang dialectic, these categories are foreign conceptions. The "individual" and the "community" are discriminable in theory, just as yin and yang can be isolated for purposes of discussing different sides of relationships, but in reality individuals and communities remain fundamentally related aspects of a full and flourishing human existence.

Indeed, yin and yang are primarily aspects of relationships; together, they comprise a dynamic unity. Again, this dynamic is suggestive of actual relations between the individual and the community, for inasmuch as the individual and the community are defined by contrast (just as the "sunny" is defined in distinction to the "shaded"), the tension between them is necessary. The novelty of a yin-yang approach is not that it eliminates tension altogether, but that the conflict excited by the contrast has been replaced by a dialectic emphasizing the active state of interdependence obtaining between the individual and the community. What has been rejected is the utter dualism and the disposition to make absolute claims about the priority of one over the other—i.e. the problems of dualism and absolutism disappear.

Actually, the yin-yang/dialectical perspective, especially in regard to health promotion, is not as novel as it may first appear. In *Rationing Health Care in America*, Churchill (1987, 21) offers a similar view:

> The individual and society are complementary rather than competing realities. To deny either or give one a fundamental moral priority or to try

to treat them separately would be foolishness. We are not concerned with an argument from an a priori notion of human nature or from the nature of society, but one based rather on the most elementary and obvious observations about the human condition and our common experiences.

Later, he adds:

> The human being is individual and social. Acknowledging this deep reciprocity between the individual and the social dimensions of human life supports neither individualism nor socialism as political ideologies. Rather it indicates the need for a sense of morality in which individual rights and social obligations are seen as mutually critical and interpretive dimensions of a single moral phenomenon.

These views are entirely consistent with a dialectical model which emphasizes the vital "reciprocity" of private and public life.

Let's deliberate further on the implications of the yin-yang practice of traditional Chinese medicine for current problems of risky behavior, not as a specific therapeutic scheme, but as a philosophical orientation useful in rethinking and assessing the circumstances and goals of health promotion—an orientation that yields novel views on such controversial matters as cigarette smoking.

Traditionally trained Chinese physicians consider imbalances of yin and yang to be the fundamental pathogenesis of disease. As the sixteenth-century physician Zhang Jiebing put it: "In diagnosis and therapy it is essential to consider yin-yang first; it is the organizing principle of the medical art. ... Only one term can cover the whole art of medicine, manifold though it is—yin-yang" (cited in Sivin 1987, 62).

The most basic principles of clinical treatment involve regulating yin and yang so as to restore relative balance and maintain yin and yang in an active, harmonious state. *The Yellow Emperor's Classic of Medicine* holds up two important principles as crucial for effective therapy: (1) The need to maintain an essential balance between yin and yang, never allowing one or the other to become excessive; and (2) the need to treat disharmonies of yin and yang in accordance with the time, place, and specific context of the illness, including such environmental factors as climate and season, domestic circumstances, and customs and religion (see Veith 2002 [1949], 129).

According to Chinese medicine, human biological and social life constitutes an organic whole that is constantly changing. Rather than generate standard therapeutic procedures, yin-yang medicine adapts specific treatments to the dynamic internal workings of the body and the changing external circumstances of life—an orientation that seems particularly appropriate in regard to behaviors such as smoking, which are rooted in a complex biological, psychological, socioeconomic, and cultural matrix. As David Altman (1990,

242) observes, current smoking-reduction programs are dominated by a perspective that emphasizes factors of personal disposition, rather than environmental circumstances, as determinants of smoking behavior. This is a perspective antithetical to yin-yang thinking, which takes issue with such bias on the grounds that individual behavior and the socio-cultural environment are interdependent and complementary domains which must be simultaneously addressed.

Analogized to health promotion, the yin-yang model we propose would not hesitate to address the larger environmental circumstances in which health behaviors occur—such ineliminable ingredients as cultural affiliation and socioeconomic status. In particular, it would support community-oriented programs that address the macro-context of health care as an orientation consistent with the holistic thinking that is a hallmark of Chinese therapeutic doctrines. However, this support should not be interpreted as a whole-hearted endorsement of the community approach. From the yin-yang point of view, effective health promotion can not be achieved by granting priority to one party or the other in deliberations about community- or individual-centered schemes. Nor is it a sufficient remedy to grant the individual and the community equal standing. Indeed, any such maneuver merely perpetuates the fallacy that individuals and communities are distinct entities whose separate interests require compromise. Rather, the yin-yang/dialectic model argues that the conflicting principles underlying these alternative orientations need to be balanced or harmonized according to the practical moral problems and concrete contexts of health promotion.

Although the individual and the community are identical in the sense that the interests of the one are identified with the interests of the other, this does not mean giving both aspects equal attention at all times. Sometimes, one or the other must receive increased attention, not in virtue of one's priority over the other, but rather in virtue of the circumstances of their relationship. In a yin-yang dialectical model, the prime directive is: sustain the relationship. Consequently, the essence of yin-yang technique is to correctly identify measures to restore the balance relative to current circumstances and protect the conditions necessary for human flourishing, which is the real goal of health promotion. An example will help to clarify this point. Bear in mind, however, that ours is a preliminary proposal, a prolegomenon to a future yin-yang program of health promotion.

When traditionally trained Chinese physicians identify maladies as a predominance of yin or a predominance of yang, they are specifying the nature of an underlying imbalance and indicating means of efficacious relief. For example, when a physician indicates that a specific disease results from a predominance of "cold-yin," this implies that relief requires diminishing "cold-yin" or elevating "hot-yang." Actual yin-yang therapeutics are far more complicated than this, but our point is simply that yin and yang are convenient diagnostic terms for referring to imbalances in relationships and for suggesting remedies to restore healthy harmony. For Chinese medical doctors, there are two ways to restore the balance of yin and yang: removing the excess or invigorating the deficiency. A common clinical practice of traditional Chinese medicine is to nourish the yin by "tonifying" yang or to "tonify" the yang by nourishing yin—meaning one can redress the deficiencies of one aspect by moderating the predominances of the other, thus restoring the normal balance. This therapeutic doctrine has novel consequences for the philosophy of health promotion, as illustrated in the following discussion.

A danger of the present concern over risky behavior is that it incites a polemic against risk-takers—unhelmeted motorcyclists, smokers, the obese—who have been castigated for the economic burdens they place on society. While these economic arguments may be sound in themselves, they promote a thin, reductive conception of human existence, trivializing the status of our fellow creatures as beings worthy of care and beneficence. Without delving into the psychology of "victim-blaming," we would point out that, far from promoting a sense of community, this view of health promotion is actually inimical to good relations–witness the hostility that anti-smoking legislation typically incites between smokers and non-smokers.

From a yin-yang perspective, such acrimony is itself pathological, since it indicates an underlying imbalance in social relations. Certainly, smokers and other risk-takers should be encouraged to evaluate their habits—for their own sake and for the sake of others—but a dialectic focused on relationships also urges the need to dampen or "tonify" the furor created by public interest claims in order to keep individuals in the community, thus preserving the conditions necessary for complete human life. We realize that the smoking issue is a provocative example. But for that very reason it emphasizes the point that a dialectical model does not assert the absolute priority of particular orientations, however worthy those orientations may appear. If circumstances call for a diminution of communal claims, so be it. In other circumstances, it will surely be the individual who gives way in order to preserve balance. The ying-yang/dialectical model makes no final claim as to the priority of the individual or the community. This is not so much because the yin-yang perspective is ambiguous as that it finds final claims to be neither possible nor warranted.

Conclusions
Toward the uncertain future

The underlying theme of this book is that a cross-cultural dialogue in the context of bioethics is necessary, possible and highly beneficial, however demanding this endeavor may prove to be. Cross-cultural meetings constitute the most striking feature of the times in which we are now living, the New Axial Age of humankind.

According to a report in the late 1990s by Martha Nussbaum, one of the most prominent public intellectuals in the United States today, a new trend in the study of non-Western cultures in U.S. universities has been evolving. It opposes a series of descriptive and normative vices such as chauvinism, romanticism, arcadianism and skepticism or relativism. It stresses a number of points about cultures which include: real cultures are pluralist, not singular; real cultures include argument, resistance, and contestation of norms; in real cultures, what most people think is likely to be different from what the most famous artists and intellectuals think; real cultures contain varied domains of thought and activity; real cultures have a past as well as a present and future. All cultures—non-Western and Western—are a complex mixture, often incorporating elements that are foreign in origin (Nussbaum 1997, 113–47). Chinese cultures and Chinese medical ethics are no exceptions. Certainly, a transcultural approach to bioethics as presented in this book recognizes, applauds, and promotes this emerging new vision of cultures.

As in cross-cultural understanding in general, cross-cultural bioethics is prone to a number of pitfalls such as dichotomizing different cultures as "radical others"; oversimplifying the differences between cultures and societies through such trite labels as "communitarian vs. individualistic"; and deeming the current dominant or official viewpoint as the only authentic representative of the culture concerned. An adequate cross-cultural understanding would not be possible at all without first overcoming stereotypes and stereotypical ways of thinking about and characterizing different cultures—whether in China, the West or anywhere else on the planet.

A main task of this book is to identify and demonstrate what I've called the "fallacy of dichotomization" or the "fallacy of dichotomizing cultures." Dichotomizing cultural differences is the major deeply-rooted and extremely popular way of thinking about cultures, in both China and the West. It is the epistemological roots of a great many empirically unfounded or problematic assumptions, normatively specious or misleading conclusions, and politically contentious or dangerous resolutions. Serious problems involved with dichotomizing cultures are the assumption of internal homogeneity, the problematic representation of the culture concerned, the grand hypothesis of a peculiar mentality omnipresent in the entire culture, false essentialism, the denial of every culture as an open system, the endorsement of the tyranny of cultural practices over ethics, the misconception of cultural incommensurability, the rejection of cross-cultural similarities or common humanity, the self-defeating prophecy of the clash of cultures as inevitable, and generating harmful social policies. Through careful examination of a series of different topics from a Chinese-Western comparative perspective, I believe I have shown sufficient empirical evidence and philosophical arguments about the fallacy and perils of dichotomization. A transcultural approach to bioethics offers a possibility to overcome this habit of thought and many other associated stereotypical ways of thinking about cultures and their differences.

Overall, in this book I've attempted to develop an "interpretative" or "transcultural" bioethics. The main characteristics of a transcultural bioethics include: to appreciate the complexities of cultural differences, to cherish the internal moral plurality that exists within every culture, to focus on both the differences and the similarities or commonalities among cultures, to promote an effective and deeper dialogue between different cultures, and most importantly, to acknowledge the necessity of normative judgments and uphold the primacy of morality. Drawing on a wide range of primary historical and sociological sources and supplied with critical philosophical analysis, I believe I have shown that—contrary to what many stereotypes have portrayed—Chinese medical ethics, along with Chinese cultures, has always been internally heterogeneous, full of diverse and contradictory elements, changing over time, influenced by and borrowing from foreign cultures, open to new possibilities, and subject to ethical scrutiny and developing moral ideals. There are captivating cultural differences as well as the fascinating commonalities exhibited by China and the West in medicine and medical ethics. As a result, a more adequate cross-cultural or transcultural bioethics is not only needed but actually possible.

In this book, I have approached medical ethics in China from an explicitly Chinese-Western cross-cultural comparative perspective. In particular, I have conducted some detailed comparisons—involving cross-cultural differences and similarities, differences in similarities and similarities in differences—of a number of subjects that include Chinese and Western approaches to medical truth-telling about terminal illness; ancient Chinese and nineteenth-century American medical attitudes to sexual overindulgence as a cause of morbidity and even premature death; and a Chinese-Western dialogue on human rights and women's rights in the context of bioethics.

This book is, nevertheless, not intended to be a systematic cross-cultural comparative study of medical ethics in China and the West. Such a study should aim to discover both the differences and similarities in the main bioethical themes and their philosophical foundations in China and the West. Among many other topics, such a study should compare and contrast the Hippocratic Oath and the Western tradition of professional ethics with the Chinese tradition as expressed in "the Excellence and Sincerity of the Master Physician" and other related Chinese documents; Confucian and Aristotelian perspectives on virtues and human life; Chinese Daoist and Western Stoic approaches to life, death and suffering; Daoist and Western liberal understandings of freedom and the authority; Chinese and Western pursuits for immortality; Chinese and Western concepts of filial piety and familism; and Chinese and Western communitarian visions. Nevertheless, I trust that this book has helped to clear the ground and even lay some foundations for more systematic and in-depth cross-cultural comparative studies in future.

In the past two decades, bioethics has been experiencing an "empirical turn" (Borry, Schotsmans and Dierickx 2005) as more and more empirical studies on almost every bioethical issue are coming out. As briefly reviewed in the introduction, most of the works on bioethics in Asia and China are empirical studies undertaken by social scientists and anthropologists. My previous study on Chinese experiences and views of abortion (Nie 2005) has joined in this turn and so does this book in some ways. Empirical studies are necessary and essential for bioethics, especially for cross-cultural bioethics, because we still know so little in this critical area. I hope that this book can serve as a call for more systematic and in-depth comparative cross-cultural studies on all bioethical issues. Meanwhile, empirical studies can never be sufficient for bioethics. They can never replace critical and judicial normative inquiries. I hope that this book has also illustrated this point.

If in this book I have seemed to claim that Chinese and Western cultures, as well as their respective systems of medical ethics, contain no real differences and enjoy an unbroken harmony, I would like to emphasize that this is not my point at all. Among the many obstacles to effective cross-cultural understanding I have discussed in this book are two common vices, each located at an opposing pole: "false opposites" (the assumed cross-cultural differences are not as dramatic as they appear to be) at one pole and "false friends" (the perceived similarities are not as real as they appear to be) at the other. While most effort of this book has focused on refuting many claims of false opposites through showing the existence of shared common values, I hope I have also exhibited the problem of real and potential false friends in Chinese-Western cross-cultural medicine and bioethics. This problem treats cultural differences as only superficial, never fundamental and significant, and uses the Western standards to measure the value (or lack thereof) of particular cultural achievements and practices found in China or other "alien" cultural domains. What I oppose are the facile generalizations, sweeping assertions, ready-made assumptions and simplistic contrasts that are all too commonly found in cross-cultural discussions. For a transcultural bioethics, Chinese-Western cultural differences are far more complex and fascinating than such familiar contrasts as a collectivistic China vs. the individualistic West and non-Western cultures vs. Western human rights.

What I do want to highlight, however, is a rather different point. To say that cultures such as Chinese and Western ones are different and contain the potential for serious conflict is one thing, but it is entirely another thing to assert that the clash, especially the violent clash, of the cultures of China and the West—or of different civilizations in general, as has repeatedly occurred throughout history—is thus inevitable. The clash of cultures and civilizations is not a matter of destiny, but the result of historical and political contingencies or simply of human choice. This is indeed one of the most serious choices that Chinese and Western peoples, individually and collectively, are faced with today. We can choose to reject the possibility of genuine cross-cultural dialogue in the name of cultural incompatibility and incommensurability and thus unleash the violent clash of cultures on the world. On the other hand, as Hai Rou (the God of the North Sea) or Zhuang Zi (see prologue) would have advised us more than two millennia ago, we can choose to sup with each other without resorting to the long spoon, and thus expand our limited cultural and ethical horizons immeasurably. So long as we are willing, genuine dialogue between different cultures—like those that take place between diverse moral traditions and viewpoints *within* every culture—is not only necessary but also possible, however difficult its realization may be in practice. I believe, and sincerely hope I have shown in this book, that the advancement of such dialogue and the prevention of the violent clash of cultures are not only necessary but possible. They constitute one of the highest moral callings of cross-cultural bioethics. A transcultural bioethics in the Chinese-Western cultural context as proposed here is, however simple and inadequate, one response to this lofty moral calling.

Primarily and foremost, this is a book about China, about medical ethics in and from the Chinese socio-cultural context. I have investigated such topics as medical truth-telling, informed consent, human rights and women's rights to illustrate how Chinese cultural norms and moral aspirations embrace and embody universal human values. I have also demonstrated how Chinese wisdom and some peculiar Chinese moral perspectives such as the notion of *cheng*, the ideal of medicine as the art of humanity, the metaphor of physician as general, and the idea of yin-yang can offer insights to develop today's professional ethics of medicine, the ethics of health promotion and bioethics in general. Nevertheless, this book has not provided a comprehensive overview or systematic study of medical ethics in China. Such a study—for example, of the distinctive features and shared elements of the major traditions (Confucianism, Daoism, Buddhism, socialism, Christianity, and the moral discourses of medical practitioners), or of the major ethical challenges faced by contemporary China in health care and biosciences in a rapidly changing socio-economic and international environment—would have to be undertaken as separate projects.

As for China, a country I was born in and have chosen to be a citizen of, my central message of this entire book, indeed most of my academic works, is expressed by the title of Chapter 2: "Taking China's Internal Plurality Seriously." At the very end of my study on the Chinese views and experiences of abortion I made the point that taking her internal plurality seriously is an urgent task, not so much in intellectual but in practical terms:

> Viewing the history of China in the past two centuries, one is struck by the turmoil, disorders, violence, and destruction Chinese people have endured. There are many complicated socio-political and intellectual reasons for this distressing history; a major but often ignored source of these conflicts is the fact that China has not worked out a way of adequately addressing the ethnic, regional, socio-cultural, economic, religious, and historical diversity of its people. On the one hand, there is the obvious, profound diversity among Chinese people in all spheres of life. On the other hand, the myth or dream or illusion of a united and homogeneous China persists. The inevitable result, as the history of modern China unfortunately proves, is either a forced unity by an authoritarian state or a country rent by disorder, chaos, and civil war. Without such diversity in all spheres of life among all her people, modern China would not have suffered so many irreconcilable civil conflicts and such internal turmoil one after another. The tragic history of China in the second half of the twentieth century proved once again that the plurality within her society cannot be destroyed or even reduced, no matter how hard people and especially official ideology may have tried. If, after two centuries of extraordinary hardship, China fails again to find an effective way of dealing with this plurality, the Chinese people will be unable to avoid another massive social upheaval.
> (Nie 2005, 252–3, slightly modified)

I repeat this point here because my most earnest dream is that this terrible historical theme will be avoided, that the inadequacy of modern and contemporary China in addressing the internal diversity will be overcome, and that the most persistent challenge Chinese civilization has always been facing—unifying China politically and culturally without undermining her great internal plurality and diversity—will be better met today and in future. What I fear most is that the vicious political circle—the swing between authoritarianism or totalitarianism and social disorder—will be continued in one way or the other. Chinese medical ethics or bioethics ought to and can serve Chinese people to help break this most vicious circle in the ancient, modern and contemporary history of China.

Epilogue
Thus spoke *Hai Ruo* (the God of the North Sea)

In the prologue, I suggested that, despite the general openness of Chinese culture and civilization (which are far more open than is usually perceived both outside and inside China), there is nevertheless a strong and persistent strand of ethnocentrism and cultural chauvinism in the Chinese mentality. However, we can identify at least one prominent alternative discourse in China which resists ethnocentrism and absolutism and advocates for difference and pluralism. This is Daoism. The two founding texts of Daoism, dating from the Axial Age, are *Daodejing* and *Zhuang Zi*. The former, comprising only five thousand words in Chinese characters, is a condensed masterpiece (arguably the shortest classic ever written); the latter is a treasury of parables and stories—probably the most playful and humorous philosophical work to survive from antiquity. As the overall aim of this book is to demonstrate the internal diversity, richness, dynamism and openness of medical ethics in China, there seemed no better way of ending the book than to cite a few stories and insights from "Autumn Floods," one of thirty-three chapters of *Zhuang Zi* (Zhuang Zi 1982 Vol II, 561–608, English translation Watson 1968, 175–89, with modifications). In so doing, I hope to offer readers a further insight into the liveliness, fascination and sheer broadmindedness of Chinese peoples and cultures.

When the time of the Autumn Floods came, hundreds of streams poured into the Yellow River (which, like the Great Wall, symbolizes China). Seeing how strong and vast his river had become, the Lord of the River (*He Bo*) was filled with joy and pride, believing that "all the beauty in the world belonged to him, to him alone." Following the powerful current, he journeyed east and finally reached the North Sea. Looking east, he could see no end to the waters. He Bo began to wag his head and roll his eyes, marvelling at the endless body of water which he had never seen the like of before. He sighed and felt a sense of shame for his previous ignorance, arrogance and conceit. He admitted to the God of the North Sea (*Beihai Ruo* or *Hai Ruo*): "If I hadn't come to your gate ... I would have forever been mocked by the masters of the Great Method!"

Then, He Bo and Hai Ruo had a long conversation in which many philosophical points and arguments were put forward and Confucianism was criticized—even made fun of, as in other parts of *Zhuang Zi*. Hai Ruo started the debate with a trio of metaphors about the limitations to which every creature is subject:

> You can't discuss the ocean with a well frog—he's limited by the space he lives in. You can't discuss ice with a summer insect—he's bound to a single season. You can't discuss the Dao (Way) with a rigid-minded scholar—he is shackled by his doctrines.

Hai Ruo well knew that, of all the waters of the world, none is as great as the sea, and that neither the Yellow River nor the Yangtze could match the ocean in immensity. But he had never, for this reason, given way to pride. He remained humble and sober, and for good reason:

> I take my place between heaven and earth and receive my breadth from the yin and yang. I sit here between heaven and earth as a tiny stone or a little tree sits atop a huge mountain. Since I can see my own smallness, what reason would I have to take pride in myself?

He continued:

> Compare the regions between the four seas with all that lies between heaven and earth—is it not like one small anthill in a vast marsh? Compare the Middle Kingdom [China] with the regions between the four seas—is it not like one tiny grain in a great storehouse? When we refer to the things of creation, we speak of them as numbering ten thousand—and man is only one of them.

Far from merely being an idea dreamed up in an ivory tower, this insight of Daoism—promoting an attitude of openness to the world and being continually aware of the limitations of one's own experience and perspectives—has, like many other Daoist concepts, long been a part of the common wisdom of China. Or to put it another way, Daoism is deeply rooted in the great storehouse of Chinese wisdom. At all events, while typing this story into my computer at my small office in a nine-story hospital block located in the South Island of New Zealand—a nation set in the vastness of the Pacific Ocean – from where I can see the blue sky merged with the vast blue waters of the ocean, a phrase from my past came to mind. I vividly remember that, many years ago and thousands of miles away, when as a child living in a small, remote village in south-central China I sometimes spoke with pride in what I had seen or done, the village elders—who were rarely well-educated by conventional standards—often responded by simply repeating the common Chinese saying, *shan wai you shan* ("There is always a mountain beyond the mountain"). For me as a boy, this phrase always aroused a keen curiosity deep in my heart to know what those mountains beyond the beautiful hills surrounding my home village were really like.

One should not, then, value only those things that appear substantial or remote and exotic and devalue the things that are small and close at hand. For Hai Ruo, "great wisdom observes both the far and the near, and for that reason acknowledges the small without considering it paltry, and acknowledges the large without considering it unwieldy, for it knows that there is no end to the weighing of things." He furthermore proposed "the Law of Difference":

> From the point of view of things themselves, each regards itself as noble and other things as mean. ... From the point of view of differences, if we regard a thing as big because there is a certain bigness to it, then among all the ten thousand things [*wanwu*, referring to the totality of created things in the universe] there are none that are not big. If we regard a thing as small because there is a certain smallness to it, then among the ten thousand things there are none that are not small. If we can know that heaven and earth are tiny grains and the tip of a hair is a range of mountains, then we have perceived the Law of Difference.

To illustrate this Law of Difference, Hai Ruo recalled a number of familiar scenarios—including the fact that East and West cannot do without one another, even though they are mutually opposed; that a beam used to batter down a city wall is useless for stopping up a little hole; that a thoroughbred horse that can gallop a thousand *li* in a day cannot compete with the wildcat or weasel when it comes to catching rats; and that the horned owl that catches fleas at night and can spot the tip of a hair, during the day cannot see a hill, even with its sharp eyes wide open.

In response to He Bo's question on what grounds should one then take action or refrain from it, on what grounds should one accept and abide or, by contrast, reject, Hai Ruo answered:

> Be broad and expansive like the infinity of the four directions—they have nothing which bounds or hems them in. Embrace the ten thousand things universally—how is it conceivable that there should be any particular one to which you should give special support? This is called "Being without Bias." When the ten thousand things are unified and equal, then which is short and which is long?

As we saw in the prologue, J. G. Herder, the first great modern Western advocate of political and cultural pluralism, regretted that the Chinese—"planted" on their particular spot on the globe and "endowed by nature" with unprepossessing physical features—could never become Greeks or Roman, even if they wished; for "Chinese they were and will remain." Yet, as Hai Ruo or Zhuang Zi would have replied to him, there is no need for Chinese to become Westerners, or vice versa, just as there is no need for Chinese Daoists to become Greek or Roman Stoics—the approximate counterpart of Daoism in the West—however similar Daoist and Stoic ethical viewpoints may be. To be comfortable in one's cultural difference is indeed one of the foundations of effective cross-cultural dialogue.

Zhuang Zi, the fourth-century BCE philosopher credited with the book that bears his name, is the greatest pre-modern postmodernist that China has produced. Deeply appreciative of the relativity and ever-changing nature of all existence, he is constantly delighted by and cherishes the wonder of difference and plurality, while mocking absolutism and a superficial universalism. However, unlike most postmodernists who subscribe to the general thesis of "incommensurability" and thus argue against the possibility of understanding between and among different cultures, Zhuang Zi, China's greatest relativist, is no nihilist or relativist with regard to the possibility of human understanding. If he lived today, he would no doubt be one of the most enthusiastic promoters of dialogue between and among different cultures, both within and beyond China—the grand dialogue that characterizes the New Axial Age in which we are now living and which accompanies the grand transformation of the Dao as manifested in the contemporary human world.

Zhuang Zi, profound philosopher and amusing story-teller whose central concern is always individual freedom, ends the bigger story in "Autumn Floods"—with a mini-story (a literary device always employed by him in masterly fashion, and one that Kafka also used in his literary works such as "The Great Wall of China"):

> Zhuang Zi and Hui Zi, a good philosopher friend of Zhuang Zi, were strolling on a bridge over the Hao River (or, according to another textual tradition, they were standing on a large stone standing out in the middle of the stream) when Zhuang Zi suddenly observed: "See how the minnows come out and dart around where they please! That's what fish really enjoy."
>
> Hui Zi, a Chinese sophist and another of China's pre-modern postmodernists, asked: "You're not a fish—how do you know what fish enjoy?"
>
> Zhuang Zi quickly responded: "You are not me, so how do you know I don't know what fish enjoy?"
>
> Taking a throughgoing relativist or postmodernist position, Hui Zi concluded: "I'm not you, so I certainly don't know what you know. On the other hand, you're certainly not a fish—so that still proves you don't know what fish enjoy."
>
> But Zhuang Zi disagreed: "Let's go back to your original question, please. You asked me how I know what fish enjoy—so you already knew I knew when you asked the question. I know it by standing here [and enjoying conversation with you] over the Hao."

Although I like this story—which on the surface appears to be just playing with words—I am unsure how to interpret it, just as I am often unsure how to interpret important issues surrounding medical ethics and cultures in China, the West or elsewhere, while still being immensely fascinated by them. In another context, Zhuang Zi once said that, rather than lying stranded and moistening each other with spit, the best life for fish is to forget each other altogether and just swim freely in great rivers, lakes and oceans. One of the numerous ancient commentaries on *Zhuang Zi*, and in particular on this story about whether we humans can ever know the joy of fish, asserts:

> All created things are different in nature, just as creatures in the water and on the land are different in nature. But to understand with the mind and to feel the feelings of different creatures, one can know the joy of fish by wandering over the Hao [with a friend, a fellow human being]. Reflecting upon and appreciating the ten thousand things of creation, you have not had to jump into the water to know what fish really enjoy, now have you?

Bibliography

Ackerknecht, E.H. (1982, rev. edn) *A Short History of Medicine*, Baltimore: Johns Hopkins University Press.
Aird, J.S. (1990) *Slaughter of the Innocents: Coercive Birth Control in China*, Washington, DC: AEI Press.
Akabayashi, A., Kodama, S. and Slingsby, B.T. (2010) *Biomedical Ethics in Asia: A Casebook for Multicultural Learners*, Singapore: McGraw Hill.
Akabayashi, A. and Slingsby, B.T. (2006) "Informed consent revisited: Japan and the U.S.," *American Journal of Bioethics* 6(1): 9–14.
Alora, A. and Lumitao, J. (eds) (2001) *Beyond a Western Bioethics*, Washington, DC: Georgetown University Press.
Altman, D. (1990) "The social context and health behavior: the cage of tobacco," in S.A. Shumaker, et al. (ed.) *The Handbook of Health Behavior Change*, New York: Springer.
Anderson, B. (1991) [1983] *Imagined Communities: Reflections on the Origin and Spread of Nationalism*, London: Verso.
Angle, S. (2002) *Human Rights in Chinese Thought: A Cross-Cultural Inquiry*, Cambridge: Cambridge University Press.
Aristotle (Anonymous) (1974, 1st edn 1913) *The Works of Aristotle, The Famous Philosopher*, New York: Arno Press.
Aristotle (1995) *The Politics*, trans. E. Barker and revised R.F. Stalley, Oxford: Oxford University Press.
Barenblatt, D. (2004) *A Plague upon Humanity: The Secret Genocide of Axis Japan's Germ Warfare Operation*, New York: Harper Collins.
Barker-Benfield, G.J. (1976) *The Horrors of the Half-Known Life: Male Attitudes toward Women and Sexuality in Nineteenth-Century America*, New York: Harper and Row.
Barthes, R. (1987) "Well, and China," trans. L. Hildreth, *Discourse* 8: 116–22.
Beauchamp, D.E. (1985) "Community: the neglected tradition of public health," *Hastings Center Report 15*, no.6 (1985): 29.
Beauchamp, T.L. and Childress J.F. (2009, 6th edn) *The Principles of Biomedical Ethics*, Oxford: Oxford University Press.
Becker, G. (1995) "Asian and western ethics: some remarks on a productive tension," *Eubios Journal of Asian & International Bioethics* 5. 31–3.
Becker, G.K. (1996) *Ethics in Business and Society: Chinese and Western Perspectives*. Dordrecht: Springer.

Becker, G.K. (1998) "Exploring the Core of Humanity," *Ethics and Society* (Newsletter of Centre for Applied Ethics, Hong Kong Baptist University), 6(2): 2–7.
Becker, G.K. (1999) (Guest Editor) A Special Issue of the *Kennedy Institute of Ethics Journal*, Vol. 9, No.40 Baltimore: Johns Hopkins University Press.
Becker, G.K. (ed.) (2000) *The Moral Status of Persons: Perspectives on Bioethics*, Atlanta, GA: Rodopi.
Becker, M.H. (1992) "A medical sociologist looks at health promotion," *Journal of Health and Social Behavior* 34: 1–6.
Beckland, E. (1859, 4th edn) *Knowing Thyself: The Physiologist; Or Sexual Physiology Revealed*, trans. M.S. Wharton, Boston.
Bellah, R.N. et al. (1985) *Habits of the Heart*, Berkeley, CA: University of California Press.
Berlin, I. (1998) "Nationalism: Past neglect and present power," in I. Berlin, *The Proper Study of Mankind: An Anthology of Essays*, New York: Farrar, Strauss and Giroux.
Bernstein, R.J. (1992) *The New Constellation: The Ethical-Political Horizons of Modernity/Postmodernity*, Cambridge, MA: The MIT Press.
Bhattacharyya, S. (2006) *Magical Progeny, Modern Technology: A Hindu Bioethics of Assisted Reproductive Technology*, New York: State University of New York Press.
BIONET (2010) *Final Report on Ethical Governance of Biological and Biomedical Research: Chinese-European Co-Operation*, Online: Freely available at http://www.lse.ac.uk/collections/BIONET/ (accessed 7 October 2011).
Blank, R.H. and Merrick, J.C. (2007) *End-of-Life Decision Making: A Cross-National Study*, Cambridge, MA: The MIT Press.
Blendon, R.J., Schoen, C., DesRoches, C., Osborn, R. and Zapert K. (2003) "Common concerns amid diverse systems: Health care experiences in five countries," *Health Affair* 22 (3): 106–21.
Bok, S. (1989)[1978] *Lying: Moral Choice in Public and Private Life*, New York: Vintage.
Borry, P., Schotsmans, P. And Dierickx, K. (2005) "The birth of the empirical turn in bioethics," *Bioethics* 19(1): 49–71.
Bray, F. (1997) *Technology and Gender: Fabric of Power in Late Imperial China*, Berkeley: University of California Press.
Burckhardt, J. (1990) *The Civilisation of the Renaissance in Italy*, London: Penguin.
Burkert, W. (1998) *The Orientalising Revolution: Near Eastern Influence on Greek Culture in the Early Archaic Age*, Cambridge, MA: Harvard University Press.
Callahan, D. (1990) *What Kind of Life: The Limits of Medical Progress*, New York: Simon and Schuster.
Carson, R. A. (1990) "Interpretive bioethics: The way of discernment", *Theoretical Medicine* 11: 51–9.
Carson, R. A. (1995) "Interpretation," in W.T. Reich (ed.) *Encyclopedia of Bioethics* (Revised Edition), New York: Simon & Schuster Macmillan.
Carson, R. A. (1999) "Interpreting strange practices," in R. Fan (ed.) *Confucian Bioethics*, Dordrecht: Kluwer.
Chan, W.T. (1963) *A Source Book in Chinese Philosophy*, Princeton: Princeton University Press.
Chen, Menglei (1991, first published in 1723) *Gujin Tushu Jicheng Yibu Quanlu* (Collection of Ancient and Modern Books, The Part of Medicine), Book 12: General Discussions (Volumes 501–520 in original), Beijing: People's Health Press.

Cheng, S. (1990) *Lunyu Jishi* (The Analects with Collected Annotations) (4 Volumes), Beijing: China Bookstore.
Cheng, S.Y., Hu, W.Y., Liu, W.J., Yao, C.A., Chen, C.Y. and Chiu, T.Y. (2008) "Good death study of elderly patients with terminal cancer in Taiwan," *Palliative Medicine* 22: 626–32.
Chung, Y.J. (2002) *Struggle for National Survival: Eugenics in Sino-Japanese Contexts, 1896–1945*, New York: Routledge.
Churchill, L.R. (1987) *Rationing Health Care in America*, Notre Dame, IN: University of Notre Dame Press.
Cohen, P.A. (2010, 1st edn 1984) *Discovering China: American Historical Writing on the Recent Chinese Past*, New York: Columbia University Press.
Comfort, A. (1972) *The Joy of Sex*, New York: Simon and Schuster.
Coney, S. (1988) *The Unfortunate Experiment: The full Story behind the Inquiry into Cervical Cancer*, Auckland: Penguin.
Cong, Y.L. (2003) "Bioethics in China," in J. Peppin and M. Cherry (eds) *Regional Perspective in Bioethics*, Lisse: Swetz & Zeitlinger.
Crawford, E. (1992) *Nationalism and Internationalism in Science 1880–1939: Four Studies of the Nobel Population*, Cambridge: Cambridge University Press.
Crawford, S.C. (2003) *Hindu Bioethics for the Twenty-First Century*, New York: State University of New York Press.
Croizier, R.C. (1968) *Traditional Medicine in Modern China*, Cambridge, MA: Harvard University Press.
Cullen, C. (1993) "Patients and healers in late imperial China: Evidence from the *Jinpingmei*," *History of Science* 31: 99–150.
Danis, M. and Churchill, L.R. (1991) "Autonomy and the common weal," *Hastings Center Report* 2: 26.
Dawson, R. (1967) *The Chinese Chameleon: An Analysis of Europeans of Chinese Civilization*, London: Oxford University Press.
de Bary, W.T. (1970) "Individualism and humanitarianism in late Ming thought," in de Bary, W.T. and the Conference on Ming Thought, *Self and Society in Ming Thought*, New York and London: Columbia University Press.
de Bary, W.T. (1998) *Asian Values and Human Rights: A Confucian Communitarian Perspective*, Cambridge, MA: Harvard University Press.
de Bary, W.T. and Tu, W.M. (eds) (1998) *Confucianism and Human Rights*, New York: Columbia University Press.
De Castro, L. (1999) Is There an Asian Bioethics? *Bioethics* 13:227–235.
de Castro, L.D., Sy, P.A., Alvarez, A.A., Mendez, R.V., and Rasco, J.K. (2004) *Bioethics in the Asia-Pacific Region*, Bangkok: UNESCO Asia and Pacific Regional Bureau for Education.
de Montaigne, M. (1965) *The Complete Essays of Montaigne*, trans. D.M. Frame, Stanford: Stanford University Press.
D'Emilio, J. and Freedman, E.B. (1998, 1st edn 1988) *Intimate Matters: A History of Sexuality in America*, New York: Harper and Row.
Deng, D. (1994) *Liang Shuoming and Hu Shi: A Comparison of Cultural Conservatism and the Thought of Westernization*, Beijing: Chinese Bookstore.
Dikötter, F. (1992) *The Discourse of Race in Modern China*, Stanford: Stanford University Press.

Dikötter, F. (1998) *Imperfect Conceptions: Medical Knowledge, Birth Defects and Eugenics in China*, New York: Columbia University Press.
Ding, C.Y. (2010) "Family members' informed consent to medical treatment for competent patients in China", *China: An International Journal* 8(1): 139–50.
Döring, O. (ed.) (1999) *Chinese Scientists and Responsibility: Ethical Issues of Human Genetics in Chinese and International Contexts*, Hamburg: Institut Fur Asienkunde.
Döring, O. (2000) "Hermeneutic dimensions of global and East Asian medical ethics," in *Proceedings of the Second Asian Bioethics Seminar*, Tokyo: 76–91.
Döring, O. (ed.) (2002) *Ethics in Medical Education in China: Distinguishing Education of Ethics in Medicine From Moral Preaching*, Hamburg: Institut Fur Asienkunde.
Döring, O. (2004) *Chinas Bioethik Verstehen*, Germany: Abera Verlag.
Döring, O. (ed.) (2009, 2nd edn) *Life Sciences in Translation–A Sino-European Dialogue on Ethical Governance of the Life Sciences*. Ethical Governance of Biological and Biomedical Research: Chinese-European Co-operation (BIONET). Online. Freely available at http://www.lse.ac.uk/collections/BIONET/ (accessed 7 October 2011).
Döring, O. and Chen, R.B. (eds) (2002) *Advances in Chinese Medical Ethics: Chinese and International Perspectives*, Hamburg: Institut Fur Asienkunde.
Dou, Y.T. (2003), "The development and treatments of late Mao Zedong's illness", *Dangshi Bolan* (Extensive Readings on the History of the Communist Party) (12): 47-53.
Du, Z.Z. (1985) *Yixue Lunlixue Gailun* (An Outline of Medical Ethics), Nanchang: Jianxi People's Press.
Du, Z.Z. (2009) *Shouzhu Yixue De Jiangjie* (Safeguarding the Boundaries of Medicine), Beijing: Peking Union Medical University Press.
Ebrey, P.B. (1993, 2nd edn) *Chinese Civilization: Sourcebook*, New York: Free Press.
Elliot, C. (1999) *Bioethics, Culture and Identity: A Philosophical Disease*, New York: Routledge.
Elliot, C. (2010) *White Coat, Black Hat: Adventures on the Dark Side of Medicine*, New York: Beacon.
Elliot, J.M., Ho, W.C. and Lim, S.S.N. (eds) (2010) *Bioethics in Singapore: The Ethical Microcosm*, Singapore: World Scientific.
Emanuel, E.J. (1991) *The Ends of Human Life: Medical Ethics in a Liberal Polity*, Cambridge, MA: Harvard University Press.
Emanuel, E.J. et al. (eds) (2008) *The Oxford Textbook of Clinical Research Ethics*, New York: Oxford University Press.
Engelhardt, H.T., Jr. (1980) "Bioethics in the People's Republic of China," *Hastings Center Report* 10(2): 7–10.
Engelhardt, H.T., Jr. (1996, 2nd edn) *Foundations of Bioethics*, Oxford: Oxford University Press.
Engelhardt, H.T., Jr. (ed.) (2006) *Global Bioethics: The Collapse of Consensus*, Salem M & M Scrivener Press.
Engelhardt, H.T., Jr. and Rasmussen, L. M. (eds) (2002) *Bioethics and Moral Content: National Tradions of Health Care Morality*, Dordrecht: Kluwer.
Faden, R.R. and Beauchamp, T.L. (1986) *A History and Theory of Informed Consent*, New York: Oxford University Press.
Fan, R.P. (ed.) (1999) *Confucian Bioethics*, Dordrecht: Kluwer.
Fan, R.P. (2009) *Reconstructionist Confucianism: Rethinking Morality after the West*, New York: Springer.

Fan, R.P. and Li, B.F. (2004) "Truth telling in medicine: the Confucian view," *Journal of Medicine and Philosophy* 29(2): 179–93.
Fei, X.T. (1999) [1948] "So-called 'Familism'," in *Collected Works of Fei Xiaotong*, Vol.5, Beijing: Qunyan Press.
Fielding, R. and Hung, J. (1996) "Preference for information and involvement in decisions during cancer care among a Hong Kong Chinese population," *Psycho-Oncology* 5: 321–9.
Finnis, J. (1982) *Natural Law and Natural Rights*, Oxford: Clarendon.
Foucault, M. (1983) "On the genealogy of ethics: an overview of work in progress," in H.L. Dreyfus and Paul Rabinow, *Michel Foucault: Beyond Structuralism and Hermeneutics*, Chicago: University of Chicago Press.
Foucault, M. (1990a) *The History of Sexuality* (Vol. I: An Introduction), trans. R. Hurley, New York: Vintage.
Foucault, M. (1990b) *The Use of Pleasure* (The History of Sexuality, Volume II), New York: Vintage.
Foucault, M. (1994) *The Order of Things: An Archaeology of Human Sciences*, New York: Vintage.
Fox, R.C. and Swazey, J.P. (1984) "Medical morality is not bioethics: Medical ethics in China and the United States," *Perspectives in Biology and Medicine*, 27: 336–60.
Freeman, D. (1983) *Margaret Mead and Samoa: The Making and Unmaking of an Anthropological Myth*, Cambridge, MA: Harvard University Press.
Freidson, E. (1988) *Profession of Medicine*, Chicago: University of Chicago Press.
Fujiki, N. and Macer, D. (1998) *Bioethics in Asia*, Christchurch, NZ: Eubios Ethics Institute.
Fung, Y.-L. (1952/3) *A History of Chinese Philosophy* (Vol. I and II), trans. D. Bodde, Princeton : Princeton University Press.
Furth, C. (1999) *A Flourishing Yin: Gender in China's Medical History, 960–1665*, Berkeley: University of California Press.
Gao, B., Zou, D. and Yang, L. (2006) "A study of the methods and times of telling elderly cancer patients," *Nursing Journal of Chinese People's Liberation Army*, No. 10.
Gao, W.L. (2003) *Wannian Zhou Enlai* (Zhou Enlai's Later Years), New York: Mirrorbooks.
Gao, Y.J. (2005) *Zhongguo Aizibing Diaocha* (An Investigation of AIDS in China), Guilin: Guangxi Normal University Press.
Gardner, A.K. (1974, 1st edn 1870) *Conjugal Sins against the Laws of Life and Health*, New York: J. S. Redfield (Reprinted Edition by Arno Press Inc.).
Garrison, F.H. (1929, 4th edn) *An Introduction to the History of Medicine*, Philadelphia: W.B. Saunders Company.
Ge, H. (Ko, H) (1967) *Bao Pu Zi: Nei Pian* (The Master of Simplicity: The Internal Chapters), trans. J.R. Ware, *Alchemy, Medicine and Religion in the China of A.D. 320: The Nei Pien of Ko Hung*, New York Dove.
Geertz, C. (1973) *The Interpretation of Culture: Selected Essays*, New York: Basic Books.
Gernet, J. (1982, 2nd edn) *A History of Chinese Civilization*, Cambridge: Cambridge University Press.
Gernet, J. (1985) *China and the Christian Impact: A Conflict of Cultures*, trans. J. Lloyd, Cambridge: Cambridge University Press.

Gilligan, C. (1982) *In a Different Voice: Psychological Theory and Women's Development*, Cambridge, MA: Harvard University Press.
Ginsburg, F.D. (1989) *Contested Lives: The Abortion Debate in an American Community*, Berkeley: University of California Press.
Glaser, B.G. and Strauss, A.L. (1965) *Awareness of Dying*, Chicago: Aldine.
Godwin, W. (1972) "The immorality of filial affection," in D.H. Monro (ed.) *A Guide to British Moralists*, London: Fontana/Collins.
Gongal, R., Vaidya, P., Jha, R., Raijbhandary, O. and Watson, M. (2006) "Informing patients about cancer in Nepal: what do people prefer," *Palliative Medicine* 20: 471–6.
Goody, J. (2006) *The Theft of History*, Cambridge: Cambridge University Press.
Gottweis, H., Salter, B. and Waldby, C. (2009) *The Global Politics of Human Embryonic Stem Cell Science*, Basingstoke: Palgrave Macmillan.
Graham, S. (1834) *A Lecture to Young Men*, Providence: Weeden and Cory.
Green, R.M., Donovan, A. and Jauss, S.A. (2009) *Global Bioethics: Issues of Conscience for the Twenty-First Century*, New York: Oxford University Press.
Greenhalgh, S. (2008) *Just One Child: Science and Policy in Deng's China*, Berkeley: University of California Press.
Greenhalgh, S. and Winckler, E.A. (2005) *Governing China's Population: From Leninist to Neoliberal Biopolitics*, Stanford: Stanford University Press.
Grene, D. and Lattimore, R. (eds and trans.) (1991), *Greek Tragedies* (Volume 1), Chicago: University of Chicago Press.
Habermas, J. (1972) *Knowledge and Human Interests*, trans. J.J. Shapiro, London: Heinemann.
Haller, Jr., John S. and Haller R.M. (1974) *The Physician and Sexuality in Victorian America*, Urbana: University of Illinois Press.
Hancock, K. et al. (2007) "Truth-telling in discussing prognosis in advanced life-limiting illness: A systematic review," *Palliative Medicine* 21: 507–17.
Hansen, C. (1996) "Chinese philosophy and human rights: an application of comparative ethics," in G.K. Becker (ed.) *Ethics in Business and Society: Chinese and Western Perspectives*, Berlin: Springer.
Hansen, C. (1997) "Do human rights apply to China? A normative analysis of cultural difference," in A.K.G. Lieberthal, S.F. Lin and E.P. Yong (eds) *Constructing China: The Interaction of Culture and Economics*, Ann Arbor: University of Michigan Press.
Hansen, C. (2000) "Why Chinese thought is not individualistic: Answer 1 of n," in G.K. Becker (ed.) *The Moral Status of Persons: Perspectives on Bioethics*, Amsterdam: Rodopi.
Hardacre, H. (1997) *Marketing the Menacing Fetus in Japan*, Los Angeles: University of California Press.
Harris, S.H. (2002, 2nd edn) [1994] *Factories of Death: Japanese Biological Warfare, 1932–1945, and the American Cover-up*, London: Routledge.
Harvey, W. (1952) "On the motion of the heart and blood in animals: On the circulation of the blood," in R.M. Hutchins (ed.) *Great Book of the Western World*, Vol. 28, Chicago and London: Encyclopaedia Britanica, Inc.
He, R., Wang, Y., Tian, Y., Zhou, C. and Wang, H. (2009) "The preference of Chinese patients and their relatives regarding disclosure of cancer diagnosis," *Chinese Journal of Clinical Oncology and Rehabilitation*. No. 3.

He, Z.X. (ed.) (1988) *Zhongguo Yide Shi* (A History of Chinese Medical Morality), Shanghai: Shanghai Medical University Press.
Herodotus (2007) *The Landmark Herodotus: The Histories*, (ed.) R.B. Strassler, New York: Pantheon.
Heywood, E.H. (1877) *Cupid's Yokes: or the Binding Forces of Conjugal Life*, Princeton: Co-operative Pub. Co.
Hippocrates (1986), *Hippocratic Writings*, ed. G.E.R Lyod, London: Penguin.
Hobsbawm, E.J. (1990) *Nations and Nationalism since 1780: Programme, Myth, Reality*, Cambridge: Cambridge University Press.
Hobson, J.M. (2004) *The Eastern Origins of Western Civilization*, Cambridge: Cambridge University Press.
Hongladarom, S. (2008) "Universalism and pluralism debate in 'Asian bioethics'," *Asian Bioethics Review*, Inaugural Edition: 1–14.
Hoshino, K. (ed.) (1997) *Japanese and Western Bioethics: Studies in Moral Diversity*, Dordrecht: Kluwer.
Hsiao, K. (1979) *A History of Chinese Political Thought*, trans. F.W. Mote, Princeton: Princeton University Press.
Hsu, F.L.K. (1970, 1st edn 1953) *Americans and Chinese: Reflections on Two Cultures and Their People*, New York: American Museum Science Book.
Huang, X., Wang, X., Zhang, Y., Lü, B. and Li, T. (2001) "Information needs of cancer patients: Whether and how to disclose the diagnosis of cancer," *Chinese Journal of Mental Health* No. 4.
Hui, E. (2008) "Parental refusal of life-saving treatments for adolescents: Chinese familism in medical decision-making re-visited," *Bioethics*, 22(2): 286–95.
Human Rights Watch (2003) *Locked Doors: The Human Rights of the People Living with HIV/AIDS in China*, Human Rights Watch 15(7).
Human Rights Watch (2011) *My Children Have Been Poisoned: A Public Health Crisis in Four Chinese Provinces*, Human Rights Watch June 2011.
Hume, D. (1998) *An Enquiry Concerning the Principles of Morals*, (ed.) T.L. Beauchamp, Oxford: Oxford University Press.
Jaspers, K. (2011, 1st edn 1953). *Origin and Goal of History*, London: Routledge.
Jennings, W.H. (1999) "Commentary [on Jing-Bao Nie's Article "The problem of coerced abortion in China and related ethical issues"]," *Cambridge Quarterly of Healthcare Ethics* 8(4): 475–7.
Jiang, Y., Liu, C., Li., J.Y. et al. (2007) "Different attitudes of Chinese patients and their families toward truth telling of different stage of cancer," *Psycho-Oncology* 16: 928–36.
Jonsen, A. (1998) *The Birth of Bioethics*, New York: Oxford University Press.
Jonsen, A. (2000) *A Short History of Medical Ethics*, New York: Oxford University Press.
Jotkowitz, A., Click, S., and Gezundheit, B. (2006) Truth-telling in a culturally diverse world, *Cancer Investigation* 24: 786–9.
Kafka, F. (1993) *Collected Stories*, trans. W. and E. Muir, London: Everyman's Library.
Kant, I. (1996) *Practical Philosophy*, trans. M. Gregor, Cambridge: Cambridge University Press.
Kass, L.R. (1985) *Toward a More Natural Science: Biology and Human Affairs*, New York: Free Press.

Katz, J. (2002, 1st edn 1984) *The Silent World of Doctor and Patient*, Baltimore: Johns Hopkins University Press.
Keown, D. (2001, 1st edn 1990) *Buddism and Bioethics*, New York: Palgrave.
Kim, J.D. (1994) "Is culture destiny?" *Foreign Affairs* 73(6): 189–94.
King, N.M.P., Churchill, L.R. and Cross, A.W. (eds) (1988) *The Physician as Captain of the Ship: A Critical Reappraisal*, Dordrecht: D Reideil Publishing Co.
Kleinman, A. (1988) *The Illness Narratives*, New York: Basic Books.
Ko, D. (1994) *Teachers of the Inner Chambers: Women and Culture in Seventeenth-Century China*, Stanford, CA: Stanford University Press.
Kwok, D.W.Y. (1965) *Scientism in Chinese Thought 1900–1950*, New Haven and London: Yale University Press.
LaFleur, W.R. (1992) *Liquid Life: Abortion and Buddhism in Japan*, Princeton: Princeton University Press.
LaFleur, W.R., Böhme, G. and Shimazono, S. (2007) *Dark Medicine: Rationalising Unethical Medical Research*, Indianapolis: Indiana University Press.
Lash, D.F. and van Kley (1965–1998) *Asia in the Making of Europe*, Multiple Volumes, Chicago: University of Chicago Press.
Lauren, P.G. (2003, 2nd edn) *The Evolution of International Human Rights: Visions Seen*, Philadelphia: University of Pennsylvania Press.
Lavery, J.V. et al. (eds) (2007) *Ethical Issues in International Biomedical Research: A Casebook*, New York: Oxford University Press.
Lee, S. and Kleinman. A. (2000) "Suicide as resistance in Chinese society," in E.J. Perry and M. Selden (eds) *Chinese Society: Change, Conflict and Resistance*, London: Routledge.
Lee, S.C. (1999) *Rujia Shengming* (Confucian Bioethics), Taipei: E-hu Press.
Lee, S.C. (2007) *The Family, Medical Decision-Making, and Biotechnology: Critical Reflection on Asian Moral Perspective*, Dordrecht: Springer.
Legge, J. (trans.) (1971) [1893] *The Confucian Analects, The Great Learning and The Doctrine of the Mean*, New York: Dove.
Lewis, D. (1874) *Chastity; or Our Secret Sins*, Philadelphia: George Mackean & Co.
Li, C.Y. (ed.) (2000) *The Sage and the Second Sex: Confucianism, Ethics, and Gender*, Chicago: Open Court.
Li, S. and Chou, J.L. (1997) "Communication with the cancer patient in China," *Annals of New York Academy of Sciences* 809: 243–8.
Li, S.Z. (1988, first published in 1592) *Bencao Gangmu* (The Great Pharmacopeias), Beijing: Chinese Bookstore.
Li, Z.S. (1994) *Mao Zedong Siren Yisheng Huiyilu* (The Private Life of Chairman Mao), Taipei: Times Cultural Press (English version, trans. H.C. Tai, New York: Random House).
Lin, Y.S. (1979) *The Crisis of Chinese Consciousness: Radical Antitraditionism in the May Fourth Era*, Madison: University of Wisconsin Press.
Little, M. (1996) "Why a feminist approach to bioethics?" *Kennedy Institute of Ethics Journal* 6(1): 1–18.
Liu, C. (1982) *Neijing de Zhexue he Zhongyixue de Fangfa* (The Philosophy and Methodology of *Neijing*), Beijing: Science Press.
Liu, L.D. (1993) *Zhongguo Gudai Xinwenhua* (The Sex Culture in Ancient China), 2 Vols., Yinchuan: Liangxia People's Press.

Liu, X.L. and Zhao, Y.F. (1986) "Our country's ancient knowledge on the circulation of the blood," *Yixue yu Zhexue* (Medicine and Philosophy) 6: 35–7.
Lloyd, G.E.R. (1990) *Demystifying Mentalities*, Cambridge: University of Cambridge Press.
Long, B. (1985, 1st edn 1963) *Huangdi Neijing Gailun* (Outline of the Yellow Emperor's Medical Classic), Shanghai: Shanghai Science and Technology Press.
Lu, G.D. and Needham, J. (1980) *Celestial Lancet: A History and Rationale of Acupuncture and Moxa*, Cambridge: Cambridge University Press.
Luk, B.H. (1977) "Abortion in Chinese law," *The American Journal of Comparative Law* 25: 372–90.
Luker, K. (1984) *Abortion and the Politics of Motherhood*, Berkeley: University of California Press.
Luo, G.J. (ed.) (2002, 1st edn 1989) *Lunlixue* (Ethics), Beijing: People's Press.
Luo, G.J., Ma, B.X. and Yu, J. (2004, 1st edn 1986) *Lunlixue Jiaocheng* (The Textbook on Ethics), Beijing: Beijing People's University.
Ma, B.Y. (1993) *Zhongguo Yixue Wenhua Shi* (A History of Chinese Medical Culture), Shanghai: Shanghai People's Press.
Ma, K.W. (1986) "Physicians in history," *Chinese Journal of Medical History* 16(1): 1–11.
Macer, D. (2004) *Challenges for Bioethics from Asia*, Eubios Ethics Institute.
Mackerras, C. (1989) *Western Images of China*, Oxford: Oxford University Press.
Macklin, R. (1999) *Against Relativism: Cultural Diversity and the Search for Ethical Universals in Medicine*, New York: Oxford University Press.
Macklin, R. (2004) *Double Standards in Medical Research in Developing Countries*, Cambridge: Cambridge University Press.
MacIntyre, A. (2007, 1st edn 1984) *After Virtue: A Study in Moral Theory*, Notre Dame: University of Notre Dame Press.
Mann, T. (1969) *The Magic Mountain*, trans. H.T. Lowe-Porter, New York: Vintage.
Marx, K. and Engels, F. (2002) [1888] *The Communist Manifesto*, New York: Penguin.
Mauss, M. (1985) "A category of the human mind: the notion of person: the notion of self," in M. Carrithers, S. Collins and S. Lukes (eds) *The Category of the Person: Anthropology, Philosophy, History*, Cambridge: Cambridge University Press.
May, L., Wong, K., and Delston, J. (2010, 5th edn) [1994] *Applied Ethics: A Multicultural Approach*, Boston: Prentice-Hall.
May, W.E. (1983) *The Physician's Covenant: Images of the Healer in Medical Ethics*, Philadelphia: Westminster.
McEvilley, T. (2001) *The Shape of Ancient Thought: Comparative Studies in Greek and Indian Philosophies*, New York: Allworth.
Mead, M. (2001, 1st edn 1928) *Coming of Age in Samoa: A Psychological Study of Primitive Youth for Western Civilisation*, New York: Harper Perennial.
Mencius (1970) *Mencius*, trans. D.C. Lau, New York: Penguin.
Meng, L. (2002) "Rebellion and revenge: The meaning of suicide of women in rural China," *International Journal of Social Welfare* 11(4): 300–309.
Miles, S. (2004) *The Hippocratic Oath and the Ethics of Medicine*, New York: Oxford University Press.
Miles, S. (2006) *Oath Betrayed: Torture, Medical Complicity, and the War on Terror*, New York: Random House.

Mill, J.S. (1998) *On Liberty and Other Essays*, Oxford: Oxford University Press.
Milwertz, C.N. (1997) *Accepting Population Control: Urban Chinese Women and the One-Child Family Policy*, Richmond: Curzon.
Milwertz, C.N. (2003) "Organizing for gender equality in China: A process of cultural and political change." Paper presented at the Ecole des Hautes Etudes en Sciences Sociales in Paris.
Mitchell. J. (1998) "Cross-cultural issues in the disclosure of cancer," *Cancer Practice* 6(3): 153–60.
Mitsuya, H. (1997) "Telling the truth to cancer patients and patients with HIV-1 infection in Japan," *Annals of the New York Academy of Sciences* 808: 279–89.
Mobeireek, A.F. et al. (2008) "Information disclosure and decision-making: the Middle East versus the Far East and the West," *Journal of Medical Ethics* 34: 225–9.
Moskowitz, M.L. (2001) *The Haunting Fetus: Abortion, Sexuality, and the Spirit World in Taiwan*, Honolulu: University of Hawai'i Press.
Munro, D.J. (ed.) (1985) *Individualism and Holism: Studies in Confucian and Taoist Values*, Ann Arbor: University of Michigan Press.
Mystakidou, K., Parpa, E., Tsilika, E., Katsouda, E. and Vlahos, L. (2004) "Cancer information disclosure in different culture context," *Support Care Cancer* 12: 147–54.
Needham, J. (1983, 1st edn 1956) *Science and Civilization in China*, Vol. II, Cambridge: Cambridge University Press.
Needham, J. (2000) *Science and Civilization in China*, Vol. 6, Part VI: Medicine, Cambridge: Cambridge University Press.
Nelson, H.L. (2000) "Feminist bioethics: Where we've been, where we're going," *Metaphilosophy* 31(5): 492–508.
Nelson, H.L. and Nelson, J.L. (1995) *The Patient in the Family: An Ethics of Medicine and Families*, New York: Routledge.
Ni, M.S. trans. (1995) *The Yellow Emperor's Classic of Medicine: A New Translation of the Neijing Suwen with Commentary*. Boston: Shambhala.
Nicholas, T.L. (1853) *Esoteric Anthropology (The Mysteries of Man)*, London: Nicols & Co.
Nie, J.B. (1986) "The historical facts and causes of underdevelopment of anatomy in ancient China," *Hunan Zhongyi Xueyuan Xuebao* (Journal of Hunan College of Traditional Chinese Medicine) 7(3): 42–5.
Nie, J.B. (1989a) "A comparative study on Wang Qingren and Andrea Vesalius," *Zhongyiyao Xuebao* (Acta of Chinese Medicine and Pharmacology) 6: 1–4.
Nie, J.B. (1989b), "Galen and modern Western medicine," *Zhonghua Yishi Zhazi* (Chinese Journal of Medical History) 19(4): 30–33.
Nie, J.B. (1990a) "Zhang Zhongjing and Gelen: The beginning of the differences of Chinese and Western medicine," *Zhongyiyao Xuebao* (Acta of Chinese Medicine and Pharmacology) (1): 2–7.
Nie, J.B. (1990b) "On Wang Qingren: His times and medical achievements," *Hunan Zhongyi Xueyuan Xuebao* (Journal of Hunan College of Traditional Chinese Medicine) 10(3): 177–9.
Nie, J.B. (1995) "Scientism and traditional Chinese medicine in twentieth-century China," *Yiyue Yu Zhexue* (Medicine and Philosophy) 16: 62–6.

Nie, J.B. (1999a) "The problem of coerced abortion in China and some ethical issues," *Cambridge Quarterly of Healthcare Ethics*, 8(4): 463–79; reprinted in B. Benett (ed.) (2004) *Abortion*, Aldershot: Ashgate; and also in L. May, S. Collins-Chobanian and K. Wong (eds) (2006, 2010), *Applied Ethics: A Multicultural Approach*, 4th and 5th edns., Englewood Cliffs, NJ: Prentice Hall.

Nie, J.B. (1999b) "*'Human drugs' in Chinese medicine and the Confucian view: An interpretive study*," in R.P. Fan (ed.) *Confucian Bioethics*, Dordrecht: Kluwer.

Nie, J.B. (2000) "Toward medical humanities centered with individual patients and the disadvantaged social groups," *Yixue Yu Zhexue* (Medicine and Philosophy) 21(10): 8–9.

Nie, J.B. (2002) "Japanese doctors' experimentation in wartime China," *The Lancet* 360: s5–s6.

Nie, J.B. (2004) "State violence in twentieth-century China: Some shared features of the Japanese Army's atrocities and the Cultural Revolution's terror," in L. Kühnhardt and M. Takayama (eds) *Menchenrechte, Kulturen und Gewalt: Ansaetze einer Interkulturellen Ethik* (Human Rights, Cultures, and Violence: Perspectives of Intercultural Ethics), Baden-Baden: Nomos.

Nie, J.B. (2005) *Behind the Silence: Chinese Voices on Abortion*, Lanham and Oxford: Rowman & Littlefield.

Nie, J.B. (2006) "The United States cover-up of Japanese wartime medical atrocities: Complicity committed in the national interest and two proposals for contemporary action," *American Journal of Bioethics* 6(3): W21–W33.

Nie, J.B. (2007) "The specious idea of an Asian bioethics: Beyond dichotomizing East and West," in R.E. Ashcroft, A. Dawson, H. Draper and J.R. McMillan (eds), *Principles of Heath Care Ethics*, 2nd edn, London: John Wiley & Sons.

Nie, J.B. (2009) "The discourses of practitioners in China," in R. Baker and L. McCullough (eds) *The Cambridge World History of Medical Ethics*, New York: Cambridge University Press.

Nie, J.B. (2010a) "On the altar of nation-state: Japan's wartime medical atrocities and postwar responses in the United States and China," in J.B. Nie, N.Y. Guo, M. Selden and A. Kleinman (eds) *Japan's Wartime Medical Atrocities: Comparative Inquiries in Science, History, and Ethics*, London: Routledge.

Nie, J.B. (2010b) "China's birth control program through feminist lenses," in J.L. Scully, L. Baldwin-Ragaven and P. Fitzpatrick (eds) *Feminist Bioethics: At the Centre, on the Margins*, Baltimore MD: Johns Hopkins University Press.

Nie, J.B. (2010c) "Limits of state intervention in sex-selective abortion: the case of China," *Culture, Health & Sexuality* 12(2): 205–19.

Nie, J.B. (forthcoming a) (ed.) *Engineering Population in East and West: A Comparative Ethical and Sociological Study*, An edited volume in progress.

Nie, J.B. (forthcoming b) *Predicaments of Social Engineering: The Ideology and Ethics of China's Birth Control Programme*, A monograph in progress.

Nie, J.B. (forthcoming c) *Morality Sacrificed, Justice Denied: Japan's Wartime Medical Atrocities and the International Aftermath*, A monograph in progress.

Nie, J.B. and Anderson, L. (2003) "Bioethics in New Zealand: A historical and sociological review," in J. F. Peppin and M J. Cherry (eds), *Regional Perspectives in Bioethics*, The Netherlands: Swetz Zeitlinger; the Chinese version, trans. L. Zheng and Q.S. Yan, appeared in *Yixue yu Zhexue* (Medicine and Philosophy) (2005) 26(9): 28–30 and 26(10): 36–8.

Nie, J.B. and A. Campbell (2007) "Multiculturalism and Asian bioethics: cultural war or creative dialogue?", *Journal of Bioethical Inquiry* 4(3): 163–7.
Nie, J.B., Guo, N.Y., Selden, M. and Kleinman, A. (eds) (2010) *Japan's Wartime Medical Atrocities: Comparative Inquiries in Science, History, and Ethics*, London & New York: Routledge.
Nie, J.B., Tsuchiya, T. and Li, L. (2009) "Japanese doctors' experimentation, 1932–1945, and medical ethics," in R. Baker and L. McCullough (eds) *The Cambridge World History of Medical Ethics*, New York: Cambridge University Press. The Chinese version translated by J. Li and X.Q. Chen appeared in *Yixue yu Zhexue* (Medicine and Philosophy) (2006) 26(6): 35–8 and reprinted in P. Liang, F. Chenn and G.G. Bao (eds.) (2008) *The Social History of Science and Technology: Science and Technology from the Imperialistic Perspective*, Shenyang: Liaoning Science & Technology Press.
Nisbett, R.E. (2003) *The Geography of Thought: How Asians and Westerners Think Differently… and Why*, New York: Free Press.
Nissenbaum, S. (1980) *Sex, Diet, and Debility in Jacksonian America: Sylvester Graham and Health Reform*, Westport: Greenwood Press.
Novack, D.H., Plumer, R., Smith, R.L., Ochitill, H., Morrow, G.R. and Bennett, J.M. (1979) "Changes in physicians' attitudes toward telling the cancer patient," *Journal of American Medical Association*, 241(9): 897–900.
Nussbaum, M.C. (1997) *Cultivating Humanities*, Cambridge, MA: Harvard University Press.
Oken, D. (1961) "What to tell cancer patients: A study of medical attitudes," *Journal of American Medical Association*, 175(13): 1120–8.
Ong, A. and Cheng, N.N. (eds) (2010) *Asian Bioethics: Ethics and Communities of Fate*, Durham: Duke University Press.
Owen, R.G. (1952) *Scientism, Man, and Religion*, Philadelphia: Westminster.
Pan, Z. et al. (1994) *To See Ourselves: Comparing Traditional Chinese and American Cultural Values*, Boulder: Westview.
Pang, M.S. (1998) "Information disclosure: The moral experience of nurses in China," *Nursing Ethics* 5(4): 347–61.
Pang, M.S. (1999) "Protective truthfulness: the Chinese way of safeguarding patients in informed treatment decisions," *Journal of Medical Ethics* 25: 247–53.
Pang, M.S. (2003) *Nursing Ethics in Modern China: Conflicting Values and Competing Role Requirements*, Amsterdam: Rodopi.
Patterson, J.T. (1987) *The Dread Disease: Cancer and Modern American Culture*, Cambridge, MA: Harvard University Press.
Pellegrino, E., Mazzarella, P. and Corsi P. (eds) (1992) *Transcultural Dimensions in Medical Ethics*, Frederick, MD: University Publishing Group.
Peppin, J.F. and Cherry, M.J. (2003) *Regional Perspectives in Bioethics*, Lisse: Swets & Zeitlinger.
Phillips, M.R., Li, X.Y. and Zhang, Y.P. (2002) "Suicide rates in China, 1995–99," *Lancet* 359(9309): 835–40.
Popper, K. (1994) *In Search of a Better World*, London: Routledge.
Porket, M. (1974) *The Theoretical Foundation of Chinese Medicine: Systems of Correspondence*, Cambridge, MA: The MIT Press.
Potter, S.H. and Potter, J.M. (1990) *China's Peasants: The Anthropology of a Revolution*, Cambridge: Cambridge University Press.

Qiu, R.Z. (1987) *Shengming Lunlixue* (Bioethic), Shanghai: Shanghai People's Press.
Qiu, R.Z. (1988) "Medicine—the art of humaneness: On ethics of traditional Chinese medicine," *Journal of Medicine and Philosophy* 13(1): 35–73.
Qiu, R.Z. (1992) "Medical ethics and Chinese culture," in E.D. Pellegrino et al. (eds) *Transcultural Dimensions in Medical Ethics*, Frederick, MD: University Publishing Group, 155–74.
Qiu, R.Z. (ed.) (1996) *Shenyu Jiankang Yu Lunlixue* (Reproductive Health and Ethics), Beijing: The United Press of Beijing Medical University and Beijing Union Medical University.
Qiu, R.Z. (ed.) (2004) *Bioethics: Asian Perspectives: A Quest for Moral Diversity*, Dordrecht: Kluwer Academic Publishers.
Ramsey, P. (2002, 1st edn 1970) *The Patient as Person: Explorations in Medical Ethics*, New Haven: Yale University Press.
Raphals, L. (1998) *Sharing the Light: Representations of Women and Virtue in Early China*, Albany, NY: State University of New York Press.
Rawls, J. (2005 [1993]) *Political Liberalism: Expanded Edition*, New York: Columbia University Press.
Raz, J. (1988) *The Morality of Freedom*, Oxford: Oxford University Press.
Rehmann-Sutter, C., Duwell, M. and Mieth, D. (eds) (2006) *Bioethics in Cultural Contexts: Reflections on Methods and Finitude*, Dordrecht: Springer.
Rigdon, S. (1996) "Abortion law and practice in China: an overview with comparison to the United States," *Social Sciences and Medicine*, 42: 543–60.
Roetz, H. (1993) *Confucian Ethics of the Axial Age*, Albany, NY: State University of New York Press.
Roetz, H. (ed.) (2006) *Cross-Cultural Issues in Bioethics: The Example of Human Cloning*, New York: Rodopi.
Said, E.W. (1994, 1st edn 1979) *Orientalism*, New York: Vintage.
Salles, A.L.F. and Bertomeu, M.J. (eds) (2002) *Bioethics: Latin American Perspectives*, Amsterdam: Rodopi.
Sarton, G. (1954) *Galen of Pergamon*, Lawrence, Kansas: University of Kansas Press.
Sass, H.-M., Veatch, R.M. and Kimura, R. (eds) (1998) *Advanced Directives in Surrogate Decision Making in Health Care: United States, Germany, and Japan*, Baltimore, MD: Johns Hopkins University Press.
Scharping, T. (2003) *Birth Control in China 1949–2000: Population Policy and Demographic Development*, London: Routledge-Curzon.
Scully, J.L., Baldwin-Ragaven, L.E. and Fitzpatrick, P. (eds) (2010) *Feminist Bioethics: At the Centre, On the Margins*, Baltimore: Johns Hopkins University Press.
Shain, B.A. (1994) *The Myth of American Individualism: The Protestant Origins of American Political Thought*, Princeton: Princeton University Press.
Shapiro, J. (2001) *Mao's War against Nature: Politics and Environment in Revolutionary China*, Cambridge: Cambridge University Press.
Sherwin, S. (1992) *No Longer Patient: Feminist Ethics and Health Care*, Philadelphia: Temple University Press.
Singer, C. (1957) *A Short History of Anatomy and Physiology from Greek to Harvey*, New York: Dover.
Sivin, N. (1987) *Traditional Medicine in Contemporary China*, Ann Arbor: University of Michigan Press.

Sleeboom, M. (2004) *Academic Nations in China and Japan: Framed in Concepts of Nature, Culture and the Universal*, London: Routledge.
Sleeboom-Faulkner, M. (2007) *The Chinese Academy of Social Sciences: Shaping the Reforms, Academia and China (1977–2003)*, Leiden: Brill.
Sleeboom-Faulkner, M. (ed.) (2008a) *Genomics in Asia*, London: Routledge.
Sleeboom-Faulkner, M. (ed.) (2008b) *Human Genetic Biobank in Asia*, London: Routledge.
Sleeboom-Faulkner, M. (ed.) (2010) *Framework of Choice: Predictive and Genetic Testing in Asia*, Amsterdam: Amsterdam University Press.
Smith, A. (1991) *The Wealth of Nations*, New York: Prometheus.
Smith, A. (2000) *The Theory of Moral Sentiments*, New York: Prometheus.
Smith, A.H. (2002, 1st edn 1894) *Chinese Characteristics*, Norwalk, CT: EastBridge.
Song, G.B. (1933) *Yiye Lunlixue* (The Professional Ethics of Medicine), Shanghai: Guoguang Bookstore.
Sontag, S. (1990) *Illness as Metaphor and AIDS and Its Metaphors*, New York: Anchor Books.
Sorell, T. (1991) *Scientism: Philosophy and the Infatuation with Science*, London: Routledge.
Spence, J.D. (1998) *The Chan's Great Continent: China in Western Minds*, New York: W.W. Norton & Company.
Stockham, A.B. (1896, new edn) *Karezza: Ethics of Marriage*, Chicago: Stockham.
Sun, S.M. (1998) *Beiji Qianji Yaofang* (Prescriptions Worth More than a Thousand Pieces of Gold), Beijing: People's Health Press.
Sun, Z. (1963) *The Art of War*, trans. S.B. Griffith, London: Oxford University Press.
Sun, Y., Li, Z., Sun, M. and Chang. L. (2007) "A study of attitudes of family members of cancer patients regarding truth-telling and possible influencing factors," *Chinese Journal of Nursing* No. 6.
Surbone, A. (1992) "Letter from Italy: truth telling to the patient," *Journal of American Medical Association* 268(13): 1661–2.
Surbone, A. (2004) "Persisting differences in truth telling throughout the world," *Support Care Cancer* 12: 143–6.
Surbone, A. (2006) "Telling the truth to patients with cancer: What is the truth," *Lancet Oncology* 7: 944–50.
Surbone, A. (2008) "Cultural aspects of communication in cancer care," *Support Care Cancer* 16: 235–40.
Svensson, M. (2002) *Debating Human Rights in China: A Conceptual and Political History*, Lanham, MD: Rowman & Littlefield.
Tai, M.C. (2008) *The Way of Asian Bioethics*, Taipai: Princeton International.
Takahashi, T. (2005) *Taking Life and Death Seriously: Bioethics from Japan*, Amsterdam: JAI Press.
Tang, S.T. and Lee, S.-Y.C. (2004) "Cancer diagnosis and prognosis in Taiwan: patient references versus experiences," *Psycho-Oncology* 13: 1–13.
Tang, S.T. et al. (2008) "Patient awareness of prognosis, patient-family caregiver congruence on the preferred place of death, and caregiving burden of families contribute to the equality of life for terminal ill cancer patients in Taiwan." *Psycho-Oncology* 17: 1202–9.
Tao, J.T.L. (ed.) (2002) *Cross-Cultural Perspectives on the (Im)Possibility of Global Bioethics*, New York: Springer.

Tao, J.T.L. (ed.) (2008) *China: Bioethics, Trust, and the Challenge of the Market*, New York: Springer.
Temple, R. (1986) *The Genius of China: 3000 Years of Science, Discovery, and Invention*, New York: Simon and Schuster.
Tissot, S.-A. (1832) *Treatise on the Disease Produced by Onanism*, New York: Collins & Hannay.
Tolstoy. L. (1986) *The Death of Ivan Ilyich*, trans. L. Solotaroff, New York: Bantam Books.
Tong, R. (1997) *Feminist Approaches to Bioethics: Theoretical Reflections and Practical Applications*, Boulder, CO: Westview Press.
Tong, R. (1998) "Feminist ethics," in R. Chadwick (ed.) *Encyclopedia of Applied Ethics*, San Diego: Academic Press.
Tong, R., Donchin, A. and Dodds, S. (eds) (2004) *Linking Visions: Feminist Bioethics, Human Rights, and the Developing World*, Lanham: Rowman & Littlefield.
Tong, R., Anderson, G. and Santos, A. (eds) (2001) *Globalising Feminist Bioethics: Cross-Cultural Perspectives*, Boulder: Westview.
Trall, R.T. (1908, 1st edn 1886) *Sexual Physiology and Hygiene: An Exposition Practical, Scientific, Moral, and Popular*, Glasgow: Kent & Co.
Tribe, L.H. (1992) *Abortion: The Clash of Absolutes*, New York: W.W. Norton.
Trilling, L. (1971) *Sincerity and Authenticity*, Cambridge, MA: Harvard University Press.
Tsai, D.F.C. (1999) "Ancient Chinese medical ethics and the four principles of biomedical ethics," *Journal of Medical Ethics*, 25: 315–21.
Tsai, D.F.C. (2005) "The bioethical principles and Confucius' moral philosophy," *Journal of Medical Ethics*, 31: 159–63.
Tse, C.Y., Chong, A. and Fok, S.Y. (2003) "Breaking bad news: A Chinese perspective," *Palliative Medicine* 17: 339–43.
Tu, W.M. (1989) *Centrality and Commonality: An Essay on Confucian Religiousness*, Albany, NY: State University of New York Press.
Tu, W.M. (1997) "Destructive will and ideological holocaust: Maoism as a source of social suffering in China," in A. Kleinman, V. Das and M. Lock (eds), *Social Suffering*, Berkeley: University of California Press.
Tuckett, A.G. (2004) "Truth-telling in clinical practice and the arguments for and against: A review of literature," *Nursing Ethics*, 11(5): 500–513.
Turner, L. (1998) "An anthropological exploration of contemporary bioethics: the varieties of common sense," *Journal of Medical Ethics* 24: 127–33.
Turner, L. (2003a) "Zones of consensus and zones of conflict: questioning the 'common morality' presumption in bioethics," *Kennedy Institute of Ethics Journal* 13: 182–218.
Turner, L. (2003b) "Bioethics in a multicultural world: medicine and morality in pluralistic settings," *Health Care Analysis* 11: 99–117.
Turner, L. (2005) "From local to the global: bioethics and the concept of culture," *Journal of Medicine and Philosophy* 30: 305–20.
United Nations Education, Scientific and Cultural Organisation (UNESCO) (2005) *Universal Declaration on Bioethics and Human Rights*.
Unschuld, P.U. (1999) [1979] *Medical Ethics in Imperial China*, Berkeley: University of California Press.
Unschuld, P.U. (2010) [1985] *Medicine in China: A History of Ideas*, Berkeley: University of California Press.

Unschuld, P.U. (1990) *Forgotten Traditions of Ancient Chinese Medicine*, Brookline, MA: Paradigm.
Unschuld, P.U. (2011) *Huang Di Nei Jing, So Wen: An Annotated Translation of Hung Di's Inner Classic*–Basic Questions (2 Volumes), Berkeley: University of California Press.
van Gulik, R.H. (2003, 1st edn 1961) *Sexual Life in Ancient China: A Preliminary Survey of Chinese Sex and Society from ca. 1500 B.C. till 1644*, Leiden: E.J. Brill.
Veatch, R.M. (1981) *A Theory of Medical Ethics*, New York: Basic Books.
Veatch, R.M. (1987) *The Patient as Partner: A Theory of Human-Experimentation Ethics*, Bloomington: Indiana University Press.
Veatch, R.M. (1991) *The Patient-Physician Relation: The Patient as Partner, Part II*, Indianapolis: Indiana University Press.
Veatch, R.M. (ed.) (2000, 2nd edn) [1989] *Cross-Cultural Perspectives in Medical Ethics*, London: Jones & Bartlett.
Veatch, R.M. (2009) *Patient, Heal Thyself: How the New Medicine Puts the Patient in Charge*, Oxford: Oxford University Press.
Veith, I. (trans.) (2002, 1st edn 1949), *Huang Ti Nei Ching Su Wen: The Yellow Emperor's Classic of Internal Medicine*, Chapters 1–34. Berkeley: University of California Press (originally published by Baltimore: Williams & Wilkings Company in 1949).
Waley, A. (trans.) (1992) *The Analects of Confucius*, New York: Book of the Month.
Waley-Cohen, J. (2005) *The Sextant of Beijing: Global Currents in Chinese History*, New York: W.W. Norton & Company.
Wang, F.L. (2005) *Organising through Division and Exclusion: China's Hukou System*, Stanford, CA: Stanford University Press.
Wang, J.L. (2001) "HIV/AIDS and prostitution in mainland China: A feminist Perspective," in R. Tong, G. Anderson and A. Santos (eds) *Globalizing Feminist Bioethics: Crosscultural Perspectives*, Boulder, CO: Westview.
Wang, Q. (1976) [1893] *Yilin Gaicuo* (Errors in Medicine Corrected) with Annotations, Beijing: People's Health Press.
Watson, B. (trans.) (1968) *The Complete Works of Chuang Tzu*, New York: Columbia University Press.
Wear, S. (2007) "Truth telling to the sick and dying in a traditional Chinese culture," in S.C. Lee (ed.) *The Family, Medical Decision-Making, and Biotechnology*, Dordrecht: Springer.
Wellmuth, J. (1944) *The Nature and Origins of Scientism*, Milwaukee: Marquette University Press.
Wertz, D.C. and Fletcher, J.C. (2004) *Genetics and Ethics in Global Perspective*, Dordrecht: Kluwer.
White, T. (2006) *China's Longest Campaign: Birth Planning in the People's Republic, 1949–2005*, London: Cornell University Press.
Williams, P. and Wallace, D. (1989) *Unit 731: Japan's Secret Biological Warfare in World War II*, London: Hodder & Stoughton.
Wong, K.C. and Lien-Teh, W. (1936, 2nd edn) *History of Chinese Medicine: Being a Chronicle of Medical Happenings in China from Ancient Times to Present Period*, Shanghai: National Quarantine Service.
Woo, K.Y. (1999) "Care for Chinese palliative patients," *Journal of Palliative Care* 15(3): 70–74.

Xia, Y. (2004) *Zhongguo Mingquan Zhexue* (The Philosophy of Civil Rights in the Context of China), Beijing: Sanlian Bookstore.
Xia, Y. (2007) [1995, 1st edn] Zouxiang Quanli de Shidai (Toward an Age of Rights: A Research on the Development of Civil Rights in China), Beijing: Social Sciences Academic Press.
Xu, T.M., Cheng, Z.F., Li, J.J., Zhang, D.Q. (1998) Zhongxifang Yixue Lunlixue Bijiao Yanjiu (*Comparative Studies of Chinese and Western Medical Ethics*), Beijing: The United Press of Beijing Medical University and Peking Union Medical University.
Yang, B. (1980) *Lunyu Yizhu* (The Analects with the Modern Chinese Translation and Annotations), Beijing: China Bookstore.
Yixue Yu Zhexue (Editorial Office of the journal *Medicine and Philosophy*) (2008), "Guiding principles on truth-telling to and consent from cancer patients," *Medicine and Philosophy* (Clinical Making Forum Edition), 29(10): 7–8.
Yu, Y.A. (1983) "Two celebrated medical works," in the Institute of the History of Natural Sciences, Chinese Academy of Sciences (ed.) *Ancient China's Technology and Science*, Beijing: Foreign Languages Press.
Zakaria, F. (1994) "Culture is destiny: A conversation with Lee Kuan Yew," *Foreign Affairs*, 73(2): 109–26.
Zeng, T., Li, Y., Chen, Y. and Fang, P. (2007) "An investigation into the attitudes of medical professional on disclosing cancer diagnoses," *Yixue yu Zhexue* (Medicine and Philosophy, Clinical Decision Making Forum Edition), 28 (11).
Zeng, T., Zhou, M., Hong, L., Xiang, L. and Fang, P. (2008) "An investigation into the attitudes of cancer patients regarding the disclosure of information on critical medical conditions," *Fuli Yanjiu* (Nursing Research), No. 17.
Zhang, D. and Cheng, Z.F. (2000) "Medicine is a humane art: The basic principles of professional ethics in Chinese medicine," *Hastings Center Report*, 30(4): S8–S12.
Zhang, L. (1998) *Mighty Opposites: From Dichotomies to Differences in the Comparative Study of China*, Stanford: Stanford University Press.
Zhang, X. and Sleeboom-Faulkner, M. (2011) "Tension between medical professionals and patients in mainland China," *Cambridge Quarterly of Healthcare Ethics*, 20: 458–65.
Zhao, H.Z. (1989) *Jindai Zhongxiyi Lunzhen Shi* (A History of the Modern Controversies between Chinese and Western Medicine), Hefei: Anfei Science and Technology Press.
Zhen, Z.Y. (ed.) (2001), rev. edn) *Zhongguo Yixueshi* (The History of Chinese Medicine), Shanghai : Shanghai Science and Technology Press.
Zhou, Y.M. (1983) *Lidai Mingyi Lun Yide* (Ancient Well-known Chinese Physicians on Medical Morality), Changsha: Hunan Science and Technology Press.
Zhou, Z.Z. (2004) *Lunlixue* (Ethics), Beijing: People's Press.
Zhu, W. (2009) *Shengming Lunlixue zhong de Zhiqing Tongyi* (Informed Consent in Bioethics), Shanghai: Fudan University Press.
Zhu, W. (2009b) Does Chinese Culture Constitue Challenges to Informed Consent? In O. Doring (ed) *Life Sciences in Translation – A Sino-European Dialogue on Ethical Governance of the Life Sciences*. Ethicial Governance of Biological and Biomedical Research: Chinese-European Co-operation. Online. Freely available at http://www.lse.ac.uk/collections/BIONET/ (accessed 7 October 2011).
Zhu, X. (2005) "A survey on whether the truth should be told to the seriously ill," *Yixue yu Zhexue* (Medicine and Philosophy), 26(8): 73–5.

Acknowledgements

As a student at Hunan College of Chinese Medicine in China in the 1980s, I once read an article introducing the philosophy of science of Bertrand Russell. I still remember, with great vividness, that the Chinese author started the article citing the beginning sentence (in Chinese translation, of course) of Russell's autobiography: "Three passions, simple but overwhelmingly strong, have governed my life: the longing for love, the search for knowledge, and unbearable pity for the suffering of mankind." Although I can never live such a creative life as Russell, I felt and feel the three simple but extremely strong passions.

Ever since I decided to give up practicing medicine and pursue an academic life in the mid-1980s, three big questions have been driving me in almost all of my research activities:

- Why has so much massive social suffering and destruction occurred in 20th century China, and in some ways continues today in the 21st century?
- What can Chinese cultural traditions, traditional medicine included, contribute to today's world?
- What are the differences and commonalities between Chinese and Western medicines—their cultural contexts, historical developments, ethical ideals and philosophical foundations?

I know all too well that any one of these three questions demands more than a lifetime of research in order to reach some good answers. But I have to try as hard as I can to make a better sense of these questions, not so much for others, but primarily, for myself.

Over the past 15 years while this book was in the making, three major research areas have occupied the largest portion of my professional career, and perhaps too much of my personal and family life. The first of these is on abortion and population control in China. Starting as a PhD thesis, my study on Chinese views and experiences of abortion culminated in a book entitled *Behind Silence: Chinese Voices on Abortion* (Rowman & Littlefield 2005). One of my current research projects, supported by a grant from the Marsden Fund of the Royal Society of New Zealand, focuses on the ideology, ethics and predicaments of social engineering as involved in China's massive and intrusive birth control program. A logical extension on this direction for future inquiries should be about the ideological sources, ethical issues, and social predicaments of engineering nature such as the Three Gorges Dam and the extensive nationwide dam buildings.

The second area, supported by an earlier grant from the Marsden Fund of the Royal Society of New Zealand, examines the ethical, historical, political and cultural dimensions of (in)humane medical experimentation conducted in Japan's wartime biological warfare programs and the lack of adequate responses from all the countries involved and the international community. The two final products resulted from this research project are: a co-edited book, *Japan's Wartime Medical Atrocities: Comparative Inquiries in Science, History and Ethics* (Routledge 2010), and an authored in-progress monograph, *Morality Sacrificed, Justice Denied: Japan's Wartime Medical Atrocities and the International Aftermath*.

The present volume gathers up some fruits of my labor in the third area of consuming research interest, that is, medical ethics in China in the broad sense. It is one of the products of my overall aim to explore the great richness, diversity, complexity, dynamism, openness, cultural roots and socio-historical contexts of medical ethics in China, as well as the necessity and possibility of a productive Chinese-Western cross-cultural dialogue in the field of bioethics.

Half of this book has been written in a very intensive month, June 2011, after I had been sick for two months and had just finished teaching for the first semester of the year. The rest of the book draws materials from some previously published book chapters and journal articles. Most of these materials, especially those about China's internal plurality, medical truth-telling, informed consent and human rights, have been significantly revised and expanded from their original form. The relevant publications are as follows:

2011. "The 'Cultural Differences' Argument and Its Misconceptions: The Return of Medical Truth-Telling in China," In Abraham Rudnick, ed., *Bioethics for the 21st Century*. Intech (Open Access Publisher);

2008. "Exploring the Core of Humanity: Cross-Cultural Perspectives on the Concept of Personhood." In Tze-wan Kwan, ed., *Responsibility and Commitment: Eighteen Essays in Honor of Gerhold K.Becker*. Waldkirch: Edition Gorz, pp. 17–27 (a revised version of a book review, "New and Eastern (Chinese) Perspectives on Personhood," published in *Medical Humanities Review* 2000 Vol. 14, No. 2: 26–34);

2005. "Cultural Values Embodying Universal Norms: A Critique of a Popular Assumption about Cultures and Human Rights." *Developing World Bioethics* 5 (2): 251–7;

2004. "Feminist Bioethics and its Language of Human Rights in the Chinese Context," In Rosemarie Tong, Anne Donchin and Susan Dodds, eds., *Linking Visions: Feminist Bioethics, Human Rights and the Developing World.* Boulder, CO: Rowman & Littlefield. pp. 73–88;

2001. "Refutation of the Claim that the Ancient Chinese Described the Circulation of Blood: A Critique of Scientism in the Historiography of Chinese Medicine," *New Zealand Journal of Asian Studies* Vol. 3, No. 2: 119–35.

2001. "Is Informed Consent not Applicable to China?: Intellectual Flaws of the Cultural Difference Argument." *Formosa Journal of Medical Humanities* Vol. 2, No. 1 & 2: 67–74 (A modified Chinese version, translated by Zhao Mingjie, was published in the Chinese journal *Medicine and Philosophy* 23 (6), 2002: 18–22);

2000. "The Plurality of Chinese and American Medical Moralities: Toward an Interpretive Cross-Cultural Bioethics," *Kennedy Institute of Ethics Journal* Vol.10, No.3: 239–60 (A modified Chinese version of this article, translated by Wang Jin and Chen Rongxia, was published in *Chinese and International Philosophy of Medicine* 2001 Vol. 3, No. 4: 135);

1996. "The Physician as General," *The Journal of the American Medical Association* 279 (13):1099–158;

1995. With Kirk L. Smith. "Individualism and Communitarianism in the Ethics of Health Promotion: The Search for a Yin-Yang/Dialectical Model," In Robert I. Misbin, Bruce Jennings, et al., eds., *Health Care Crisis? The Search for Answers*, Frederick, Maryland: University Publishing Group, 1995. pp 235–45.

I thank all the publishers and/or editors of these materials for allowing me to incorporate them into this book. Special thanks go to my good friend Kirk Smith for co-authoring the last chapter (but earliest written) of this book and especially for supping, studying and lecturing together in the United States and China.

Although by personality and choice I enjoy a solitary and contemplative life, human beings are by both nature and nurture social animals. Without any deep and sophisticated reflection one knows that we all are dependent upon each other and exist for each other. I really do not know how to thank all the people upon whom this book, and my life, depends. But I know how blessed I am. I also know that the best way to thank is to exert myself to give back as much as I can, however small this may be, to what I have received and am receiving.

I wrote my Master's thesis in the history of medicine on Zhang Zhongjing and Galan, two great physicians in the second century. This book is a kind of continuation of inquiries that had started in that thesis. I am always in debt to my Chinese mentors, Ma Kanwen, Yuan Lida and Zhou Yimou.

My work in China would not be possible without the generous support from many Chinese colleagues and friends including, but far from limited to, Du Zhizheng, Tang Kaling, Cong Yali, He Yuming, Hu Lingyin, Li Lun,

Qiu Hongzhong, Peng Jian, Wang Yongguang, Wang Yifang, Zhang Daqing, and Zhao Mingjie. To Qiu Renzong, Du Zhizheng and Tang Kaling, I thank them for opening my mind's eye through their pioneering works in the philosophy of science and bioethics, medical humanities and ethics in China, and Chinese ethics respectively.

Intellectually, I am deeply indebted to Mencius and Kant for their life-changing insights on the nature of human morality; to Tang Junyi, Mo Zongsan and Qian Mu who had produced the first class scholarship on Confucianism and traditional Chinese cultures when they were forced to be on exile from mainland China after the success of Mao's revolution; to Amartya Sen for his great works on social philosophy and Indian cultures; to Arthur Kleinman for his paradigmatic studies in medical anthropology and China studies; to Mark Selden for his eye-opening works on China and Asia. Their influence upon my scholarship has been significant.

My deep gratitude goes to Robert Veatch for his paradigm-building works in bioethics (a patient-centred bioethics), for his generous support to my work, and for his kindness in writing the foreword to this book.

For my German and Dutch colleagues and friends Ole Döring and Margaret Sleeboom-Faulkner, I thank them for their exemplary works—philosophical and anthropological or sociological respectively—on bioethics in China and Asia and especially for their encouragements whenever I fell into the mood of the Chinese proverb "*baiwu yiyong shi shushen*" (A scholar is the most useless in the world).

To Carl Elliott, I am always grateful for, among many others, his creative and incisive inquiries into medicine and bioethics in the American socio-cultural context and his direction for me to come to Dunedin.

Coming to work and live in New Zealand twelve years ago realized a dream of mine as a young student in China, a dream I then never thought could come true. The dream was to live in a beautiful countryside ("*shiwai taoyuan*", a peaceful land away from the maddening world, dreamed of by an ancient Chinese poet) and yet simultaneously pursue my intellectual and academic interests.

I am very grateful to the University of Otago and the Bioethics Centre for granting me tenure and for giving me their generous support. The earlier research this book is based on was supported by a University of Otago Research Grant. It has been a privilege and pleasure to work with all my colleagues including, but far from limited to, Gareth Jones, Lynley Anderson, Donald Evans, Sandy Elkin, Jacob Edmund, Mike King, Vicki Lang, Brian Moloughney, Charlotte Paul, Takashi Shogimen and Xiahuan Zhao; and I highly appreciate their generous support. Special thanks go to Grant Gillett, Neil Pickering and Simon Walker for offering helpful suggestions. Such imaginative phrases as "supping with foreign devils," "cultural norms embodying universal values," and "truths of cultures" were suggested by Grant and Neil. Moreover, when I intensively worked on completing this book under the pressure of the final deadline in June 2011, Grant so kindly took up much of my marking task.

This Bioethics Centre has been blessed with a very stimulating intellectual environment and many wonderful postgraduate students. One of my new postgraduate students, Samuel Ujewe, helped with the preparation of the early version of the bibliography. Some of the materials in this book have been used in my teachings, especially in the two courses I have been coordinating, "Introduction to Bioethics" (for undergraduates) and "Theories of Biomedical Ethics" (for postgraduates). I am very thankful to the students in these two courses for their questions and comments.

The wonderful editing (of most manuscripts) undertaken by Paul Sorrell and always highly appreciated by me has been essential for the good English of this book and many other English publications of mine. His professional editing and Samuel's assistance have been supported by a PBRF (Performance-Based Research Funding) Publication Grant from the Otago University.

It is my honor to have this volume published in the "Biomedical Law and Ethics Library" by Routledge. The series editor, Sheila MacLean, has generously supported this book and other works of mine. I thank Katie Carpenter and Stephen Gutierrez at Routledge for their interest in this project, their willingness to accommodate my need to have this book published by the end of 2011 and their kind extension of the final deadline so that I could have the crucial month (June) to complete the manuscript. I am also grateful to Jack Webb for his editorial help and Thomas Lodge for his efficient management to produce this volume in less than five months. The comments and suggestions of three anonymous reviewers chosen by Routledge have been very helpful.

Also, I need to thank my family physician Jenny Lewis and quite a few specialists and nurses for having restored my health and probably saved my life without which the completing of this book would not be possible.

What all the above scholars, colleagues, friends and many others have so generously given me has demonstrated, far more concretely and convincingly than my words in this book, that humanity and morality are always transcultural.

My whole life and career to date, including any useful words that I have so far published, would not be possible without the unfailing love, support, understanding, and tolerance from my wife Lüjia (Xu Zhi), my daughter Luxi, my son Luke, my parents Nie Mao-Chu and Su Feng-Ying, my parents-in-law Xu Tie-Qiang and Cai Su-Chun, my brother Jing-Pei, my sister Jing-Jing, and other members of my whole extended family. Luxi, an earnest lover of the English language, has edited some materials of this book. My life and career would be unimaginable without the unsung sacrifice given especially by Lüjia. This book is dedicated to her and the two other very special Ls of mine.

Whilst finishing this book, I listened again to Beethoven's 9th Symphony, several times over. Whilst proofreading I listened to it in a concert by the NZ Symphony Orchestra and the City of Dunedin Choir, along with a glorious

NZ product *Kaitiaki* inspired by European as well as Maori/South-Pacific cultural elements. If only this book could help to add a tiny bit to the joy (the joy of learning in particular) and love that sustains humankind and of which I have been so blessed as a recipient!

About the author

JING-BAO NIE, BMed, MMed, MA, PhD

Jing-Bao Nie is an Associate Professor at the Bioethics Centre, Division of Health Science, University of Otago, Dunedin, New Zealand. He is also the Furong Visiting Professor at the Centre of Moral Culture, Hunan Normal University, and Adjunct Professor at the Institute for Medical Humanities, Peking University, China.

He obtained a PhD in the medical humanities from the University of Texas Medical Branch (UTMB) in the USA (1999), an MA in sociology from Queen's University in Canada (1993), and a Master of Medicine (in the history of Chinese medicine) and a Bachelor of Medicine (functioning as an MD) from Hunan College of Chinese Medicine in China (1986, 1983). He was the postdoctoral fellow in bioethics at the University of Minnesota (1998–99) and a lecturer at Hunan College of Chinese Medicine (1988–91). He was a visiting scholar at the National University of Singapore, Hong Kong Baptist University and Bonn University.

Dr Nie is the author of *Behind the Silence: Chinese Voices on Abortion* (Rowman & Littlefield, 2005), (chief editor) *Japan's Wartime Medical Atrocities: Comparative Inquiry in Science, History and Ethics* (Routledge, 2010), and three chapters in *The Cambridge World History of Medical Ethics* (Cambridge University Press, 2009). He co-authored *Chayi, Kunhuo yu Xuanzhe* (Differences, Perplexities, and Choices: Comparative Studies on Chinese and Western Medicine) (Shenyang Press, 1990). He has published numerous journal articles and other book chapters and given many invited addresses and conference presentations worldwide. Currently, he is editing a volume about the Eastern-Western comparative ethics of Population governance and completing a monograph about the ideology and ethics of China's birth control program.

Dr Nie is a consulting editor of *Asian Bioethics Review* and serves on the editorial/advisory boards of such journals as *Bioethics, Kennedy Institute of Ethics Journal, Open Ethics Journal, Eubios Journal of Asian & International Bioethics, Medicine and Philosophy, Medicine and Society*, and *Ethical Studies* (the last three in Chinese). He was a co-editor of the *"Liuyedao"* book series (Qingdao Press, 1998–2000) and the *Journal of Bioethical Inquiry* (2006). He co-chaired the organizing committee of the 6th International Congress of Feminist Bioethics (2006) and served on the Board of Directors of the International Association of Bioethics (2005–2009).

Dr Nie was born and grew up in a remote village in Hunan, South-Central China, and worked as a "peasant" there. Married to Xu Zhi (Lüjia), he has two children, Luxi and Luke.

He loves reading poetry and literature. His favorite authors include Tao Yuanming, *ci* poets, Hunan writer Shen Congwen, Hai Zi, the trio-Greek tragedy playwrights, Hölderlin, Dostoyevsky, Thoreau, Kafka, Camus, and Dunedin writer Janet Frame. He always enjoys seeing beautiful New Zealand landscapes and having holidays at the snow-covered Mt. Cook.

Index

abandonment: babies 165; medical truth-telling 123–4
abortion: China 41–6, 51, 95, 154, 165, 170–2, 173, 203–4; United States 33–4, 95
Ackerknecht, E.H. 81
acupuncture 70, 72, 181, 183, 199
Aeschylus 27
Africa 49
AIDS/HIV 158
Aird, J.S. 6
Akabayashi, A. 4, 117
Alora, A. 5
Altman, D. 222–3
American Medical Association 100, 130–1, 195
analytic and experimental medical tradition 81–2
anatomy 80–1
Anderson, B. 202
anger 65
Angle, S. 155
animals 189, 207
anthropology 27–8, 41–2, 46–7, 143, 206
Antigone 101–2
Aquinas, Thomas 102
Aristotle 27, 220
'Asian Values' 49, 151–3, 213; fallacy of 151-3
assumptions: homogeneity 46, 152, 226; human rights 150–1, 153; incommensurability 48, 136, 152, 226, 233; *see also* internal moral plurality
Au, Derrick 207
Augustine 101, 102
authoritarianism 49, 50, 151–3, 167–8
autonomy 123, 135, 140, 167, 206, 207, 215; professions 183
Axial Age 1–2, 35, 91, 155, 230; New 2–6, 225, 233

Bacon, Francis 102
Baker, Thomas 71
'barefoot doctors' 96, 174
Barenblatt, D. 5
Baring, Evelyn 111
Barthes, R. 51, 67
Beauchamp, D.E. 215
Beauchamp, T.L. 10, 140, 207
Becker, G.K. 4, 206–7, 208–9, 213
Becker, M.H. 215
Beckland, E. 64
Bellah, R.N. 33, 215
Berlin, I. 202
Bernstein, R.J. 47
Bible 142
bioethics: in the new Axial Age 1-6, 225-9; five major themes of transcultural or interpretative 8-13

birth control program 6, 41–6, 169, 170–2, 173, 203; *see also* abortion
Blank, R.H. 4
Blendon, R.J. 141
blind spots 12
blood: circulation of *see separate entry*; collection industry 158; oath 183, 186, 199; *xue* 63
Bok, S. 102, 125
BonHoeffer, D. 102
Borry, P. 227
British Medical Association 101
Buber, Martin 210
Buddhism xxii, 2, 5, 35, 94, 152, 175, 212; *cheng* 183; *ci* 182–3; fetal life 43, 44, 45; pre-modern China: medical ethics 91–4, 189, 191, 204; Sun Simiao 189, 191
Burkert, W. 2

Callahan, D. 33, 216
Canada 32
cancer 66, 117, 119, 120–1, 122; *see also* medical truth-telling
capitalism 66, 94, 144–5, 158, 159
Carson, R.A. 7
Chadwick, Ruth 207
Chan, Jonathan 207
Chan, W.T. 175, 191, 192, 193, 194
Chen, Menglei 106–7, 184, 185, 194, 200, 201
Chen Shigong 185
cheng 106–7, 115, 126, 127–9, 130, 140, 183, 187, 191–4, 200
Cheng, S. 128
Cheng, S.Y. 99
Christianity 2, 22, 33, 94–5, 126, 176, 196; fetal life 44; honoring parents 142; informed consent 140, 142; personhood 206, 207–8, 209, 210; wrongfulness of lying 101

Chuang Tzu (Zhuang Zi) 2, 38, 50, 144, 155, 167, 175, 186, 228, 230–4
Chung, Y.J. 5
Chunyu Yi (popularly known as Cang Gong) 104–5
Churchill, L.R. 221–2
Ci, J. 209, 211
circulation of blood 69–86; Chinese interpretations of *Neijing* 78–80; lack of empirical and intellectual foundations 80–1; *Neijing* in contrast to Galen and Harvey 81–2; not circulation described in *Neijing* 74–8; origin and development of historical claim 70–3; refuting historical claim 73–4; sources of historical misjudgement 82–5
civil rights 135
clash of cultures 7, 228; self-defeating prophecy of 48, 152, 226
Cohen, P.A. 25
colonialism 35, 152
Comfort, A. 66
commercialization of medicine 201–2
common humanity 9–11; rejection of 48
commonalities 9-11, 54-9, 120-2
communitarian China vs individualistic West 21, 35–6, 135–6, 154, 209–11; dichotomizing East and West 26–8; distortion of Western realities 32–4; fallacy of dichotomizing cultures *see separate entry*; human rights and women's rights 166–9; individuality and individualism in China 34–5; myth in China 28–32; Western attitudes 22–6
communitarianism: dichotomizing

see communitarian China vs individualistic West; health promotion: beyond individualism and 214–24; justification for informed consent 139–42
complementary medicine 181
Coney, S. 101
confidentiality 142
Confucianism xxiii, 2, 10, 35, 94, 103, 135, 182, 184–5; abortion 42, 45; Americans and Confucian values 33, 143; *cheng* 106–7, 115, 126, 127–9, 130, 140, 183, 187, 191–4, 200; craftmanship 199–200; economic and social conditions and morality 96–7; ethical governance 204; filial piety 142; human rights 155, 168; informed consent 140; knowledge of 187; *li* 126–7, 128; longevity 187; medicine as the art of humanity 130, 131, 140, 181, 198–204, 205; medicine as craft 199–200; Menicus 2, 10, 153, 162, 194, 204; personhood 209, 210, 211–12, 213; pre-modern China: medical ethics 91–4, 191; primacy of morality 13, 132, 156; *ren* 126–7, 128, 130, 140, 149, 155, 182–3, 199, 201, 210; self-deception 130; status of physicians 199–201; Sun Simiao 191, 192; truthfulness 40, 106–7, 108, 109, 115, 116, 126–31; Universal Declaration of Human Rights 155, 168; women 175–6; *xin* 108, 127, 128; *yi* 126–7, 128, 149, 155; Zhuang Zi 230–1
Confucius 2, 107, 162, 184, 231; Golden Rule 130; truthfulness 108, 109, 127–9
Cong, Y.L. 42
consent *see* informed consent
consumer economy 66

Crawford, E. 202
Crawford, S.C. 5
Croizier, R.C. 85, 183
Cromer, Lord 111
Cullen, C. 93
Cultural Craze 32
cultural differences: in China and the West simplified and stereotyped, xxi-xxiii, 21-6, 37-43, 51-4, 98-99,117-119, 135-6, 150-1, 166; fallacy of dichotomizing 32-36, 37-50, 55-68; 225-6; complexities of 7-8, 98-115
"cultural differences" argument: against medical truth-telling, informed consent, human rights and women's rights in China, see the concerned separate entries.
cultural relativism 7, 151, 155–6
Cultural Revolution 29–30, 32, 149, 157, 175, 182

D'Emilio, J. 66, 67
Danis, M. 217
Daoism 2, 94, 103, 212; anti-paternalistic 38–9, 140, 144, 167; death 35; family 126; human rights 155; individualism 35, 38–9, 144, 152, 155; informed consent 140, 144; knowledge of 187; Lao Zi (Lao Tzu) 2, 155, 175, 190, 218; pre-modern China: medical ethics 93–4, 191, 204; primacy of morality 13, 132, 156; rights-related concepts 167; sexuality 35, 62; Stoicism 35, 38, 232–3; women 175; Zhuang Zi (Chuang Tzu) 2, 38, 50, 144, 155, 167, 175, 186, 228, 230–4
Dawson, R. xxii, 25
de Bary, W.T. 35, 155, 167
de Montaigne, M. 194death: cause-of-death patterns 174;

Daoist philosophy 35; terminal illness *see* medical truth-telling
deception vs concealing truth 108, 109, 129–30
definitions: China and Chinese 90–1; medical morality 90
democracy 31, 49, 152–3, 159, 168, 169
Deng, D. 32
Dewey, John 193
dialectical materialism 85
dialogue: cross-cultural 11, 225-9, 230-4
dichotomization *see* communitarian China vs individualistic West and fallacy of dichotomizing cultures
dichotomizing cultures see fallacy of dichotomizing cultures
Dikötter, F. xxi, 6
Ding, C.Y. 144
disclosure *see* medical truth-telling
discrimination 13, 188; rural people 96–7, 174, 176; women 163–9
diversity *see* internal moral plurality
Döring, O. 6, 7
Dou, Y.T. 138
Du, Z.Z. 30
dualism 24, 219, 221
Duffy, Eliza 60

Eastern Europe 117
Ebrey, P.B. 142
economic and social conditions and morality 96–7
economic development 157, 158
egoism 2, 32, 213
Elliott, C. 33, 202
Elliott, J.M. 5
Emanuel, E.J. 4, 33
empirical turn 227
Engelhardt, H.T., Jr 4, 23, 25, 89, 206, 209
environment and human body 61–2
equality 10, 188; *see also* inequality

essentialism, false 47, 136, 152, 166, 226
Euripides 27
Euro-centrism 159–60
Europe 32, 117
experimental methods 81–2

Faden, R.R. 136, 140
fallacy of dichotomizing cultures 37, 46–50, 152, 225–6; Chinese and Western bioethics dichotomized 37–41; informed consent 136; internal plurality: Chinese attitudes to fetal life 41–6; list of oppositions 37–8; medical truth-telling 110–13, 131
family 33; consent 142–5; cross-cultural distinction: role of 126; medical truth-telling 109, 117, 118, 120, 121–2, 125–6
family planning/birth control program 6, 41–6, 169, 170–2, 173, 203; *see also* abortion
famine 157
Fan, R.P. 4, 6, 98, 99, 105, 117, 130, 209
Fan Zhongyan 200–1
fear 65
Fei, X.T. 143
Feinberg, Joel 206
Fejoo Montenegro, Benito Geronimo 71
feminism 4, 33, 143, 163–4, 176–7; condition of Chinese women 164–6; Confucianism and 175–6; reproductive rights as human rights 169, 170–2; significance of human rights and women's rights 166–9; toward Chinese feminist bioethics 172–6
fetal life: China 41–6, 51, 95, 154, 165, 170–2, 173, 203–4; survey results in China 44; United States 33–4, 95

Fielding, R. 120
Fingarette, Herbert 209
Finnis, J. 9–10
Fletcher, Joseph 206
foot-binding 13
Foucault, M. 52–3, 67, 69
Fox, R.C. 23–4, 29, 33
Freeman, D. 28
Freidson, E. 183
Freud, S. 102
Fujiki, N. 4
fukou (household registration) system 96
Fung, Y.-L. 2

Galen 74, 81–2
Gao, B. 121
Gao, W.L. 139
Gao, Y.J. 158
Gardner, Augustus 57
Garrison, F.H. 81
Ge, H. (Ko, H.) 59, 62
Ge Youli 165–6
Geertz, C. 8
gender issues *see* women
Germany 13, 202, 203
Gernet, J. 9, 91
Gilligan, C. 167
Ginsberg, Robert 208
Ginsburg, F.D. 34
Godwin, W. 142
Goethe, Johann Wolfgang von 102
Golden Rule 130
Gong Tingxian 185, 201
Gongal, R. 117
Goody, J. 159
Gottweis, H. 4
grabbism (*nalai zhuyi*) 47
Graf, Friedrich-Wilhelm 208
Graham, Sylvester 56, 58, 60, 64–5
grand hypothesis of peculiar mentality 46–7
Green, R.M. 4

Greenhalgh, S. 6
Grene, D. 102
grief 65
Guantanamo Bay 203
Gujin Tushu Jicheng Yibu Quanlu (A Collection of Ancient and Modern Books) 102–3, 105
Guoyu 104

Habermas, J. 84, 85
Haller, J.S., Jr 60
Han Dynasty 62, 104, 128, 175, 183
Han Yu 199
Hancock, K. 117
Hanfei Zi 193–4
Hansen, C. 167, 209, 210–11
Hardacre, H. 5
Harris, John 207
Harris, S.H. 5
Harvey, William 70, 71, 72, 73, 74, 75, 78, 79, 81, 82
Hauerwas, Stanley 33
He, R. 122
health promotion 214; individualism and communitarianism in conflict 215–17; practical implications of yin-yang approach 220–4; yin-yang/dialectical approach 217–20
Hegel, G.W.F. 22, 102
Herder, J.G. xxii–xxiii, 232
Herodotus 27
Heywood, E.H. 60
Hippocrates 64, 100
historical misjudgement, sources of 82–5
HIV/AIDS 158
Hobsbawm, E.J. 202
Hobson, J.M. 159–60
holistic orientation of traditional Chinese medicine 85, 223
Homer 27
homosexuality 66

Hong Kong 90, 98, 116, 120, 144, 208
Hongladarom, S. 38
Hongloumeng (Dream of the Red Chamber) 107
Hoshino, K. 5
household registration (*fukou*) system 96
Hsiao, K. 2
Hsu, F.L.K. 28
Hu Shi 31
Hua Tuo 104
Huang, X. 120
Huangdi Neijing (The Yellow Emperor's Classic of Medicine) 2, 199; acupuncture 183, 184, 199; circulation of blood *see separate entry*; physician as general 197; sexual passion 58; yin and yang 222
Huangfu Mi 200
Hui, E. 144, 209, 210
human rights 8, 49, 114, 140; as a Chinese value 149–62; ethical universals 10; negligence and violations 156–8; significance of women's rights and 166–9; UDBHR *see* Universal Declaration on Bioethics and Human Rights; Universal Declaration of Human Rights 150, 155, 168; women's reproductive rights as 169, 170–2
Hume, D. 161–2

incommensurability, assumption of 48, 136, 152, 226, 233
individualism 159; 'Asian values' 151–2; communitarian China vs individualistic West *see separate entry*; health promotion: beyond communitarianism and 214–24; informed consent 135, 140–1, 145; medical truth-telling 117, 118, 125

inequality 13, 188; rural people 96–7, 174, 176; women 163–9
infanticide 42, 43, 45
informed consent 49, 119, 123–4, 131, 134–6, 145; abortion 170–1, 172, 203–4; communitarian justification 139–42; 'cultural differences' argument 8, 135–6, 145; empowering patients 136–9; family consent 142–5; sterilization 170, 171; trust between patients and medical profession 141–2; Western countries 134–5, 136–7
interpretative bioethics 6-7
interpretative cross-cultural bioethics, characteristics of 7-13
internal moral plurality 8–9, 36, 46, 50, 89–91, 97, 136, 154, 226, 229; 'China' and 'Chinese' 90–1; comparisons with West 95–7; contemporary situation 94–5; fetal life 41–6; traditional China 91–4, 186; use of term 'medical morality' 90
International Covenant on Civil and Political Rights 169
Islam 2, 94

Japan 5, 157, 186, 203; abortion 45; medical truth-telling 117, 209
Jaspers, K. 1, 2
Jennings, W.H. 42
Jesuit missionaries 22
Jiang, Y. 122
jing 63–4, 65
Jinpingmei (The Golden Lotus) 93, 105–6, 186
John Paul II, Pope 208
Jonsen, A. 134, 182, 199
Joyce, James 102
Judeo-Christianity 196, 206, 207–8, 209; role of family 126; wrongfulness of lying 101

Kafka, F. xxiv–xxv 233
Kant, I. 102, 129, 167, 206
Kass, L.R. 33, 194
Katz, J. 100, 123–4, 136, 140
Kennedy Institute of Ethics 22–3
Keown, D. 5
Kim, D.J. 152–3
King, N.M.P. 196
Kipling, Rudyard 21
Kleinman, A. 98
Ko, D. 176
Ko, H. (Ge, H.) 59, 62
Korea 186
Kuhse, Helga 207
Kwok, D.W.Y. 84

LaFleur, W.R. 5, 45
Lai Fuyang 200
Lao Zi (Lao Tzu) 2, 155, 175, 190, 218
Lash, D.F. xxii
Latin America 3
Lauren, P.G. 155, 158–9
Lavery, J.V. 4
lead pollution and poisoning 158
Lee Kuan Yew 49, 151, 152
Lee, S. 165
Lee, S.C. 4, 182, 199, 213
legalism 2, 212
Legge, J. 127, 128–9
Leibniz, G.W. xxii
Levy-Bruhl, Lucien 28
Lewis, D. 54–7
li 126–7, 128
Li, C.Y. 175
Li, S. 98
Li Shizhen 200
Li Yan 106–7, 201
Li, Z.S. 138
Liang Shuming 31–2
Liaozhai Zhiyi (Strange Stories from a Chinese Studio) 106
Lie Zi 184
Lin Zhao 149

Lindermann, Hilde 33
Little, M. 163
Liu, C. 82
Liu Shaoqi 139
Liu, X.L. 72, 80
Lloyd, G.E.R. 46
Locke, J. 206
Long, B. 70, 71–2
longevity 35, 57, 59, 62, 187
Lu, G.D. 70–1, 72, 73, 80, 83
Lu Xun 47
Luk, B.H. 42
Luker, K. 34
Lun Dayi Jingcheng (On the Proficiency and Sincerity of the Master Physician) 186–7, 188–90, 191
Luo, G.J. 32
Lusitaus, Amatus 102
lying or deceiving vs concealing truth 108, 109, 129–30

Ma, B.Y. 198
Ma, K.W. 199
McCann, Dennis P. 208
Macer, D. 4
McEvilley, T. 2
MacIntyre, A. 89, 217
Mackerras, C. xxii
Macklin, R. 4, 10, 99, 117, 131, 137, 168, 211
Macmurray, John 210
malpractice liability 144
Mann, Thomas 22
Mao Zedong 22, 35, 51, 138–9, 155, 157, 168
Marcel, Gabriel 210
market economy 141
Marx, Karl 3, 202
Marxism 29–30, 31, 94, 96, 143, 164, 212
masturbation 56, 64, 66
Mauss, M. 206, 212, 213
May, L. 3

May, William 33
Mead, M. 27–8
medical truth-telling in China 39–40, 49, 113–15, 116, 131–3; Confucianism: truthfulness 40, 106–7, 108, 109, 115, 116, 126–31; 'cultural differences' argument against 116–18, 119–20, 132; cultural differences oversimplified 98–102, 132; current debate 118–20; ethical rationales for 106–7; family role 109, 117, 118, 120, 121–2, 125–6, 130–1; forgotten tradition 102–7; harm: secrecy and untruthfulness 122–5; lying or deceiving vs concealing truth 108, 109, 129–30; may conceal truth in certain situations 108–9, 119; medical sages 103–5, 106, 109; mendacious Oriental vs truthful Occidental 110–13; patients want to know truth 120–2; primary sources 102–3; professional duty 130–1; surveys 120–2, 130; trust in medical professionals 121, 123, 125; Western influence and its limits 107–10
medical truth-telling in the West 39–40, 98, 117, 123; mendacious Oriental vs truthful Occidental 110–13; new phenomenon 99–102
medicine as the art of humanity 130, 131, 140, 181, 198–201, 205; physicians as agents of states and nationalism 201–4
Meng, L. 165
Mencius 2, 10, 153, 162, 194, 204
Middle East 117
Miles, S. 194, 203
military imagery 196–8
Mill, J.S. 34
Milwertz, C.N. 6, 166, 171–2

Mitchell, J. 117
Mitsuya, H. 117
Mo Zi 2
Mobeireek, A.F. 117
Moism 2, 126, 213
Moskowitz, M.L. 6, 45
motorcycle helmets 216, 224
multiculturalism 95–6
Munro, D.J. 35
murder 141
Murray, Thomas 33
Mystakidou, K. 117

nationalism 83, 202–4, 205
natural environment and human body 61–2
Needham, Joseph 23, 69, 70–1, 72, 73, 80, 83, 86, 184
Neijing see *Huangdi Neijing*
Nelson, H.L. 143, 163–4
Nepal 117
New Culture Movement 32, 126, 175
New Zealand 32, 101, 134, 137, 141–2; organ transplantation 143
Ni, M.S. 197
Nicholas, Thomas 57, 60–1
Nie, J.B. 2, 5, 6, 7, 25, 34, 38, 42–3, 50, 78, 81, 82, 85, 91, 101, 132, 134, 142, 154, 170–1, 172, 173, 174, 184, 199, 203, 205, 211, 227, 229
Nisbett, R.E. 28
Nissenbaum, S. 56
non-disclosure *see* medical truth-telling
Novack, D.H. 100
Nuremberg Code 134–5
Nussbaum, M.C. 225

obesity 128, 214, 224
Oedipus the King 101
Oken, D. 100
Ong, A. 4–5

openness xxii, 94, 118, 231
organ transplantation 143
orgasm 58–9, 60, 61, 64, 65
Orientalism 26, 111–13
Owen, R.G. 84

Pan, Z. 33, 143
Pang, M.S. 6, 98
Pascal, Blaise xxiv
passions and disease 65
paternalism 98, 100, 109, 126, 134; Daoism 38–9, 140, 144, 167; health promotion 215, 216
patients' rights 114, 134, 135, 136, 137, 196, 210; medical truth-telling 119, 123; New Zealand 142; *see also* informed consent; medical truth-telling; trust in medical professionals
patriarchy 12, 164, 165, 168
Pellegrino, E. 4, 33
Peppin, J.F. 3
personhood 140, 206–13
pharmaceutical companies 202
Phillips, M.R. 165
Plato 129, 153
plurality *see* internal moral plurality
political ideology 32; dichotomization: generating contentious and harmful social policies 48–9
Polo, Marco xxii, 23
Popper, K. 26
population/birth control 6, 41–6, 169, 170–2, 173, 203; *see also* abortion
Porket, M. 82
positivism 84
postmodernist discourse 9, 23, 25, 26, 37, 41–2, 142, 209; incommensurability 48, 233
Potter, S.H. 41–2
power relations: empowering patients 136–9; family 143–4

pragmatism 30
primacy of morality 11–13, 156, 226; tyranny of cultural practices over morality 7, 13, 47–8, 132, 152, 226
problematic representative 46; *see also* internal moral plurality
professional ethics of traditional Chinese medicine 181–6, 194–5, 205; *cheng* in Confucianism: philosophical and spiritual basis of 115, 140, 181, 191–4, 195; medicine as the art of humanity 130, 131, 140, 181, 198–204, 205; physician as general 196–8; proficiency and sincerity 186–91
protective medical treatment (*baohuxing yiliao*) 119, 121
psychology 28, 47

qi (energy in all life and in universe) 63, 72, 73, 74–8, 79–80
Qianjing Yaofang (The Thousand Golden Prescriptions) 54, 55–6
Qin Dynasty 91
Qin Yueren (popularly known as Bian Que) 104
Qiu, R.Z. 4, 29, 31, 42, 169, 172–3, 182, 184, 199, 200, 209, 210
Quante, Michael 207

racism 96, 202
Ramsey, P. 33, 140
Raphals, L. 176
Rawls, J. 10
Raz, J. 140–1
Rehmann-Sutter, C. 4
relativism 7, 13, 151, 155–6, 225
ren 126–7, 128, 130, 140, 149, 155, 182–3, 199, 201, 210
representative, problematic 46; *see also* internal moral plurality
Rhijne, Willem ten 70–1

Rigdon, S. 42
Roetz, H. 2, 4, 155
Rousseau, Jean Jacques 102
rule of law 29
rural–urban divide 96–7, 164–5, 169, 174

Said, E. 26, 111
Salles, A.L.F. 3
Samoa 27–8
Sanguozhi (Records of Three Kingdoms) 104
Sarton, G. 82
Sass, H.-M. 5
Scandinavian countries 32
Scharping, T. 42
scientism 83–6
Scully, J.L. 4
self-deception 130, 192
self-defeating prophecy of clash of cultures 48, 152, 226
self-interest 193–4
sexual excess as a cause of disease in China and US 51–4, 67–8; cross-cultural similarities 54–9; cross-cultural differences in similarities 59–65; repression to freedom 65–7
Shain, B.A. 33
Shakespeare 102
Shapiro, J. 157
sheng (spirit) 63
Sherwin, S. 33, 163
Shiji (Records of the Grand Historian) 104
Shin Ohara 209
Shituoji (Story of the Stone) 107
side effects of medicine 197
Sima Qian 184
Singapore 49
Singer, C. 82
Singer, Peter 206
Sivin, N. 63, 218, 220, 222
slavery 12, 13

Sleeboom, M. 83
Sleeboom-Faulkner, M. 5, 83
Smith, Adam 194
Smith, A.H. 111–13
smoking 214, 222–3, 224
social contract 196–7
socialism 2, 30, 32, 94, 109–10, 126, 212
sociology 28, 46–7, 143, 206
Socrates 129
Solzhenitsyn, A. 122
Song, G.B. 107–9, 126, 129
Sontag, S. 66, 198
Sophocles 101–2
Sorell, T. 84
Southern Europe 117
Soviet Union 202
Spaemann, Robert 207
Spence, J.D. xxii
sterilization 170, 171
Stockham, Alice B. 64
Stoicism 35, 38, 232–3
Su Shi xxiii, xxiv
suicide 96, 109, 164–5, 174; medical truth-telling 119
Sun, Johannes H.C. 207
Sun Simiao 10, 54, 55–6, 61, 62, 182, 185, 186–91, 192, 199
Sun, Y. 122
Sun Zi (Sun Tze) 197, 198
Surbone, A. 117
Svensson, M. 155, 167–8
Swazey, J.P. 23–4, 29

Tai, M.C. 4
Taiwan 45, 90, 98, 116, 120
Takahashi, T. 5
Tang, S.T. 98
Tao, J.T.L. 4, 6
Taoism *see* Daoism
Telfer, Elizabeth 207
Temple, R. 70, 72, 73
terminal illness *see* medical truth-telling

themes of transcultural bioethics 7–13, 226
thick description/narrative 8–9
Three Gorges Dam 157
Thucydides 113
Tissot, S.-A. 64
Tocqueville, Alexis de 33
Tolstoy, L. 122, 124, 125
Tong, R. 4, 33, 163, 164
Tooley, Michael 206
totalitarianism 2, 35, 202, 216, 229
transcultural bioethics: characteristics of 7–13, 226
Trall, R.T. 60
Tribe, L.H. 41
Trilling, L. 102
trust in medical professionals: informed consent 141–2; medical truth-telling 121, 123, 125
truth-telling *see* medical truth-telling
Tsai, D.F.C. 195
Tse, C.Y. 98
Tu, W.M. 157, 193
tuberculosis (TB) 66
Tuckett, A.G. 117
Turner, L. 10
tyranny of cultural practices over morality: see primacy of morality

UNESCO *see* Universal Declaration on Bioethics and Human Rights
United Nations 161
United States 5, 24–5, 32–3, 157, 160, 202, 203, 207; abortion 33–4, 95; communitarianism 32–4; family values 33, 143; health promotion 214, 215; medical truth-telling 99–100, 130–1; profession of medicine 183; sexual excess as a cause of disease in China and US *see separate entry*; universities 225
Universal Declaration on Bioethics and Human Rights (UDBHR) 149, 161–2; assumption 150–1; fallacy of 'Asian values' argument 151–3; human rights as a Chinese value 153–6; international nature of human rights 158–60; suggestions for amending 160–1
Universal Declaration of Human Rights 150, 155, 168
Unschuld, P.U. 2, 6, 58, 64, 73, 83, 92, 93, 182, 184, 185, 191, 193, 197, 199, 200
urban–rural divide 96–7, 164–5, 169, 174
utilitarianism 208

vagina 58, 65
van Gulik, R.H. 53, 58, 59, 61, 62
Veatch, R.M. 3, 140, 196–7
Veith, I. 218, 222
Vesalius 82
violence against medical professionals 141
Voltaire 23
Vossius, Issac 71

Waley, A. 127
Waley-Cohen, J. xxii
Wang, F.L. 96
Wang, J.L. 173
Wang, Q. 78–9, 80
Wang Yangming 162
war: art of war and art of medicine 196–8
Warren, Mary Anne 206
Watson, B. 50, 167, 175, 230
Wear, S. 125
Weizhi (Records of the State of Wei) 104
Wellmuth, J. 84
Wertz, D.C. 4
White, T. 6
Whitehead, Alfred 22
Williams, P. 5

women 12, 49, 105, 134, 144, 163–4, 176–7; abortion *see separate entry*; condition of Chinese women 164–6; pre-modern medical practitioners 93; reproductive rights as human rights 169, 170–2; significance of human rights and rights of 166–9; suicide 96, 119, 164–5; toward Chinese feminist bioethics 172–6
Wong, K.C. 70, 71, 74, 78
Woo, K.Y. 38
World Medical Association 135, 150, 195

Xiao Jing (The Classic of Filial Piety) 142
xin 108, 127, 128
Xu Chunfu 185, 200
Xu Dachun 58, 63, 197
xue (blood) 63
Xun Kuang (Xun Zi) 2, 42

Yang, B. 128
Yang Quan 184
yang see *yin-yang*
Yang-Zhu 2
Yellow Emperor's Classic of Medicine see *Huangdi Neijing*
yi 126–7, 128, 149, 155
Yi He 104
Yi Huan 103–4
Yi Xin Fang (Prescriptions of the Medical Mind) 58, 59, 61, 62
yide (medical morality) 90
yin-jing 63, 65

yin-yang 2, 24, 65, 175, 181; model on the ethics of health promotion 214–24; *yang* 62, 65, 75, 76–8, 79, 175; *yin* 63, 65, 75, 76–8, 79, 175
Yiye Lunlixue (The Ethics of the Medical Profession) 107
Yu Luoke 149
Yu, Y.A. 72

Zakaria, F. 151
Zeng, T. 98, 121
Zhang, D. 182, 199
Zhang Gao 185, 200
Zhang Jiebin 79–80, 200, 222
Zhang, L. 53
Zhang, X. 141
Zhang Zhongjing 82, 104, 184
Zhang Zixin 149
Zhao, H.Z. 183
Zhe Cheng 198
Zhen, Z.Y. 73
Zhou Dengyi (Chou Tun-i) 192
Zhou Enlai 138, 139
Zhu Huiming 185
Zhu, W. 145
Zhu, X. 98, 121
Zhu Xi 199, 220
Zhu Zhenheng 63, 65
Zhuang Zi (Chuang Tzu) 2, 38, 50, 144, 155, 167, 175, 186, 228, 230–4
Zou Xinxing 133
Zuozhuan (The Chronology of the State of Lu) 103–4

Printed in Great Britain
by Amazon